D1339729

Understanding Governance Series

General Editor: **R.A.W. Rhodes**, Professor of Government, University of Tasmania and Distinguished Professor of Political Science, Australian National University

Understanding Governance encompasses all theoretical approaches to the study of government and governance in advanced industrial democracies. It has three long-standing objectives:

1. to understand the process of change;
2. to develop theory to explain why change occurs; and
3. to set this change and its causes in comparative perspective.

The series includes titles that adopt post-structural and post-modern approaches to political science and challenge such notions as hollowing-out, governance, core executives, policy networks and the new institutionalism. It also publishes material with traditional institutional and historical approaches to such topics as prime ministers, ministers, the civil service and government departments. All titles not only meet the conventional standard of theoretical and empirical rigour but also seek to address topics of broad current interest that open the field of study to new ideas and areas of investigation.

Titles include:

Anika Gauja
THE POLITICS OF PARTY POLICY
From Members to Legislators

Michael Rush and Philip Giddings
PARLIAMENTARY SOCIALISATION
Learning the Ropes or Determining Behaviour?

Paul 't Hart and John Uhr (*editors*)
HOW POWER CHANGES HANDS
Transition and Succession in Government

Robert Hazell, Ben Worthy and Mark Glover
THE IMPACT OF THE FREEDOM ON INFORMATION ACT ON CENTRAL GOVERNMENT
IN THE UK
Does FOI Work?

David Richards, Martin Smith and Colin Hay (*editors*)
INSTITUTIONAL CRISIS IN 21st-CENTURY BRITAIN

Ann Scott
ERNEST GOWERS
Plain Words and Forgotten Deeds

Chris Skelcher, Helen Sullivan and Stephen Jeffares
HYBRID GOVERNANCE IN EUROPEAN CITIES
Neighbourhood, Migration and Democracy

Kevin Theakston
AFTER NUMBER 10
Former Prime Ministers in British Politics

Titles previously published in the Transforming Government series include:

Simon Bulmer, Martin Burch, Caitríona Carter, Patricia Hogwood and Andrew Scott
BRITISH DEVOLUTION AND EUROPEAN POLICY-MAKING
Transforming Britain to Multi-Level Governance

Nicholas Deakin and Richard Parry
THE TREASURY AND SOCIAL POLICY
The Contest for Control of Welfare Strategy

Neil C.M. Elder and Edward C. Page
ACCOUNTABILITY AND CONTROL IN NEXT STEPS AGENCIES

Oliver James
THE EXECUTIVE AGENCY REVOLUTION IN WHITEHALL
Public Interest Versus Bureau-Shaping Perspectives

David Marsh, David Richards and Martin J. Smith
CHANGING PATTERNS OF GOVERNANCE IN THE UNITED KINGDOM
Reinventing Whitehall?

Iain McLean
THE FISCAL CRISIS OF THE UNITED KINGDOM

Edward C. Page and Vincent Wright (editors)
FROM THE ACTIVE TO THE ENABLING STATE
The Changing Role of Top Officials in European Nations

Hugh Pemberton
POLICY LEARNING AND BRITISH GOVERNANCE IN THE 1960s

B. Guy Peters, R. A. W. Rhodes and Vincent Wright (editors)
ADMINISTERING THE SUMMIT
Administration of the Core Executive in Developed Countries

R. A. W. Rhodes (editor)
TRANSFORMING BRITISH GOVERNMENT
Volume One: Changing Institutions
Volume Two: Changing Roles and Relationships

David Richards
NEW LABOUR AND THE CIVIL SERVICE
Reconstituting the Westminster Model

Martin J. Smith
THE CORE EXECUTIVE IN BRITAIN

Kevin Theakston
LEADERSHIP IN WHITEHALL

Kevin Theakston (editor)
BUREAUCRATS AND LEADERSHIP

Patrick Weller, Herman Bakvis and R. A. W. Rhodes (editors)
THE HOLLOW CROWN
Countervailing Trends in Core Executives

Understanding Governance Series
Series Standing Order ISBN 978–0–333–71580–2
(*outside North America only*)

You can receive future titles in this series as they are published by placing a standing order. Please contact your bookseller or, in case of difficulty, write to us at the address below with your name and address, the title of the series and the ISBN quoted above.

Customer Services Department, Macmillan Distribution Ltd, Houndmills, Basingstoke, Hampshire RG21 6XS, England

---

Institutional Crisis in 21st-Century Britain

Edited by

David Richards
Professor of Public Policy, Department of Politics, University of Manchester, UK

Martin Smith
Professor of Politics, Department of Politics, Derwent College, University of York, UK

and

Colin Hay
Professor of Government and Comparative Public Policy at Sciences Po, Paris, France

palgrave
macmillan

First published 2014 by
PALGRAVE MACMILLAN

Palgrave Macmillan in the UK is an imprint of Macmillan Publishers Limited,
registered in England, company number 785998, of Houndmills, Basingstoke,
Hampshire RG21 6XS.

Palgrave Macmillan in the US is a division of St Martin's Press LLC,
175 Fifth Avenue, New York, NY 10010.

Palgrave Macmillan is the global academic imprint of the above companies
and has companies and representatives throughout the world.

Palgrave® and Macmillan® are registered trademarks in the United States,
the United Kingdom, Europe and other countries.

ISBN 978–1–137–33438–1

A catalogue record for this book is available from the British Library.

A catalog record for this book is available from the Library of Congress.

Transferred to Digital Printing in 2014

Dedicated to the memory of Steve Buckler
(1960–2013)

Contents

Tables and Figures

Tables

Figures

Preface and Acknowledgements

Institutional Crisis in 21st-Century Britain emerged from a conference we organised during the summer of June 2012. It sprang from our sense of frustration that while there had been various commentary pieces appearing by then in the written media discussing the broader nature of the various crises examined throughout this volume, the focus in the academic literature tended to be rather narrower, reflecting instead on the problems besetting individual institutions. There was then an obvious lacuna – a need for a more rigorous exploration of the extent to which the wave of perceived institutional crises revealed over recent years might in some way be collectively related, as opposed to simply being a matter of serendipitous coincidence. The aim of this edited volume is to address this lacuna.

There were two obvious challenges that we, as editors, faced in plotting how best to approach this task. The first concerned the range and variety of institutions confronting potential crises. Such breadth meant that in terms of contributors, should we draw on expertise from political science alone, or adopt a broader strategy casting our net right across the social sciences? We opted for the latter with the view that such plurality would add a greater richness and wider perspective to our understanding of the relationship between institutions and the effect(s) wrought by crisis narratives. This in turn presented a second challenge concerning the issue of coherence. It is the norm in most collections of this kind for the editors to try and impose a common conceptual framework, ensuring a degree of continuity in the way in which each contributing author distils her or his analysis. But in our case, given the diversity of the contributors' disciplinary fields, such an option did not appear readily available. As such, it was not clear we would be able to achieve the usual levels of coherence for this type of enterprise. As outlined in the volume's Introduction, our strategy was then to ask the authors to each consider a common set of questions regarding the institutions they were writing on with the hope that, in the least, some common themes might emerge.

Yet if hindsight is one of the vices within the social sciences, so be it. For when we came to reflect on the synergies to emerge on receipt of the individual chapters, it became apparent that the crisis pathologies underpinning many of the accounts they offered chimed with themes discussed elsewhere in a more exclusively political science literature concerning what can be referred to as a 'critical approach towards the British political tradition' (Hall 2011). So, when subsequently penning the book's Introduction and Conclusion, we were retrospectively afforded the luxury of being able, in true inductive fashion, to appeal to the literature on the British political tradition (BPT) to offer what we regard as a coherent analytical framework round which much of the book is organised. This provided the coherence we originally believed would elude us. The tenets of this literature are set out in more detail in the introductory chapter. But to give the reader some flavour of the arguments it alludes to, it touches on themes of elitism, hierarchy, secrecy and the absence of real transparency and accountability. These were all characteristics that were regularly referred to throughout the individual chapters concerning the problems besetting each respective institution.

Having then been given the opportunity to present the BPT as a common conceptual approach interwoven, in various ways, throughout the volume, it is also useful to reflect on the antithesis to such a tradition, as offering a potential diagnosis to the problems discussed forthwith. One obvious attempt to break from the BPT was that made by America's Founding Fathers, and their normative appeal to popular sovereignty, a separation of powers, a system of checks and balances and, of course, federalism. Over 200 years on from the Declaration of Independence, numerous other, more participatory, delegative, transparent and pluralist approaches to the way both systems of government and their related institutions organise themselves are now in operation.

The UK, we therefore conclude, in addressing its own crises, needs to move on from the iron-cage of its own history and with it the various 19th-century trappings we identify as continuing to underpin both the organisational forms and cultures of many of its key institutions. To quote from Abraham Lincoln in his first inaugural address from Washington DC in 1861,

> This country, with its institutions, belongs to the people who inhabit it. Whenever they shall grow weary of the existing government, they can exercise their constitutional right of amending it, or exercise their revolutionary right to overthrow it.

If we could indulge for a moment, by lifting this musing and transposing to a modern-day setting, our hope is that the current wave of institutional crises afflicting UK institutions garners more than just a weariness (and with it potential apathy), but rather acts as a catalyst for a wave of reforms, suggesting that sometime in the near future change, rather than continuity will win the day.

Finally, in the process of compiling this edited volume, some heartfelt thanks are long due. First, to all the contributors, thank you for your forbearance, responsiveness (in most cases) and reflexivity. Your collective participation has undoubtedly enriched the final product. A special mention also to Vivien Lowndes (Nottingham) who attended the initial conference and who provided a number of thought-provoking insights. Thanks to the editorial team at Palgrave Macmillan – Amber Stone-Galilee and Andy Baird in particular – for the support and assistance offered throughout the various stages of production. Thanks also to Rod Rhodes, the editor of the *Transforming Government* series for his receptive, but incisive comments when we first approached him with the idea for this book and for allowing us to contribute to what is one of the outstanding series in political science. Also, of course, deep thanks to our nearest and dearest – for all your tolerance and forbearance – it is really appreciated.

Finally, a brief note on the person to whom this book is dedicated. Sadly, in January 2013, at far too young an age, Steve Buckler lost an all too brief battle with cancer, that most pernicious of diseases. At the time of his passing, he was the longest serving member of the Department of Political Science and International Studies at Birmingham University and a political theorist of eminent repute. His academic forays had also led at times to some noteworthy contributions to the literature on British politics. More importantly, he was both a sometime colleague and good friend to a number of us who have contributed to this book. We know he would have been sympathetic to the over-arching critique presented within this volume and it is to his memory that this book is most appropriately dedicated.

DR, MJS and CH, January 2014

Contributors

Sadiya Akram is a Research Fellow at the ANZSOG's Institute of Governance, University of Canberra. She is currently working on an ARC-funded project examining citizen engagement and political participation, which will focus on case studies taken from Australia, Denmark and the UK.

Paul Cairney is Professor of Politics and Public Policy at the University of Stirling. He is the author of approximately 30 articles on Scottish and British Politics and public policy. Recent books include *Understanding Public Policy* (2011), *Scottish Politics* (with Neil McGarvey, 2008) and *Global Tobacco Control* (with Donley Studlar and Hadii Mamudu, 2012).

Charles Dannreuther is Lecturer in European Politics at the University of Leeds and has held previous positions in Manchester, London School of Economics and Warwick. He works on regulation approaches to political economy and has just published the *Political Economy of the Small Firm* (with Lew Perren, 2013).

Patrick Diamond is currently a Post-Doctoral Research Fellow at the University of Manchester. He is the author of numerous books on British politics and public policy, most recently *Governing Britain: Power, Politics and the Prime Minister* (2013).

Daniel Fitzpatrick is currently a Research Associate at the University of Manchester. Previously, he was a Research Assistant in the Department of Politics at the University of Sheffield following the award of his PhD in 2011.

Colin Hay is Professor of Government and Comparative Public Policy at Sciences Po, Paris. He is the author of a number of books including, most recently, *The Failure of Anglo-Liberal Capitalism* (2013) and *The Legacy of Thatcherism* (2014, with Stephen Farrall). He is an editor or co-editor of the journals *New Political Economy*, *Comparative European Politics* and *British Politics*.

David Judge is Professor of Politics at the University of Strathclyde. He is the author, co-author or editor of 12 books, the latest of which is *Democratic Incongruities: Representative Democracy in Britain* (2014).

Simon Lightfoot is currently Senior Lecturer in European Politics at the University of Leeds. Before coming to Leeds, he worked at Liverpool John Moores University. He has been a visiting fellow at the National Europe Centre, Australian National University and the Corvinus University of Budapest. He is the author of *Europeanising Social Democracy: The Rise of the Party of European Socialists?* (2005) and co-editor of *Teaching Politics and International Relations* (2012).

David Marsh is Professor at the ANZSOG's Institute of Governance, University of Canberra. He is currently working on a variety of projects on citizen engagement, political participation and governance.

Brendan McCaffrie is a Research Fellow at the ANZSOG's Institute for Governance, University of Canberra. He is currently working on an ARC-funded project examining citizen engagement and political participation in Australia, the UK and Denmark.

Ralph Negrine is currently Professor of Political Communication in the Department of Journalism Studies at the University of Sheffield. He is the author of various books on political communication and media policy, British politics, governance and public policy including *The Transformation of Political Communication* (2008), *The Political Communication Reader* (with James Stanyer, 2007) and *European Media* (with Stylianos Papathannassopoulos, 2011).

David Richards is currently Professor of Public Policy at the University of Manchester. He has previously held posts at the Universities of Strathclyde, Birmingham, Liverpool and Sheffield. He is the author of numerous articles and books on British politics, governance and public policy including, most recently, *New Labour and the Civil Service: Reconstituting the Westminster Model*.

Layla Skinns is Senior Lecturer in Criminology, School of Law and a member of the Centre for Criminological Research at the University of Sheffield. Her main research areas are police, policing and police legitimacy, in the context of the police custody process in England and Wales, and in other common law jurisdictions. She has published various articles and books including, most recently, *Police Custody: Governance, Legitimacy and Reform in the Criminal Justice Process* (2011).

Martin Smith is Anniversary Professor of Politics at the University of York. He was previously Professor of Politics at the University of Sheffield. He has published widely on British politics, public policy and state transformation. His most recent book is *Power and the State* (2009).

Helen Thompson is Reader in Politics at the University of Cambridge. She is the author of various books on different aspects of international political economy, most recently *China and the Mortgaging of America: Domestic Politics and Economic Interdependence* (2010).

Adam White is Lecturer in Public Policy at the University of York. His research focuses on security governance, legitimacy, regulation and the public good. He is the author of *The Politics of Private Security: Regulation, Reform, and Re-Legitimation* (2010).

Introduction: A Crisis in UK Institutions?

David Richards and Martin Smith

Introduction

There is an obvious, but striking contrast between the 1950s, an age often framed against a back-drop depicting popular, widespread deference, respect and trust towards the 'great' institutions of the state such as parliament, Whitehall, the judiciary, the armed forces, the established Church, etc., and today, where rarely a week passes when one or other institution is not being drawn into publicly defending itself against accusations of nefarious practice, corruption or maladministration. To give a flavour, in the brief time it has taken to pen this introductory chapter, the media have carried a variety of stories – either real or alleged – concerning:

- failures in child protection
- unacceptable practices in various NHS primary care trusts
- a smear campaign against the Stephen Lawrence family organised by the police
- the failure of the Liberal Democrats to properly investigate sexual harassment within their party
- union manipulation in the selection process of Labour MP candidates
- the Conservative MP Patrick Mercer resigning from his party over concerns surrounding cash for questions
- the conviction of the BBC presenter Stuart Hall for child-sex offences following on from the arrest of other current or former BBC employees on similar charges in the wake of the Jimmy Saville affair
- the arrest and prosecution of a number of media figures as part of the Eleveden and Weeting operations investigations into illegal media practices

- three UK banks being investigated for shutting exchanges out of the credit derivatives market.

The list is by no means exhaustive and it may be that the substance behind some of the above accusations is less than solid. What is clear is that many of these crises are pervading what were once seen as venerable and trusted institutions in both a contiguous and recurrent fashion. As Figures 0.1 and 0.2 illustrate, people increasingly see politicians as self-serving and there has been a clear decline in the trust of once highly regarded institutions. In the current climate, deference and trust appear long gone. The new zeitgeist is framed by a climate of public distrust and suspicion forged on a view that institutions prioritise self-interest over the public good.

Such a transformation in the perception and status of institutions over a relatively short period of time prompts the question why? Is it, for example, the result of a set of pathological institutional problems; rising expectations of the electorate; or the 24-hour media cycle? Indeed, one of the themes alighted on in this volume, which surveys the landscape of institutional crisis across the UK, is whether these events really are symptomatic of a broader institutional malaise and whether the recurring crises which seem to affect public institutions are symptomatic of a broader crisis. Is there any connection between these apparent crises and, if there is, what does it tell us about the UK political system?

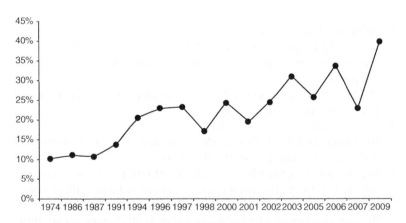

Figure 0.1   Percentage who 'almost never' trust UK governments (of any party) to place the needs of the nation above the interests of their own political party
Source: Cousins (2011).

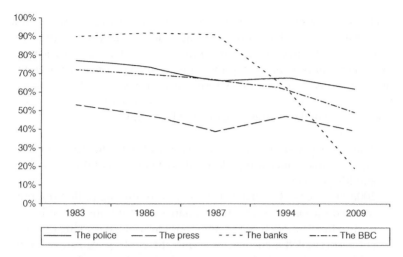

Figure 0.2   Trust in UK institutions
Source: Cousins (2011).

For some, crises are seen as being linked to the financial crisis to emerge in 2007–8, which has subsequently had a profound effect on the political economy of the developed world. This, of course, is not unique to the UK context. The extent of the economic downturn has created sizeable problems for various governments in terms of continuing to provide the level of public services citizens have come to expect throughout much of the latter half of the 20th century. In countries such as Greece and Spain, there have been dramatic reductions in public provision and public sector pay, coupled to large increases in unemployment. This has led to the prospect of wider political crises as voters question the ability of their political leaders, in some cases unelected technocrats, to deal with the scale of the problems that they face.

If we return to the UK context, at the same time that the financial crisis has unfolded, there is the perception of a domino effect, a crisis contagion spreading across a range of different institutions – parliament, Whitehall, political parties, local government, Europe, the police, the media, the Union (of UK nations), etc. – potentially culminating in what we might label a more general crisis within UK institutions. While the notion of crisis itself could clearly be contested, the common perception to take root is that the status quo is challenged in various ways and in different areas that would have been unthinkable half a century ago.

This sense of crisis is raising a series of fundamental questions, not only over the formal and informal rules and current working practices surrounding key institutions within the UK state, but more particularly over their claims to legitimacy and perhaps more pertinently the ability of institutions to adapt to new forms of governance, and the implications of new media. A brief, more generic survey of some of the key events associated with this dynamic might include:

- 2006–7 – the so-called (by certain parts of the media) 'cash for honours' scandal concerning alleged links between political donations and life peerages
- 2008 onwards – the financial crisis, and its aftermath, that not only revealed the extent to which key financial institutions had embraced unsustainable models of risk and poor governance working practices but also revealed inadequacies within the existing regulatory framework coupled to a dysfunctional relationship between key oversight bodies – the Treasury, the Financial Service Authority and the Bank of England
- 2009 – the MPs' expenses scandal exposed the pathology within Westminster of an embedded culture of self-regulation, secrecy and club-like government that rendered it, in the eyes of many, as not fit for purpose and further added muster to an existing debate over arguments concerning the lack of legitimacy engulfing the formal arenas of UK politics
- late 2009 onward – an emerging European sovereign debt crisis and its impact on domestic politics across a range of areas
- 2011 – the 'hacking scandal' to emerge from parts of the UK media, but most notably the News International organisation, which revealed a set of informal, insider, elite, networked relationships between the political class, the media and the Metropolitan Police. This prompted a range of questions over the way these different institutions interact with one another and the 'hidden' effect these interactions have had on institutional working practices
- October 2011 – the Liam Fox affair once again raised the spectre of nefarious practices associated within the lobbying process across Whitehall and beyond, reigniting questions that had previously been raised more than a decade earlier over the 'cash for questions' affair and the subsequent creation of the Nolan Committee to examine standards in public life
- winter 2011–12: the move towards a 2014 referendum on Scottish independence, triggering the potential emergence of a crisis of the Union

- 2012 – a growing debate about the UK's membership of the European Union, with the Conservative Party committing itself to an in–out referendum after 2015 if returned to power
- 2013 – UKIP win 25 per cent of the vote in the local elections, symbolising a loss of faith in the major parties, reflected for example in the earlier electoral success of 'minority' party candidates elected to parliament in Bradford and Brighton.

It has been argued that the real importance of these apparently 'contingent' crises is that they have in different ways revealed a set of more embedded, long-term, though more subtle and complex crises afflicting the UK political system concerning issues of representation, parties and participation. This rather different set of crises may be clustered round the general theme of a 'crisis of legitimacy'.

The aim of this edited volume is to examine the nature of these supposed crises and to address an overarching question:

- To what extent is there a general crisis of institutions in the UK?
  In the context of this issue, this volume also sets out to consider:
- What, if any, links exist between the different perceived crises?
- And, more specifically, is there any relationship between the more recent 'contingent crises' and the notion of a set of longer term, embedded 'crises of legitimacy'?

Understanding crisis

There is a sense in the United Kingdom that crisis is always with us. At the national level, there have long been arguments about the sustainability of the UK economy and indeed much of the post-war historiography of UK politics is focused around the issue of decline and the sense of crisis that such decline has created for institutions (Kenny and English 2000). In some approaches, crisis was endemic to the UK revolution due to the failure of a satisfactory bourgeois revolution (Anderson 1964) and the deeply embedded consequence of empire (Douglas 1986). Here, crisis was more often than not depicted as a structural aspect of the failure of the UK political system to properly modernise post hegemony. For Anderson (1964), the UK state was in crisis in the 1960s as a consequence of its historical development since the English civil war of the 17th century. However, Thatcherism was supposed to have unshackled the UK economy and indeed much of the 1990s and 2000s saw the UK economy growing faster than its continental partners.

Traditionally, the decline debate focused on the economy. Yet, in its more recent manifestation, it is seen in broader terms as a crisis enveloping social, political and economic institutions. The question is whether the crisis is one of a particular institution, of institutions in general or a broader social and economic crisis.

Much of the extant literature focuses on crisis at a systemic level; a broad crisis of the political and social system. The development of what may be called a meta-theory of crisis exists within the context of the notion of the 'risk society' developed in the work of Beck (1992) and Giddens (1998). In essence Beck (1992) and Giddens (1998) link our existential need for security to the uncertainties and challenges of later modernity. The paradox of late modern capitalism is that as the basic human needs are met, we create a new set of risks through technological developments 'which no one absolutely understands and which generates a diversity of possible futures' (Giddens 1998: 25). In the context of the risk society, we develop a whole raft of new threats from overpopulation to environmental disaster, all of which could provoke a widespread crisis for human kind. In a sense, the argument from Beck is that we are over-attenuated to risk. From this perspective, crisis becomes part of modern life and interestingly Gamble (2000) sees the fatalism provoked by a wider sense of crisis as leading to political apathy. Beck (2005) also sees these risks being globalised and moreover, as nation states are increasingly unable to resolve global problems, the legitimacy of the nation state is undermined.

These general senses of politics as crisis or as a response to crisis have generated approaches and understandings that can be seen to be drawn from three broadly defined positions. Interestingly, Power (2007: 4–5) sees risk becoming embedded within managerial and regulatory modes of governing. He argues, 'A stream of apparent failures, scandals, and disasters from the 1990s have challenged and threatened institutional capacities to organise in the face of uncertainty, suggesting where a world is out of control, where failure may be endemic.' The response is risk management in order to control this world of uncertainty and infinite possibilities. The assumption of the risk society approach is that late modernity creates new types of risks that often provoke political mobilisations and hence risk becomes acutely present within the polity. From this perspective, it could be that the recurrent crises of UK institutions are a manifestation of the risk society stemming from the audit society and citizens' greater sensitivities to risk.

Yet what we set out to highlight in this volume is that this uncertainty and risk (and the subsequent institutional failure) do not necessarily result from a more complex world but are essentially political. That what we in fact see are not rising expectations for institutions to deliver (as the risk theorists suggest) but a continued defensiveness on the part of institutions threatened not by 'risk' but by more informed citizens and the demand for greater information. The uncertainty for organisations is that they are faced with increasing oversight, which reveals poor practice or indeed failure. In this sense, the world has not become riskier but increased information makes it more difficult for organisations to control their policy domains. It is certainly the case that a number of the crises in the modern UK (e.g. the horsemeat scandal) are related to greater sensitivity to risk, but also to more rigorous mechanisms of accountability that exposed once hidden decisions.

If we return to the explanations of crisis, in the 1970s, the focus was located very much at the wider state level. In many ways, the same remains the case today, but in their more recent guise, crisis narratives are more often than not organised round two contrasting approaches: one set of critiques tends to frame crisis as being predominantly that of 'demand' (in terms of the expectations of citizens); conversely, there are those that regard crisis predominantly as a matter of 'supply' (in terms of the state and its related institutions' ability to deliver).

A crisis of demand: Conservative conception of crisis

The conservative approach to crisis essentially locates the cause of the crisis with the citizen and in that sense politics has failed because the citizen demands too much (Flinders 2010). The roots of the conservative position lies in the 'overload' debate of the 1970s where the clamour of special interests was seen to have created excessive demands on the state which politicians were unable to fulfil (King 1975, Birch 1984). These perceptions fed into rational choice and New Right conceptions of government which saw citizens acting rationally to demand more from government and politicians acting rationally by supplying more in order to win re-election. The subsequent overload led to government failure and a wider critique of legitimacy crisis. Such approaches also link in with Putnam's (2000) sense of citizens bowling alone and so disengaging from their civic responsibility or, in Flinders' (2012) words, becoming 'decadent'.

The conservative approaches adopted by the contributions from the likes of Flinders and Putnam draw parallels with the fictional rulers in José Saramago's novel *Seeing* who, when faced with mass blank votes, decide that the people have to be taught a lesson and shown that they need to appreciate what the rulers do. Their failure to vote is subverting and betraying the democratic process. Hence the problem is not the process or the government but the voters. For Flinders, for example, the failure to engage is not a refusal to abide by the current democratic rules of the game, but a rejection of politics and democracy. Yet it is arguable that, at least for some, non-voting is a democratic act because to vote is to legitimise a system that voters do not see as democratic, fair or operating particularly effectively. Indeed, England and Wales experienced their own *Seeing* moment when only 15 per cent turned out to vote for the first ever election of police commissioners in 2012. Whilst this could be regarded as an act of modern decadence, it may also be a sign of an intelligent and reflexive electorate not prepared to vote for an ill-explained and ill-justified politicisation of police decision-making. From this perspective, the case of non-voting for police commissioners was, for many, a highly political act. Indeed, in Bedfordshire, the number of spoilt ballots reached a sizeable 8.47 per cent of the vote, suggesting a sophisticated rather than decadent electorate.

In Saramago's tale, the main aim of the political leaders is to persuade 'the degenerates, delinquents and subversives who had cast the blank votes, to acknowledge the error of their ways and to beg for the mercy and the penance of a new election to which, at the chosen time they would rush en masse to purge themselves of the sins of a folly they would never dare to repeat' (Saramago 2004: 50). Likewise for Flinders (2012a: 18), the public do not hate politics 'but they do not understand it'. The nature of this argument reflects a conservative emphasis on the need to respect traditions and with it established institutions. As such, if the electorate are enlightened, they will look on the UK's democratic settlement in a new benign light and the normal process of politics where people dutifully vote for, and respect, their leaders can resume.

Problems of supply: Critical conceptions of crisis

The critical perspective emphasises a supply-side approach by seeing crisis as endemic to the capitalist system. For critical theorists, there are many ways of narrating crisis, but here we briefly highlight three dominant strands:

- the potential of a 'crisis of accumulation' as a consequence of the tendency of the rate of profit to fall and the ability of labour to resist, producing tendencies towards economic crisis
- the potential for a fiscal crisis of the state because of its dependence on capitalist accumulation for income and therefore the difficulties for states to maintain their welfare systems (Offe 1984)

- wider crisis of hegemony or legitimacy as a consequence of ruling elites failing to maintain broader support for their strategies.

From a critical theorist perspective, crisis is inevitable for two reasons. First, there is contradiction between welfare and markets (Offe 1984) with the state needing to provide welfare to maintain capitalism, but welfare undermining the profitability of capitalism. This is what O'Conner saw in the 1970s as a fiscal crisis of the state where the state is unable to pay for the level of welfare and, for Gough (2011), the 2008 financial crisis has reproduced a further fiscal crisis. Second, the continuation of class conflict means that crisis is a mechanism to push back the claims of the working class (Wahl 2011) and indeed the fiscal crisis is used as an argument for reducing wages and cutting services. Whilst, for a period in the late 20th century, critical approaches were for many regarded as an increasingly moribund intellectual and political venture, the 2008 financial crisis has seen a rejuvenation and a return to many of the core themes underpinning a Marxist approach – the contradictions between welfare and markets and a return to material as opposed to post-material politics. From a critical perspective then, crisis is located in the economic system not the political institutions.

Locating crisis within an institutional framework

The problem with these macro-theory approaches to crisis is that they tend to see crisis as a broader crisis of politics or legitimacy. They may be accurate, but do not really help to explain or understand the sorts of problems that are occurring within institutions. Rather, the crisis is located at the level of the system (seen either as the state or the citizenry) and consequently the explanations are deterministic and reductionist. What we seek to understand in this volume is why problems are occurring at the level of a particular institution and whether there is a general explanation for these crises that does not exist only within the social structure as a whole.

One means of approaching this question is offered by the elitist perspective. For example, in terms of political crisis, the elitist approach regards it as a consequence of both the structure of the political system and the ways in which decisions are made with citizens essentially disengaged from the political process. The main thrust of the current elitist approach argues that what is occurring are growing perceptions of crisis as a consequence of an increased dissonance between the activities and everyday lives of citizens and the functioning of the political system and the political class.

The most obvious enunciation of this approach is revealed in the literature on the British political tradition (BPT). It is a literature that, while sizeable, lacks coherence and is certainly not defined by a single, agreed narrative. What can be regarded as a 'classical' wave (Hall 2011) consists of various disparate commentaries reflecting on the origins of the nature of modern-day UK politics, organised round a set of shared assumptions (Oakeshott 1962, Birch 1964, Beer 1965, Greenleaf 1983a, 1983b, 1987). These orthodox accounts of UK government tended to celebrate the virtues of the BPT, which was predominantly established in the 19th century, and praise it for its ongoing stability, continuity and ingenuity. Their depiction of an essentially uniform, elitist and top-down system that delivered strong, seamless but democratically accountable government was presented as normatively good and to be emulated elsewhere.

Yet a more critical wave within the BPT literature was later to emerge (Tant 1993, Evans 2003, Marsh and Hall 2007, Richards 2008, Hall 2011). These accounts questioned the substantial accruement of power at the centre of UK government, sustained by a bi-partisan consensus which has remained largely unchallenged. It highlights the closed and secretive ways in which decisions are made. By invoking the concept of a dominant political tradition, the elitist approach focuses on how the UK political system derives its character from specific historical processes which reflect elitist notions of responsible and representative government (Tant 1993, Evans 2003, Marsh and Hall 2007, Richards 2008, Hall 2011). From this perspective, the UK's representative model of government is still organised on the basis of 19th-century precepts. Essentially, the notion of democracy, the executive, voting and representation that exist in the UK are 19th-century constructs. Crucial to the normative ideas underpinning this approach is the idea that both the executive and the legislature should operate within a self-regulating arena to protect against outside, potentially undemocratic, influence (Judge 1993, Moran 2003). This *modus operandi* can be traced back to the 19th century, where, alongside the emergence of a new democratic settlement, was the embedding first of what Moran (2003) refers to as a system of 'club regulation' among the UK's political elite, but also what Vincent (1998) identifies as the principle of 'honourable secrecy' (see Chapter 6 of this volume).

From this elitist perspective, the argument can be made that the perceived crises within institutions now occurring are linked to the emergence of 21st-century expectations, technologies and transparency challenging a 19th-century model of democracy and participation.

On one level, freedom of information (FoI) has played a crucial role in this debate as it has challenged two of the key elitist tenets crucial to the BPT, that of 'club-like' government and secrecy. Prior to FoI, there were only certain specific moments when revealing glimpses of the actually practices within the black box of UK politics were made available. Normally, these arose out of episodic crises or scandals such as BSE or the arms to Iraq affair, where subsequent government inquires at least offered some insights into the inner works of the UK's political institutions (Smith 1999).

But if, for example, we take the MPs' expenses crisis, this was played out in the new climate of FoI and offers a revealing example of 19th-century practices grating against 21st-century expectations, technologies and views on transparency. MPs were allowed to claim block expenses as a consequence of recognition that the public would not countenance large pay increases. This system was able to function effectively when enveloped in a veil of secrecy. However, FoI ultimately led to the revelation of these expenses in public and with that a sense of shock and outrage from individuals and the media at the nature of the claims. The response of many MPs was one of surprise at such a reaction. There was considerable dissonance between what MPs and the public saw as appropriate. Exposure had revealed a problem with the existing status quo.

Similarly, in the case of the death of Ian Tomlinson in 2009, the police faced an apparent crisis because they initially denied any involvement in his death until mobile phone videos revealed the police assault. Here, advances in technology and therefore new forms of transparency exposed what was traditionally a closed and secretive code of practice underpinning key state institutions. As one police officer pointed out at the Leveson inquiry, 'The police are struggling to keep apace of social media. He says that some social media accounts could jeopardise the professional image of the police force' (*The Guardian*, 5 March 2012).

Aims of the book

The aim of this book then is to investigate whether there is a general crisis of UK institutions. If so, to what degree can it be understood from an elitist perspective, as part of a crisis of the BPT? Alternatively, if there is not a crisis, what is going on? Why are political institutions being exposed in this way? Is there a series of unlinked, contingent events and exposures that institutions will overcome or is there a more profound crisis of a political system and culture established in the 19th century and unable to adapt to the bright lights of 21st-century politics? Are these crises or traumas causing citizens to lose faith and to look to alternative forms of political engagement? Are events like the riots of 2011 an indication of a more fundamental crisis in the UK political process? Can we point to a widespread crisis of UK institutions or will the long-term resilience of the UK state and political class see traditional modes of politics bounce back? Is any perception of crisis merely the public taking the political class for granted? Is it a crisis of expectations or a further example of media exaggeration? Do we need to be more realistic about politics or is this (another) opportunity for democratic renewal?

The book is organised in two parts. Part I adopts a thematic approach to understanding crisis in which the first three chapters explore a set of more generic arguments concerning, in turn, a crisis of expectation, participation and politics. These chapters seek to set out in detail the broader contours of various debates and approaches underpinning our current understanding of crisis. Part II then adopts a more institutional focus – offering accounts of many of the key UK institutions and their current relationship to crisis. The nine institutions explored forthwith are: parliament, political parties, Whitehall, the Union, the European Union, the financial sector, regulation, the media and policing. This list is by no means exhaustive – the NHS, the welfare state, the judiciary and child protection, for example, are not included, predominantly due to the constraints of space presented by a single volume. Nevertheless, the aim of undertaking what is a sizeable survey of most of the key UK institutions is to allow for a depth of analysis leading to a series of reflective responses to the questions posed at the outset of this introductory chapter.

Part I

A Thematic Approach to Crisis

1
A Crisis of Expectation

David Richards

Introduction

Much has been made about the current conduct of contemporary UK politics. There is a perceived malaise, reflected more often than not in terms of a rising tide of anti-political sentiment directed towards mainstream politics and disengagement by the general public from the formal arenas of politics – party membership or voter turnout – as the oft-cited examples. It is a theme the former Labour Foreign Secretary David Miliband reflected on when giving the Speaker's Lecture at the Palace of Westminster in June 2012. His address, *Ministers and Politics in a Time of Crisis* offered a series of thematic comparisons with the 1970s, a decade, he observed, that had a similar:

> debate about 'fiscal crisis of the state', the rise of separatist parties in the form of the SNP and Plaid Cymru, the birth of extremist parties like the National Front. The sociologist Daniel Bell claimed in the middle of that decade that the nation state 'was too big for the small problems and too small for the big ones'. There was even a name for the crisis: 'the ungovernability thesis'. Britain, it was claimed, was too divided to be governed.

Miliband went on to suggest that, similar to the 1970s, contemporary debates over a perceived crisis of politics reflect a sense of 'broken promises' on the part of the political class towards the electorate.

Those familiar with the now sizeable literature on the various problems besetting the conduct of contemporary liberal-democratic politics in the UK will recognise that Miliband's contribution concerns the emergence of what is often referred to as a 'crisis of expectation' (Stoker 2006, Hay 2007, Flinders 2012a). It is formulated on the notion that there is an ever-widening gulf or 'expectations gap' (Flinders 2012a: 57) between what is promised by or expected of the political class and what it, in turn, can offer. Here it is argued that the gap between what is depicted as the demand- and supply-sides of democratic politics has exponentially grown. Recently, this figurative gap has been further widened by the financial crisis and the emergence of a new austerity age, further fuelling a growing sense of anti-political sentiment and cynicism surrounding the conduct of politics.

Addressing the symptoms of this crisis tends to invoke two broadly contrasting responses. The first is predicated on the need to change the way in which contemporary politics operates, stressing the need for reform in terms of the nature and practice of the institutions, processes and actors involved in delivering or supplying politics (Stoker 2006, Hay 2007). The second seeks 'to map and diagnose the contemporary condition of disaffection and disengagement ... as resting not with changes in the supply of political goods so much as with changes in the responsiveness to, and desire for such goods by their potential consumers' (Hay 2007: 40). In terms of the latter, blame is mainly apportioned in the direction of what is characterised as an increasingly sectional and selfish electorate who hold 'unreal-ideals' and expectations of what democratic politics can offer. Flinders (2012a: vii) provides the starkest enunciation of this type of account, depicting the emergence of a 'bad faith model of politics', caused by a surge in demand-side pressures.

Hay (2007: 39) observes that demand-side explanations concerning a contemporary crisis of expectation currently form the dominant approach within the academic literature.[1] As such, much of this chapter is focused on this particular set of arguments and approaches, but not in an uncritical manner. For if we are to use the past to help illuminate our understanding of the present, the experience of the 1970s and the response to the first-wave crisis of expectation offers some crucial insights. As Miliband (2012) pointedly observes:

> if these are the lessons of the 1970s, there is one seismic difference that is relevant. It concerns the political conditions in which the economic crisis has to be addressed. The 1974 Labour manifesto talked of a 'crowning test of our democracy' in confronting the economic perils facing the country, but there was little thought that the political system itself needed reform. Today we do not have that luxury.
>
> (Miliband 2012)

The stress here, which forms the overarching theme of this chapter, is on the need to re-examine the way in which contemporary democratic politics is currently supplied. In so doing, it seeks to challenge those accounts that predominantly preference demand-side explanations concerning the current problems besetting politics. The argument presented below avers that contemporary demand-side narratives concerning a crisis of expectation are miscast, as they essentially offer a defence of the existing political settlement and in so doing perpetuate the very crisis they seek to address.

In terms of the organisation of the chapter, attention is first paid to the response to the first-wave, 1970s crisis of expectation in the shape of Thatcherism. Here, it is argued that what ensued was a series of economic and social reforms, but crucially not any substantive alteration to either the existing political settlement or with it the conduct of UK politics, which instead continued to operate in much the same way. This is explained by the ongoing commitment by post-1979 governments to the British political tradition (BPT), a theme already touched on in the introductory chapter to this edited volume.[2] It then explores the various dimensions of the second-wave crisis of expectation currently enveloping the conduct of UK politics, suggesting that the dominance of demand-side accounts to addressing this issue is not unproblematic. The argument developed here concerns themes of causality, correlation and sequencing. It is suggested that primacy must first be given to reforming the way in which politics is currently supplied, which in turn has the potential to render a shift in demand-side perceptions of what mainstream politics can offer. This chapter concludes by arguing that if such sequencing in the reform process is ignored, and with it the plea made by Miliband above overlooked, then there is a strong chance that, as with the 1970s, this second-wave crisis of expectation will be regarded as another missed opportunity to bring about a crucially needed remodelling of the existing political settlement.

We've been here before: The 1970s and the first-wave crisis of expectation

The current perceived crisis of expectation besetting UK politics is by no means a new phenomenon. A similar set of themes concerning an expectations gap first appeared in the course of the 1960s, culminating in the emergence of a more fully blown crisis in the 1970s. It led to the portrayal of the UK state as 'ungovernable'. As Pierson (1991: 141) observes:

> It was in this period of the early and mid-1970s that social democratic confidence in the competence of the mixed economy allied to greater

social equity came under increasing challenge. It was also...the period of the flowering of New Right and neo-Marxist accounts of the welfare state, both of which concentrated on the ubiquity of crisis arising from the inherently unstable and contradictory elements within the post-war welfare capitalist consensus.

Various explanations were offered as to the causes underpinning the emergence of this state of ungovernability. One of the most prominent approaches was that of a crisis of expectation and what was labelled as the 'overload thesis'. The concept of overload first emerged in two articles, published in the same year by Crozier (1975) in his analysis of the USA and Tony King's (1975) account of the UK. The key theme of the overload thesis was predicated on the view that following the turn to more statist and welfarist programmes adopted by many advanced-liberal democracies in the aftermath of the Second World War, there had occurred a clearly identifiable rise in public expectations (demand) of what public goods government should provide. It was argued that, inevitably, governments had failed to deliver (supply) on many of these expectations, which in turn had resulted in a serious decline of public confidence in government.

In the UK context, Anthony King (1975: 166) captured the essence of the overload thesis in a striking aphorism which laid the failure to meet the expectations of the nation clearly at the door of the government:

> Once upon a time, then, man looked to God to order the World. Then he looked to the market. Now he looks to government. The differences are important. God was irremovable, immutable. The market could be removed or mutated but only, it was thought at a very high price. Government by contrast, is removable, mutable – and corporeal. One blames not 'Him', or 'It' but 'Them'.

It was a thesis that was to attract a number of exponents (Brittain 1975, Rose 1975, Douglas 1976, Moss 1976, Jay 1977, Barnes and Kaase 1979, Richardson and Jordan 1979, Parsons 1982, Birch 1984). Rose (1975: 14) succinctly sums up the main theme to emerge in these accounts and in so doing the emphasis they each placed on the demand-side:

> Governments become overloaded when expectations are in excess of national resources, the government institutions, and the impact that its outputs can achieve. *Such an overload arises from decision of citizens*

individually and in organized groups to ask more of government than it can in total provide [italics added].

Different elements of the overload critique were embraced by the Left (Habermas 1975, Offe 1975), but more crucially by the emergent New Right, which drew on them to explain what it depicted as a wider crisis of the state (Dorey 1995). The New Right claimed that if the trend towards governments attempting to satisfy the ever-increasing expectations of society was not arrested, then eventually both author-ity and legitimacy of government and the political system would be undermined:

> Although 'legitimation crisis' is a concept usually associated with the Left, it does tie in very closely with much of the neo-conservative critique, for as the economist Samuel Brittan observes: 'If a succession of governments ... stir up expectations only to disappoint them, there is a risk of the whole system snapping under the strain'.
>
> (Brittan 1983: 17)

Accounts of overload underpinned by a crisis of expectation narrative have subsequently received a number of revisionist critiques. Hay in par-ticular (1996, 2007) offers a challenge to the overload thesis, identifying a key paradox; he notes how on one level the account seeks to frame a rational choice-based portrayal of self-interested voters open to political bribery in the 1970s. Such an image he avers is essentially patronising of the electorate, who are depicted as greedy, unprincipled and oppor-tunistic. Yet, at the same time, by calling for a decisive break from the past, which had supposedly led to a crisis of expectation, overload the-orists were 'appealing precisely to the good sense of the electorate that they have previously just dismissed' (Hay 1996: 136).

The validity of such criticisms of the overload thesis is important, but it should not detract from the extent to which, as Hay (1996) indeed recognises, the sense of crisis in the 1970s was very real. From this perspective, what can be understood as the discursive construction of crisis had a very real or tangible impact. The context of this crisis narra-tive was employed by the New Right to depict the various governments of the post-war era as collectively the guilty party (supply-side empha-sis) in their pandering to and attempting to appease the exponential growth in self-interested, sectional demands placed on them by soci-etal groups (demand-side emphasis). It is in this sense that both the crisis narratives of overload and ungovernability were distilled into a broader crisis of expectation organised around a dialectical set of *both* demand- and supply-side forces. In so doing, the New Right could position itself to offer a potent challenge to the embedded Keynesian-welfare settlement pursued by different governments since 1945 by linking the growing expectations of the electorate to a range of economic and political crises. Such positioning afforded the New Right the opportunity to offer an alternative to the existing orthodoxy, a challenge taken up by key actors in the Conservative Party after 1975.

The Thatcherite response to crisis and the shadow of the BPT

Much has been written about the late 1970s ushering in a new neo-liberal political settlement under the auspices of Thatcherism. The literature on Thatcherism tends to embrace two binary positions: a set of transformative accounts depicting the 1970s as a critical juncture leading to a radical break embodied in the exceptionalism of the Thatcherite project; and those narratives stressing a more evolutionary or path-dependent approach emphasising historical continuity. Such a distinction is both well-rehearsed and remains as contested today as it was a few decades ago.[3]

In the context of this chapter, it is argued that from the late 1970s, the Conservative leadership appealed to a sense of crisis to justify a programme to transform what it regarded as an over-extended state. It proposed the withdrawal of the state to be replaced by non-state actors to meet the demands of the electorate. In governance terms, this involved reducing the size of the public sector, combating inflation not unemployment, disengaging from the economy and cutting direct taxation (supply-side solutions in both a monetarist and governance sense). In so doing, the demands of the electorate would shift from the state towards the marketplace to satisfy its expectations. Hence, the problems of both overload and the related crisis of expectation would be resolved.

Yet, in practice, there was a contingency that shaped the subsequent character of the reform programme pursued by the various Conservative administrations between 1979 and 1997. That contingency emerges in the shape of the BPT. Here, it is useful to disaggregate and go beyond what Marsh (1995) sees as a tendency in the literature towards 'uni-dimensional explanations' of Thatcherism. In so doing, in public policy terms, debate over the extent to which the post-1979 reforms in areas such as political economy and state welfarism are exceptionalist or evolutionary remains unresolved. But where there is far less contestation concerns the limited impact of Thatcherism on the existing political settlement. Here, there emerged a notable continuity with the past. There was a discernible lack of reforming zeal in such areas as the constitution or the broader system of governance as reflected in the Westminster model, much to the chagrin of some on the New Right (Hoskyns 2000).

Why? Thatcherism was to all intents and purposes constitutionally conservative, concentrating much of its political capital on addressing economic and welfare rather than political reform (Gamble 1994b). Indeed, it is worth noting that Thatcherism regarded what Barry (1965) referred to as the UK's 'power-concentration' constitution, or what is now more commonly depicted as the core executive's power-hoarding approach to governance, as particularly useful in pursuing its economic and social-welfare reform programmes. The more 'high politics' areas concerning the UK's parliamentary state were left relatively unchallenged because Thatcherism had little interest in rejecting the Westminster model and starting afresh.

Throughout its period in office, the Conservative Party instead embraced a Burkeian position, remaining committed to parliamentary conservatism, an unwritten constitution, the existing model of representative democracy and a neutral civil service. Consequently, there was never an attempt, for example, to embrace a specific New Right model of bureaucracy that would have challenged the edifice of the parliamentary state. Thatcher, for example, when speaking about civil servants as individuals rather than Whitehall as an institution, was keen to praise their commitment and professionalism (Richards and Smith 2000). This view was recently reaffirmed by the current Cabinet Secretary Jeremy Heywood and Head of the Civil Service Bob Kerslake (2013): 'Despite her "Iron Lady" image and her conviction politics... Margaret Thatcher mostly held a rather traditional view of the Civil Service.' Thus, no alternative to the Westminster model was sought or developed during the 1979–97 Conservative administration. The Thatherite legacy was one that had limited effect on the way in which UK politics was to be supplied and, as such, continuity with the BPT was maintained (Richards 2004).

What this brief overview of both the literature and the events of this period illustrates is that in the course of the late 1970s and the ensuing period of Thatcherism, a crisis of expectation was used predominantly as a rhetorical tool by the New Right to delegitimise the previous postwar epoch of UK politics and so agitate for change. At one level then, it is operating as a narrative to challenge, not sustain the status quo. But the change that ensued was both contingent and focused on certain areas, notably in the economic, social and welfare spheres. This was because the diagnosis to a crisis of expectation offered by the ensuing Conservative administration was mediated through an approach that sought predominantly to alter the contours of the state, to affect a shift, in paraphrasing Greenleaf (1987), from collectivism to individualism. But elsewhere, there were clear continuities. Thatcherism placed little emphasis on reforming the Westminster model or with it the BPT, both of which remained predominantly intact (Marsh and Tant 1989, Tant 1993, Richards 2008, Hall 2011). Such a perspective helps reveal the contingencies to Thatcherism and with it the ongoing dichotomy between transformative and evolutionary accounts of its legacy.

Crisis redux: The second-wave crisis of expectation

One of the overarching themes, reflected in the different contributions to this edited volume, is the number and variety of interrelated crisis narratives presently at play. Of course, as we have seen above, the same was also true in the 1970s. Yet, in the current context, a perceived crisis of expectation has resurfaced, but with a slightly different emphasis. This time it has predominantly been distilled through a broader debate coalescing round the notion that contemporary politics is failing (e.g. Stoker 2006, Hay 2007, Riddell 2011, Flinders 2012a). Much of this debate centres on a wider legitimation crisis drawn from a growing body of evidence signalling the exponential decline in engagement by the public with traditional or formal arenas of politics.[4]

As was the case with overload in the 1970s, the issues currently being raised are not exclusive to UK politics, but are part of a wider set of challenges facing many advanced liberal-democratic states. For example, one of the earliest but still dominant demand-side explanations to the current crisis is offered by the US political scientist Robert Putnam (2000). His 'social capital thesis' draws on a variety of evidence to suggest that the erosion of civic participation and public duty by individuals in society has led to disengagement from the formal political process. This explanation is shaped by the view that it is not existing democratic models and their related institutions but citizens that should bear the brunt of the blame for contemporary failings in politics.

The current 'failure' of politics and a new emergent crisis of expectation

In the context of the UK, there are some notable contributions to the demand-side literature concerning a contemporary crisis of politics

(Bentley 2005, Bale et al. 2006, McHugh 2006, Stoker 2006, 2010, 2011, Flinders 2010, 2012a, Fox 2010, Riddell 2010, 2011, Hatier 2012). Like Putnam, and before him Almond and Verba (1963), these accounts are predominantly drawn to the civic realm focusing on evidence drawn from changing patterns in the behaviour, actions and attitudes of the public.

The idea that citizens are less willing to participate has led to Flinders' notion of a 'bad faith model of politics'. From this perspective, a 'corrosively cynical' public view of politics and politicians has taken root:

> We must not allow our political system to become synonymous with failure because public apathy and distrust places a mighty weight on those who have stepped forward on behalf of society in order to attempt to deal with the wave after wave of crises (social, economic, environmental, etc.) that crash upon the shore of politics with ever increasing frequency.
>
> (Flinders 2010: 309–10)

The focus is not primarily concerned with the nature or the way in which politics is currently being supplied in the form of the existing system, its related institutions or actors, but instead, the behaviour of the electorate. Such accounts preference a demand-side focus for the current perceived failings in politics:

> The public have become politically decadent in their expectations about what politics should deliver, how politicians should behave and their own responsibilities within society. I want to suggest that people 'hate politics' because they simply do not understand it; and they are generally not helped to understand it by the media (or university professors of politics for that matter). There may also be a demographic factor at play: this contemporary climate of anti-politics is arguably rooted in a generation that has become complacent and parochial, and in doing so has forgotten the alternatives to democratic politics.
>
> (Flinders 2010: 310, 2012a: viii)

Central to this approach is the view that the public has a general mis-understanding of how representative democracy operates. As Stoker (2006: 1) reminds us, democracy is 'inevitably destined to disappoint' given that it is about 'squeezing collective decisions out of multiple and competing interest and opinions'.

At the broadest level, current problems besetting politics are framed in terms of the waning of a more deferential, less cynical era of politics (Nevitte 1996, Inglehart 1999, Marquand 2004).[5] In its place has emerged a more critical, atomistic citizenry (Giddens 1990, Norris 1999, 2011, Stoker 2010), that possess a rising set of expectations over what politics can offer (Stoker 2006: 45, Flinders 2012a). For Flinders (2012a: 57), this has led to 'an ever increasing "expectations gap" between what is promised/expected and what can realistically be delivered by politicians and democratic states'.

This notion of a widening expectations gap within the literature essentially draws on two countervailing dynamics. The first is a rising demand on the part of the electorate, but the second concerns the growing constraints currently operating on the political class, hampering its ability to supply political goods because of a range of events, many of which are beyond their control: globalisation; information technology; a post-ideological/post-material age; the risk society, etc. Moreover, an emerging climate of austerity has compounded the problem of supply, leading to the claim that there is currently too much voice in an age of diminishing choice. The demand-side diagnosis thus alights upon the need for the electorate to undergo some form of a reality check, or *in extremis* (re)-education over what democratic politics can realistically offer: 'Saving politics from itself and embracing a more honest account of politics therefore demands accepting that focusing on supply is less important than focusing on demand' (Flinders 2012a: 59). It is this set of themes that are examined in detail below.

The dynamics of a demand-driven expectations gap

Crucial to the notion of an expectations gap is the argument that ' voters have unrealistic beliefs and hopes about what the political system can deliver for them' (Riddell 2011: 3). There are various dimensions to this argument, the more prominent of which include:

(i) Rise of the citizen consumer

One strand of the literature highlights a growing trend towards the 'citizen consumer' (Leys 2003, Pattie, Seyd and Whiteley 2004, Stoker 2006). It alights on such themes as marketisation and commodification of the state and politics, emphasising materialism and choice which have 'encouraged people to demand levels of service provision that would commonly be provided only in the private sector ... thereby inflating public expectations far beyond what the state or politics was intended, expected or resourced to provide' (Flinders 2010: 317, Riddell 2011: 63).

(ii) Governance, complexity and rising expectations

Another central theme concerns the range and complexity of issues governments are now expected to address. Flinders (2012a: 21), for example, when reflecting on the 1970s overload debate claims that 'One crucial element of the changing nature of politics since the 1960s and 1970s is that the public's expectations of politics have grown even greater, as have the range of issues which politicians are expected to shoulder responsibilities'. The main thrust of this approach suggests governing in the 21st century is a more complex and demanding task. The last quarter century has witnessed a shift in governing from a traditional Weberian, top-down, hierarchical and bureaucratic approach to a mode involving an eclectic mix of states, networks and markets.

To compound this issue, not only does government have to operate in an increasingly complex, multi-level governance setting, but the often individualised and specialised challenges laid at its door have also exponentially grown and in some cases become nigh on intractable to resolve (Gamble 2000, Stoker 2006). Stoker (2006: 66), for example, cites: 'the impact of globalisation and the technological challenges we face [means] that doing politics in the twenty-first century is hard'. Or for Flinders (2012a: 21), the advance of science has heightened 'social anxieties' and in so doing by implication heaped added pressure onto government. Elsewhere, the erosion of 'fate' means politicians are now also expected to 'prevent, manage and respond... to natural disasters... to alleviate both the likelihood and consequence of events... which would for most of the twentieth century have existed beyond the realm of democratic politics'. The cumulative effect of these various forces has led to an exponential growth in public expectations placed on government.

(iii) Decline in civic virtues and the need for democratic (re)-education

A third central theme of this argument concerns a perceived decline in civic virtues and the rise of an 'anti-politics' generation. For example, Flinders (2010, 2012) suggests that the older generation, who experienced total war, had a greater respect for and appreciation of the value of democracy. This is then contrasted with the disengagement and 'anti-politics' predisposition of a younger generation 'that has become complacent and parochial, and in doing so has forgotten the alternatives to democratic politics' (Flinders 2010: 310). The net result, Bentley (2005: 16) suggests, is that the electorate ends up with the type of politics (and politicians) it deserves: 'The decline of deference is not a bad thing, but when it sweeps away all kinds of public legitimacy we have a fundamental problem. That's why I say that we get the politicians we deserve, because our opt-out from politics inevitably reduces the legitimacy of leaders.'

Another dimension to this approach is offered by Franklin (2004), Clarke et al. (2004) and Park (2005). Their various surveys of the decline in younger generations' participation in formal arena politics – party membership, voting, etc. – invoke a variety of debates concerning changing life-style choices that are seen as habit-forming at an early age and have a subsequent path-dependent effect on levels of civic engagement.

Finally, Bale et al. (2006), McHugh (2006) and Riddell (2010) make the case using evidence drawn from a number of Audit of Political Engagement surveys conducted by the Hansard Society and the Electoral Commission to suggest that there is a gap between the rhetorical commitment by citizens to act and the reality of their propensity to actually engage (Fox 2010). This particular critique is a rebuff to those calling for institutional (supply-side) reforms through the introduction of new or more participatory deliberative mechanisms, instead arguing that the inherent danger of such reforms is that they may:

> only succeed in engaging those already over-represented amongst voters and party members – that is, the educated, affluent and middle-aged. Mechanisms designed to provide greater opportunities for citizens to participate more directly in decision making as a means of increasing legitimacy and reducing the perceived democratic deficit may therefore have the opposite effect.
>
> (McHugh 2006: 551)

What binds these various approaches together is a shared view that an increasingly skewed relationship between the governors and the governed has arisen in which individuals have a very acute sense of their rights but an underdeveloped understanding of their reciprocal responsibilities to the democratic process (Stoker 2006, Riddell 2011, Flinders 2012a). As Hatier (2012: 468) in somewhat contrarian style avers, 'There is a clear imbalance in the relationship between politicians and voters: whilst unhappy voters can remove the government in place at the next election, representatives cannot ask for better citizens.'

The conclusion is that the UK's existing model of representative democracy, warts and all, remains the 'least worst' form of government. Thus, in their analysis, there is a common rejection of the need for a major overhaul in the UK's existing democratic and governance arrangements. Some offer an olive branch to limited, more delegative, bottom-up and participatory reforms, but this is often pitched only at the local level (Stoker 2011). For the underpinning driver of each of these various accounts is that ultimately democratic politics is about a political class having to making difficult, often unpopular choices over the allocation of a set of (for some, increasingly) scarce resources. Riddell (2011: 101–2) encapsulates this view:

> Whenever the People are invoked, I wonder which People? The vocal and active minority, or the majority? That is why I am sceptical about citizen's juries and deliberative assemblies ... Participatory democracy has attractions at a local, neighbourhood level, but not nationally in reconciling conflicting preferences and pressures on public spending, taxation and borrowing. That job is for politicians elected by, and acting on behalf of, all the people.

Their diagnosis then to a current crisis of expectation falls mainly on the need to (re)-educate the demos in what it can and should expect from contemporary democratic politics.

A critique of a demand-driven expectations gap

Two themes emerge from the above discussion on an expectations gap: first, the claim that demand by the electorate for what government should be delivering has exponentially grown over recent decades; second and relatedly, that the seeds of anti-political sentiment result from a decline in deference on the part of the public linked to a reciprocal rise in cynicism, particularly among younger generations, emanating from a misunderstanding of what representative democracy can and actually does. Each of these themes is addressed below.

Great state expectations

It may well be the case that the range of issues politicians are now expected to bear (some) responsibility for has increased over the last 40 years ago. Unfortunately, the evidence to support such a claim in the current literature is more often than not pitched in a rather broad-brush and impressionistic manner with little attempt to offer any form of systematic analysis addressing actual change over time. Flinders (2012a: 21) exemplifies this approach. 'Science, to take one example, has raised social anxieties and placed new demands at the door of politicians that simply did not exist 50 years ago – human embryology, regenerative stem cell technology, xenotransplantation, nanotechnology etc.' The wholly subjective nature of this list and others like it comprises of scientific developments that could be interpreted in terms of advancements addressing social problems and so aiding society, rather than developments increasing demands on government. But beyond such ad hocery, there are a number of wider points here:

- First, to resurrect an old-fashioned pluralistic adage, for every such development or issue laid at the government's door, others similarly drop-off.
- Second, complex social issues such as teenage pregnancy, homelessness and narcotic abuse are by no means new. In terms of the latter, it could be that one consequence of the decline of deference is that issues that were once dealt with behind closed doors, like teenage pregnancy, are now politicised and are much more in the public realm. So what we see here is a potential 'politicisation' rather than a 'de-politicisation' effect. Either way, what is clearly required is much greater empirical investigation than is currently available within the existing literature.
- Finally, natural disasters and wars have been an ever-present feature of life. The issue within these accounts is potentially one of ahistoricism. This is brought into sharp focus if, for example, we are reminded of the dislocation caused by two periods of total war during the course of the 20th century. To make good on earlier commitments by the state, most notably that of deferred gratification to prosecute the war effort, each period culminated in a groundswell of expectations placed at the government's door, the manifestation of which was the promise of 'homes fit for heroes' after 1918 or a 'new Jerusalem' after 1945.

The crucial question then remains, not simply is government doing more today than it was 30 years ago, but more precisely, do people look more to the state now than they did previously? In addressing this question, Whiteley (2012: 15–33) offers both a revealing and detailed account of the changing attitudes of citizens over time towards what

Table 1.1 Changes in perceptions of government responsibility 1985–2006

Government definitely should do the following	1985 (%)	1990 (%)	1996 (%)	2006 (%)
Provide healthcare for the sick	86	85	82	71
Provide a decent living standard for the old	79	78	71	60
Impose strict laws to protect the environment	–	–	62	48
Provide financial help to students	–	49	37	34
Keep prices under control	61	49	42	32
Help industry to grow	54	43	40	29
Reduce income differences between the rich and the poor	48	42	35	27
Provide affordable housing	–	–	62	48
Provide a job for everyone who wants one	38	24	28	17
Provide a decent living standard for the unemployed	45	32	28	11

Note: Dashes indicate missing data in those years.
Source: Whiteley (2012: 12).

they expect from government. His analysis is particularly relevant in this context, as it is not a simple, synchronic snapshot based on recent polling, but has a more diachronic overtone to it, drawn from the extensive data sets provided over a 20-year period by the International Social Survey Programme Role of Government Studies collected in 1985, 1990, 1996 and 2006. Crucially, this time-series data (see Table 1.1) reveals that overall individual perceptions of what is expected from government over time have declined, not risen.

Whiteley (2012: 29–32) concludes that there has been a cumulative decline in the electorate's expectations on what government should be providing compared to 30 years ago:

Over a period of years the UK population has grown more conservative in feeling that government should do less ... The trends suggest that Britons are gradually moving away from the belief that the state should provide health, welfare and education ... The very large reductions in support for job creation, unemployment benefits and the provision of affordable housing, together with the drop in support for redistribution suggests that people are less inclined to turn to government to solve their problems.

Such evidence is hardly surprising if we reflect on the subsequent response to the 1970s debates surrounding overload and ungovernability. The rhetorical response of Thatcherism was to roll back the frontiers of the state, let the market in and, in so doing, seek to resolve an expectations crisis by breaking the previous post-war cycle of party competition and with it state growth. Of course, the evidence concerning the degree to which state retrenchment over the subsequent period occurred remains contested (Marsh et al. 1999). But perhaps less controversial is the view that the state today is, in relative terms, less directly active than in the heady corporatist days of the 1960s and early 1970s. What the evidence from Whitely highlights is one of the legacies of the Thatcherite and indeed post-Thatcherite eras; a shift in individuals' expectations of what governments should be providing or, to invoke Greenleaf (1983a), a re-orientation from collectivism to individualism. In many areas, people are more accepting of looking less to the state than in the previous Keynesian-Welfare era. Crucially, of course, this challenges the notion of a demand-driven 'expectations gap' acting as a key driver in explaining the current failure of politics.

'*I wasn't learnt proper*': Anti-politics and the myth of the model democratic citizen

There is something rather paternalistic, indeed patronising, in some of the claims sketched above, which suggest that more recent generations of the public have become increasingly 'politically decadent' or 'illiterate' and so fail to understand the essence of what democracy is for. Certainly, such accounts make little attempt to substantiate such a view. Their tendency is to construct an argument based on a narrow understanding of what constitutes 'the political', from which is developed a set of assumptions depicting a causal relationship between declining voter turnout, in particular among younger sections of the electorate, and a perceived rise in political and civic apathy (see Chapter 2). Underpinning such claims is a Putnam-style assertion that cumulatively there has been a decline in social and political capital within recent emergent generations of the electorate.

The issues and arguments here are complex and go beyond simple, unidimensional accounts that lack sufficient survey data to reveal what or how people think politically. There is a tendency to treat the electorate as a monolithic entity, rather than as a set of complex, reflexive actors making individual rational decisions on whether to vote or not, or even vote for traditional mainstream parties. Nevertheless and contra some of the assumptions presented above relating in particular to younger peoples' relationship with the formal political arena, a recent large-scale, survey-based study by Tonge, Mycock and Jeffrey (2012: 599), assessing the impact of citizenship classes since their introduction in England in 2002, concludes that:

> citizenship education *has* made a significant impact upon political understanding and engagement...Our study demonstrates that young people who have received Citizenship classes are more likely to engage in civic activism, contributing to a healthier polity. The political literacy and 'taught democracy' ambitions for citizenship education espoused particularly by Crick–Blunkett...may be being realised.

Here, it is important not to read off a lack of formal political engagement, especially by younger generations, as a symptom of increased political illiteracy. For if our focus goes beyond the narrower confines of formal arena politics, then, as outlined in more detail in both Chapters 2 and 5, there is a sizeable body of evidence highlighting the changing patterns in the way in which younger generations still continue actively to engage politically. They do so, however, in such a way that falls outside traditional channels. Indeed, the evidence offered in the more reflexive accounts by the likes of Norris (2011) and Stoker (2006, 2012) rightly alights upon a set of debates concerning the rise of the 'critical citizen' in a post-deference age, rather than the emergence of a generation of politically illiterate subjects. The extensive data drawn over time from the annual Democratic Audit reinforces such a view:

> evidence that turnout in UK elections is falling and that party membership levels are now a fraction of what they were half a century ago, these stark declines are clearly not reflected in other forms of political and civic activity...Indeed, our findings reinforce longer-run UK evidence that levels of engagement in most forms of political and civic activity have held up well since the late 1960s.
>
> (Wilks-Heeg et al. 2012: 5)

This returns us to one of the key problems to emerge in the more prominent demand-side accounts presented by those such as Riddell (2011) and Flinders (2012a) – a tendency throughout to adopt only a narrow view of politics. The overarching claim within these accounts is the need to defend democratic politics against a rising anti-political tide. But in so doing, the underpinning approach is a tendency to conflate a defence of politicians with a defence of the Westminster (power-hoarding) model. For example, Riddell observes that 'throughout this book I have treated the case for representative democracy and politicians as synonymous' (Riddell 2011: 143).

One of the issues this raises is a lack of proper disaggregation between people's views of politicians as individual actors and their broader views on the nature and efficacy of the current democratic and political system. As opinion-poll data collected over time reveals, the public has always held a sceptical view of politicians and what motivates them. For example, a survey conducted in 1944 during the latter stages of the Second World War asked:

Question: Do you think British politicians are out merely for themselves, for their party, or to do their best for their country?

Results: (per cent) Themselves 35, Party 22, Country 36, Don't know 7

> Source: Gallup. Reported in George H. Gallup (1976),
> *The Gallup International Public Opinion Polls: Great
> Britain 1937–1975* (Random House, New York),
> Volume I, p 96. cf. Healey et al. (2005).

Elsewhere and more recently, the eight reports so far published by the Hansard Society (2003–11) on public attitudes towards politicians draw together an array of both quantitative and qualitative data sets collected over time to reveal the following:

- In the 1970s, 60 per cent of the public believed that people involved in politics told the truth only some of the time.
- In 2007 (pre-expenses scandal), the 2007 Eurobarometer Survey of public attitudes found that only 34 per cent of the UK public trusted Parliament.
- The Committee on Standards in Public Life has consistently found in its biennial Trust in Public Life surveys that politicians are among the least trusted of professions when it comes to telling the truth.
- Qualitative focus group research in 2005, well before the expenses scandal, found that politics was viewed 'as the pursuit of an exclusive and disreputable elite of "hypocrites and liars"'.

• The 2009 Audit of Political Engagement showed that 26 per cent of the public trust politicians either 'a great deal' or 'a fair amount', a decline of just 1 per cent on the number who reported the same in 2004.

Not surprisingly, the Hansard study concluded, 'Politicians have rarely been trusted. The expenses scandal did not therefore lead to a collapse in trust in politics and politicians because levels of trust were already so low' (Fox 2010: 1). The public has always rather than recently held a sceptical view of politicians. What is most revealing in the collective evidence produced by these various Hansard Society reports is the degree to which:

> the average citizen in Britain could be described as disappointed and disengaged by politics: disappointed by the practitioners, practice and outcomes of politics, and not actively engaged in the regular processes of politics. The picture painted of the beginning of the twenty-first century...suggests the overall pattern is relatively stable but negative in terms of the story it tells, providing a less than ringing endorsement of the British political system.
>
> (Stoker 2012: 32)

Cause and effect: Bringing the supply of politics back in

This returns us to the real issue presented by demand-side accounts drawn from the sizeable evidence now available concerning civic engagement and a perceived crisis of expectation. It is, as Hay (2007: 45) observes, a problem of confusing correlation with causation:

> To account for an exhibited decline in political participation by reference to a broader decline in civic virtue or respect for the duties and obligations of citizens in a democratic polity is rather like blaming the seasonal cull of turkeys on the latter tendency to put on weight in the run-up to Christmas.

Crucially, as was the case in the post-1970s reforms, there is an absence of a serious consideration of the problems thrown up by the UK model of democracy and, with it, a nuanced understanding of the nature of elite power and the problems it incurs in 21st century politics.

As we saw in the introductory chapter to this volume, the literature on the BPT highlights the way in which the current UK model of democracy is organised round a 19th-century set of ideas advocating an essentially elitist, top-down form of government, constructed on a power-hoarding rather than a power-dispersing approach. It is a democratic settlement that offers only limited channels for wider engagement in the political process. Such insights help explain why in a post-deference political era, as we see in the chapters throughout this volume but in particular in Chapters 2 and 5 on participation and parties, people are increasingly switching away from formal political arenas to pursue alternative forms of political expression and engagement.

The often unwitting, but implicit defence of both the BPT and the Westminster model underpinning many of the demand-side accounts reviewed above potentially acts as a constraint on engaging what Stoker refers to as 'the citizen as amateur' or Henrik Bang calls the 'everyday maker'. The net result is what King (2007: 355), the original author of a crisis of expectation in the 1970s, identifies as the emergence of a 'discrepant power' paradox:

- In an era of modern governance, the power commanded by the traditional political class has increasingly been challenged by an array of multi-level governance forces – globalisation, Europeanisation, devolution, judicial activism, etc.
- Yet the same political class has continued to operate within the contours of both the BPT and the associated 19th-century constitutional settlement that is, as noted above, essentially power-hoarding in outlook.

It is this paradox that helps explain why those embracing a predominantly demand-side set of explanations regarding a crisis of expectation miscast their analysis, or more particularly fail to properly diagnose its root cause. As King (2007: 355) observes, there exists a:

> discrepancy between people's expectations of central government and central government's inability to fulfil many, probably most of those expectations. It manifests itself in central-government ministers' unwillingness to admit that they cannot fulfil those expectations. Ministers, including Prime Ministers, still speak the language of Palmerston, Gladstone, Disraeli and Churchill, but their capacity to influence events is but a pale shadow of their predecessors.

The political class's tendency to invoke the language of the Westminster model through rhetorical appeals to 'strong government' or 'taking tough, unpopular but important decisions' on the part of the people has certainly exacerbated the problem.

But the real issue remains with the model itself. For it is formulated on a traditional, unrealistic and outdated conceptionalisation of the UK electorate found in the musings of J.S. Mill, Sir Ivor Jennings, the Fabians and Douglas Jay's 'the Man in Whitehall really does know best' in which the ordinary voter does not have the knowledge or aptitude to engage in the finer principles of decision-making. The individual is therefore kept at arm's length in the policy-making process and in so doing feeds a sense of alienation in terms of possessing any capacity to shape outcomes (Power Inquiry 2006, Whiteley 2012, Wilks-Heeg et al. 2012).

Reforming the supply of politics then is crucial. Yet, as Hay and Stoker's (2013: 2) extensive qualitative, survey-based study on democratic renewal reveals, 'citizens and elites are on different wave lengths when it comes to reforming politics'. Their study underlines a 'substantial mismatch' between the reform agenda currently being pursued by the political class (and outlined by both Smith and Judge's contributions elsewhere in this volume) and the ideas emerging from citizens. For example, only five per cent of the current reforms being pursued by the Coalition are ones that form part of the reform agenda of citizens. Elsewhere, their data reveals that what citizens are most seeking includes:

- reform ideas to find ways of ensuring that those who made decisions, especially elected representatives, are open in what they do and accountable for their performance
- improving communication and ensuring that fair and accessible information about decisions and why they are made is provided
- strong support for a greater say (Hay and Stoker 2013: 13).

A gap between the current reform programme and public expectations of what should constitute change, shown by the Hay and Stoker study, is hardly surprising. For, as Marsh, Richards and Smith (2001), Richards and Smith (2004), Richards (2008) and Diamond (2014) highlight elsewhere, the BPT and the Westminster model are both features that the UK political class has consistently defended over time. Any top-down reform then is filtered through a narrow spectrum of what the BPT is able to accommodate before it reaches a point of elasticity.

Conclusion: A crisis of expectation and the need for a smarter democracy

There is clearly a different tenor to the debate surrounding a crisis of expectation as it was narrated in the 1970s compared to the present day. What this chapter offers is a revealing contrast in the way in which during and immediately after the 1970s, a crisis of overload and expectation was co-opted by the New Right to challenge the status quo. Albeit mainly to affect change in the economic and social sphere. Whereas today, the response to the second-wave expectation crisis by both the political class and the dominant demand-side accounts emerging in the academic literature is one that is being mediated predominantly through a broad defence of existing institutional arrangements, certainly at the national level.

This chapter recognises the important contribution demand-side accounts have made in invigorating the debate over what the future vision for the practice of democratic politics in the UK should be. But, as Gainsborough (2012: 24) observes, it is 'one thing to "defend politics", but as political scientists we need to be able to do so in such a way that our capacity for getting to the heart of how elite power is exercised in the UK is not diminished.'

In developing Gainsborough's mantle, at the crux of this debate should be a re-evaluation of the inadequacies surrounding the existing model of democracy. For it remains in outlook a 19th-century model of elitist democracy that in a previous era did what it was intended to do – deliver stability, continuity and order. Yet, as King observes (2007: 54), it is organised round a set of principles that do not 'so much disdain deliberation as ignore it altogether... [and is] not concerned with promoting the value or principle of citizen participation.' Unsurprisingly then, in a post-deference age, failure to adapt properly has led to a stoking up of discontent.

The paradox then is that current demand-side accounts have the potential to sustain the very problem they seek to address. For in the same way that half a decade ago the likes of Oakeshott (1962), Birch (1964), Beer (1965), Greenleaf et al. (1983a, 1983b, 1987) offered in their various accounts of the BPT, a mythologised model of UK democratic best practice that other nations elsewhere in their transition to democracy were advised that they would do well to replicate, so there is a current generation who are effectively seeking to largely sustain this same democratic model and with it, the non-participatory, non-delegative and non-deliberative tenets that are in themselves fundamental to understanding and explaining the real contours of the present crisis.

This is not to suggest that the need to nurture the demand-side is in itself not a vitally important task in ensuring a healthy, vibrant and active civil arena that operates as the 'space between the public and private spheres where civic action takes place' (Grugel 2011: 89). Yet, sequencing here is everything. Emphasis first has to be placed on ensuring that the democratic structures and mechanisms available are capable of harnessing the energy and enterprise of the civic arena, or else the sense of drift in the public's dislocation and alienation from politics will continue. It is important not to forget the lessons of the 1970s. To return to Miliband (2012):

> The point of the 1970s comparison is to say that the country faces choices the like of which it has not had for a long time. My argument is that the economics will not be resolved without political reformation of a profound kind. Reform of government; reform of parliament; reform of the political parties; and reform of the way we do politics. I say this because I have learnt it. We elect a government of politicians, not an administration of technocrats. But government for the people needs to be complemented by government by the people.

The diagnosis then for the issues raised in this chapter concerning a second-wave crisis of expectation is one that should, in the first place, preference reform to the supply of politics. Crucially, this requires willingness by the political class to abandon the BPT and instead seek out a smarter democracy appropriate for the 21st century emphasising much greater deliberation and participation.

Notes

1. The literature on demand-side approaches for explaining electoral disengagement in advanced liberal-democracies is substantial, although for a useful summary see Hay (2007: 1–61). In terms of the more specific literature focused on current debates concerning the UK, see for example Bentley 2005, Stoker 2006, Flinders 2010, 2012a, 2012b, Riddell 2010, 2012, Campbell 2012, Hatier 2012, Wood and Flinders 2012.
2. See the introductory chapter of this volume for an overview of the literature on the BPT. The interpretation of 'BPT' employed throughout this chapter draws from the 'critical wave' identifying an embedded elitist governance tradition preferencing responsible and representative government over more pluralistic, participatory or delegative approaches.

3. See Marsh et al. (1999) and Kerr (2001) for an overview of this wide-ranging literature on transformative versus evolutionary accounts of Thatcherism.
4. Details of the extensive empirical data concerning, for example, declining voter turnout and the collapse of mass party membership are presented in Chapters 3 and 5.
5. Here it is worth noting that while there has been much work done on the growth of cynicism, the literature on the collapse of deference, particularly within the UK context, is much more limited and is more often than not simply asserted as an accepted phenomenon.

2

A Crisis of Participation

Sadiya Akram, David Marsh and Brendan McCaffrie

Introduction

Concerns over declining levels of political participation in the UK, particularly in traditional activities such as voting and political party membership, have led many to argue that political apathy is increasing and that democracy is at risk (Putnam 2000, Macedo et al. 2005). Reading this literature one could assert that there is a general crisis of political participation. This chapter questions this interpretation and argues that the mainstream participation literature only provides a partial account of trends in political participation because it operates with a narrow understanding of politics. While there has certainly been a decline, both in the UK and other mature, liberal democracies, in traditional forms of participation, which might be characterised as producing a crisis of participation, at the same time there has been a rise of new forms of political participation that operate outside of the established formal arenas. Consequently, this chapter argues that the decline in traditional forms of participation must be located within a broader understanding of the rise of alternative forms. Additionally, it is critical of the mainstream literature's rather simplistic account of decline and crisis, arguing instead, first, that there is a growing crisis in engagement, resulting from an uncoupling between citizens and the state and, second, that this has important implications for state/citizen relations, which need to be addressed in order to strengthen democracy.

The chapter begins by briefly outlining the extent of the decline in traditional forms of political participation. Subsequently, it shows that the mainstream literature on participation is limited and exhibits three distinct, if related, problems: first, as already suggested, it operates with a narrow definition of politics; second, it imposes this definition on its respondents; and, third, non-participation in mainstream forms is equated with political apathy. There is an increasing recognition that new forms of participation have emerged and that, although they differ from traditional forms in significant ways, they deserve recognition (Norris 2002, Pattie, Seyd and Whitely 2004, Dalton 2008, Marsh 2011). As such, this chapter also examines and critiques Bang's (2009, 2011) key concepts of the Everyday Maker (EM) and the Expert Citizen (EC) as they raise crucial issues for political science, particularly in relation to contemporary participation, modes of governance and forms of democracy. The chapter avers that Bang's work succinctly highlights our central argument that there is a crisis in engagement, which is occurring as a result of an uncoupling between citizens and the state. Whilst we welcome Bang's important contribution to this literature, we suggest that the concept of the Everyday Maker, in particular, requires further conceptual refinement if it is to accurately reflect the nature of contemporary forms of political participation.

Examining the decline in conventional forms of political participation

As Chapters 4 and 5 highlight in greater detail, voter turnout in the UK at general elections has been in steady decline since the post-war period (Hay 2007, Marsh 2011). After the post-war high of 83.9 per cent in the 1950 election, turnout declined to 59.4 per cent in the 2001 general election. Despite increases in 2005 to 61.4 per cent and again in 2010 to 65.19 per cent, turnout overall remains much lower (the Electoral Commission[1]). This pattern is broadly replicated across the world in countries where voting is not compulsory. In the USA, for example, Macedo and Alex-Assessoh (2005: 1) suggest that American voter turnout ranks 'near the bottom among democratic nations' and Putnam highlights that participation in presidential elections has declined by 'roughly a quarter over the last thirty-six years' (2000: 32).

In a similar vein, all three of the UK's main political parties have experienced a dramatic decline in membership levels since the 1960s (Pattie, Syed and Whitely 2004). The Democratic Audit,[2] which conducts regular audits of political party membership in the UK, highlighted a 75 per cent decline in party membership in the UK over the same period. As a consequence, the share of the UK electorate belonging to a political party now ranks among the lowest in Europe (Driver 2011). Similarly, Van Biezen et al. (2011) estimate that since the 1980s, party membership has declined by around 50 per cent or more in France, Norway, Sweden,

Finland, Switzerland and Ireland. Conventional forms of political participation are thus clearly declining, although explanations for why this is occurring differ, as is discussed below.

Explaining decline in conventional forms of politics

Political participation is considered to be critical to democratic citizenship because, without public involvement in the process 'democracy lacks both its legitimacy and its guiding force' (Almond and Verba 1963, Dalton 2008: 76). Political participation as a principle of a healthy democracy was enshrined in Almond and Verba's (1963) model of 'civic culture', which has been influential in the mainstream literature on participation (Norris 2002). This model is based on a five-nation study of mass attitudes and values and identifies three broad types of political culture: the participatory culture; the parochial culture; and the subject culture. Almond and Verba (1963: 79) argue:

> A participant is assumed to be aware of and informed about the political system in both its governmental and political aspects. A subject tends to be cognitively oriented primarily to the output side of government: the executive, bureaucracy, and judiciary. The parochial tends to be unaware, or only dimly aware, of the political system in all its aspects.

This model associates political participation with engaging with the government or the political system and it is the loss of this engagement which is lamented by most of the mainstream literature on political participation. Clearly, there has been a decline in traditional forms of political participation and it is important to acknowledge that this is occurring (Putnam 2000, Macedo and Alex-Assessoh 2005, Stoker 2006, Hay 2007). However, this chapter emphasises that this is only a partial reading of trends in political participation today.

Historically, mainstream approaches have held a narrow definition and understanding of political participation. These approaches have two main features: first, they concentrate on a limited range of forms of participation, which are primarily conventional and individualised, such as voting, election activity and political party and interest group membership. Only a minority of these forms are unconventional, for example, involvement in protest actions (Norris 2002). Second, it emphasises citizen attempts to influence officials. As such, it operates with a narrow 'arena' definition of politics, focusing on formal political institutions, and neglects 'process' definitions, which are concerned with the '(uneven) distribution of power, wealth and resources' which may occur in a range of institutional and social environments (Leftwich 2004, Hay 2007: 73).

As Chapter 1 notes, Putnam's famous book *Bowling Alone* (2000) provides a good example of the mainstream literature's explanations of this decline in political participation. He argues that, since the post-war period, there has been a significant decline in social capital across America. This decline has led to disengagement from politics and disenchantment with political processes. Putnam's view is that weaker civic engagement will lead to a weaker, and less effective and responsive, government. Whilst Putnam's empirical analysis of declining levels of political engagement is important, we would argue that he operates with a narrow arena definition of politics, focusing exclusively on conventional forms of political participation. As in much of the mainstream participation literature, individuals are held responsible for their disengagement with the state and there is a neglect of new and alternative forms of participation as valid modes of political behaviour.

Elsewhere, Stoker's plea for a re-engagement with politics in *Why Politics Matters* (2006) is similarly typical of the mainstream literature's approach to political participation. Stoker assumes widespread disengagement from politics, laments a decline in formal political engagement and is disparaging about new forms of political participation. For example, whilst Norris (2002) describes signing petitions and boycotting as novel and important forms of political participation, Stoker (2006: 10) sees them as examples of market-based consumerism: 'what counts as "politics" for most people is not much more than an extension of their activities as a consumer'. Given this view, Stoker preferences what Richards refers to in Chapter 1 as a demand-side approach, whereby he identifies individuals as being responsible for declining rates of participation. Indeed, his solution to the problem of disengagement is to argue that people should be more self-critical and reflective about their approach to politics and be more committed to formal politics and political institutions. At the political level, he argues for the importance of reforming wider political institutions and a wider civic culture to enable people to engage in politics more effectively, without needing them to become 'model citizens'.

In contrast, Hay (2007) disputes the thesis that there is a rising tide of apathy in Western democracies and shows that a significant proportion of those who have withdrawn from formal politics are engaged in other modes of legitimate political activity. He defends a broader and more inclusive conception of the political that is far less formal, less state-centric and less narrowly governmental than in most conventional accounts. However, he also accepts that there has been a rejection of traditional politics by many people and that this stems from their distrust of politicians and of the political process.

Interestingly, unlike much of the mainstream participation literature, which adopts a demand-side approach that lays the blame for declining political participation at the hands of a non-voting electorate, Hay holds politicians, economists and the political and economic system accountable. He identifies an increase in the number of policy areas where politicians have abdicated responsibility, either through choice or force of circumstance. Hay's main explanation for declining levels of participation suggests that a process of 'depoliticisation' has occurred which is a consequence of the dominance of a neo-liberal ideology that values market-based decision-making over democratic solutions involving an active and participating electorate.[3] Arguably, Hay provides a more balanced critique of the current situation in political participation. However, in our view, an argument which emphasises the growth of widespread depoliticisation is, despite its protests, still firmly rooted in an arena and state-focused approach to political participation. Once we broaden our definition, it becomes clearer that, while participation is changing, this does not necessarily imply a crisis of participation itself.

New forms of politics: What is changing?

Moving beyond the mainstream approach to political participation, there has been an increasing recognition in the literature that there have been important changes in the types of political actions in which individuals are engaging, the reasons for their actions and the outcomes of these actions. Norris (2002), in particular, provides a helpful conceptual framework for understanding these changes. She argues that the mainstream approach to participation has diversified in terms of acknowledging that there have been distinct changes in the 'agencies' (the collective organisations through which people mobilise for the political), the 'repertoires' (the ways in which they choose to express themselves politically) and the 'targets' (the actors towards whom participants are attempting to direct their action) of political participation. Here, we examine each of these changes in turn before focusing particularly on the issue of how they affect young people.

Agencies

Norris (2002) points out that, whilst the agencies of political actions were traditionally characterised as interest groups or parties, they have now diversified and broadened to include social movements and transnational advocacy groups (TAGs). The Fawcett Society, the National Farmers Union (NFU) and the Royal Society for the Protection of Birds (RSPB) are good examples of traditional UK interest groups. These groups are formal organisations which usually have well-established organisational structures, formal membership rules and fairly easily measurable activities. Their main aim is to influence government and policy processes, whilst also providing direct information to, and representation of, members. These formal agencies certainly continue to exist, but, more recently, new social movements and TAGs are emerging as popular avenues for informal political mobilisation, protest and expression (Snow and Soule 2010, Tarrow 2011).

In contrast to traditional interest groups, social movements and TAGs have more fluid and decentralised organisational structures and more open membership criteria. Occupy,[4] UK Uncut[5] and 38 Degrees[6] are typical of this type of broad-based and networked organisation.They do not necessarily oppose formal decision-making processes, but favour looser coalitions with more informal modes of belonging, focused on shared concerns about diverse issues, community building and identity politics. They tend to use a range of alternative repertoires in their political actions, involving, for example, internet communications, internet activism or influencing lifestyle choices.

Repertoires

There is increasing recognition in the more recent political participation literature that there is a need to move away from a focus on conventional repertoires, such as voting and joining interest groups or political parties. This strand of the literature acknowledges that recent decades have seen a diversification in the types of activities or repertoires used for political expression (Karpf 2010, Vromen and Coleman 2011, 2013). Perhaps the most significant way in which the repertoires of political action have changed involves the use of communication-based, technological innovation and, specifically, internet activism (for examples of this see Vegh 2003, Bang 2009, Van Laer and Van Aeslts 2010, Bennett and Segerberg 2012). Whilst the earlier literature drew a line between conventional and protest forms of activism, it is not clear whether this distinction remains appropriate today (Verba and Nie 1972). In this vein, Norris points out that new social movements may be adopting action repertoires which combine traditional actions, such as voting and lobbying, with a variety of alternative modes, such as internet networking, street protests, consumer boycotts, direct action and political violence. 38 Degrees in the UK, GetUp![7] in Australia (Vromen and Coleman 2011, 2013) and MoveOn[8] in the USA (Karpf 2010) are all good examples of online multi-issue, campaigning, organisations which use a range of online methods and, in particular, mass emailing, alongside more traditional repertoires, such as taking part in local actions, to mobilise action. This issue is complicated by the relationship between more traditional and newer repertoires. For example, in their analysis of GetUp!'s 2010 election campaign, Vromen and Coleman (2011) found that almost one-third of all member emails were invitations to participate in offline local actions. As such, newer repertoires have not replaced older forms, but may enhance their effectiveness.

Direct action strategies have also broadened to include lifestyle politics, which raises interesting questions about the overlap between the social and the political, whilst also pointing to the need for a process definition of politics (Norris 2002). Such activities would include volunteering at recycling cooperatives, helping at battered women's shelters or fund-raising and protesting against animal cruelty. In these activities, the distinction between the public and private remains problematic, as has long been argued by feminists.[9]

Targets

According to Norris, a key difference between the mainstream literature and the more recent literature on political participation is that the targets of participation have widened beyond the nation-state. Traditional theories of representative government claim that citizens hold elected representatives and governments to account directly through regular elections. Norris explains that, whilst these activities remain important, there has been a 'shrinkage' of the state through globalisation, privatisation, marketisation and deregulation, which has meant that decision-making has flowed away from public bodies and official government organisations to complex private agencies working at local, national and international levels. Consequently, the former focus on representative government signifies an excessively narrow conceptualisation of participation that excludes some of the most common targets of civic engagement.

Based on findings from extensive empirical analysis, Norris highlights increasing non-state orientated activities directed towards diverse actors in the public, non-profit and private sectors. Here, non-governmental organisations (NGOs) and human rights organisations can become the focus of agents' attentions. The targets can also be multinational companies (MNCs), which may face economic boycotts or protests. An interesting example of this type of mobilisation is provided by the actions of UK Uncut, which was established in October 2010 following the global financial crisis and in response to significant cuts in government expenditure. UK Uncut has organised a range of protests against MNCs such as Vodaphone, Boots, Arcadia and Barclays based on their belief that these MNCs are not paying enough tax in the UK, and that, if they did so, this could help to relieve some of the financial troubles the UK is facing without requiring public sector cuts (Marsh and Vromen 2013).

Norris' conceptual clarification, and particularly the distinctions between agencies, repertoires and targets, is important and enhances our understanding of political participation. However, it only begins a necessary reconceptualisation of current political participation. Norris and the broader literature on alternative modes of political participation have begun to accommodate the changes in participation patterns by including informal organisations. However, in our view, this literature retains a bias towards traditional voluntary associations with measurable, institutionalised and structured activities which aim to effect policy change (Bang 2009, Marsh 2011). Indeed, Bang has criticised Norris directly for this reason (Bang 2009: 127).

Young people

The extent to which recent changes in political participation refer specifically to young people is an important question which has been considered in some of the political participation literature (Pattie, Seyd and Whitely 2004, Marsh, O'Toole and Jones 2007, Vromen and Collin 2010). Pattie, Seyd and Whitely (2004) contend that young people are less interested in, and knowledgeable about politics, and feel limited levels of efficacy. They are also less likely to vote or join political parties. As a result, young people are often labelled 'apathetic'. However, in contrast, they are more likely to demonstrate or to protest and to engage in internet-based activities on particular issues. Similarly, Norris emphasises that it is particularly among the young that one can see cause-orientated activities (2003: 17).

Whilst young people may not be wholly responsible for changes in the agencies, repertoires and targets of political participation, it is certainly important to gain a better understanding of how this issue relates to them. For example, the recent UK riots in 2011, together with the previous riots of 2005, provide an interesting example of why there is a need to operate with a broader understanding of politics and of political participation in relation to young people. As Marsh and Vromen (2013) argue, the riots in the UK in August 2011, which mainly involved young people, might be regarded as political, but the looting would probably be seen as criminality and not political action. In contrast, and if one operates with a broader approach to political participation, such action might well be seen as evidence of alienation from the political system (Marsh, O'Toole and Jones 2007, Akram 2009). Young people's involvement in rioting highlights the need for a broader understanding of the political and should, in turn, lead to a questioning of how the government attempts to engage with young people.

Duty norms and engagement norms

Changes in forms of political participation relate to broader changes in the structure of society and, in particular, to changes in citizenship norms (Dalton 2008). For Dalton, norms regarding citizenship shape political behaviour and he identifies a shift from duty-based citizenship to a more engaged citizenship. Duty-based norms of citizenship encourage people to participate as a civic duty and include activities such as voting, acceptance of state authority and reporting a crime. Conversely, engaged citizenship involves an expressive, participatory emphasis on individualised and direct forms of action. The engaged citizen is willing to act on her principles, be politically independent and address social needs. Dalton's engaged citizenship, then, identifies many of the repertoires Bang sees as pursued by Expert Citizens and Everyday Makers, discussed in more detail below.

Dalton points to rising levels of education, changing generational experiences and other social forces as being responsible for a decreasing respect for authority and traditional forms of allegiance based on duty-based citizenships. Simultaneously, these same forces have resulted in more expressive and reflexive identities and lead to more direct participation in cause-orientated politics. Dalton argues that there has been a 'renaissance', rather than a decline, in democratic participation; it is just that it takes different forms (2008: 85).

His observations regarding changes in citizenship norms are important. In our view, the argument for a shift from duty to engagement norms is strengthened further if we accept that a decline in conventional forms of political participation, and specifically voting, is related to a decline in duty norms and, in particular perhaps, to a decline in deference. Historically, political participation has been based to a significant extent on duty norms, with people engaging in politics, in large part, because they believe it is their duty to do so. Such duty norms were reflected in high levels of voting and respect for the rule of law. This understanding supports Almond and Verba's (1963) analysis of UK political culture, which they saw as characterised by acceptance of the authority of the state and a commitment to participation in civic duties. Almond and Verba (1963) also identified deference as a key feature of UK political civic culture, which stemmed from a pronounced subject culture in the UK. As such, we would argue that a decline in an authoritative state, together with increasing reflexivity in society, has led to a decline in the importance of, and consequent decline of, deference and duty norms in UK political culture (Nevitte 1996).

Henrik Bang: Explaining the rise of new forms of political participation

Henrik Bang has made a significant contribution to the debate on political participation through his work on networks, governance and alternative forms of participation (2009, 2011). The crux of Bang's argument is that the nature of politics, and thus political participation, is changing and that new forms of participation need to be acknowledged. Bang contends that whilst there have been some developments in the mainstream literature on political participation, much of it still suffers from a commitment to state-centric politics and continues to neglect, and indeed deny, alternative forms of politics as being legitimate and important.

Drawing on Castells, Bang's starting point is that we are living in a period of late modernity, in which we have moved from an industrialised and hierarchical society to one based on networks (Castells and Cordosa 2006). Here, it is axiomatic that globalisation has occurred and is a process with economic, social and political consequences.[10] In the political sphere, Bang argues that the nation-state has been replaced by a network state and governance has replaced government (Bang 2009, 2011).

On an agential level, and following Beck (1992) and Giddens (1994), Bang accepts that society is generally more complex, as are individuals, who are described as being more reflexive and risk-taking. In such a society, individuals' identities are no longer linked to preconstituted interests, such as class and political party affiliation. Instead, they are free to debate and choose their identity. In this scenario, politics becomes a contested issue and changes associated with the transition to a network society have crucial consequences for politics. These changes help to explain the decline in traditional forms of participation, but also the concomitant rise of alternatives.

Project politics and project identities

Bang disputes the mainstream political participation literature's argument that political participation is characterised by political apathy or free riding, instead identifying political exclusion as the main problem facing politics today. Political exclusion, he suggests, leads to an uncoupling of political authorities from ordinary citizens (2009, 2011). One of Bang's key contributions to the political participation literature is his contention that participation today is characterised by project politics and project identities. He highlights the 2009 Obama campaign as an illustrative example of individuals organising in such a way:

> [A]t its high point, mybarackobama.com (MyBO) had 2 million active users, more than 100,000 profiles and 35,000 affinity groups, and was the co-ordination point for 200,000 events. In addition, 70,000 people raised $30 million using MyBO, while in the last four days of the campaign users made 3 million telephone calls as part of the get-out-the-vote effort...
>
> (Bang, 2009: 118)

Given such large-scale involvement in a recent national political campaign, Bang questions the mainstream political participation literature's central premise that political apathy is widespread and participation is declining. Bang argues that mainstream political science and the political participation literature have failed to document or acknowledge the importance of such activity. This failure results from a limited definition of the political and an enduring commitment to a state-centric model of political participation, which focuses almost solely on participation through conventional means.

In his analysis of data accessed through the MyBO website, Bang (2009) finds that, of the 28,000 groups and circles that one could choose to join to be involved in the Obama campaign: 9735 people joined groups concerned with local campaigns; 5248 joined groups concerned with specific people; 4938 joined groups based on specific issues; 4291 joined groups based on interests; and 3926 joined groups concerned with national issues. Bang points out that this data reflects the myriad forms of participation that interest people, which suggests a mix between project and identity politics, the personal and the communal, and the local and global. Based on these findings, he argues that a new political community approach to participation has emerged which emphasises immediate and concrete political community action and combines identity politics with project politics. In his view, this undermines mainstream political science's traditional dichotomy and hierarchy separating *small* and *big* politics.

Bang identifies the emergence of a new form of political participation that differs from traditional forms because it emphasises project politics and project identities. Notwithstanding Bang's characterisation, it is also important to note that the Obama example serves to highlight peoples' continuing commitment to traditional forms of political participation. Whilst the Obama campaign may have utilised new repertoires of political action, such as encouraging engagement through the MyBO website, public involvement in national election campaigns is a long-standing feature of conventional forms of political participation. Consequently, we argue that contemporary political participation is not necessarily characterised by a choice between mainstream and alternative forms of political participation. The boundary between traditional and non-traditional forms is porous and people may choose to use both, or either, when it suits them. But it is an observation that is important because, in contrast to Bang's position, which points to a 'hollowing out' of the state, our position accepts that both the state and alternative modes of political participation can co-exist and both have a role to play in political participation today.

For Bang, late modernity and the network society is characterised by highly reflexive individuals who have a project politics and project identities. Unlike previous generations, individuals' identities are not shaped by social structures, such as class, gender and ethnicity, instead their identities are fluid. Given these characteristics, people can choose which political projects to engage in and which aspect of their identity to express through those projects. Whilst we do not think that Bang denies the existence of structured inequality in individuals' lives (Bang 2011), it certainly seems that he underplays its importance in favour of reflexivity and choice (Marsh et al. 2007, Marsh 2011). Consequently, Marsh argues that the stress on fluid identities in the late modernity literature is 'overdone' (2011: 82). In their research on young people, class and politics in the UK, Marsh et al. (2007) found that although their respondents rarely talked about class, 'they lived it'. These findings suggest that their respondents' lifestyle choices were not open and were strongly constrained by their access to forms of capital (Bourdieu 1986, Marsh 2011: 82). In particular, within the UK context, Marsh et al. (2003) see class, ethnicity and gender themselves as a lived experience, which is clearly rooted in, but not determined by, structured inequalities. We agree that a focus on identity politics and lifestyle choices neglects the continued importance of structured inequality in shaping the options and chances of the disadvantaged. As such, we caution against over-emphasising the fluidity of identity in contemporary forms of political participation and reiterate the importance of recognising the impact of structural inequalities on individuals.

This point is easily made if we turn to another contemporary 'crisis'; the on-going financial crisis discussed in greater detail in Chapters 3 and 9, but which forms a key backdrop to the issues presented in this chapter. Certainly, the alternative forms of political participation utilised by UK Uncut and Occupy were, in a large part, a response to the structural inequalities reflected within capitalism which were thrown into stark relief by the aftermath of the 2008 financial crisis. In addition, the actions by UK Uncut and Occupy, in many ways, exemplify the broader uncoupling that is occurring between states and citizens. In effect, these groups operate outside the formal political processes, but engage with it to the extent that they are highly critical of the state's response to the current financial and economic crisis; a response which, in their view, has had an adverse effect on citizens' lives.

From politics-policy to policy-politics

According to Bang, the shift to late modernity and to new and alternative forms of political participation is a reflection of a shift from a polity operating in a politics-policy framework to one operating in a policy-politics framework. Bang sees politics-policy as reflecting an input-output model of politics in which the focus is on how pre-constituted political agents gain access to, and also recognition in, political decision-making processes. This framework emphasises sectional and partisan competition over practical policy considerations. In contrast, policy-politics is rooted in a 'flowput' model, where the focus is on how political decisions emerge through consultation with people.

Bang welcomes a policy-politics approach, in which private and voluntary sectors are networking to produce and deliver the policies wanted by the reflexive individuals characteristic of late or high modernity. Whilst this approach certainly has benefits in terms of incorporating the viewpoints of citizens in the design of policy, we argue that it is too simplistic to claim that late modernity has initiated a shift from politics-policy to policy-politics. Rather, we would suggest that both are involved in policy-making and that, whilst we of course welcome greater citizen engagement in policy creation, there is an important role for the state in this process.

Introducing the Everyday Maker and the Expert Citizen

It is Bang's classification of Everyday Makers (EMs) and Expert Citizens (ECs) that offers one of the most important recent contributions to the mainstream political participation literature, which it fundamentally challenges (2009, 2011). Bang introduces the EC and EM as the two new types of citizens who engage in political participation in late modernity.

EMs and ECs are governed by a project identity, which means that they put concerns for 'immediate and prudent action' (Bang 2009) above worries about decision-making. Whether they engage in protests, collaborate in public, private or state and civil society partnerships, make alliances with the media, or do voluntary work in their neighbourhoods, EMs and ECs repeatedly engage in concrete projects. EMs and ECs can be pro-system, anti-system or both in different contexts, as this flexibility helps their causes and enables them to pursue their own projects. They adopt oppositional or legitimating identities only if it is functional to developing their project and to meeting specific life plans or policies. Whilst they may share some characteristics, EMs and ECs differ in significant ways, as they reflect different forms of political participation. Below we consider the EC first, before moving on to the EM.

(a) Expert Citizens (ECs)

Bang defines ECs as strategic individuals who use their expert knowledge and understanding of traditional political processes to influence outcomes. As such, ECs may be new professionals, particularly in voluntary organisations, but not within political parties or trade unions. ECs are familiar with the traditional processes of representative democracy or big politics, which they know as input politics, but they deliberately choose to develop small tactics for making a difference outside of the formal institutions of democratic government. They deal with all types of elites and sub-elites, both political and corporatist. To ECs, politics is a fusion between representation and participation, a new form of political participation in which they use their knowledge and skills to influence others. They build networks of negotiation and cooperation with politicians, administrators, interest groups and the media; as such, they develop 'network consciousness'.

Typically, the ECs' identity is not based on either protecting or fighting the system, as they aim to be competent partners in the exercise of good governance. However, Bang expresses concerns about the relationship between the political system and ECs, arguing that political authorities often need ECs and may incorporate them into expert networks as representatives of the opinions of citizens (in Bang's terms 'lay people'). In such a scenario, the government seeks to 'incorporate to emasculate' and, potentially, this can exacerbate the existing problem of the uncoupling between the state and lay people (Bang 2009). In addition, while ECs usually claim to speak for lay people, they often do not listen to them. As such, for Bang, the emergence of the EC reflects a demo-elitist ethos in which the key principle of democracy becomes the need to rationalise and legitimate the discourses of the experts, who are controlling policy-making in an increasingly complex economy and polity.

(b) Everyday Makers (EMs)

EMs are aware of ECs as they may come into contact with them in nearly all of the institutions, networks or projects that they experience in their everyday lives. Arguably, the EM has emerged in response to the existence of the EC and it is these EMs who represent a particularly interesting new development in ordinary peoples' contemporary political participation.

For Bang, the key focus for the EM is to act in an everyday way, to act locally, although they may also think globally, and to act because it matters to them. Like ECs, EMs do not feel defined by the state; they are neither apathetic about it nor opposed to it. They may be interested in 'big politics', but do not derive their primary political identity from it. The boundaries between their politics and lifestyle may not be clear, as EMs do not make a distinction between participating to feel engaged and to develop oneself, and participating for specific causes. Political participation for them is certainly not associated with acquiring influence and success and they draw a clear line between participating in policy-politics as citizens or as professionals. They aim to encourage more spontaneous or little-organised forms of involvement than the ECs, who typically will seek to professionalise all spontaneity, by, for example, collaborating with the media. Whilst they may act collectively, their commonality does not build on an idea of common good, but rather on the acceptance and recognition of their common capacities for making a difference.

For Bang, the EMs have a number of key mantras:

- Do it yourself.
- Do it where you are.
- Do it for fun, but also because you find it necessary.
- Do it ad hoc or part time.
- Do it concretely, instead of ideologically.
- Do it self-confidently and show trust in yourself.
- Do it with the system if need be. (Bang 2009: 132)

Whilst EMs do not engage directly with the state in their politics, Bang argues that they *are* political and are engaged in political processes, albeit these processes are different from the ones that are the focus of the mainstream participation literature. Bang contends that ECs and EMs demonstrate the way in which political participation is moving from the input to the output side and away from a focus on the formal arenas of government towards more direct forms of action. In Bang's view, EMs, like ECs, are concerned with creating political capital by enhancing political capacities for self-governance and co-governance in, and through, various projects.

To date there has only been one attempt to identify and analyse EMs quantitatively. Li and Marsh (2008) used the UK 2001 Home Office Citizenship Survey data to establish the number and characteristics of the EMs. They acknowledge that their data has major limitations because they do not have attitudinal data and so cannot establish whether individuals' actions are non-ideological or whether they participate for fun, two characteristics of EMs. Despite these limitations, their results are both interesting and revealing. They identify 14.5 per cent of the respondents as ECs and 37.3 per cent as EMs. Unsurprisingly, Li and Marsh also found two further categories of political participants, political activists and non-participants. Given this finding, Li and Marsh argue that more work needs to be done to refine Bang's characterisation of alternative forms of political participation and examine how citizens' activities relate to the porous boundary between traditional and new forms of political participation.

There have been a number of qualitative attempts to identify EMs. However they also suggest that there is room for refinement of the concept (Hendriks and Tops 2005, Blakely and Evans 2009, Marsh and Vromen 2013). For example, Marsh, O'Toole and Jones (2007) found evidence of EMs in a qualitative study of young people and politics in the UK. Few of their respondents were involved or even interested in formal politics, but some became involved in local issues which concerned them; in Bang's terms their activity was local, *ad hoc* and non-ideological. For example, the authors highlight the case of two single mothers in a hostel for the homeless who led a protest to the local council about the poor state of the local park, which was unsafe for their children. However, Marsh, O'Toole and Jones (2007) argue that, although some of their young respondents exhibited characteristics of EMs, many, and especially the more disadvantaged ones, were involved with the state, largely because they had no choice as recipients of benefits. As such, Marsh, O'Toole and Jones (2007) suggest that some EMs may, consistently, have more contact with the state than Bang envisages. In a similar vein, Marsh and Vromen (2013) argue more broadly that it is important to recognise that there are many participating citizens who demonstrate some, but not all, of the characteristics of EMs, and there is a need to distinguish between different types of EMs, or alternatively to recognise that we need more categories.

(c) EMs and the state

The EMs' disengagement from the state raises critical questions over the current debate concerning a crisis of participation in the UK discussed elsewhere in this volume and about the role of the state and the future of UK state–citizen relations. Attempts by the state to re-engage with citizens will be difficult if EMs are reluctant to engage with it. The state's engagement with EMs will be exacerbated by the EMs' scepticism about the state's strategy of co-opting ECs into expert networks as representatives of the opinions of citizens. If the government is to reverse the uncoupling that is occurring between the state and citizens, it needs to engage with EMs, and indeed ECs, on mutually negotiated platforms. Engagement with EMs and ECs, as a first step, requires an understanding of the grievances felt by these individuals and recognition of the legitimacy and importance of alternative forms of political participation.

A further factor, which affects the state's re-engagement with citizens, is the increasing demonisation of politicians, the state and politics (Fawcett and Marsh 2013). Stoker (2006) and Hay (2007) both, separately, identify people's distrust of politicians as one of the key reasons for increasing depoliticisation in society and, whilst they recognise that politicians and the state are necessary for democracy, they end up blaming politicians and the state for citizen disengagement from politics.

Bang also recognises that individuals express high levels of scepticism regarding their elected representatives (2009, 2011). However he questions why politicians are blamed or othered, when they nevertheless remain crucial to the policy process and the output side of politics. In our view, whilst politicians and the state clearly need to work harder to gain people's trust, demonising them will only result in further uncoupling between the state and citizens. Consequently, we are critical of the depoliticisation literature's tendency to demonise politicians and the state, and argue that the state and politicians are essential for good governance and, as argued in Chapter 1, attempts must be made to work with and improve the state's engagement with citizens (Fawcett and Marsh 2013).

From duty norms to engagement norms revisited

Like Dalton, Bang explains the changes in political participation in late modernity in terms of a shift from duty norms to engagement norms (Bang 2011). It is Bang's contention that the change to late modernity is increasingly associated with a shift to engagement norms, where people are engaged in alternative modes of political participation that correspond to their project identities and project politics. This norm change corresponds with a concomitant move away from the traditional dichotomy between legitimating and oppositional norms, which has a strong basis in democratic theory and has been the dominant paradigm in the mainstream political participation literature. Bang argues that the shift from duty to engagement norms is increasingly apparent for young people, but it is questionable whether one can extrapolate from this that young people are also more likely than the rest of the population to be EMs or ECs (Li and Marsh 2008).

It is important to consider the implications of a change from duty to engagement-based norms for the neo-liberal state. Bang suggests that the neo-liberal state is aware of this shift and, as a result, increasingly 'operates with a politics of threat' (2011: 440). For Bang, a shift to engagement-based norms poses a challenge to democratic theory and its reliance on the twin core propositions of acceptance of authority and obedience to hierarchy. He also contends that democratic theory presumes that recognition of authority equates to active consent and a belief in legitimacy. EMs challenge this model, because, while they routinely accept authority as a fact of their everyday life, they may question its legitimacy and do not obey or submit to commands and duty norms. EMs recognise authority as necessary to the pursuit of their own life projects and often pretend to consent to, and collaborate with, hierarchical authority, because they recognise their dependence on it for survival, as well as for realising their own projects.

Where next for the study of Everyday Maker?

Clearly, to the extent that Bang has identified new forms and modes of political participation, this has consequences for both the practice and recognition of citizen engagement and, more broadly, the future of politics and democracy. Overall, we would argue that the concept of the EM is one of the most interesting developments in recent conceptual work on political participation, a view shared by others (McFarland and Michelleti 2011, Furlong and Cartmel 2012). However, we would argue that there needs to be further detailed empirical exploration of both the EM and EC to enable a clearer understanding of the role and activity of EMs. Certainly, the mainstream argument that there is a crisis in political participation, particularly in the way it has been played out within the UK context, is difficult to defend given the variety of new forms of political participation. We suggest that, if there is a modern UK crisis in the relationship/interaction between citizens and the state, it is one of uncoupling, in which government is unwilling or unable to engage with new types of participants on their own terms. However, until scholars of political participation can be clearer about exactly how EMs and ECs operate, it is difficult for government to know how best to engage with them. Nevertheless, as argued in Chapter 1, rather than blame citizens for being apathetic, we need to focus on how governments can re-engage with citizens.

Conclusion: Re-coupling citizens and the state

This chapter has questioned the mainstream political participation literature's approach to a crisis in participation. We have drawn from our own research-based evidence of the evolving nature of forms of participation within the UK, but in a way that the mainstream participation literature seems unable or unwilling to recognise. Currently, much of the literature remains committed to a paradigm that only accepts conventional forms of participation as legitimate. Further, we have highlighted that the growth of alternative forms of political participation reflects a crisis in engagement or an uncoupling between the state and citizens and suggest that this is of concern if we are to have a more engaged citizenry.

Clearly, the crucial question is how to address the process of depoliticisation (Fawcett and Marsh 2013, Flinders and Wood 2013) or, in our terms, the uncoupling that has occurred between the state and citizens. In separate books, Stoker (2006) and Hay (2007) address the depoliticisation issue. Both argue for the importance of politics and for repoliticisation in the face of increasing levels of depoliticisation in society, an argument which we wholeheartedly endorse. It is important to note that Hay operates with a broader conception of politics than Stoker and acknowledges the rise and importance of alternative forms of political participation. However, both offer disappointing solutions to the problem of depoliticisation. For Stoker (2006), citizen disengagement from the state can only be remedied by institutional change and, thus, his approach is reliant on an arena definition of politics and input politics rather than output politics. In contrast, Hay argues that repoliticisation can only occur if neo-liberal hegemony, as expressed through discourses of globalisation, is undermined and if there is a shift in both the perception and, to a certain extent, the reality that politicians are self-serving individuals. As such, Hay's defence of politics is also limited because it is focused on the state and input politics, rather than on output politics.

Following Bang, we place a much greater stress than Stoker or Hay on the importance of alternative forms of political participation, but argue that they must be integrated within a broader process of recoupling between the state and citizens. In our view, much of the uncoupling problem results from the demonisation of politics and politicians, where the politicians are seen as the problem and greater participation is seen as the solution (Fawcett and Marsh 2013). While much of the mainstream literature sees citizens and their apathy as the core reason for disengagement from conventional forms of political participation, most of the more critical political participation and almost all of the depoliticisation literature regards politicians and government as the main culprits. In contrast, we would argue that the crisis has two sides. As such, we agree with Bang that within the context of the UK, the key task is to convince citizens that government and politicians are necessary, and that politics is a difficult, if essential, occupation, while, at the same time, persuading the political class that it needs to be more honest about the problems it faces and about its capacity to solve them. Not an easy task, but a crucial one.

Notes

1. The Electoral Commission – www.electoralcommission.org.uk/faq/elections/ turnout-general-elections – accessed on 09.02.13

2. Democratic Audit uses a range of sources such as political party membership data and figures disclosed to the Electoral Commission in conducting its regular audit into political party membership – www.democraticaudit.com – accessed on 09.02.13.
3. See Fawcett and Marsh (2013) for a discussion on the relationship between depoliticisation, governance and political participation.
4. www.occupylondon.uk
5. www.ukuncut.org.uk
6. www.38degrees.org.uk
7. www.getup.org.au
8. www.moveon.org
9. MamaBake in Australia (www.mamabake.com) and Mumsnet in the UK (www.mumsnet.com) provide excellent examples of online communities which have come together for the pursuit of issues relating to motherhood and women. For both of these communities, the focus is on developing a platform where women can engage in discussions, share advice and help each other in a manner that blends lifestyle issues with politics, thus highlighting that the personal is most definitely political.
10. See Hay (2001) for a critique of the extent to which globalisation has occurred.

3
A Crisis of Politics in the Politics of Crisis

Colin Hay

Introduction

The global financial crisis which first began to make itself apparent in 2007 and then broke with full force in the autumn of 2008 has generated an intense debate in academic, business, journalistic and political circles alike about what went wrong and how things might be repaired. Yet, to date at least, it has failed to generate a wider political crisis. The Coalition administration, which many saw as potentially flaky from the moment of its inception, now seems destined to see through its full parliamentary term and, though the Labour opposition has persistently retained a lead in the opinion polls, there is little sense of the imminent arrival after the next election of a paradigm-changing administration.

The argument of this chapter is that much of the reason for this stems from the politics of crisis narration. In short, this crisis has come to be conceived of, by at least all of the major political parties, in paradigm-reinforcing rather than crisis-challenging terms, as a crisis of debt to which entrenched neo-liberal austerity is the answer rather than a crisis of growth to which a new growth model is the answer. That, I suggest, is not particularly surprising; but it has profound political and economic consequences which I seek to explore in the following argument.

A crisis of growth not debt

It is a necessary but not in itself a sufficient condition of getting the responses to the crisis right that we get our diagnosis of the crisis right. And this is not easy. For the crisis has been understood in a variety of rather different ways – most of them credible in at least some respect. Is this the UK's crisis or a global financial crisis or a crisis of the West or, perhaps, a crisis of the Eurozone and its immediate hinterland from which the UK is largely exempt? There is a great deal at stake in our answer to these questions.

For if this is an external or exogenous crisis and the UK is and has been exposed to it only through contagion effects, then the solution is as much about managing exposure to future shocks as it is about managing the transition to a different model of political economy. Yet if the UK's crisis is a largely internal or endogenous crisis, then a much more serious dose of domestic reform may be required to address the pathologies it has exposed.

It is perhaps unsurprising that policy-makers, from all parties, have been so keen to emphasise the external character of the crisis – appealing to the UK's affliction as the local manifestation of a global phenomenon. But they have been in very good company in doing so. Indeed most journalistic and broader public commentary on the crisis has assumed it to be largely external in origin – even if it has exposed some domestic frailties (e.g. Brummer 2009, Cable 2009, Davies 2010, Mason 2010, Buckley 2011). This, I suggest, is wrong.

For in a way this is an internal and an external crisis – a UK crisis, a Eurozone crisis (of sorts), a crisis of the West, even a global crisis. But, from a UK perspective, it is also far worse than that. Why? Because the origin of *all* of these associated crises lies in the Anglo-American capitalism of which the UK, since at least the 1980s, has been perhaps the key architect. It is a crisis of Anglo-liberal excess and of a globalisation couched in this image.

A fiscal crisis *of* and *for* the state?

Politically, the crisis has manifested itself first and foremost as a severe constriction in the taxation base. And, in seeming confirmation of the truism that it never rains but pours, this occurred at precisely the moment at which the recapitalisation of the banking sector placed an almost unparalleled call on the public purse (see Chapter 9).

In this respect, the crisis might well be argued to have precipitated a full-scale fiscal crisis of the state – or, perhaps more accurately, a fiscal crisis *for* the state (cf. Gough 2010). The distinction might seem narrowly academic, but it is important. For to suggest that this is a fiscal crisis *of* the state would be to implicate the state directly in the generation of the fiscal shortfall that now threatens the public programmes with which we associate it. To appeal to a fiscal crisis *for* the state is to make no such assumption. Indeed, it is to suggest that the fiscal deficit which now threatens public expenditure cannot be attributed to any dynamic internal to the state itself since its origins lie elsewhere. That is far more accurate.

The origins of such a fiscal crisis for the state are, in fact, readily comprehensible and can be traced clearly to the global financial crisis. They arise from the worsening of the condition of the public finances associated with: (i) the decline in fiscal revenue (the 'tax take') arising from the sharp downturn in economic output (GDP); (ii) the decline in fiscal revenue associated with tax reductions designed to stimulate demand (temporary VAT reductions, stamp duty 'holidays' and the like); (iii) the costs of underwriting the banking sector with public funds; (iv) the costs associated with sector-specific subsidies designed to support parts of the economy that were hit disproportionately (such as car scrappage schemes); and (v) the increased costs associated with meeting social and welfare needs as the number of those eligible for benefits rose as a consequence of the dislocating effects of the crisis.

What is striking, and somewhat at odds with the tenor of public debate, is that by far the greatest contributory factor in the UK, as elsewhere, was not the extent of the recapitalisation of the banking sector, but the simple reduction in the tax return arising from the sharp decline in taxable economic activity. Had taxation revenue continued to grow at pre-crisis levels, it would have exceeded the actual tax take by around £35 billion in 2008–9 and £92 billion in 2009–10. This equates to an 8 per cent reduction in taxation revenue arising directly from the crisis in 2008–9 and a 23 per cent reduction in 2009–10. The UK's budget deficit was around £49 billion in 2008–9 and £107 billion in 2009–10. In other words, approximately 70 per cent of the current account deficit in 2008–9 and 86 per cent in 2009–10 is attributable to lost taxation revenue alone (Hay 2012).

Is it not, of course, difficult to see how such a profound destabilisation of the public finances might occur? For most of the state's outgoings are, in essence, the product of long-standing commitments – citizens, after all, have a right to receive those benefits, and to consume those public services for which they are eligible, regardless of the rate of growth of economic output. If the public finances are in modest balance before the onset of a crisis of this magnitude, then they are most unlikely to remain in balance during and immediately following the crisis – since it is practically impossible for the state to reduce the size of its commitments proportionally to its loss in revenue as the crisis unfolds. But the point is that any failure to match reductions in the revenue stream with an equivalent and immediate rationing of welfare and other spending commitments will result in a growing current account deficit. A further factor merely compounds the problem. As growth turns negative, unemployment is bound to rise, albeit once again with some time-lag effect. The result, inevitably, is that, without any change in the eligibility criteria, the number of legitimate welfare claimants and total welfare expenditure both rise – with increased numbers of citizens claiming unemployment and associated benefits, a variety of means-tested payments and subsidies, and access to a range of public services to which they were not previously entitled.

The politics of the crisis: Brown's recession, Cameron's austerity

So what were the political ramifications of this? It is to this question that we can now turn directly, considering in turn the character and effectiveness of the interventions made by, first, the government of Gordon Brown and then the Cameron-Clegg Coalition to shore up the old growth model, the likely political legacy of the recession, and the prospects for the resumption of growth in the years ahead.

Perverse though it might seem, the government of Gordon Brown had a good recession (see especially Thain 2009; and, for similar judgements, Pemberton 2009, Gamble 2009a: 108, for a contrasting view see Coates 2009). It acted swiftly, decisively and with some degree of creativity in responding to a set of challenges that it had not anticipated in any way and which cut to the heart of the growth model on which it had come to rely. Brown, in particular, played a key role in setting the tone and temper of what proved a perhaps surprisingly coordinated international response. Indeed, that it is even possible to suggest the public rescue of the global banking system from the precipice marks the return to an era of Keynesian economics owes much to the influence of Brown himself (Krugman 2008: 185). But that does not make it true.

Though we did not see the return of the Keynesian economic paradigm, we did see something interesting – and strangely reminiscent of economic policy-making, at least in the UK, in the mid- to late 1970s. For just as the Labour government of Jim Callaghan sought to deploy monetarist techniques in an attempt to consolidate the prevailing Keynesian growth model, so that of Gordon Brown engaged in a bout of what might be termed inter-paradigm borrowing – in using a repertoire of at least quasi-Keynesian techniques to shore up the existing growth model. But the point is that both episodes of inter-paradigm borrowing were characterised by the attempt to stabilise, rather than to replace, the existing model; as such, neither marked a paradigm shift

(Gamble 2009a). This was 'foul weather Keynesianism' – a dipping into the repertoire of Keynesian techniques in recession only for such instruments to be abandoned as and when – indeed, alas, well before – growth was firmly re-established.

Indeed, that Cameron's Conservatives emerged as the largest party in the 2010 General Election almost guaranteed such an outcome – an impression only confirmed by the Coalition's Emergency Budget in June 2010. For, as was repeatedly emphasised before, during and after the election campaign, the Conservatives' priority in office was – and has subsequently been to make immediate cuts in public expenditure to appease market sentiment. In this respect, as in many others, Cameron's Conservatives and their coalition partners were no more carriers of an alternative economic paradigm than the government of Gordon Brown they replaced.

But there were during the election campaign – as there remain today – significant differences in emphasis between the parties on economic policy. Indeed, perhaps predictably, as time has passed so these differences have increased. First, although they did not explicitly deny that they would have engaged in the same public underwriting of the banking sector, the Conservatives were clearly much more uneasy about deficit financing and the associated ratcheting up of public debt.

In this context it is interesting that they did, and still do, refer to the recession as a crisis, but they do so in a very particular way. The crisis, for them, is a debt crisis – 'Labour's debt crisis' – and that, of course, implies that the solution to the crisis is to restore balance to the public finances through a combination of tax raising and unprecedented cuts in public spending (on the extent of the debt, see Helen Thompson's chapter in this collection). Yet it is by no means the only significant difference between the parties. Interestingly, in their 2010 election manifesto, the Conservatives were far more sanguine about the degree to which the UK growth model was broken than Labour. Its economic chapter opened with a stark question: 'Where is the growth to come from?' What is less clear is that either party offered much of an answer. For Labour, it seems growth rested on resuscitating the old growth model. But for the Conservatives, it was – at least during the campaign – very clear that this will not suffice. As they boldly stated at the time,

> We cannot go on with the old [growth] model ... built on debt. An irresponsible public spending boom, an overblown banking sector and unsustainable consumer borrowing on the back of a housing bubble were the features of an age of irresponsibility that left Britain

so exposed to this economic crisis. They cannot be the source of sustainable growth for the future.

(Conservatives 2010: 3)

Yet this has not at any point led to a clear sense of what is to be done. Instead we were simply told, as we are still told today, that the UK must make the transition to a new growth model based on saving rather than borrowing, investment rather than conspicuous consumption, and a balance of trade surplus in place of an existing deficit – as well as a greatly reduced role for financial services. But the problem remains that the Coalition government simply disavows the kind of intervention and, indeed, the degree of public investment necessary to secure any such transformation (clinging conveniently to a faith in the capacity of the market, if left to its own devices, to find for itself a new growth trajectory). Whilst this remains the case, the new growth model remains almost entirely aspirational – and, in all likelihood, elusive.

But things have undoubtedly moved on since the election. For one thing, a crisis discourse is now firmly established – and it would seem to have a strong hold over government and opposition policy alike. More significantly, that crisis discourse is essentially that of the Conservatives during the election campaign – and it is paradigm-reinforcing rather than paradigm-threatening. However obvious that might seem, it is a crucial point and one that bears repetition. For it is not something for which the existing literature, in its typical (and perhaps understandable) concern to link crises with episodes of paradigm succession, prepares us well (Hall 1993, Blyth 2002, Pemberton 2009).

The crisis discourse that has consolidated in the UK in recent years is one of a crisis of (public) debt – to which, of course, austerity and deficit reduction is the solution. And that, in itself, is interesting – in at least two respects. First, this remains true despite Moody's credit rating downgrade for the UK economy in February 2013 and despite the criticisms, in an interview with the BBC, of the International Monetary Fund's (IMF's) Chief Economist, Olivier Blanchard (BBC News 24 January 2013; IMF 2013). What is also interesting is that this is, in effect, a second-order crisis discourse in that it would seem to posit a primary or originating crisis (typically referred to simply as the 'global financial crisis'), the domestic effect of whose (mis)management has been to generate the present crisis of public debt which now needs to be addressed. As this suggests, seen in such terms the debt crisis is itself a symptom of the originating (and presumably more fundamental) crisis out of which it arose; and deficit reduction is revealed as a form of symptom amelioration rather than crisis resolution. We will return in rather more detail to the implications of this presently. But suffice it to note for now that were the crisis constituted differently, as a (first-order) *crisis of growth* not a (second-order) *crisis of public debt*, then austerity and deficit reduction would be no solution at all. Indeed, they would almost certainly be seen likely to compound the problem. No less significantly, were the crisis accepted as a crisis of growth, a paradigm shift might be rather more imminent.

Crisis discourses, as this suggests, are no more politically neutral today than they were in, say, the late 1970s (Hay 1996). Unremarkably, whether a crisis proves paradigm-challenging or paradigm-reinforcing depends on how it is perceived – specifically whether it is seen to signal an exhaustion of the paradigm or (as here) to emerge from a violation of its core precepts.

Yet we need to be careful here. For the current debt crisis discourse – though firmly established in the UK – has not gone unchallenged; and that challenge, though to some extent still implicit, is growing in intensity. This is certainly not as yet the pitting of competing crisis narratives against one another. But, under the leadership of Ed Miliband, Labour has increasingly counterposed a 'Tory cuts' discourse to the Coalition's 'Labour's debt' discourse. The former might be taken to imply an understanding of the crisis as one of growth rather than debt. Yet, thus far at any rate, that alternative crisis discourse has not been articulated publicly and it has certainly not led to the positing of an alternative growth strategy – the corollary of such an alternative. But the point is that it could be ... and perhaps it still might be.

What makes this more likely is that we are now entering a period where the effects of deficit reduction are starting to bite after an extended period in which they have been promised, yet largely deferred. And we do so at a time when there is an almost palpable sense that the public is starting to tire of the blame attribution that forms a part of the Coalition's broader debt crisis discourse.

Yet it is clearly possible to reject the suggestion that the deficit is to any significant extent a simple product of Labour's profligacy in office, whilst retaining the notion of this as a crisis of debt. The former is evidently (and evidentially) wrong (Dolphin 2011); the latter is at least a matter of interpretation (there is, after all, a substantial deficit and private debt remains at unprecedented levels). But the point is that such blame attribution is a key part of the Coalition's debt crisis discourse – and, it seems, it is the part of that discourse which most lacks public credibility.

The question of Labour's culpability: falling out of love with prudence?

This brings us to a key theme of the unfolding politics of the crisis – the question of Labour's culpability in and for the crisis (for contrasting views of which, see Coates 2009, Pemberton 2009, Thain 2009). This is a tricky issue. For, in the end, what matters politically is not whether and to what extent we, but the electorate, held, hold and continue to hold Labour, when it was in office, culpable – and, perhaps, no less significantly whether and to what extent that sense of culpability persists. Whether it *deserves* to be held culpable is a secondary and a more narrowly academic consideration.

Consider first public attributions of culpability. Surprisingly, perhaps, and despite presiding over the onset, at least, of the longest and deepest recession the UK has endured since the 1930s, Labour has avoided much of the blame – the contrast with the experience of Fianna Fail in Ireland is surely telling (Hay and Smith 2013a). It did far better at the polls in 2010 than, in a sense, it had any right to do. Thus, even if the electorate had by this time become convinced of the need for deficit reduction (on which, of course, there was cross-party consensus), it seemed reluctant to assign responsibility for carrying this out to the opposition. The Conservatives, it appears, were deemed just a little too enthusiastic to be entrusted with what was clearly seen as the unfortunate necessity of deficit reduction. Moreover, as we have seen more recently, significant portions of the electorate are also deeply sceptical of the claim that the deficit is a product of Labour's fiscal imprudence – the reflection of an ideological commitment to public expenditure growth at the expense of sound economic management.

If this is right, then Labour would appear to have been quite fortunate, certainly when compared with the ostensibly analogous administration of Jim Callaghan or, indeed, its immediate Irish counterpart. To what might we attribute this comparative good fortune? Perhaps two things. First, certainly in contrast to such comparators, Labour had a good crisis. Brown, in particular, got most things right – and, perhaps more significantly, he was *seen* to get most things right, certainly internationally (e.g. Krugman 2008: 185). In a manner that clearly belied his hardly enviable domestic reputation at the time, he was – and was seen to be – both decisive and influential internationally. He led, in effect, a surprisingly coordinated if short-lived proto-Keynesian counter-offensive to the crisis. Second, and no less significant, was the absence of a clearly articulated political alternative. However vociferous their general criticism of the then government and its handling of the crisis, it was never made clear during the 2010 General Election what (if anything) the Conservatives would have done differently had they been in office at the time. Moreover, with all the parties committing themselves during the campaign both to deficit reduction and to a broadly similar time frame for its delivery after the election, the economic stakes of the contest appeared at the time surprisingly low. Lacking a clear sense of what had gone wrong, how the Conservatives might put it right, and what kind of change in economic policy trajectory this might entail, the Conservatives were not well placed to exploit and reinforce any loss in Labour's perceived economic competence and credibility. The crisis has, then, proved far less economically discrediting for Labour than one might well have anticipated; if one is in any doubt, one need only consider the position of Fianna Fail today.

But if Labour was fortunate, in effect, in the opposition it faced, then did it deserve such good fortune? To what extent *should* it have been held more culpable for the crisis? That, as already indicated, is a difficult question to answer definitively and there is arguably little to be gained by dwelling on it at any length here. But a few points can nonetheless be made that are relevant to the lessons we might draw from the crisis.

First, there is clearly plenty of culpability to go around. If any part of the broader analysis of the UK case on which I draw is correct (e.g. Watson 2010, Hay 2011, 2013, Hay and Wincott 2012), then the UK growth model was peculiarly exposed to this kind of a crisis in a manner that was not at all difficult to anticipate (and which was shared with other economies reliant on demand generated by equity release or asset appreciation – see Hay 2006, 2013). At minimum, then, the New Labour administrations of both Blair and Brown were culpable, along with the Monetary Policy Committee of the Bank of England (MPC), for their failure to appreciate and mitigate the fragility of the growth model they were nurturing and for their failure to anticipate a crisis that was eminently predictable (at least in outline form). Yet, what is also clear is that the largely private debt-financed growth model that expired with the crisis predated New Labour's tenure in office. What makes the question of culpability altogether more difficult to answer is that what we might now describe as its growth model remained unacknowledged for some time after New Labour came to power – in effect the government remained largely unaware of the role of easy credit, private debt and asset-price appreciation in the generation of the growth for which it was taking credit. The growth model was much more the product of serendipity than of conscious design (Hay and Smith 2013b). That must surely temper Labour's culpability to some extent; it would, after all, seem harsh to hold it culpable for things of which it was unaware. But this 'innocence through ignorance' defence is time-delimited. From around 2000 onwards it was clear, not least through its open advocacy of an 'asset-based' model of welfare, that New Labour was both acutely conscious of, and keen to nurture, the 'privatised Keynesian' growth model (Crouch 2008, Watson 2010, Hay 2013; see also Thompson, this volume). The inherent fragility of that model neither it nor its MPC allies seem to have considered. For this, both must surely bear some significant responsibility.

The contemporary politics of the crisis

But this is to dwell on the past. That is the easy bit. Altogether more difficult, and altogether more pressing, is to reflect on how alternative understandings of where we are now and how we have got here might lead to rather different responses to what ails us as we go forward.

Here it is useful to return to the most obvious current conflict between the Coalition and the opposition on economic policy. This increasingly pits, as I have suggested, the 'Labour's deficit' discourse of the Coalition again the 'Tories' cuts' discourse of the opposition. As we have also already seen, much of this discursive battleground concerns the attribution of political responsibility for our afflictions. It is about blaming others for our past, present and (perhaps) future ills. But as narratives, these competing accounts rest on rather different and in fact antithetical assumptions – about the crisis itself and hence the nature of those afflictions. It is useful to tease these out for it shows that the stakes of inter-party competition have grown significantly in the years since the election.

Labour certainly now seems to understand the crisis differently to the Conservatives – in ways that are clearly crucial to how we should respond to it. That may not be terribly surprising, but it is extremely important, as we begin to see if we start to tease out the implicit alternative understanding of the crisis on which its 'Tories' cuts' discursive offensive is predicated.

There are at least three implicit premises to Labour's 'Tories' cuts' discourses: (i) that cuts, at least on this scale and at this pace, are unnecessary and hence a political choice rather than an economic imperative; (ii) that things would be different were Labour exercising that political choice; and (iii) that cuts, or at least cuts on this scale and to this time frame, are not only unnecessary but themselves damaging. A final and more narrowly political premise is that the deficit reduction agenda is in fact a foil for a Conservative (rather than Coalition) ideological offensive on the public sector. In the present context, however, it is the third of these premises – that deficit reduction on this scale is itself economically damaging – that is by far the most important. Yet there remains much ambiguity about this in Labour's discourse, not least because the party remains ostensibly committed to a very similar time frame for deficit and debt reduction to that of the Coalition. That is, of course, difficult to reconcile with the idea that the Coalition's programme of public spending cuts is economically damaging. But at times it has been possible to detect in Labour's thinking more of a Keynesian influence – with growth rather than deficit reduction becoming the focus and with deficit and debt reduction being seen less as the primary goal of policy than as a happy bi-product of policies to nurture growth. Only time will tell if this crystallises into a more obviously Keynesian alternative crisis discourse; but there is some potential for it to do so, especially once the effects of public spending cuts start to become evident.

Were it to do so, we would have two very different understandings of the crisis with very different implications for the appropriate policy set to respond to it and very different expectations of the consequences of the Coalition's current programme of deficit reduction.

Such an alternative crisis discourse might note the fiscal origins of the UK's current predicament. If the crisis is seen as a crisis of growth (of which debt is merely a symptom) rather than a crisis of public debt per se, then the dangers of deficit reduction as a putative solution become very obvious. No less significantly, this leads to very different expectations about what may now come to pass. Indeed, the more Keynesian 'crisis of growth' theory and the more orthodox 'crisis of public debt' theory generate wildly divergent expectations about levels of growth in the months and quarters ahead.

As this perhaps suggests, had the Labour opposition the courage of its (admittedly, recently rediscovered) Keynesian convictions it might even challenge the Coalition to a contest over economic predictions. It would not be difficult to put such divergent expectations to the test publicly. In such a context and following such a contest, if rapid deficit reduction did indeed produce negative growth, then it would be far easier to discredit both the policy and the economic theory on which it was predicated. And what would make such a battle of expectations even more difficult for the government is the systematic bias in its growth projections to date. As Alan Budd conceded shortly before stepping down from his role as Chair of the Office for Budget Responsibility (OBR) in 2010, its own growth projections have consistently erred on the side of optimism – for fear that too much realism might spook the markets.

Suffice it to note that the Treasury, the MPC and the OBR have spent considerably more time revising downwards their growth projections in recent months than they have revising them upwards. At minimum, then, a public contest over economic expectations might lead to a rather greater dose of economic realism.

This begins to look like something of an alternative economic strategy for Labour. But as a strategy, it lacks one key thing. For what such an alternative crisis discourse calls for is a new growth model to replace the one that is broken. And herein lies the problem. For although, in their different ways, all of the principal parties acknowledge the need for an alternative growth model, none appear to have a clear sense of what one might look like. It is certainly tempting to suggest that what the UK needs is a heavy dose of Keynesianism – or at least a government with the courage of Keynesian convictions. Such an administration might warn of the dangers of compounding the UK's problems with swinging public sector spending cuts in the absence of a clearly articulated growth strategy, set out precisely such a growth strategy, and link deficit reduction clearly and explicitly to the growth such a strategy might produce, pre-committing itself to different levels of deficit reduction depending on the growth rate attained. But this in itself is not sufficient. For, in the absence of an alternative growth model, it still falls far short of the minimum required to animate an alternative economic strategy.

It is, of course, not too difficult to imagine what an alternative growth strategy for the UK economy might look like – with, for instance, the channelling of credit out of the housing market and into what are identified as strategically significant (and export-oriented) sectors of the economy. But there has, to date, been virtually no public discussion of the options available, there would seem to be remarkably little academic or other preparatory work to draw on in the UK context in developing such a strategy and, whilst the growth dividends from such a strategy might be considerable, they are unlikely to come on stream in the short term. Genuine comparative advantages are not easily or rapidly acquired, especially in a world economy only slowly recovering from recession.

It is to what we might do in such a context that we now turn.

Getting what went wrong right ... and putting it right

A crisis of debt not of growth

Crises, as I have suggested, are to a large extent what we make of them. For what we do in response to a crisis depends to a very considerable extent on how we perceive the problem – we respond not to the condition itself but to our diagnosis of it. What is clear is that the dominant discourse conceives of our affliction as a crisis of debt. But, as I have argued, this is not the only way in which the crisis could be understood – and it is not how the crisis *should* be understood.

The point is that it is our seemingly shared conviction that this *is* a crisis of debt that makes austerity and deficit reduction the logical solution. Change our sense of the crisis and we change the range of responses considered appropriate. Thus, were the crisis conceived of differently, as a crisis of growth not a crisis of debt, then austerity and deficit reduction would be no solution at all. Indeed, they would almost certainly be seen as likely to compound the problem.

Yet it is precisely the implication that I draw from the preceding analysis that the dominant account misdiagnoses the current UK crisis. And, if we are to put right what went wrong, it is first imperative that we get our diagnosis of the affliction correct. The implication of the preceding argument is, then, that this is not a crisis of debt. To see the UK crisis, or indeed the Eurozone crisis, as one of debt is to mistake a symptom for the condition itself; and the risk is that, in mistaking the symptom for the condition, we choose a course of medicine only destined to reduce further the life expectancy of the patient.

Yet wrong though it may be, it is not at all difficult to see why a crisis of debt discourse might have taken hold in the UK. It is not very threatening; it does not entail a change in economic paradigm; and it leads readily to a simple diagnosis – deficit reduction and austerity – which is arguably quite in accordance with the liberal market disposition of recent UK governments. The alternative crisis of growth discourse is, in a sense, a far more challenging one. For it would entail a rejection of the prevailing economic paradigm informing policy since at least the 1980s. More significantly still, it would almost certainly require a rejection of the old growth model and the search for a new one.

As this suggests, whilst the crisis of debt discourse is paradigm-reinforcing, the crisis of growth discourse is paradigm-challenging. And, if there is one thing that we have learned from previous crises, it is that prevailing economic paradigms are not readily abandoned. They tend, if anything, to be tested to destruction. Arguably, this is what happened in the 1930s; and it may well be what is happening today. The point is that the dominant crisis of debt discourse has led both the Coalition government and, to the extent that it accepts it too, the Labour opposition to search for growth principally by seeking to revive the old (broken) model of growth.

But there are serious impediments to the resuscitation of the old growth model. There are essentially six of these. Together they must lead us to question the extent to which growth, even in the short to medium term, can be revived in this way and, in fact, the longer term desirability of any such revivification, were it to prove possible.

1. *The heightened sensitivity of demand to interest-rate variations.* The first impediment to the return to growth by recently conventional means relates to monetary policy. The point here is simple – the dependence of the old growth model on private debt increased the sensitivity of demand in the economy to interest-rate movements and, in the process, the threat to growth posed by inflationary pressures.
2. *Interest rate spreads on consumer and commercial lending.* This is compounded by a second factor – the size of the mortgage and commercial lending-rate spreads which opened up during the crisis. Though not much commented on, these have yet to close up again in the way that inter-bank lending rates did. It has, in short, become more costly to borrow at a given base rate; or, in other words, the monetary authorities have allowed the banks to pass on a significant part of the cost of their recapitalisation to borrowers, crowding out both consumer demand and investment in the process.
3. *A looming crisis of housing affordability.* A third factor is long-standing – indeed, it is intergenerational. Sustained house price inflation at 10 per cent per annum over a number of decades was always going to create a crisis of affordability for new entrants into the housing market at some point. That point has, of course, been brought forward, dramatically, by the crisis – and the intergenerational problem of affordability is now being compounded by a step-level increase in the cost of mortgage lending over the base rate, the increased levels of personal debt that will follow the withdrawal of state funding for higher education and, indeed, the comparative risk aversion of the banking sector following the crisis.
4. *Likelihood of currency depreciation in the absence of growth.* A fourth factor relates, in a way, to the first – it is a feedback effect. If growth continues to prove elusive in the UK whilst it starts to return to other leading economies, then it is likely that the exchange rate will suffer at precisely the point at which oil prices (themselves largely denominated in dollars) start to rise. The result can only be inflation and upward pressure on interest rates – in short, a return to the condition of 'stagflation' that afflicted the UK economy in the 1970s and again during the early part of the crisis itself.

5. *Prospects for the re-regulation of financial markets.* In at least one respect, the performance of the UK economy since the crisis has been better than was envisaged by most commentators. At the time, for instance, there seemed nothing terribly remarkable about Martin Weale's (2009: 3, 8) comments in 2009 that 'it is most unlikely that the financial services industry can in the future act as the sort of motor of growth that it has done in the past ... if the sector returns to the importance it had in 2000, GDP is likely to be reduced permanently by about 1.9 per cent'. But this step-level reduction in the contribution of financial services to UK GDP has simply failed to materialise – and that is of course no bad thing. But the point is that it might yet still happen. For what Weale had envisaged by now is the systematic re-regulation of financial markets – and, in particular, limits on short-selling – which have yet to arise, but which arguably the prudential governance of global financial markets requires. Such regulations might be very good for the stability of the global economy going forward; but they would merely serve to accentuate the size of the hole in the UK's model of growth that needs filling.

6. *The cost of austerity.* Finally, however bad things may already be, if the above analysis is correct, then they are only likely to get worse before they get better. First, as we have seen, however beneficial for the world economy any re-regulation of financial markets might prove, it is likely to come at some considerable price in terms of the contribution of financial services to UK GDP. And, second, with the lion's share of the public spending cuts associated with the move to public austerity still to come, demand in the economy and hence the contribution of consumer spending to economic output is almost bound to fall before it improves.

As this suggests, the immediate prospects for the resumption of a model of growth resembling that which came to characterise the UK economy since the early 1990s look bleak indeed.

Impediments to a new growth model

So what can be done? Well, the above analysis would seem to lead inexorably to a simple conclusion – the need for an alternative growth model, the search for which has scarcely begun. But this is no manifesto of despair. For there is much that follows from the preceding analysis by way of practical policy suggestions that can make a substantial difference in the long-overdue search for a new, more sustainable and, indeed, inclusive model of growth – in which the proceeds of economic success are more evenly distributed. The following is merely an outline of the implications of the analysis I have sought to present.

1. *Politicising the cost of borrowing.* First, if the economy is to be 'rebalanced', then the government and the Bank of England need to be putting concerted downward pressure on the actual cost of borrowing (independent of the base rate), particularly in sectors where a clear link to the growth strategy for the economy can be made and substantiated. The banks, I contend, have in effect been allowed to recapitalise themselves by charging commercial borrowers, mortgage holders and those servicing consumer debt a sizeable interest-rate premium, relative to the base rate to compensate them from their investment banking losses during the crisis. This is both intolerable and a significant drain on the growth prospects of the commercial and consumer economy. The banks need to be named and shamed and held publicly to account for their behaviour.

2. *The private to public investment.* A corollary of this is that there is a strong argument to be made for not just private but *public* investment in support of a clearly articulated growth strategy built on identifying and supporting growth in a series of key export-oriented sectors. Apart from anything else, the cost of financing long-term public borrowing is significantly lower than for commercial lenders. Moreover, public infrastructure projects are likely to be key to any reconfiguration of the economy which might more closely align its structure to a new (and more clearly export-oriented) growth strategy. Public investment might, in other words, be a highly cost-effective way of providing the public goods on which the transition to a new model of growth relies.

3. *Hypothecated investment or growth bonds.* This is all very well, but how might it be funded? There are many options which might be considered here. But one of these is the use of public investment or growth bonds – a form of hypothecated government debt and, in effect, an ethical form of investment available to financial institutions and private citizens alike. The funds secured in this way would be ear-marked for public infrastructural projects or might be distributed through a range of national or regional investment banks, perhaps even including a green investment bank. The latter might fund investments in sustainable technologies or the human capital to utilise such technologies.

4. *Conditional deficit reduction.* A further implication of the analysis presented here is that we cannot afford to consider deficit reduction as a

goal in itself – and certainly not the principal goal guiding economic policy. Indeed, a powerful implication of the preceding discussion is that deficit reduction in a context of stagnant or negative growth is self-defeating and threatens only to produce a vicious circle of declining economic output. But this is not to suggest that there is a simple trade-off between deficit reduction and growth promotion – merely that deficit reduction must be made conditional on growth. Governments, in such a conception, would need to be clear about their strategy for securing growth and to make a strong public pre-commitment both to an explicit growth target and to a sliding scale of deficit reduction.

5. *International coordination of debt and growth management.* The economic case for conditional deficit reduction is, I would contend, a very strong one; but it undoubtedly has its political difficulties. To announce the end of deficit reduction in one economy alone, especially in the current global economic climate and in a context of the timidity of financial institutions, threatens a run on the currency and a steep rise in the cost of servicing (short-term) national debt. Consequently, it is imperative that steps are taken at an international (and, ideally, a global) level (under the auspices of the IMF, for instance) to agree a coordinated strategy for managing debt and growth – as well as, in time, to move away from a simple notion of output growth as the global currency of economic performance.

The above five points do not, of course, constitute a growth model for the UK economy – nor are they intended to. But they do suggest a way forward if the UK is not to lock in the kind of comparative poor economic performance from which it suffered in the 1960s and 1970s.

Conclusion: A crisis of politics in the politics of crisis

We have travelled a fair distance in the preceding pages – considering the nature of UK capitalism itself, the Anglo-liberal growth model to which it has given rise since the 1990s and the culpability of both in the global financial crisis and our own domestic crisis. We then turned to consider the consequences of the crisis and the prospects for the return to growth in the years ahead, concluding with a set of proposals for the way forward in the years ahead – the potential path from crisis, as it were.

But there is one question in all this that we have not considered. And it is to this that we now turn in conclusion. That question is a simple one: Is it even correct to refer to this as a crisis in the first place? And, strange though it might seem, our argument is that the more one reflects on this, the less self-evident it is that we have witnessed a crisis.

It is clear that the language of crisis has, if anything, been cheapened in recent years. Everything these days is a crisis. So surely this is? Well, it is certainly bad enough; but in a sense that is precisely the point. For if we return to the (Greek) etymology of the term, we find that a crisis is a moment of decisive intervention – medically, the critical point at which the doctor's intervention proves decisive, one way or the other, in the course of the illness and the life of the patient (Hay 1996). Insofar as this is a relevant analogy, we are not yet at that point. For although the patient may well be suffering more than ever, the condition does not seem to be improving; but this is not because of the failure of any decisive intervention, for there simply has not been one. If this is what a crisis is – a moment of decisive intervention – then we have simply yet to get to the moment of crisis. What we have seen is instead the accumulation of a series of largely unresolved contradictions – not that the significance of this should be underemphasised. For in many respects this is far worse; it would surely be better were we able to talk about this as a moment of decisive intervention.

So what possibility is there of our situation of radical indecision becoming one of decisive intervention? For, perverse though it might seem, the best that we can hope for is a crisis – at least a crisis thus understood.

Here there are grounds for optimism and pessimism alike.

For the optimist, crises understood as moments of decisive intervention and paradigm shift are rare, though they typically post-date the emergence of the symptoms they ultimately seek to resolve, often by a decade or more. In short, we may be too impatient in expecting the crisis point to have been reached already. This was certainly the case in the 1930s – with the transition to Keynesianism taking at least a further decade from the advent of the great depression; and a similar kind of time lag can arguably be identified in the process of change initiated in the 1970s. It seems that the transitions we now associate with crisis periods take a long time to arise – typically a decade or more. It is perhaps ever more likely the more the condition remains resistant to the current medicine – medicine, of course, prescribed by doctors trained and versed in the operation of the old paradigm.

Yet there is only so much optimism one can draw from such historical analogies. For there can be no guarantee that alternative doctors with alternative medicines will be summoned simply because the patient remains unwell and the condition is not responding to current treatments. Searching for solutions is no guarantee that they are found nor that they are implemented. Above all this is a political problem. For us to respond to the crisis differently we need a different politics of crisis narration. The problem we face politically is that, to far too great an extent, we have either not been looking for solutions (certainly not for alternatives to the prevailing paradigm) nor, to the extent that we have been looking for solutions, have we been looking in the right places and in the right way. My hope is that in this chapter I have made a compelling case that we need first to get right what went wrong in order to put it right and to suggest at least some of what getting it right and putting it right might entail. Whether we do so or not is politically contingent – and that is the basis of any and all of the optimism we might have.

Part II
Surveying Institutions in Crisis

4
A Crisis of Parliament

David Judge

Introduction

The words 'parliament' and 'crisis' have often been linked in single sentences, in different time periods, in different countries and in the pronouncements of politicians and academics alike. The impression is often given that crisis is endemic to parliaments and parliamentary systems for, as Bracher (1967: 245) noted nearly 50 years ago, 'The phrase "crisis of parliamentarism" is nearly as old as the phenomenon of parliamentary democracy'. Indeed, a random selection of analyses of parliaments over this period produces references to 'modern crises of parliaments' (Loewenberg 1971: 4) or 'a crisis of representative democracy?' (Alonso et al. 2011: 7). What these random quotations point to, respectively, is that parliaments and parliamentarianism may be confronted with possible multiple crises, and, when a question mark is appended, the notion of 'parliamentary crisis' becomes a contestable proposition and is not simply a matter of fact. What they also point to is that the institution of parliament needs to be located within the broader analytical frames of parliamentarism and parliamentary democracy.

The objective of this chapter, therefore, is to examine the contestability of the idea of parliamentary crisis in the UK and to do so by making a basic distinction between parliament as an institution, parliamentarianism as a system of government and parliamentary democracy as a form of representative democracy. Although inextricably interlinked in practice, these terms are capable of being disaggregated analytically, in which case, 'crisis' may manifest itself differently, disproportionally, or not at all, across different analytical layers. 'Crisis', for the purposes of this chapter, is taken as a social construction of what constitutes 'a conjunction of undesirable circumstances beyond the norm' (Drennan and McConnell 2007: 16; see also Nohrstedt and Weible 2010: 5). In this sense what constitutes an exceptional threat, the level of intensity of the threat to the status quo and the urgency required in responding to such threats are open to interpretation and contestation.

Threaded through the analysis of this chapter are the concepts of legitimacy and legitimation. Just as these concepts are central to any understanding of the institutional purpose and standing of parliament, equally they are crucial to a conceptualisation of crisis. Indeed, as Boin (2004: 167) notes, 'the currency of crisis is legitimacy' (see also 'tHart and Boin 2001: 31; Stark 2010: 4). Thus a crisis manifests itself when a marked decline in legitimacy incapacitates an institution:

> At the heart of crisis is an unremitting discrepancy between external expectations and perceived performance... If we take shifts in legitimacy as a key indicator of disruption it can be argued that any kind of rapid decline in the legitimacy of institutional structures that were previously widely valued helps us to identify a... crisis.
>
> (Boin 2004: 168)

The argument is advanced that if there is a crisis, or a series of interconnected crises, then it might well be that what the UK is witnessing is a conceptual crisis: a crisis that stems from the counter-positioning of established notions of representative democracy and legitimacy derived from electoral processes against countervailing conceptions of democratic representation and representative claims which are not focused upon, or do not privilege, the institutional form of parliament or electoral representation. In one sense, this argument simply reformulates historic questions about the nature of representative democracy and notions of democratic legitimacy. In answering these questions, the distinctive nature of the 'legitimation claims' of parliament (or more precisely the elected element of the House of Commons) is addressed and located within a discussion of diffuse systemic political support.

The discussion is structured in the following manner. It starts by examining empirical evidence of 'a crisis of public confidence and popular trust' in the institution of parliament, before considering levels of diffuse support for the wider system of parliamentary democracy in the UK. Concerns that the Westminster parliament has been residualised in the system of UK governance are then examined within a broader discussion of the Westminster model and its continuing significance as a legitimating frame for UK government. The crisis dimensions of this frame, which are encapsulated in a closed logical loop interred in the disjunction between the idealised prescriptions of the Westminster model and the practice of governance in the UK, are then analysed. The final section of the chapter moves the focus of the discussion away from a perceived 'crisis of government' to a 'crisis of parliamentary representation'. This latter 'crisis' has manifested itself both in theory, in a 'reconceptualisation of representation' that asserts the legitimacy and authenticity of non-electoral representative claims, and, in practice, in the implementation of 'democratic innovations' and the increased importance of non-electoral modes of representation beyond the conventional institutional configurations of elections and parliamentary institutions.

Parliament as an institution: Indicators of crisis – trust/confidence

Specific indicators

When popular trust in the UK parliament has been probed, levels of public support/trust have been found to be worryingly low (for a broader analysis of trust in UK institutions, see Chapter 2). Indeed, low trust is combined with low public knowledge thresholds about the workings of parliament. Thus, for example, when respondents to the Hansard Society surveys have been asked how much they know specifically about the UK parliament, 61 per cent on average claimed to know nothing or not very much about parliament (across the six surveys in which this question was asked), with 15 per cent claiming to know nothing at all about the UK parliament (Hansard Society 2013: 32).

When members of the public have been asked specifically about their 'trust' in parliament the results, in successive Eurobarometer surveys, have consistently recorded a marked propensity 'to tend not to trust' the UK parliament rather than 'to tend to trust'. In 2012, 25 per cent tended to trust in contrast to 70 per cent who tended not to trust (average across Eurobarometer 2012a, 2012b). This marked a nearly 50 per cent decline in those trusting parliament within the space of a decade (down from 47 per cent in 2001) and a nearly 40 per cent increase in those tending not to trust parliament (up from 43 per cent) in the same period (Eurobarometer 2001). Interestingly, for all that the furore over MPs' expenses in 2009 was deemed to constitute a 'crisis', especially in the media, public reaction 'did not manifest itself, contrary to conventional wisdom, in collapsing levels of trust in politics and politicians' (Hansard Society 2009: 126, Fox 2010: 6). In this respect, although the scandal surrounding MPs' expenses served as a 'focusing event' in subjecting the activities of MPs to unremitting public scrutiny and no little ridicule, it did not mark a catastrophic drop in trust levels. In part, the failure to stimulate such a 'collapse' was because of the perilously low pre-existing levels of trust. It should be noted, however, that there was an 11 per cent drop in trust in parliament, as an institution, at the height of the expenses scandal between Eurobarometer 70 (October–November 2008) and Eurobarometer 71 (June–July 2009); and that the level of trust in parliament has not yet recovered to the institutional trust levels immediately prior to the scandal (30 percent in Eurobarometer 70, and 34 per cent in Eurobarometer 68 between October and November 2007). These low institutional trust scores also reflect 'confidence' assessments of the UK parliament, with, for example, only 23 per cent of respondents to the European Values Survey of 2008 recording a great deal or quite a lot of confidence in the Westminster parliament.

A caveat should, however, be entered at this stage by noting that it is unclear from these surveys exactly what respondents were assessing in making their confidence judgement, or what was their cognitive basis for scoring levels of trust (Hooghe 2011: 270, Marien and Hooghe 2011: 3). Nonetheless, despite this caveat, and no matter what was being measured, levels of trust and confidence in the UK parliament are distinctly lower in the UK than in all but four of the relatively well-established parliamentary democracies in the EU (Greece, Spain, Italy and Portugal, excluding post-2004 accession states). Moreover, although there were trendless fluctuations in most of these EU states across time, the UK (along with Portugal) stands out for 'a significant growth of cynicism' towards parliament since the 1990s (Norris 2011: 73). For many, these findings are sufficient evidence of a 'crisis of public confidence' in the UK parliament.

General indicators

Yet, surveys in the UK also reveal that citizens are capable of making discriminatory trust-judgements amongst and between politicians and political institutions (even if survey questions use single item indicators). Moreover, the more astute analysts of political behaviour acknowledge the multi-dimensionality of trust. Thus, for example, Pippa Norris – in her analysis of trends in citizens' attitudes towards democratic governance – makes a distinction between specific trust (at the level of political actors or public policies) (2011: 61) and diffuse trust (as a form of 'institutional confidence' which reflects more enduring and general orientations than trust in particular actors or policy programmes

(2011: 66)). Even at the level of institutional confidence, different trust judgements may conceivably apply from one institution to another and, indeed, are empirically observable (Norris 2011: 70–82). In this sense, Norris locates a conception of political trust in close proximity to Easton's broader conception of political support: with its specific and diffuse dimensions (Easton 1965; and see below).

This point can be illustrated in relation to the UK parliament. There remains relatively limited confidence in parliament's specific capacities with, for example, only 47 per cent of respondents in the 2013 Audit of Political Engagement agreeing that parliament held government to account (Hansard Society 2013: 57). Yet, when asked whether the UK parliament was essential to UK democracy, over two-thirds (68 per cent) of respondents agreed, with 30 per cent strongly agreeing. Only seven per cent disagreed. In fact the 2013 figure marked an eight per cent increase on the 2010 result of 60 per cent who found parliament 'worthwhile' or 'essential' (Hansard Society 2010: 41). This might be taken as an indication of a relatively high level of general or diffuse support or trust for the institution when located within the wider system of representative democracy. Indeed, generalised support for such a system continues at relatively high levels. Evidence of this is provided in a YouGov poll in 2012 which repeated a question asked in a 1969 Gallop Poll, 'Would you describe Britain as a democratic country or not?' (Kellner 2012: 2). The respective positive answers were 68 per cent in 1969 and 67 per cent in 2012. The negative answers revealed a small decrease across the two surveys from 20 per cent to 17 per cent. When pushed still further about their assessment of British democracy, 63 per cent of respondents to the 2012 YouGov poll were prepared to support the statement 'For all its faults, Britain's democratic system is one of the finest in the world.'

The significance of these empirical findings for the following discussion is two-fold. First, there is a distinction to be drawn between attitudes to parliament as an institution and parliament as part of a system of representative democracy. Second, specific public concerns about institutional competence (controlling government) linked to specific trust and specific aspects of MPs' roles, sit alongside general recognition of the 'essential' categorical role of the UK parliament in defining 'our democracy'. David Easton's notion of 'diffuse support' is of resonance here. Diffuse support for Easton encompasses 'rudimentary convictions about the appropriateness of the political order of things' (1965: 279) and generalized beliefs, no matter how inarticulate, 'that the authorities and the order within which they operate is right and proper' (1965: 280).

The significance of these generalised beliefs will be discussed below, but first specific aspects of parliament's institutional roles and capacities need to be examined.

Parliamentarism as a system of government

Specific crises

Loewenberg (1971: 4), as noted above, identified 'modern crises' (in the plural) of parliaments. These crises emerged as the expectations associated with pre-democratic parliaments – of the representation of a narrowly defined 'political nation' of vested socio-economic interests, collective institutional behaviour and an egalitarian organisational structure – came increasingly to be at odds with the institutional characteristics of parliaments in an age of the mass franchise. The first crisis emerged from the role of political parties in the wake of the development of the mass franchise. Parties sought to 'mobilize the new electorate, to recruit representatives from it, and control these representatives after their election' (1971: 5). The second was the expansion of the demands made upon parliaments as the scope of government increased almost exponentially, as public policies became increasingly complex, and as specialized oversight and interventions by parliament became more imperative. The third was the enhanced position of executive leadership in the political system and its corollary of the 'executive domination' of parliaments (1971: 12).

It is the third 'crisis' that has attracted most attention in the UK, but the other two are inextricably linked and continue to sustain elemental percussive backbeats to the 'crisis' in executive-legislative relations. The third dimension of the crisis was presented in a particularly stark form in the Power Commission Report in its conclusion that the UK was confronted by a 'crisis of a nineteenth-century political system facing twenty-first-century citizens' (Power Commission 2006: 108). At the centre of this crisis was the purported fact that '[t]he Executive in Britain is now more powerful in relation to Parliament than it has been probably since the time of Walpole' (Power Commission 2006: 128). While the Power Commission Report distilled the essence of broader, longstanding public and parliamentarian fears of an over-dominant executive, it attracted criticism from Flinders and Kelso (2011: 257) who sought to argue that such fears were overblown (for a critique of this position see Chapter 1). According to them, the Power Commission Report, along with most of the Political Science profession in the UK, failed 'to take account of the complexities of parliament' (2011: 257) and the 'complex resource interdependencies that actually exist' (2011: 259) between the executive and legislature. They also claimed that 'scholars may have contributed to an erosion of public support in politics in general and declining levels of public confidence in parliaments in particular' (2011: 250). The general thrust of their argument is that public cynicism about parliament and MPs (which is often taken as an indicator of an attitudinal crisis) may have increased in an 'over-inflation' of public expectations (fuelled by inaccurate conceptualisations of parliament's position in the UK state) alongside a deflation of the results of 'detailed empirical research' (which provide practical contestations of those erroneous conceptualisations).

Even if, as Flinders and Kelso suggest, the imbalance between executive and parliament is not quite as lopsided as often portrayed in caricatured accounts of UK governance, there is still widespread concern that parliament has been residualised in the system of government. Although, as the next section reveals, simple arguments that the Westminster model no longer accurately describes the reality of contemporary UK governance have been moderated, and replaced with arguments that the Westminster model remains of importance as a validation of the activities of a centralised executive, the position of parliament in these arguments remains tenuous. Parliament as an institution may not be in 'crisis', but when located within broader conceptualisations of governance and the British political tradition (BPT) (see Introduction), it may be at the epicentre of a crisis of parliamentarism.

The Westminster model

For a model that has attracted sustained criticism from political scientists for most of the past three decades or so, and one that provides the counterpoint for a self-proclaimed new 'conventional wisdom' of policy communities (Jordan 1990: 471) or a 'new orthodoxy' of a differentiated polity (Marsh 2010), the Westminster model has proved remarkably resilient.

In part this resilience stems from the simple fact that there is no agreed definition of the Westminster model, and no real agreement whether it is an 'organising perspective' (Gamble 1990: 404–6), part of a 'political tradition' (most recently Hall 2012: 92–120) or a descriptive model. Similarly, the fact that some 14 key beliefs and core institutions can be, and have been, identified as constituent elements of the Westminster model at various times (Rhodes et al. 2009: 7) makes it relatively easy to identify some continuities of 'key beliefs' or institutional configurations over time. Conversely of course it also makes it relatively easy to identify discontinuities or disjunctions of some other elements over time, as indeed critics of the model have demonstrated persistently.

It is instructive that the most recent, and most detailed, examination of the Westminster model identified at its core a set of four interrelated components which not only echoed those identified earlier by Gamble (1990: 407) but which, more significantly, reflected the central ideas of the Westminster model 'as understood by its constitutive actors' (Rhodes et al. 2009: 10). The four components were: responsible government with political executives drawn from parliament and ultimately dependent upon sustaining the legislature's confidence; an executive whose members are individually and collectively accountable to parliament; a professional, non-partisan and 'permanent' public service; and, in the UK at least, a legally sovereign parliament (Rhodes et al. 2009: 10). They are deemed to be core ideas in that they have the deepest historical roots and 'typically gravitate' (Rhodes et al. 2009: 9) around the constitutional fusion of the executive and legislature (see also Richards and Smith 2002, Richards 2008: 15–16).

Over time other ideas have been 'grafted on' to this core: some for categorical/taxonomic reasons, in the sense of being used to categorise and differentiate majoritarian from consensual systems (Lijphart 1999: 1–8), and some for descriptive accuracy in the sense of reflecting changed practices in relation to electoral processes, party systems and inter-institutional interactions. Yet the emphasis upon inserting more elements into the model to bolster its descriptive accuracy skewed the debate towards empirical positivist analysis and towards measuring the degree of separation between model and political practice. In this respect, critics started from the premise that the Westminster model constituted an accurate representation of political reality. Not surprisingly they discovered that it was not. What the Westminster model sketched, in the pivotal period of its inception in the second half of the 19th century, was an idealised 'liberal view of the constitution' that constituted 'a theory of legitimate power' (Birch 1964: 65). As such, from the outset, it was an artificial contrivance that arose out of the conflation of liberal theories of representation with a Diceyean view of liberal government (Judge 1993: 138–40). The brief and exceptional convergence between the prescriptions of the liberal view of the constitution and the practice of liberal government in the mid-19th century became petrified in seminal academic writings, most notably those of Dicey, despite the manifest erosion of the precepts of the liberal view after 1867. Indeed, for much of the period thereafter 'adherents to the Liberal theory of the state [encapsulated in the Westminster model] have been regretfully aware that political practice has departed from [these] principles' (Birch 1964: 80).

Just such awareness has, since the late-1970s, been an analytical stem cell in the genetic development, mutation and transmutation of models of policy communities, networks, governance, multi-level governance, differentiated polity and asymmetric power (e.g. Richardson and Jordan 1979, Rhodes and Marsh 1992, Rhodes 1997, Bevir and Rhodes 2003, Marsh et al. 2003, Bache and Flinders 2004, Richards 2008): all of which started from the premise that they provided 'alternatives' or posed a 'direct challenge' to the Westminster model (Marsh 2012: 46–8). The 'challenge' was empirical insofar as these alternatives sketched a more realistic representation of the UK polity (e.g. Bevir and Rhodes 2003: 198–9).

Initially such 'corrective' accounts were dismissive of parliament's contribution to governance narratives, with parliament variously being seen to be insulated from networks, or residualised in the policy process, or in fact superseded in a 'post-parliamentary' polity (e.g. Jordan and Richardson 1987: 288, Rhodes and Marsh 1992: 13, Richardson 1993: 90, 2000: 1006, Rhodes 1997: 38). Notably, for the present discussion, the residualisation of parliament in these alternative models was not treated as 'a crisis' but something lower down the Richter scale of normative anxiety. There was certainly acknowledgement that, if these alternative models better encapsulated the processes of UK governance, then there were 'normative grounds for concern' (Grant 2000: 51). Similarly, Rhodes and Marsh (1992: 265), in recognising that normative questions about the extent to which networks undermined existing notions of parliamentary democracy remained largely unexplored in their model, nonetheless raised a concern, bordering on pessimism, at the extent to which the 'output legitimacy' claimed by networks served to insulate their activities from the 'constraint of political, especially electoral, legitimacy'.

In part, such relative normative sanguineness might have been because new modes of governance were not as insulated from electoral representative processes as network analysts made out (Judge 1993: 120–30, 2005: 106–14). More importantly, however, was a claim that networks were nested in a process of parliamentary representation and the legitimation of government and government outputs flowing from that process. Indeed, the legitimating frame provided by the Westminster model is now widely recognised even by those intent on demonstrating that political practice does not correspond to the political prescriptions of the Westminster model. Such recognition is to be found in Rhodes et al.'s (2009: 29) statement:

> In Westminster systems traditions provide a set of maps, a language, and historical narratives about government that over time captures those essential features we would now group under the heading 'the Westminster model'... We disagree that Westminster is a fantasy... it is better seen as a set of evolving traditions couched in myth.

More precisely Rhodes et al. identify the Westminster model as a 'legitimizing interpretation' which allows 'various actors' to provide legitimacy and context for their actions (2009: 228). Similarly, other contemporary analyses of UK governance are replete with reference to the Westminster model as a 'legitimising mythology' (Richards 2008: 199, Diamond and Richards 2012: 192, Hall 2012: 12); a 'legitimating tool' or a 'legitimating framework' (Flinders 2010: 25).

This framework is strikingly evident too in official descriptions of UK governance. Official views – recently enunciated in the *Cabinet Manual* (Cabinet Office 2011: 2–4) – still proclaim the four key elements of the Westminster model. These are not false statements, as the term 'myth' might suggest (Keating 2008: 111) but reflect instead the ideas of legitimate government as refracted in the vision of the executive. What is important about these official statements is that they combine statements about 'what is' with 'what should be'; and these ideas extend beyond formal official pronouncements. Of particular relevance, Richards (2008: 199) noted, from his interviews with ministers and civil servants, that 'it is important to appreciate the extent to which actors from the core executive have continued to draw from the Westminster model in defining, shaping and legitimising their behaviour'. Diamond and Richards (2012: 182) also reaffirmed the 'continuing salience of narratives that have emerged from within that [Westminster] model which still condition the mindset of ministers and civil servants' (see also Bevir 2010: 125, Richards and Mathers 2010: 516–18,). In case it is suspected that the salience of the Westminster model for members of the executive pertains mainly to the centralisation/hierarchical dimensions of the model, it is worthy of note that the responsibility/accountability dimensions continue to feature predominantly in the mindset of ministers and civil servants (e.g. Rhodes 2011: 38, 229, Stark 2011: 1151).

In parallel to this internal executive recognition of the continuing significance of parliament, academics, many of whom started as parliamentary sceptics, were willing to concede – even if grudgingly – the importance of parliament to legitimation processes in the UK (Richardson 1993: 90, Daugbjerg and Marsh 1998: 62–3, Marsh et al. 2001: 244–7, 2003: 314). Yet, even if there is now a broader acknowledgement that the four key notions of the Westminster model serve as a framework of ideas through which the members of the core executive in the UK seek to legitimise their institutional position and their policy preferences, there is equally a consensus that the UK polity does not necessarily adhere closely to those ideas in practice. Smith (2008: 150) makes this point neatly in his observation that 'as a myth the Westminster model may represent how officials and ministers present the political system, but however strong their beliefs... it does not represent the truth about either the power of ministers or of officials [or how the system works]'.

Obviously Smith's statement throws up questions about 'truth' and about 'myth'. This is not the place to engage in the deconstruction of the term 'myth'. What is important instead is to disinter from this brief consideration of the Westminster model, the crisis dimensions that stem from the analysis. These can be specified within a closed logical loop. First, there is a disjunction between the idealised prescriptions of the Westminster model and the practice of governance in the UK. Second, all contemporary governments describe, and so define, UK state institutional interactions in terms of the 'representative and responsible' core of the Westminster model. Third, this definition still 'conditions the mindset of ministers and civil servants'. Fourth, the Westminster model cements into the political institutional architecture of the UK the pivotal importance of parliament in providing the legitimating frame for executive action: for, as Judge (2006: 369) noted, in the UK an 'executive-centric state has been justified in terms of a legislative-centric theory of parliamentary sovereignty'. Fifth, in spite of points two to four, point one still pertains. In this loop, an inherent conceptual 'crisis' is embedded. Executives depend upon a model of legitimation, the practical deficiencies of which possess the capacity to undermine the very claims to legitimacy incorporated within the model. Yet executives are unable to prescribe or incapable of articulating – either theoretically or expediently – an alternative model without dissipating the 'legislative-centric theory of parliamentary sovereignty'. This is why the executive remains insistent that 'Parliament is sovereign [even if]... in practice... Parliament has chosen to be constrained in various ways' (Cabinet Office 2011: 3 para 9). This very insistence fuels disbelief and dissatisfaction. In this manner, the executive is locked into a 'conceptual crisis'. This is why the Blair and Brown Labour governments – in their repeated declarations that 'there is no intention to begin from first principles' (HL Debates 21 June 2001: col 52) – consistently defended their actions and formulated institutional change within the parameters of the Westminster model (Judge 2005: 273–9, 2006; Richards 2008: 196–203; Flinders 2010: 279–86). Equally this is why critics of those governments lamented, and continue to lament, a failure to provide a 'new narrative' (Hazell 2007: 18–19), an 'explicitly defined governing theory' (Diamond 2011: 68) distinct from the Westminster model, a 'discernable conception of an alternative constitution' (Flinders 2010: 285) or an 'overarching theory of government' (Diamond and Richards 2012: 191).

Parliament, electoral representation and non-electoral representative claims

In the unmediated principal-agent view of responsibility in the Westminster model, power flows serially from electors to parliament, and from parliament to the executive. So far in this chapter attention has been focused primarily on the parliament-executive nexus and the challenges posed by decentred network governance to the Westminster model. What has attracted far less attention, but what is ultimately at the heart of network governance analysis, is 'representation'. Simply stated: networks incorporate non-elected representatives into decision-making processes. This redirects our attention 180 degrees away from the executive to the representative linkage between 'the people' and state decision-makers. If the UK is not facing a 'crisis of government', it might yet be facing a 'crisis of representation' (Saward 2008: 93).

The problem with formulating such an argument, however, is, as Mainwaring et al. (2006: 15) note, 'the notion of a crisis of democratic representation is underspecified'. A meaning of crisis is to be found at the end of a continuum of democratic representation 'at which citizens do not believe they are well represented' (Mainwaring et al. 2006: 15). Mainwaring et al. maintained that a crisis of democratic representation had two basic components: attitudinal/subjective and behavioural. The attitudinal component manifested itself in the perceptions of citizens when 'large numbers of citizens are dissatisfied with the way in which they are represented, or they feel not represented at all' (Mainwaring et al. 2006: 15). In many respects, these perceptions are independent of whether representatives do or do not act on behalf of constituents or in the 'public interest'; what matters is whether electors *perceive* that their representatives are acting on their behalf (as individual constituents or as part of a collectivity of the 'political nation'). Importantly,

Mainwaring et al. proceed to argue that even if there is widespread citizen dissatisfaction with elected representatives there has also to be a behavioural response to that disaffection. This would take the form of 'repudiation': of citizens rejecting existing electoral representative processes (Mainwaring et al. 2006: 15). In analysing five countries in the Andean region of Latin America, Mainwaring et al. were well aware that their choice of cases placed their comparator countries at the 'unambiguous' end of a continuum of crisis. Moreover, they were aware of the difficulty of conceiving of crisis as a continuum: insofar as there is 'no precise cut point that enables one to categorize case A as a crisis and case B as a non-crisis' (2006: 16). In which case, Mainwaring et al. conceded that the concept 'crisis of democratic representation' is 'not useful for intermediate cases' (2006: 16). The UK would fall within this intermediate category.

In this intermediate position, there is clear attitudinal evidence in the UK of specific public disquiet with the formal representative processes (in seeming contradiction of the buoyant diffuse support noted earlier). A YouGov Poll in 2012 found, for instance, that only 15 per cent of respondents agreed that the Westminster parliament 'does a good job in representing the interests and wishes of people like you' (Kellner 2012: 2). This response was relatively consistent across the regions and nations of the UK. Moreover, 66 per cent of respondents believed that 'most MPs end up becoming remote from the everyday lives and concerns of the people they represent'. When asked which groups of people 'MPs generally pay most attention to', 'the people' (conceived as 'voters who live in their own constituency' or 'people like you') played a relatively insignificant role. Only 27 per cent believed that MPs paid most attention to constituency voters, and an even starker finding was that only 5 per cent believed MPs paid most attention to 'people like you'. When asked to choose one specific focus to which 'MPs nowadays pay most attention', only one in 25 respondents (4 per cent) identified that focus as the 'majority view among voters in their constituency' (Kellner 2012: 14). The significance of these findings, when refracted through Mainwaring et al.'s lens of the attitudinal/subjective component of representational crisis, is that 'the point [of such findings] is not whether the bad reputation of MPs and Parliament is deserved or undeserved. It is what people think' (Kellner 2012: 8).

When combined with behavioural changes by mass publics towards the institutions of representative democracy – evident in decreased levels of turnout at parliamentary elections, steeply declining memberships of UK nationally focused political parties, low knowledge thresholds of the purpose, functions and activities of parliament and parliamentarians, in fact in most of the indicators of 'why people hate politics' (Stoker 2006, Hay 2007) – it is possible to move the UK further towards the crisis end of Mainwaring et al.'s continuum.

Yet, in order to prevent further drift of representative democracy in the UK towards the negative end of this crisis continuum, successive attempts have been made to redress some of the perceived imbalances of parliamentary representation (for a critique of these attempts see Chapters 2 and 5). These have included strategies to enhance the 'representativeness' of parliament through programmes (primarily implemented through political parties) to improve the 'descriptive representation' of the Commons in terms of gender, ethnicity and sexual characteristics; transmit the views of constituents more directly to their elected representatives through e-petitions and advisory referendums; increase control over representatives through proposals for the recall of MPs; and engage electors more actively in understanding parliament through improved parliamentary outreach services. Yet, as the YouGov poll evidence suggests, these proactive programmes appear to have had little impact on the attitudinal dimensions of crisis.

At the same time, examination of the behavioural dimensions points to an increased privileging of non-electoral modes of representation over electoral forms of representation. At a practical level, UK governments have deployed some 'state sponsored' non-electoral modes of representation – citizens' juries, focus groups, citizens' assemblies, deliberative forums, consultative forums – to 'supplement' formal electoral representation. The case is made that the addition of non-electoral representation alongside electoral representation is 'positive-sum' (Saward 2009: 21). Such non-electoral initiatives are deemed 'typically [to] function not as alternatives but rather as supplements to elected representative bodies' (Urbinati and Warren 2008: 405). Certainly, Labour governments before 2010 saw the use of deliberative mechanisms as an enhancement of representative processes (McLaverty 2009: 384). Yet the compatibility of electoral and non-electoral representative forms might be as much a construct of wishful thinking as empirical observation. As Beetham (2011: 125) notes, many of these state-sponsored non-electoral modes of representation result in parliament being bypassed as a representative channel. Indeed, it is worth quoting Beetham at some length:

What is noticeable about most of these [non-electoral] initiatives, and the discussion of them in the academic literature, is that they completely ignore or bypass parliaments. While at first glance they might seem to be complementary to the formal representative process, there is a danger that they only serve to diminish its significance and public legitimacy . . . Proposals for re-engaging citizens in politics through new forms of participation are likely to further this erosion if ways cannot be found to incorporate them into the established representative process.

(Beetham 2011: 134, 138)

As noted in Chapter 2, in many other instances, however, non-electoral claims are voiced, often out of necessity, beyond the formal representative processes: literally on the streets outside of representative institutions. In recent times, streets around Westminster have reverberated to claims of 'not in our name' (Iraq war demonstrations), 'we are the 99 per cent' (Occupy LSX demonstrations), 'all together for public services' (TUC anti-cuts rally), or to a host of more delimited claims by students to 'fund our future' or of public sector workers to 'save our pensions'. In essence, these are 'representative claims' by non-elected political actors. Similarly, the 'performance protests' coordinated by, for example, UK Uncut in campaigns against, variously, corporate tax avoidance and NHS cuts, or by Plane Stupid against the expansion of Heathrow airport, constituted clear, non-electoral, representative claims. In making these representative claims, such groups often sought to address non-parliamentary audiences and to construct non-electoral constituencies (see also Chapter 5).

Non-electoral representation and the distinctiveness of electoral representation

Saward has been at the forefront in the UK of the reconceptualisation of representation. In particular, he has been determined to show that 'legislatures, formal territorial constituencies and the institutions they support are not all that matters to political representation' (Saward 2010: 31). More importantly, for the present discussion, he also maintains that any prior assumption – that elected representatives are the sole or '*fully* legitimate representatives' (Saward 2010: 167, emphasis in original) – needs to be questioned; as does the notion that 'the unelected are automatically *illegitimate* representatives' (Saward 2010: 167). It is the claiming rather than the possession of the attribute of legitimate authority that is important: 'What needs to be generated is a sense of legitimacy' (Saward 2011: 77). This allows Saward to conceive of democratic representation as a diffuse set of political practices and performances whereby democratic representation can plausibly be seen in 'many manifestations of non-statal political representation' rather than being identified with a specific set of institutions (Saward 2011: 93). In this reformulation, the essence of democratic legitimacy 'is understood as "perceived legitimacy" as reflected in the acceptance of claims over time by appropriate constituencies under certain conditions' (Saward 2010: 84). Thus, recognition of legitimate representative claims beyond the institutional configurations of elections and representative assemblies is a key part of reconconceptualisations of representation (Urbinati and Warren 2008: 391). As such they hold the potential to deprivilege parliamentary representation, to question the legitimacy of electoral representation and so to contribute to a perception of parliamentary crisis.

But, even Saward (2010: 167) acknowledges that his approach does not constitute a 'black-and-white alternative' to conventional conceptions of electoral democracy and that 'Elections and parliaments and the forms of due authorization and accountability they offer still matter, of course.' In fact he observes that those representative claims that are held to be compelling, or which have particular resonance among relevant audiences, 'will be made from "ready mades", existing terms and understanding that the would-be audiences at a given time will recognize' (Saward 2010: 84). This is of significance in differentiating electoral from non-electoral claims as one of the 'ready mades' of 'modern democratic constitutional design' is the 'centre-staging' of electoral representation, which is 'often now taken to be the paradigm of democracy'. Indeed, for present purposes, it is worth reiterating that elections underpin the 'perceived legitimacy' of electoral representation, and provide recurring opportunities where the represented assent to being represented – whether assent is based upon prospective or retrospective judgements of representatives' performance, or both (Rehfeld 2006: 188). In other words, electoral representation is identified as 'the received (and adaptable) frame within which we understand and interpret politics' (Saward 2010: 178), and 'it matters hugely for us to acknowledge and understand claims we accept more or less unthinkingly' (Saward 2010: 60).

At this stage in the discussion, it is worth noting the parallels with David Easton's notion of 'diffuse support' noted earlier. Such support is dependent upon evaluations of the pertaining political 'rules of the game'; the continuing validation of which is underpinned by a 'legitimating ideology'. In the general case of liberal democracies this ideology – as the 'ethical principles that justify the way power is organized, used and limited' (Easton 1965: 292) – is enunciated in the language of electoral representation. In the specific case of the UK, 'the general belief, *whether based on reason or not* ... that public policy should be sanctioned and authorized by a representative body still pervades the ... polity' (Judge 1999: 141, emphasis added). Such diffuse support is often tacit, even covert (Easton 1965: 161), unthinking, but, nonetheless, profound in the sense that, as noted above, it gives the elected representative 'a head start in terms of familiarity and perceived legitimacy'.

What also gives parliament a head start is that at 'a strongly abstract level, representation in its most familiar contemporary guises, is "One to All" ... This oneness is positive. It provides an answer to the basic political question – who resolves issues when they are contested?' (Saward 2010: 90–1). In the case of liberal democracies, it is a state's legislature that 'brings the nation together symbolically under one roof' (Saward 2010: 90). Indeed, opinion poll data suggests that there remains overwhelming public support for such a national focus in the UK (Committee on Standards in Public Life 2011: 30). On average, 93 per cent of respondents in the period 2004–10 believed that MPs' decisions should be guided by 'what would benefit people living in the country as a whole'. This national focus outstripped both a party focus (84 per cent support) and a constituency focus (84 per cent support) in the same period.

The symbolism and reality of contemporary parliamentary deliberation in the UK may be severely mismatched, but the symbolism has a practical significance in that it enables elected representatives, and especially governments derived from national representative assemblies, to claim to speak for the collective entity of 'the nation'. While non-elected representatives may wish to claim that they too speak for a 'higher level' national interest (or even 'higher levels' beyond the state), what differentiates their claim from that of the elected representative is the manner in which the visions of the collective interest is constructed. Sidestepping here the protracted debate about the terminological differences between 'the national interest', 'the public will', and 'the general will', and how each is conceptualised and deployed in political theory, the important point for present purposes is that a national representative assembly is required to justify, through deliberation, the vision of the national interest propounded therein (Judge 2013; see also Chapter 7). In this respect, justification is a form of accountability or responsibility. What distinguishes electoral forms of representation, ultimately, is that 'only the elected have both deliberative and decision making power' (Urbinati 2006: 15).

Conclusion: a conceptual crisis?

So where does the preceding discussion leave us? Contradictory answers have been provided across three dimensions of parliamentary interaction: first, public attitudes, second, state governance and, third, the practice of representation.

The first dimension points on the one hand towards a 'crisis of public confidence' in terms of specific indictors of public support and trust in the UK parliament. Yet, at the same time, generalised support for parliament within a broader context of representative democracy indicates continuing high levels of general or diffuse support in an Eastonian sense.

The second dimension identifies contemporary modes of governance at variance with the prescriptions of 'representative and responsible' government focused upon a sovereign parliament at Westminster. Yet, all contemporary governments have consistently defended UK state institutional interactions in terms of the 'representative and responsible' core of the Westminster model. Executives have thus defended a model of legitimation, the practical deficiencies of which challenge the very claims to legitimacy incorporated within the model. In so doing, they have been locked into a mindset incapable of conceiving of an alternative governing model without dissipating the 'legislative-centric theory of parliamentary sovereignty'. If a 'headshift' (see below) is required to break out of this logical loop of crisis, it would be confronted with the fundamental paradox that such a reconceptualisation would presumably entail devising a different model to one based upon traditional principles of electoral representation and responsibility. In other words, it would be a post-parliamentary system. Yet, even those models that profess to be 'post-parliamentary' (as noted above and below; see also Chapter 2) recognise that such an alternative is premised upon a 'dependence' on parliamentary institutional forms.

The third dimension distils the essence of this conceptual crisis. As noted above, non-electoral claims are made with increasing intensity. Non-electoral modes of representation are both advocated and deployed with increasing vigour. Yet electoral representation is still distinctive. The problem is that in seeking to make this form of representation less distinctive, a challenge is posited at a conceptual level and promoted at a behavioural level through notions and modes of non-electoral representation. Thus to claim that non-electoral representation supplements and enhances electoral representation somehow misses the point that in the process of supplementation the latter would become less distinct. To paraphrase Dubnik's (2011: 712) statement on accountability, 'Any effort to enhance representation also alters representation'.

Indeed, those theorists, such as Keane (2009a: 697), who call for 'a headshift' and 'a break with conventional thinking' do so out of a belief that a more empirically realistic model of 'actually existing democracy' (Keane 2011: 212) is required to acknowledge the 'morphing' of representative democracy into 'a new historical form of "post-parliamentary" democracy' (Keane 2011: 212). In common with other analyses of non-electoral representation examined earlier in this chapter, Keane's own model of 'monitory democracy' is based on the premise that existing descriptions of representative democracy are 'just too simple' (2011: 231). While this is not the place to examine the intricacies and convolutions of this model, all that needs to be noted here is that 'monitory democracy' encapsulates a vast array of extra-parliamentary, often non-elected, scrutinising institutions – both formal and informal. In this model, political legitimacy is nested in multiple demoi, reflecting a vast diversity of interest; with decision-makers 'subject constantly to the ideal of public chastening, tied down by a thousand Lilliputian strings of scrutiny' (Keane 2009b).

Keane is adamant that monitory democracy 'operates in ways greatly at variance with textbook accounts of "representative", "liberal" or "parliamentary democracy"' (Keane 2009a: 706, 2011: 221). Yet, in calling for 'a headshift' and a reconceptualisation of representative democracy, he insists, repeatedly, that 'legislatures neither disappear, nor necessarily decline in importance' (2011: 213), that 'monitory democracies depend upon legislatures' (2011: 218) and that monitory democracy 'thrives on representation' (2009a: 699). However, if monitory democracy is to be conceived as 'something other and different' (2011: 231), it necessarily poses a challenge 'to the legitimacy of institutional structures that were previously widely valued' (Boin 2004: 168). In this sense, linking back to 'tHart and Boin's claim that legitimacy is the currency of crisis, this challenge gives rise to a conceptual crisis: insofar as the disjunction confronting governance analyses (noted above) is also manifest in the contradictions embedded in a 'headshift' required to make sense of non-electoral and monitory modes of representation in a political system still legitimised by electoral representation and parliamentary institutions. In which case, conceptualising 'something other and different' (a new democratic institutional topography) is ultimately dependent on retaining 'something the same and similar' (namely parliamentary institutions and processes of electoral representation). The historic legitimation expectations associated with the latter and the changed legitimation claims of the former hold the potential, to paraphrase Boin (2004: 168), to be unremittingly discrepant. Therein lie the roots of a conceptual crisis.

5
A Crisis of Political Parties

Martin Smith

Introduction

The idea of a crisis of political parties is not new. In the UK, and comparatively, there has been a long debate about the decline of parties (Rokkan 1970, Crewe, Sarlvik and Alt (1977), Selle 1991, Daalder 1992, Whiteley 2011). Crisis is in many ways endemic to parties as they battle over losing elections, retaining members and finding suitable leaders. Indeed, it is easy to mistake the everyday waxing and waning of parties' fortunes for a more profound crisis. Parties within the UK political system have considerable resilience and continue to be the main structuring element of politics in the UK. Indeed much of the party literature suggests we cannot write parties off and they continue to be central mechanisms of political organisation (Fisher et al. 2014). However, the argument of this chapter is that there is currently a particular problem with the major UK political parties and their role in the process of representation that has become critical because it is beginning to undermine the legitimacy of the political elite and consequently reinforces the wider process of political disillusionment. Parties and party leaders view politics in self-referential terms and see little alternative to parties as the framework of politics, while the electorate is increasingly distanced and disillusioned by the existing party system. Indeed, the key point is that parties are 19th-century political institutions that have increasingly less relevance to how people practise politics day to day. This is the point which Katz and Mair (1995: 15) highlighted two decades ago when they pointed out:

> we see the emergence of a new type of party, the cartel party, characterized by the interpenetration of party and state, and also by a pattern of inter-party collusion. In this sense, it is perhaps more

accurate to speak of the emergence of cartel parties, since this development depends on collusion and cooperation between ostensible competitors, and on agreements which, of necessity, require the consent and cooperation of all, or almost all, relevant participants.

However, while for some this is seen as an adaption of parties to new circumstances (Ignazi 1996), the problem is that parties are losing their role as representatives of citizens and in a sense becoming 'parties-for-themselves'. They exist to win power for themselves and to remain in government and hence ensure that the party leadership have political careers. This disconnect with the public is undermining the faith of the voters which creates a crisis of legitimacy for the parties. Hence, whilst the parties can sustain themselves by becoming integrated within the state, they are unable to engage citizens in political activity.

This chapter suggests that a number of factors have led to a growing dissonance between the elite practice of politics through parties and the way politics is experienced by citizens. It argues that whilst political elites are trying to maintain the traditional parties as the main mechanism for organising politics, citizens are increasingly bypassing parties, and the parties are in danger of losing their legitimacy. Moreover, the public dissatisfaction with the two-party duopoly is producing a fractured party system. We have already seen a decline in party identity, party membership and party funding (Katz and Mair 1995). In addition, it is increasingly clear that the three main parties are losing their ability either to attract a wide range of activists or to continue as national parties. Consequently, we have seen a dual politics. On one side, the three main parties are in ideological terms becoming increasingly homogenised, whilst on the other, citizens are focusing more on issue politics, independent candidates and non-traditional forms of participation. As set out in Chapter 3, there is a growing crisis of ideas as the main parties fail to develop ideas to cope with the pressures of economic crisis. The point is that parties are not representing citizens and they are conducting politics in a self-referential system that fails to take account of the perceptions and interests of voters. As Chapters 1–3 each in different ways conclude, the net result is that we are seeing a growing disillusionment with traditional politics. This chapter begins by outlining the traditional position of parties within the UK political system.

Parties and the UK political system

Political parties have been, and still are, a key structuring factor within the UK polity. Politics both within and outside Westminster has been

conducted through and by parties and hence much of the political process has been shaped within the context of the two or two-and-a-half
party system. Moreover, as Judge (1993) points out, UK parties were created within the confines of the parliamentary system and hence they
are top-down parties that extended outwards to the electorate. They did
not, even in the case of the Labour Party, start as mass political mobilisations which were institutionalised as parties. Consequently, parties
are intimately linked to the Westminster model and the 19th-century
conception of representative democracy that continues to dominate UK
politics. Like much else in UK politics, parties were shaped and created
in the 19th and early 20th century and reflect the social cleavages and
view of representation that was prevalent at that time.

Traditionally parties have been seen as having a particular set of
functions in relation to the political system in terms of simplifying
political choices and providing personnel for government and allowing
accountability to function. According to Berrington (2004), 'The party
is essentially a link between the citizen and the state; party is one of the
devices which makes possible citizen influence on the policies of government'. Parties are seen as a key element of the democratic process
and competition between parties is fundamental to the viability of the
political system. They formalise and institutionalise conflict and hence
underpin a stable and democratic political system.

However these functions were carried out within the context of the
Westminster model and as a result they took on a number of particular
ways of structuring the political process:

- Parties were essential to the reproduction of the Westminster model
  in terms of being a mechanism for reinforcing the UK governing
  code. As Marquand (1988) highlights, the UK system has been one
  of club government and parties governed through reproducing the
  club rules. This explains both the tardiness of constitutional reform
  and the ways in which radical parties like Labour quickly accommo-
  dated to the governing system. What is striking is how the parties,
  and especially Labour, embraced the Westminster system without
  challenging it and in so doing reproduced the rules of the game. As
  Fielding (2010: 104) points out, the way the franchise extended:

  > allowed the Liberals and the Conservatives to retain their
  > Westminster basis, merely adding on subordinate constituency
  > elements. Despite its initial outsider status, Labour leaders eventu-
  > ally accepted the established parameters, much to the frustration
  > of a minority within its ranks hostile to 'Parliamentarianism'.

To all intents and purposes 'politics' in twentieth-century Britain meant representative politics – and that meant (to paraphrase Schumpeter's maxim) the rule of the Westminster party politician.

Probably the clearest example of this process is the way in which Labour, by becoming part of the Westminster system, abandoned not only its Marxist elements but also its radical pluralist traditions which were highly critical of existing conceptions of the state and sovereignty and could have provided an alternative way of constructing politics and participation (Richards and Smith 2010).

- Within the Westminster model parties have been able to institutionalise the representation of class interests. Labour has always played the dual role of representing and containing working-class interests. Labour's relations with the unions continue to be about trying to ameliorate the demands of labour and to reconciling class politics to a parliamentary system (Miliband 1961). Middlemas (1979) illustrated how adept the UK political system was at accommodating class conflicts and ensuring that they did not dissolve into violent conflicts. Parties were central to this process in that they clearly had class interests and represented class groups but they also had to accommodate cross-class interests to achieve votes outside of their constituencies and to ensure the maintenance of the Westminster system.
- The Westminster system has provided a legitimate form of elite politics contained within clear and continuous institutional boundaries. Parties have been central to this elite politics by supporting the institutional underpinnings and through ensuring a two-way circulation of elites. The first is horizontal circulation between Labour and Conservative (or between broadly working-class and middle-class representation) and the second is a vertical circulation as parties acted as a mechanism for renewing the political elite. In many ways, the vertical circulation was the most important in terms of legitimisation because it allowed people to enter the political system. For Labour, this in particular allowed working-class representation in parliament through the trade-union link and trade-union sponsorship, and the local selection of candidates, which often ensured that local working-class candidates were selected. Consequently, party and parliament was a system that allowed structured working-class participation in the political system.
- The Westminster system is based on a notion of indivisible sovereignty not only of parliament, but also of the UK, and parties were crucial to the support and underpinning of the Union of

England with Scotland, Wales and Northern Ireland. One of the most neglected aspects of the role of the three main parties – but particularly Labour and Conservative – has been their importance to the integration of the Union, at least until the 1970s. The parties ensured national representation and with the assistance of the electoral system (another part of the Westminster model armoury) were able to prevent the development of regional representation (except of course in Northern Ireland in the 1970s where Labour and Conservatives withdrew from electoral politics). Essentially Labour and the Conservatives developed their own particular narrative to support a national politics. For Labour, this was based around the notion of a national project of redistribution and citizenship through a universal welfare state. Labour were crucial to tying the working class into the Union (most notably in Scotland and Wales) through the fruits of social democracy. For the Conservatives, the Union was central to the idea of nation and built up through the idea of the empire state, which shared the rewards of empire with the elites of the whole of the UK. The Conservative Party was always the Conservative and Unionist Party – their notion of nation was an expanded territory of the UK and Ireland. In many ways, parties (and the monarchy) were the key elements of nation-, rather than state-, building. Parties tied Scotland and Wales into the Westminster system and through a UK-wide voting and party membership legitimised the rule of a London-based parliament. It is perhaps hard to believe today but the Conservatives were the largest party in Scotland in the elections in 1951, 1955 and 1959. In 1955 they even had a majority of the vote (Jones and Scully 2006: 117).

The parties were essential to the maintenance of the Westminster model; in effect they legitimised the system through their role in the transmission of ideas and people, and as an accountability mechanism. As we saw in Chapter 4, the Westminster model is a system of elite rule; MPs are representatives not delegates (as conceptualised by the Conservative thinker Burke) and the executive is accountable to parliament. Parties have been the mechanism that legitimises this closed system by allowing voters access to parliament and government. The parties have been the tool for a circulation of elites that was legitimised through the electoral process where most people accepted the governmental structures. In this way, parties were crucial to validating an elite system of politics by allowing enough people in and by transmitting citizens' concerns to the centre (as voters, members and candidates). Through mass memberships, a significant proportion of the electorate had some sort of engagement in the political process. However, the problem is that if parties are failing to represent or allow transmission into parliament and government, the processes of legitimation will start to break down and it is this breakdown that is the key crisis of parties.

The continuous crisis of parties

At one level, the crisis of party is not new. It has always been with us (Fielding 2010). As Crewe, Sarlvik and Alt (1977: 129) pointed out the problems of party have long existed:

> In the general election of 1951 almost nine out of ten eligible electors turned up at the polls, the vast majority (96 per cent) to vote Labour or Conservative, thereby giving them all but twelve seats in the House of Commons. In the quarter century that has since elapsed, the absolute and relative fortunes of the two parties have fluctuated, albeit with increasing volatility... In their three election victories of the 1950s the Conservatives won almost half of the vote; by October 1974 the Conservative figure was down to only a little more than a third (36–7 per cent), the lowest level in its history as a mass party.

There is then problem of longevity and scale in relation to the parties around the extent to which trends started in the 1970s have continued; the combination of factors; and, more importantly, the ways in which the parties are no longer operating effectively in terms of their relationship to the Westminster model. What we have seen is a significant change in the party system with the decline of the two-party duopoly. As Figure 5.1 illustrates, the two main parties have seen their share of the vote decline from a 1950s high of 98 per cent to 65 per cent in 2010. There are now effectively different party systems according to the election being fought and the geographical location with UKIP challenging in EU elections and nationalist parties the main parties in Scotland and Wales. Even in national elections the share of Labour and Conservative votes is declining significantly.

The problem is that not only are parties in the UK declining in their political role but they are even failing to provide their legitimising role for elite politics. The decline of the two-party system undermines the notion that the Westminster system allows a clear choice. In addition, their electoral strategies, which are increasingly aimed at capturing the median voters, are undermining their policy strategy and leading to

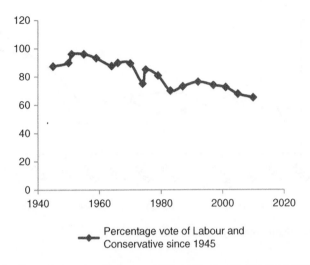

Figure 5.1 Percentage vote of Labour and Conservative Parties since 1945

a poverty of ideas which further reinforces the voters' disengagement with traditional party politics. Parties are failing in their functions of representation and legitimation and, consequently, we can see a loss of faith with the traditional mechanisms of representation. One of the most fundamental indicators of this loss of faith is the decline in party membership (see Figures 5.2 and 5.3).

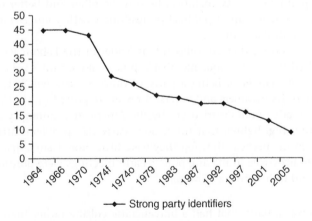

Figure 5.2 Strong party identifiers 1964–2005
Source: http://blogs.lse.ac.uk/politicsandpolicy/files/2010/03/Party-ID.jpg.

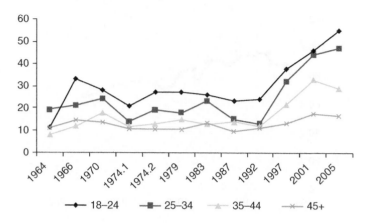

Figure 5.3   Non-voters by age group 1964–2005

The decline in party membership

That party membership has declined is taken for granted but the scale of the decline is dramatic. In 1955, 1 in 11 voters were party members and today it is 1 in 100 (Wilks Heeg and Crone 2010: 9). Whilst it is the case that the decline in party membership is European wide, the UK with a membership of just 1 per cent of the electorate is amongst the lowest in Europe (Beizen, Mair and Pognutke 2012). It also seems that those who continue as party members are a particular group. As Beizen et al. (2012) point out, party members tend to be older and better off and increasingly made up of political professionals with younger members having political ambitions.

It is interesting that Ed Miliband, as leader of the Labour Party, has recognised that the Labour membership base has shrunk to the extent that it is in danger of being a party of office seekers which is out of touch with its members and voters. A review (reported in *The Guardian* but not made public) carried out by the American community activist Arnie Graf highlighted that the Labour Party had problems attracting new members because they felt they were little more than apparatchiks who had little role in making policy. Party meetings were bureaucratic, closed and uninviting; as Graf said:

> This was a party that had a bureaucratic culture rather than a rela-
> tional culture. At the end of meetings I'd rather chew off my arm
> with my own teeth than go back. I thought the smartest people are

the ones who didn't come. Going to the pub afterwards seemed to be the best part.

(Davis 2012)

There is an important point here. From this analysis, the problem of 'anti-politics' is not the decadence of the voters but the failure of the parties to be accessible or meaningful to ordinary people who do not centre their lives around political activity. For Graf, the Labour Party is top down when it needs to be bottom up (Davis 2012).

This is a fundamental problem in the sense that there is a growing detachment between citizens and parties. As research by the Labour MP Gloria de Piero illustrates, people see politicians as 'other' (Jowitt 2013). Whereas once parties were the link between the citizen and government, this is no longer the case. Traditionally the link existed through identification, membership and activism. For instance, party membership was always important to parties not necessarily for funding or for providing future politicians but for campaigning. It was parties that provided the foot soldiers of elections. At the very least, people would be in receipt of party literature or party canvassing but many were members of parties – even if it was just as part of the social club. The point is that parties were embedded in the everyday of civil society. Most people had some contact with parties. However, increasingly parties and citizens operate in separate spheres. As Fisher and Denver (2009) demonstrate, there has been a considerable reduction in the number of party members at constituency level (see Figure 5.4). They illustrate that with the decline in members and the development of new technology parties have started to change their campaigning strategies moving away from traditional campaigning and developing a modern, focused campaign using call centres, computers and direct mail.

These signs of decay are reflected in recent elections. In by-elections in Bradford in 2012 and in Eastleigh in 2013, the main parties won only 35 per cent of the vote with Respect winning in Bradford and UKIP coming second in Eastleigh. In the 2013 council elections, UKIP won 25 per cent of the vote and ensured for the first time that all three of the main parties received less than 30 per cent of the vote in a national election (and turnout was only 30 per cent). The Democratic Audit's report on the Bradford by-election suggested that:

The recent political history of Bradford West has been marred by patronage, neglect, bad organisation and even electoral fraud. Both

Labour and the Conservatives are implicated in this state of affairs. Local politics in Bradford has been about mutual accommodation between elites of each community ('Asians', city whites and suburbanites) rather than real diversity, and voters have found this alienating.

(Baston 2013)

The point the report makes is that local people no longer felt that the parties represented them or had any interest in their concerns. Their votes were taken for granted and there was little attempt to build a local party organisation that represented the interests of the community. An Ipsos/Mori poll in June 2013 found that only 21 per cent trusted MPs (http://www.ipsos-mori.com/Assets/Docs/Polls/June2013_trust_charts.pdf)

The modernisation of campaigns allows more people to be contacted with fewer resources. Until the early 1980s, the majority of funding was spent by candidates locally. Despite parties increasing the amount of funding that they have, this is increasingly being spent at the central level rather than by candidates in their particular campaigns (Wilks Heeg and Crone 2010). These resources are being increasingly focused on marginal seats leaving those in safe seats without any contact with the campaigning process. Moreover, campaigning is increasingly remote rather than face to face. It is interesting that in the 2012 elections for police commissioners, there was almost no contact with candidates and a risible turnout of 15 per cent.

A key point made by Wilks, Heeg and Crone (2010: 17) is that 'Political parties have effectively become a broken link in the chain which connects voters to their representatives.' Even in election campaigns, parties are failing to engage with voters except through national campaigns which, by their very nature, are distant from the lives of ordinary people. The conclusion that Whiteley (2012: 19) points to is the 'long running decline in voter attachment to political parties'. There is no doubt about the decline of party members, the decline of party attachment and the limits of party campaigning but there has been little or no recognition of what this means. If parties are not connecting people to the political process, the horizontal circulation of elites is detached from any vertical circulation and the gap between people and politician becomes wider. As parties shift from mass parties to cartel parties, the process of politics is being transformed. As Bolleyer (2009: 1) confirms, parties are increasingly 'perceived as driven by the professional calculus

of their elites and as such built upon the distribution of selective benefits rather than ideological beliefs'. The problem that Bolleyer identifies
with the cartel development is:

> that the tightening of party – state linkages can equally be read
> as a response to the vulnerability of the cartel party as organisa-
> tional actor. More than other party models, it needs outside resources
> to generate internal support which reinforces its resort to selective
> benefits (i.e. political appointments, patronage)

In other words, as parties develop as elite-based organisations cut off
from voters and members, they increasingly rely on either the state
or other donors to provide support for the parties. This reinforces the
absence of links with society and undermines the transmission roles of
parties, and further diminishes their legitimacy. Interestingly one of the
key factors that has led to the general disenchantment with politics has
been the relationship between parties and donors. This has been a significant problem for the three major parties: Labour had problems with the
donations of Bernie Eccelstone and cash for peerages; Liberal-Democrats
over receiving money from a convicted fraudster; and the Conservatives over cash from non-domiciles and cash for access. The parties need
large sums of funding to run national campaigns and the problematic
dependence on large donations has led to a growing clamour for state
funding rather than any attempt at renewing party membership as a
way of sustaining parties.

As Biezen et al. (2012) point out, the changing relations between
voters and parties 'inevitably calls into question our dominant way of
thinking about party as a powerful organisational linkage between the
mass public and the institutions of government'. This is a fundamental
issue. The political institutions in the UK work on the basis of parties as
a linkage mechanism in the political process and indeed there has not
been a fundamental evaluation of how the political system should adapt
to the decline in party membership. Hence, the UK parties are becoming
shell organisations that run the political process from the top downwards. These cadre parties work in sustaining the Westminster model –
indeed they enable the system to be even more closed – but they fail in
their legitimising role as the parties are not seen to represent voters and
increasingly they are seen as just ensuring the circulation of an ever-
diminishing elite. This is illustrated by the breaking down of their role
in transmission (see Figure 5.4).

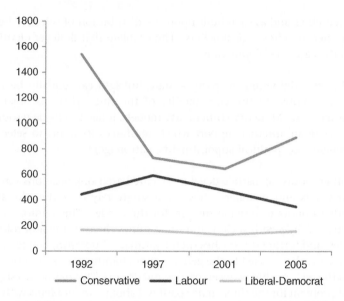

Figure 5.4   Mean number of party members per constituency 1992–2005
Source: Fisher and Denver (2009).

The failure of political transmission

The consequence of the declining party membership is that the role of parties in transmission is being undermined. When parties were functioning, they were a mechanism for transmitting ideas and people to government. This was also within a limited framework of elite politics, but nevertheless there was some symbolic representation of working-class citizens. Parties have always structured the political process but increasingly they are becoming structures that restrict rather than enable participation. The extent of the structuration is demonstrated by the Pathways to Power Report, which highlights the exclusion of a range of groups from the process. As the report points out, the barriers to participation are many and varied including explicit prejudice in selection process to subtle understandings of what a good candidate should be, to barriers such as the cost in time and money required to be elected (Durose et al. 2011). Even when candidates are selected outside of the norm, they tend to do so when they conform:

> We found that under-represented groups do not find their way into national politics on the basis of their difference but rather by their

conformity to particular aspects of the archetypal candidate. For example, candidates from under-represented groups can conform to the stereotype of candidates by means of sharing the same political motivations, being from a political background, being university educated, being part of a professional elite or by being involved in local or national politics.

(Durose et al. 2011: 25)

For Durose et al. (2011: 65), the pathways into politics are increasingly professionalised and 'while the composition of the House of Commons has become more diverse, those elected conform closely to the new but still very narrow pathway of the professional politician'. As the Sex and Power (Centre for Women and Democracy 2013) Report illustrates, there continue to be high barriers to women entering politics, not least the fact that women do not feel represented by parties.

In the past, parties did allow a way for groups that were not necessarily privileged access to the political process. Most significantly the working-class route into parliament has declined. As Mills (2010) points out:

a BBC poll last year showed that almost 60% of white working-class people felt unrepresented in parliament. Labour, the traditional home for that social group, saw their share of the lower income DE demographic at the last election fall by a third to 40% according to recent analysis. This cannot be mere coincidence.

(Mills 2010)

Allen (2012) highlights how this process of transmission has become narrowed even once people get into parliament:

For MPs who want to get anywhere fast, it would seem that being close to your party, and being part of the Westminster village, is everything. MPs who worked in politics and around Westminster prior to their election to the Commons also dominate the most important governing roles in the country (those frontbench positions in all parties). Of the 242 MPs elected for the very first time in 1997, 51.7 per cent of those MPs who made it to Cabinet-level positions had this sort of insider experience compared to only 10.3 per cent who had experience on local councils. 44.8 per cent of those MPs whose only political experience was having served on local councils remained backbenchers for the thirteen years following their initial election or until they left the Commons, whichever came first.

Table 5.1   Social background of MPs 1979–2010

Occupational group	1979	1983	1987	1992	1997	2001	2005	2010
Professions	278	278	278	258	272	270	242	218
Business	138	162	161	152	113	107	118	156
Journalists	46	45	42	44	47	50	43	48
Farmers	23	21	19	12	7	6	8	10
Politicians/political organisers	21	20	34	46	60	66	87	90
White-collar workers	9	21	19	12	7	6	8	10
Manual working class	98	74	73	63	56	53	38	25

Source: Adapted from McGuinness (2010).

Parties are changing in how they structure political recruitment. They used to be a mechanism for transmitting some working-class representation into politics (but clearly excluding women and ethnic minorities). However, they are increasingly becoming very similar and recruitment is increasingly from a narrow group (see Table 5.1). As the table indicates, not only are the working class considerably underrepresented but the level of representation has declined significantly since 1979 and almost mirrors the increase in those whose occupation was politician/political organiser. Hence, the failure to transmit 'non-traditional' groups into parliament and government highlights further this distance between the political class and the ordinary voters. It is interesting that minor parties attempt to illustrate how they are in touch with the concerns of ordinary voters. It is illustrative that before the 2010 General Election, the Conservative Party introduced open primaries in a pilot number of constituencies in order to widen the pool for MPs. However, not only have the Conservatives forestalled plans for widening primaries, but one of the MPs selected by this method, Sarah Wollaston, feels that she is viewed as a rebel for taking independent positions and that:

> people who come through the political sausage machine are like fish in water here. From day one they arrive understanding how the system works, whereas someone like me spends a lot time banging their heads against a wall and soon you realise that a lot of things happen here in rooms to which you are not invited.
>
> (Helm 2013)

The system is not particularly adept at accepting MPs who do not come through the 'normal' routes.

Issue politics and minor parties

The combination of the decline in party membership, party alignment and failure of the transmission function has led to an increase in issue politics and growing support for minor parties (which are often issue focused rather than social cleavage focused). In the post-war period, minor parties were essentially squeezed out of the political system. Even once dealignment was relatively well established in the 1980s, the electoral system prevented third parties translating votes into seats. So, for example, the Social Democratic Party won 25 per cent of the vote in 1983, only slightly less than Labour, but won only 23 seats in the Commons. However, in recent years with sustained voting for minor parties and different electoral systems used in non-parliamentary elections, minor parties and independents have had an increasing impact, not least the apparent growing support for UKIP.

Parties tend to package a range of policy issues into some sort of ideological consistency but that consistency may not resonate with voters who are not necessarily concerned with a coherent set of ideas or party positions. There have long been questions over the degree of ideological consistency of voters (Ansolabehere, Rodden and Snyder 2008). In addition, the debate about the end of class voting has been ongoing since the 1960s (Abrams and Rose 1960, Franklin and Mugan 1978). There is however little doubt that the class–party alignment of the 1950s and 1960s is considerably weaker. In particular Labour has seen a significant decline in its working-class vote. In 1945, 62 per cent of the working class voted Labour. This went up to 65 per cent in 1966 but by 1983 it had declined to 42 per cent. In the 2010 election, 40 per cent of class DE voted Labour and only 29 per cent of C2 (less than voted Conservative). As Clarke et al. (2009: 634) confirm, 'Viewed in terms of their empirical range, the class × vote and class × party identification correlations appear to have dropped precipitously over time'. In the 1966 election, Labour had eleven million working-class votes and only 2 million middle class but as Kellner (2011: 157–8) pointed out in 2010, '8.6 million people voted Labour. YouGov found that they divided as follows – 4.4 middle class, 4.2 working class. For the first time, Labour's middle-class vote exceeded its working-class vote.' The ties of identity between individual and groups and parties seem to have dissolved almost completely over the last 30 or 40 years.

There is now growing evidence that people participate in politics on an issue basis rather than through ideological or party ties (see Chapter 2). As Milne (2005: 15) suggests, 'Research shows that the percentage prepared to go on a protest demonstration has risen from 20 per cent in 1979 to 33 per cent in 2000'. Consumer boycotts are growing as a form of political action. For example, in 2012 a consumer boycott of Starbucks forced the company to pay £20 million in taxation after consumers expressed concern at the way the company avoided paying taxation in the UK. People have a diminishing loyalty to parties and their political interests are issue- rather than class- or party-based (Achterberg and Houtman 2006). Organisations such as 38 degrees are providing an internet-based forum for issue-based, progressive campaigning which is able to organise citizens around particular policies in a way that draws particular interest to the views of parties. Of course, this is an important general point that is highlighted in this volume: that disillusionment with parties and politicians is not the same as a disengagement from politics or a sign of a decadent citizenship. It may be that people are actually being more reflexive in their political choices and have abandoned their faith in parties as the mechanisms for political activity (see Chapters 1 and 2).

As a result, there is a growing (or may be continuing) political mobilisation around single issues whether it is opposition to GMOs or road building, protest against the Iraq war or hunting. It is campaigns such as Make Poverty History, the Countryside Alliance or opposition to student fees that have mobilised people and not parties. Whiteley (2011) highlights how the number of people giving donations to political organisations or becoming involved in boycotts is much higher than those who join political parties. What is interesting is that the political parties are often equivocal on these sorts of issues. As catch-all parties, they will not adopt positions that alienate sections of the electorate and therefore policies that are controversial tend not to win the support of the major political parties.

In addition, there is growing evidence of the internet impacting on the conduct of politics and political participation. Whilst for Flinders (2012: 165):

> To me the promise of digital democracy and on-line engagement appeared not simply to be an excuse for laziness but, more importantly, it completely overlooked the central and defining essence of democratic politics. Politics revolves around building relationships ...

However, it is possible to see the internet having some positive impacts on political engagement. For example, the Pew Internet and Life project illustrates that in the USA 'Groups and their members are using all kinds of digital tools to bind themselves together' (Raine, Purcell and Smith 2011: 4)

More interestingly, their research also illustrates that groups have used the internet both to support getting candidates elected and to raise issues. The key point about the internet is that first it lowers the cost of political participation. At the minimum, people can easily express their views through Twitter or blogs. Second, this form of political participation operates outside the field of parties. People are able to express a political position that is not framed either by the organisation or ideology of parties. Until the spread of the internet, this was probably done only through the letters' pages of newspapers. The internet allows thousands of opinions to bloom. There is also some evidence that social information provided through the internet can influence decisions to participate politically (Margetts et al. 2011). So whilst it remains embryonic and the impact of the internet may be diffuse and exaggerated, there is a potential for it to change processes of political participation and create alternative channels to political parties.

Whilst the internet provides one new route for participation, it also appears that minor parties and independents are starting to have a significant political role. In the 2009 European Elections, UKIP came second and in the 2012 elections of police commissioners independents won 12 out of the 51 positions. There has been a growing number of independents at local and national level and the growth of the Greens and UKIP as established parties. Without the traditional duopoly, the party system does not operate according to the Westminster model. Parties were 19th-century vote-collecting machines which legitimised elites; they are no longer working this way. Elites continue to expect to operate with parties but parties are not connecting with citizens. This disconnection is extended by the debate on state funding.

As Katz and Mair (1995) predicted, as party membership declines parties increasingly seek state funding as a way of preserving their position. Indeed, the more they gain state funding, the less they need party members (Whiteley 2011). However, the more they seek state funding and are seen as state organisations, the less people feel the need to join. Hence a strong indicator of the crisis of the parties is that they are no longer looking to members to sustain their activities but to state funding. What we have seen recently is parties relying increasingly on institutional and individual donations for party finance. It is interesting that in the late 1990s and early 2000s, when Labour seemed to be developing as a successful election winning party, it was able to diversify funding and, once Brown became leader and its electoral prospects declined, then the range of contributions declined (Fisher 2010). There is an argument – that in many ways fits neatly with the Westminster model – that parties are essential to democracy and that they have never had sufficient funding from members to sustain their activities (Fisher 2011) (and indeed they lack the finance for all their activities). Therefore to retain independence, they need state funding. So within this context, the Kelly Report on future party funding is interesting as it tacitly embraces this assumption:

> Political parties play an essential role in this country's democracy. The public may be cynical about them. But they affect all our lives in important ways. They produce the platforms and leadership between which electors choose when casting their votes at elections. They provide and support the individuals who make up the government, the opposition and the membership of hundreds of local authorities. They develop policies. They build support for those policies by engaging with the electorate. When in opposition, they scrutinise and debate government policy and hold the Government to account.
>
> (CM8208 2011: 1)

Hence, the assumption of the report is that the parties are essential (in essence as they exist) and they need support. The second assumption is that large donors should be removed as they do not have legitimacy and so the recommendations of the committee are that donations should be capped and state funding should be increased. So on one side the independence of parties is safeguarded but their future is reassured. The solution to party membership and the rise of issue politics is a view that the state should support the existing parties as an essential aspect of democracy, but of course state funding further breaks the link between the party and the voters and ensures that the increasing focus on politics concentrated within a centralised elitist arena is further reinforced. Fisher makes the point that parties cannot be expected to rely on small donors as the UK is not a giving culture (Fisher 2010), but this is again a reinforcement of the UK notion of passive democracy; parties can rely on the state and allow people to get on with their lives. For Fisher (2010), 'Public opinion is a very poor guide on public funding' on the basis that people are ignorant about the issues. Parties in this model are cut from the populace and this is justified paradoxically as a mechanism to maintain democracy. The point well made by Aitcheson (2012) is that state funding further isolates elites from the populace:

> Such a reform would ossify politics – institutionalising even more the dominance of the established parties. Insofar as party elites could depend on state subsidies, they would become even more insulated from any need to engage with their grassroots, and what is left of inner party democracy would remain in tatters. Meanwhile voluntary political associations would, in effect be turned into quangos.

The problem has become more acute for Labour in that in trying to distance itself from the unions, it is in danger of losing a significant part of its funding and so become more inclined towards state funding. In addition, its claims to working-class representation become even weaker.

The decline of national parties

One of the most critical elements in the changing position of the parties is the fact that they are no longer national parties. Labour and Conservative are becoming parties of regions, rather than the whole, of the Union. Labour is increasingly the party of the northern cities and the Conservatives are becoming the English (rural and southern) party. Whilst Labour has maintained strong support in Scotland, the election of an SNP Scottish administration – with a majority of seats in the parliament – means even Labour's grip on the Union is weakening, and it cannot rely on the working-class vote in Scotland. The 2010 election provides a very strong indication of a trend that has been developing since the 1970s. In Scotland, the Conservatives were the fourth party with 16 per cent of the vote, a dramatic decline from the 50 plus per cent of the 1950s. In the south of England, Labour has again been reduced to a rump with almost no Labour seats outside of London, south of the line from the Bristol Channel to the Wash.

There are two significant points here. First, many votes are wasted or they are surplus votes as Labour and Conservatives build up large majorities in their heartlands. Second, this creates a two-way problem of legitimacy. On one side, Conservatives in the northern cities effectively have no representation. They do not have MPs and their votes do not affect electoral outcomes (and similarly for Labour voters in the south). Furthermore, governments can govern without the support of large parts of the country. This has been the situation with regard to the Conservatives and Scotland (and some degree Wales) since 1979. The problem for the Conservatives is that they are a Unionist party but their governing strategy is undermining the Union. Paradoxically the Conservatives have rejected the mechanism which would resolve the problem of national representation – proportional representation (PR). If voting was proportional, the problem of wasted votes would decline and Labour and the Conservatives would have national representation which may help to legitimise their rule in Scotland and, of course, make it more likely that Nationalist parties could be represented in a Westminster government. In many ways, the core crisis of parties is that they are unable to represent the whole country in government and the Westminster model of representation no longer works without national parties. The only solution is actually some form of electoral reform that would allow governments with wider support. It is little wonder that there is a sense of disillusionment amongst voters when the only form of participation in government – elections – is not working as it should. In Italy, the disillusionment with politics led to 25 per cent voting for the comedian Beppo Grillo and his anti-politics position, and a similar sort of process may be occurring in the UK with the growth of support for UKIP. In the UK, the recent successes of UKIP and Respect indicate that the possibility of voters rejecting the mainstream parties exists unless they find ways of reconnecting with the electorate.

The failure of ideas

If voters no longer have class or party loyalties, how do the parties attract votes? The main UK parties are now a combination of cartel parties in terms of governing but catch-all parties in terms of elections. The breakdown of party alignment means that both the Conservatives and Labour have recognised that they cannot get elected on a 'core supporter strategy'. Consequently, they are therefore dependent on a catch-all strategy to build the electoral alliance necessary for the 40 or so per cent of votes to win an election. This is perhaps best illustrated by the Philip Gould approach to politics which built Labour's electoral strategy round focus groups which could be used to gauge the response of voters to each nuance of Labour Party policy. It has been suggested that Cameron was influenced by the Blairite approach and saw the need to detoxify the party and hence the policies around 'hugging hoodies' and protecting spending for the NHS and overseas development. However, McAnnulla (2010: 292) points out that for Labour, 'much of the effort was not so much about accommodating to the preferences of particular voters (though this was of course significant) but about making Labour's ideas and policies understood as "centrist" and nonthreatening'.

What is interesting here is the focus not on Conservative and Labour adopting the same centre ground – as there are clearly major ideological differences between the parties (Smith 2010, 2013) – but that they are concerned to develop policies that do not frighten voters. The result is not necessarily consensus but anodyne policy and the failure of parties to challenge policies that seem popular. So for instance, in the 2005 election neither Conservative nor Liberal-Democrats would challenge Labour's economic policy because it seemed successful (even though in retrospect it is clear there were many flaws) (Smith 2005). Likewise during the 2010 election campaign, Labour and the Conservatives had a different conception concerning the role of the state in relation to the economy, but their analysis of economic problems was remarkably similar (see Chapter 3). Both in effect saw a response to the economic crisis of 2008 based on reducing the deficit through cutting expenditure. Neither party has been prepared to challenge the assumptions of the policy or to propose anything that is radically different. This position is clearly illustrated by the contrasting problems that Labour and Conservatives have got themselves into in relation to immigration and gay marriage. In both cases, in order to widen their appeal, they have attempted to move away from their traditional positions. In the case of Conservatives and gay marriage, the desire to present itself as a modern liberal party is alienating its core voters and potentially strengthening the position of UKIP to attract 'traditional Conservatives'. Likewise Labour sees that its liberal position on immigration is alienating working-class voters and has therefore tried to take a harder line. The main parties are increasingly finding it difficult to retain an ideological anchor. Preference accommodating rather than preference shaping has become the default mind-set of the different party leaderships, hence their policies shift round following their perception of voters' views. What we see in terms of the mainstream party reaction to UKIP's 2013 relative electoral success is not a reasoned attack on UKIP's policies, but the parties scrabbling to be seen to be taking the issues raised by UKIP seriously.

The parties are creating policy on the basis of fear; it is a fear of frightening the electorate and so all policy developments are marginal rather than radical. It is a policy of marginal gains: tiny differences will give just enough votes to win an election (especially in the context when a party can win with a small percentage of the electorate). This is illustrated by Labour's economic policy. Labour's ideological anchor is a different conception of the role of the state to the Conservatives and yet Ed Balls is prepared to state:

> My starting point is, I am afraid, we are going to have keep all these cuts. There is a big squeeze happening on budgets across the piece. The squeeze on defence spending, for instance, is £15bn by 2015. We are going to have to start from that being the baseline. At this stage, we can make no commitments to reverse any of that, on spending or on tax. So I am being absolutely clear about that.
>
> *(The Telegraph* 14 January 2012)

Labour has to appear 'reasonable' in relation to the economy and they have to be able to win a large tranche of middle-class votes. The fundamental problem is that the parties are trying to bundle together electoral alliances by appealing to a broad range of groups. As this is the basis of their electoral strategy, they are failing either to develop distinctive political agendas or to thinking about incorporating issue politics into their policies. They fear adopting strong positions because of the danger of offending potential voters. Perhaps the best illustration of this approach is the rapidity with which the Coalition government is prepared to abandon policies that it thinks are unpopular or contentious and subject to media criticism.

Conclusion

The crisis of parties is much more profound than politicians are prepared to admit. Parties are 19th-century organisations with particular functions: to represent classes; to ensure a horizontal and vertical circulation of elites; to bind together the union and to develop policy. They are failing in all these functions and as citizens no longer see parties as the mechanisms for representing their political interests. Traditionally, parties structured politics in the very real sense of shaping the way in which day-to-day politics operated at both the mass and elite level. However, that structuring of politics is now operating almost solely at the elite level. The Westminster model was and is an elite system of governing, but one legitimised by party representation that enabled voters to affect the outcome. However the failure of parties to engage people as members means they are not acting as organisations embedded in civil society. Moreover, with the increasing loss of national representation and the rise of minor parties, the electoral system means that votes now affect very few seats and so the electorate cannot hold politicians to account in the Westminster model form. The Westminster model has always been a legitimising myth, but it is moving a destructive distance away from the realities of politics, voting and governing. The 'main' parties are faced with four key problems:

- They are unable to distinguish themselves to the voters other than as vote-gathering machines.
- The rise of alternative political parties such as the Greens, UKIP and Respect that are able to connect with particular constituencies and disrupt the normal patterns of electoral outcomes is a threat to the traditional parties and is increasingly fragmenting the party system.
- There is a growing group of people disaffected by politics and disconnected from the political system (as illustrated by the very low turnouts amongst the youngest groups). The disaffected create a long-term threat to the legitimacy of the political system and can create situations of disorder (as in the 2011 riots).
- Political participation is increasingly focused on issue politics and social movements rather than political parties. Parties are becoming increasingly divorced from the issues that excite citizens. Parties are no longer the main source of politics and increasingly people are by-passing them in terms of representation and influencing politics.

Citizens are no longer members of parties; their voting attachments are weak. Parties are failing to support the process of transmitting normal people into the elite. Hence, parties structure the elite part of the Westminster model – they provide the political leadership but they have lost the legitimising aspect by not enabling citizens to access politics. As a consequence, voters are disillusioned with party politicians and looking to other forms of political activity and increasingly supporting independents and minor parties. The parties are burying their heads in the sand by looking to state funding and failing to think seriously about the electoral system and its failings. The problem is that parties, despite declining support, still control government, and legitimacy can only be restored through citizens being more involved in the process of determining who governs and what they do once in power. Moreover, the centralised nature of power, in England at least, means that mechanisms for participation are not well developed outside of the

Westminster system and consequently people can exercise little control over their day-to-day lives. As was argued in Chapter 1, the conservative approach is to attack voters as being anti-politics and to look to the state to defend parties. The radical approach is to re-imagine the political process so that the traditional parties no longer structure the nature of politics and define the form of democracy that exists in the UK.

6
A Crisis of Whitehall

Patrick Diamond

Introduction

The concept of crisis has been periodically applied to Whitehall since the 1970s encapsulating the decline of confidence in the UK state's ruling institutions. The era in which UK government resembled a club, 'whose members trusted each other to observe the spirit of the club rules' (Marquand 1988: 178), has long ago passed into abeyance. Senior civil servants claim that the UK government, engulfed by a culture of 'spin' and politicisation, is in crisis (Foster 2005). Ministers vilify the mandarins, slamming Whitehall's incompetence and failure to deliver (Blair 2010). The language of crisis is a staple of journalistic commentary on the civil service (Cameron 2009). The concept of crisis, nonetheless, is still obliquely defined. As Gamble attests, even in the theoretically informed literature, crisis 'is thrown around fairly indiscriminately' (2009: 7).

At the core of this volume is the framing and interpretation of institutional crises in contemporary politics. Boin and t'Hart (2000: 10) define crises as 'intense media scrutiny, public criticism, political controversy, and calls for reform'. This definition of crisis is somewhat nebulous, underplaying the structural and institutional underpinnings of crisis, alongside the process of crisis narration. More recent accounts emphasise that crises are politically manufactured, constructed through narratives that legitimate particular remedies and programmes of action (Gamble 2009a, Hay 2011). Hay and Gamble are concerned with how neo-liberal governments have used the financial crisis and previous crises such as the winter of discontent in the late 1970s to legitimate the reform and retrenchment of the state. Hay uses the 'punctuated equilibrium model' to highlight that long periods of stability are broken by bursts of high-octane reform.

Despite influencing a number of influential accounts of the post-2008 financial crisis (Gamble 2009, Hay 2011), there are weaknesses in the conception of crisis as narration. As Marsh (2010) elaborates, this notion of crisis leads Hay to interpret continuity and change as a dualism. In Hay's (1996) conception of crisis, long periods of relative stasis are 'punctuated' by brief moments of radical change. There is a tendency to underplay the constraints on actors: agents operate on a prestructured terrain shaped by the prevailing ideological and material context. As was observed in the introductory chapter, there is a dominant political tradition in the UK underpinning political institutions which appears remarkably stable and resilient over time. The Thatcher governments left the state substantially intact in order to liberalise the economy and force through reforms of the post-war settlement. Changes to the constitution and the civil service were limited; where reform did occur, such as creating 'arms-length' agencies in Whitehall, it was incremental rather than revolutionary. As this chapter argues, notions of 'crises' do not sit easily with the empirical analysis of continuity and change in the Whitehall paradigm. Of course, institutions are always changing, but the impact of stasis and inertia is too often underestimated. Moreover, the extent to which structural change emerges out of, and is reinforced by, the dominant political tradition is underexplored in the literature (Marsh and Hall 2007).

Hay's account emphasises that there are always overlapping and contradictory narratives of crisis. This chapter reflects on the interpretations of 'crisis' promulgated by ministers and officials, assessing the impact of the post-2008 crisis on the institutions and practices of the UK state. Despite innumerable attempts to recast the Whitehall model since the New Public Management (NPM) reforms of the 1980s, the permanent bureaucracy is still resistant to change. This chapter assesses whether fiscal retrenchment and the Coalition government will permanently reshape the Whitehall paradigm for an era of austerity.

The aims of the chapter are three-fold. The first section outlines what is meant by the Whitehall paradigm, briefly charting the history of UK civil service reform. Whitehall is a metonym for the UK government's administrative centre (The Economist 2012). The reform process is characterised as much by continuity as change: ministers and officials uphold central axioms of the Westminster model, underwriting their status and power within the UK political system.

The chapter considers how the discourse of 'crisis' emerged in Whitehall during the New Labour era, paving the way for the Coalition's post-2010 reforms. Both the Conservative Party and the Liberal

Democrats are committed to an agenda of governance reform, shifting from a centralised, monolithic state to a post-bureaucratic society. While the Coalition's approach emphasises the changing role of the state, the imperative is for historically unprecedented retrenchment in the capacities of the central bureaucracy.

Finally, the chapter considers whether the Coalition's reforms represent a fundamental challenge to the Whitehall model and the dominant tradition of UK politics, symptomatic of a 'critical juncture' in the evolution of the UK state. The central argument is that, somewhat paradoxically, the core institutions and practices of the Whitehall model are being strengthened and reinforced by the post-2010 reforms. The window of opportunity for change thrown up by the financial crisis is unlikely to result in far-reaching institutional recalibration.

The core theme of the chapter is that Whitehall exhibits 'pathology without crisis'. Innumerable weaknesses are identified in the political and administrative machinery of government. All governments since the 1964–70 Wilson administration have espoused a rhetorical commitment to modernising the institutions and practices of the state. However, relatively few concrete programmes to radically overhaul the Whitehall machinery are driven through and implemented. Ministers are reluctant to renegotiate the strategic compact between politicians and the civil service. Taking on vested interests depletes the core executive of political capital: Whitehall reform rarely features in a party's vote-seeking strategy.

At root, this chapter avers that Whitehall remains a predominantly static institutional landscape characterised by organisational inertia. Fundamental change in the practices of the permanent bureaucracy takes place only where ministers and civil servants proselytise a shared conception of reform, a window of opportunity which has occurred rarely in post-war UK politics.

The Whitehall paradigm

The concept of the Whitehall paradigm refers to key institutional relationships within the UK system of government (Campbell and Wilson 1995, Richards 2008, Page 2010):

- First, a permanent bureaucracy that does not change according to the political affiliation of the government of the day. This contrasts with the Australian and Canadian systems where ministers appoint senior officials who are judged ideologically sympathetic to the administration. In New Zealand, there is a contractual relationship where permanent secretaries meet performance objectives set by ministers.

- The second characteristic of the paradigm is a core tenet of the mid-19th-century Northcote-Trevelyan Report (1853), namely, a set of values concerned with public service and neutrality which enables officials to give objective advice to ministers and 'speak truth to power'. Moreover, civil servants are 'generalists' who apply competencies forged through a (predominantly English) liberal education to governing challenges. Only rarely do officials resort to specialist knowledge and expertise.

- Third, the permanence of the civil service means it offers a 'career for life', a vocation to which officials devote their careers. There is little permeability or movement between professions, minimising the risk of corruption while making levels of trust in the UK civil service among the highest in the world (Foster 2005). Officials operate in a disinterested and neutral environment untainted by private interests.

- Finally, the Whitehall model is predicated on the notion that civil servants maintain a 'monopoly' in providing policy advice to ministers. This is the 'public service bargain' on which relationships within the UK system of government are predicated. Civil servants offer loyalty to ministers in return for oversight of the policy process and anonymity.

As Campbell and Wilson attest, 'To understand British executive politics, one needs to understand the world of the politician, the world of the bureaucrat and the interaction between the two' (1995: 9). The Whitehall paradigm operates in a system in which power is concentrated, where the core executive has an asymmetric role in decision-making.

The Whitehall paradigm is embedded within the Westminster model, a constitutional doctrine and a system of government predicated on territorial centralisation, executive dominance and majoritarian democracy (Lijphart 1999, Flinders 2010). Nonetheless, there is a disjuncture between the idealised characteristics of the Whitehall paradigm and the actual practice of governance (Judge 1993). The Whitehall paradigm was shaped by waves of *ad hoc*, pragmatic and evolutionary reform (Burnham and Pyper 2008). Northcote-Trevelyan established the principle of a neutral and meritocratic civil service. The Haldane Committee on the machinery of government (1918) codified the symbiotic relationship between ministers and civil servants, inaugurating Whitehall's federated structure based on departments. The Wilson government affirmed its commitment to civil service modernisation in the Fulton Report (1968), enunciating contemporary principles of managerial and organisational efficiency.

However, the reforms rarely questioned the status of the civil service within the institutional architecture of the UK polity. They did not diverge from constitutional orthodoxy and the dominant political tradition. As we saw in the Introduction, the role of the British political tradition (BPT) emphasises the sustaining of an elitist, top-down and centralised system of government. According to Evans (2003: 18), 'The Westminster model forms the basis of the British Political Tradition and in the course of the nineteenth and twentieth centuries became the political orthodoxy of British government.' The UK state's expansion in the 20th century drew on an ethos of 'club government', in which public administration was conducted through closed elites in accordance with central tenets of the BPT (see Chapter 1, but also Marquand 1988, Tant 1993).

This reinforced the evolutionary character of UK political development, privileging conservatism and continuity over change (Kerr 2001). The consolidation of various initiatives is reflected in how civil service reform plans have evolved across time, notably *Next Steps* (1988), *Continuity and Change* (1994), *Modernising Government* (1999), *Civil Service Reform: Delivery and Values* (2004) and *Putting the Frontline First* (2009). It is striking that similar themes and reform agendas re-emerge throughout these White Papers on Whitehall modernisation.

Inevitably, there are literatures which aver that the Whitehall paradigm is characterised by discontinuity. Campbell and Wilson (1995) posit 'the end of Whitehall' view, arguing that NPM[1] has eroded the allegiance between ministers and civil servants. This is augmented by a literature alluding to the impact of politicisation and pluralisation in UK government (Richards 1997, 2008, Foster and Plowden 1998, Marquand 2004, Foster 2005). Politicisation refers to the growth of special advisers and the influence of Number Ten and the core executive in departmental policy-making. This was borne out by high-profile conflict during the New Labour years, particularly Robin Cook and Clare Short's resignations over Iraq and the alleged manipulation of intelligence material relating to weapons of mass destruction (Cook 2004, Seldon 2006). On the domestic agenda, Estelle Morris resigned as Secretary of State for Education and Skills in 2002 over allegations that Number Ten was interfering in departmental policy (Rawnsley 2006). Such cases of open dissent between 10 Downing Street and departmental ministers were, nonetheless, relatively unusual.

The process of politicisation was accompanied by a shift towards pluralisation: a range of external actors from interest groups to think-tanks challenged the dominance of civil servants in policy-making. This allegedly triggered an erosion of the Whitehall model and the UK's 'Rolls Royce' system of government.[2] This view is augmented by Rhodes' claim of 'hollowing-out' and the emergence of a differentiated polity where the capacity of the executive to drive through policy change is circumscribed as power drifts upwards to the European Union, sideways to the private sector, and downwards to local delivery agencies (Rhodes 1994).

Nonetheless, the evidence for any fundamental erosion in the Whitehall 'paradigm' is contested. There is a tendency to conflate separate events and processes. The controversy surrounding the emergence of 'sofa government' and the build up to the Iraq war, for example, is distinct from the imposition of targets and marketisation in the public sector. New Labour's approach to public sector reform was not borne of sofa government. The reform agenda encapsulated disparate ideas that emerged during the 1990s: the need to reconcile the Thatcherite inheritance of public choice and quasi-markets[3] with more traditional social democratic goals. Moreover, targets characterised Labour's 'command bureaucracy' in the first term (1997–2001). However, diversity of provision and contestability emerged as the central narrative of the second term (2001–05), encapsulated by an enhanced role for the private sector in service delivery (Riddell 2007, Barber 2007).

Within the Whitehall system, Page (2010) finds little evidence of an escalation in day-to-day conflict between ministers, civil servants and special advisers. Similarly, Smith (2009) concludes that the autonomy of departments has not been greatly diminished. Marsh Richards and Smith (2001) challenge the claim that central government has been hollowed-out. There may be evidence of an emerging 'minister-dominated paradigm', but the extent of change has been overstated.

An alternative perspective is that Whitehall has seldom been amenable to structural reform (Marsh Richards and Smith 2003, Wrisque-Cline 2008). The underlying drivers of continuity and bureaucratic inertia in Whitehall are multi-faceted. Hood insists that the political class has rarely focused on driving through change:

> We have seen this movie before – albeit with a slightly different plotline – with a rash of attempts to fix up the bureaucracy, with the

same pattern of hype from the centre, selective filtering at the extremities and political attention deficit syndrome that works against any follow-through and continuity.

(2007: 12)

Hood infers that politicians rarely discern strategic advantage in using institutional power resources to drive through state reforms. Elsewhere, it is claimed that ministers and civil servants conspire to maintain the status quo: the Westminster and Whitehall model confers prestige, power and resources (Richards and Kavanagh 2001). The symbiosis between officials and ministers encourages both to uphold the existing constitutional settlement. This was the backdrop to discussions about Whitehall during the New Labour years and under the Coalition since 2010. While the epithet of crisis is regularly applied to Whitehall, it is within the context of the stability, continuity and permanence afforded by the BPT.

New Labour and Whitehall

Nonetheless, the epithet of 'crisis' had been regularly attributed to the formal apparatus of central government and the civil service following Labour's 1997 victory. While an ethos of shared purpose between officials and politicians to some extent continued, there was frustration about the inability of Whitehall to implement the government's landmark reforms (Blair 2010, Mandelson 2010). The then Prime Minister made an infamous speech in 1999 about the 'scars on my back', underlining Labour's mistrust of the civil service (Blair 2010). Peter Hyman, a senior adviser in Number Ten (1997–2003), alludes to the antiquated nature of Whitehall:

The civil service as a whole... was stuck firmly in the approaches of the past. What we discovered in 1997 was not the Rolls-Royce service of popular myth but an organisation ill-equipped to deal with the demands of a fast changing world. Civil servants were still being recruited with far too narrow a set of skills. There were few project managers which meant that many government IT projects ran into the ground and wasted vast amounts of taxpayers' money... Few departments had modern communication departments able to understand the views of the public or communicate adequately with frontline staff... Most civil servants moved jobs so frequently within departments they were never held accountable for delivering anything. Success was measured by any criteria other than the one that mattered: delivery. There was huge resistance to outsiders coming into the civil service, yet some of our best successes proved to be when outsiders and existing civil servants worked together in teams.

(Hyman, 2004: 73–4)

This is endorsed by Lord Birt, Blair's senior adviser on strategy (2000–06):

There is too much invested – and this is a general truth in a lot of public policy – in the status quo. Do not under-estimate the extraordinary inertia within the departments and within the Civil Service itself on many questions. It is honest and it is well intentioned but it is inertia and it is the enemy of change.[4]

Similarly, Andrew Adonis, Schools Minister and former Secretary of State for Transport (2009–10), insists, 'The biggest obstacle I faced was the weakness of the Whitehall machine' (Adonis 2012: 43). The institutions and practices of the permanent bureaucracy were seen as no longer 'fit for purpose'. The Home Office provides an illuminating case study of how crisis narratives were manufactured and proselytised during the New Labour years (Painter 2008).

As Painter (2008) recounts, successive Home Secretaries struggled to impose reforms following a series of high-profile 'fiascos' under David Blunkett (2001–04), Charles Clarke (2004–06) and John Reid (2006–07). The spiralling number of asylum claims and fears about loss of control in the immigration system were exacerbated by security shocks such as '9/11' and '7/7'. This culminated in a succession of mishaps: lapses in probation service orders; a scandal over foreign prisoners' visas which meant offenders were never deported; a crisis of prison numbers leading to greater use of non-custodial sentencing; and a debacle over the vetting of criminal records (Painter 2008).[5] As a result, there were a barrage of headlines referring to 'meltdown' and 'chaos' in the Home Office. The view of ministers was that 'policy fiascos' could not be blamed on contingency or the contentious terrain on which the Home Office operates. Blair's advisers fastened onto Whitehall's inefficiency and incompetence, underlined by an anecdote from the Number Ten Chief of Staff, Jonathan Powell:

A Home Office team came to make a Power Point presentation to the Prime Minister in the Cabinet Room on crime, complete with multi-coloured graphs showing that the crime rate would rise inexorably. When Tony asked why crime would rise, the officials replied that it was because the economy was growing and that put temptations in the way of criminals. We scratched our heads. I asked the team what would happen if the economy were to go into recession. Without missing a beat, the officials replied that crime would rise because people would be deprived and more of them would have to resort to robbery to survive.

(Powell 2010: 72)

Similarly, Blunkett (2006) criticised the lack of operational effectiveness in the Home Office. These problems were made worse by a lack of coordination between the Home Office and criminal justice agencies. Ministers narrated the 'crisis' in terms of a dysfunctional management culture which justified systemic reform, reallocating policy responsibilities from the Home Office to the Ministry of Justice (MoJ), and clarifying the operational responsibilities of ministers and civil servants. A similar diagnosis ensued following the 'foot and mouth' crisis at the Ministry of Agriculture, Fisheries and Food (MAFF) in 2001, the loss of personal data by the Inland Revenue in 2008 and the failed procurement of a single NHS IT system.

Nonetheless, ascribing the notion of 'crisis' to Whitehall may lead to misdiagnosis, imposing reforms which accentuate problems rather than ameliorating them. This alludes to criticisms of New Labour's governing style (Foster 2005). There are suggestions that ministers paid too little regard to due process. Whitehall was overly centralised, as power was amassed at the centre around Number Ten. A culture of 'hyperactivity' led to ill-considered initiatives out of sync with the reality at the front line. Fewer checks and balances were in place as the result of Cabinet government's decline. The politicisation and pluralisation of the policy process threatened to undermine constitutional relationships at the heart of the Whitehall model. These claims are contentious, but are influential in the wider literature (Foster and Plowden 1998, Butler 2004, Marquand 2004, Foster 2005):

- Mandarins aver that Whitehall had been thrown into 'crisis' by ill-considered reforms which failed to address the dilemmas and trade-offs characterising public administration.
- New Labour's focus on the politics of performance inferred that productivity and quality in public services would be improved through competition and quasi-markets. The emphasis was on 'permanent revolution': as it became apparent that the public sector

'target and command' regime was yielding diminishing returns, New Labour redirected its reforms towards competition and contestability between providers, further destabilising the machinery of government.

- Legislative hyperactivity and demands for 'attention-grabbing' policy initiatives from Number Ten confused the civil service, risking institutional overload and making departments more vulnerable to delivery failure and policy fiascos.
- The development of the strong state encouraged a centralised implementation strategy (Gamble 1994b). UK governments have traditionally relied on local agencies to deliver public services and social welfare through the territorial dispersion of power (Bulpitt 1986). As a consequence of centralisation over two decades, Whitehall departments were operationally accountable but the lines of responsibility were increasingly ambiguous. Agencies were charged with delivering 'front-line' targets rather than departments; however, there was confusion about whether ministers, mandarins or managers should answer to Parliament on operational questions (Flinders 2008).

These accounts draw attention to how the governing process was being fundamentally restructured by the dynamics of risk, blame and performance (Hood and Lodge 2010). The competence of the contemporary state is judged by its capacity to manage and control various facets of *risk*. Ministers and officials are less concerned about taking credit for policy success and more focused on avoiding the attribution of *blame*. All governments are concerned with the ability to deliver improvements in public sector *performance*, operating within strict public expenditure limits alongside the imperative of fiscal consolidation and state restructuring.

This chapter argues that ministers and civil servants are strategically calculating agents who narrate distinctive accounts of 'crises'. The role of Political Science is not merely to accept these interpretations, but to challenge and contest their underlying assumptions. Politicians sought to create consensus for a shake-up of Whitehall. Officials harnessed the discourse of 'crisis' to defend the Whitehall model from ill-considered and counter-productive reforms (Foster 2005). Moreover, while agents construct and promulgate crisis narratives, this chapter avers that articulating an account of crisis does not inevitably lead to change. There may be continuous pressure and desire for change, but this will not necessarily lead to reform.

Like all post-war governments, Labour's appetite for Whitehall reform was matched by a reluctance to overhaul the constitutional rules of the game determining the relationship between ministers, the civil service, Parliament and the state. The Blair and Brown governments were deeply ambivalent about overturning inherited institutions and practices. The Westminster model offered an apparently seamless view of the policy-making and delivery process for an incoming administration with relatively little governing experience. Power was amassed in a strong executive, the basis on which the governing party was able to deliver its manifesto commitments. There was little enthusiasm for bottom-up and participatory governance reforms, imposing serious obstacles to structural modernisation in the machinery of the state (Cook 2004).

Governance after crisis: From the big state to the post-bureaucratic society

This chapter argues that while narratives of 'crisis' are constantly manufactured by agents, fundamental continuities in the Whitehall model remain. Nonetheless, the case for reform has attained wider currency given the Coalition's response to the post-2008 crisis. The Coalition's strategy draws on a critique of New Labour's centralising approach to state–society relations, alongside the imperatives of fiscal consolidation and deficit reduction (Smith 2010). As the Cabinet Office minister Francis Maude argued in a speech to the think tank Reform, 'The era of big government has come to an end not just because the money has literally run out, but it is also shown to have failed'.[6] The Conservative and Liberal Democrat programme is concerned with harnessing the financial crisis and the consequent pressures on the UK public finances to engineer a radical restructuring of the state.

The antipathy to the centralising state reflects separate but by no means contradictory strands of the UK liberal tradition. On the one hand, the 'Orange Book' tendency within the Liberal Democrats emphasises decentralisation and local autonomy within a dynamic market economy. One of the book's authors, David Laws, argued that the 'Liberal belief in economic liberalism' ought to be rescued from 'soggy socialism and corporatism' (2004: 11).

On the other hand, the 'liberal conservatism' lauded by David Cameron prioritises social duty and compassionate paternalism over the centralising state: 'the old, top-down, big-government approach has failed'.[7] The disquiet within both parties about Labour's centralised, statist approach led to the notion of a post-bureaucratic society (Norman and Ganesh 2006, Smith 2010).

Prior to the crisis, Cameron's Conservatives sought to challenge the legacy of 'Whitehall knows best', particularly in social policy (Bale 2010, Blond 2010). The principle of a post-bureaucratic state was about 'bottom-up' solutions to social problems, breaking with the top-down, centralising approach adopted by previous Labour governments. This was consistent with the principle of subsidiarity: governments should perform those functions that individuals and civic associations could not provide themselves, according to Keynes' (1926: 9) dictum in *The End of Laissez-Faire*:

> The most important items on the Agenda of the State relate not to those activities which private individuals are already fulfilling, but to those activities which fall outside the sphere of the individual ... The important thing for Government is not to do things which individuals are doing already, and to do them a little better or a little worse, but to do those things which at present are not done at all.

The legitimacy and power afforded by the centralised state is rejected in favour of mobilising civil society and the private sector (Kenny 2009, Smith 2010). The Conservatives insisted that state-driven models of social reform rarely succeeded, reinforcing passive dependency on the welfare state. The challenges of an ageing society require new delivery tools, reducing citizen's reliance on state provision and forging 'pro-social' attitudes, behaviours and incentives (Thaler and Sunstein 2008, Halpern 2010). The growth of the state under Labour between 1997 and 2010 is depicted in Figure 6.1.

While Labour's bureaucratic state allegedly 'crowded out' voluntary initiative, the Conservatives advocated a strategy of decentralisation among local agencies and actors. The post-bureaucratic society appeared to fit rationally with the imperative of the post-2008 crisis towards fiscal retrenchment and a redrawing of the parameters of the state. Nonetheless, the Coalition government was confronted by a strategic dilemma. Public opinion surveys indicate that the UK electorate have continued to support universal public services free at the point of use (Curtice et al. 2010). The 2010 Conservative Manifesto pledged to sustain rising real-terms expenditure on the NHS to reassure voters.[8] As such, reform was concerned with integrating a range of actors into the delivery of public services without sacrificing the principle of universality in public provision. The strategy was to reconcile retrenchment in the

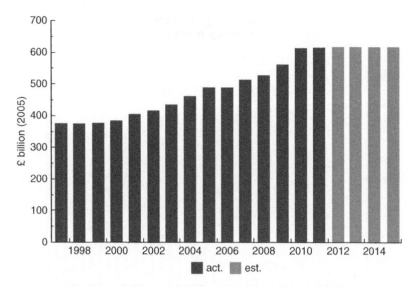

Figure 6.1   UK state spending 1997–2015[9]

UK public finances with a commitment to social cohesion and a fairer society (Smith 2010).

Ministers sought to portray the post-bureaucratic state as a necessary decentralising reform, challenging the nostrum that 'the man in Whitehall knows best': government programmes failed to ameliorate poverty and social deprivation (Norman and Ganesh 2006). Moreover, cuts in public expenditure were needed to maintain confidence in the UK economy, and to safeguard the UK's status as a 'safe haven' with international investors. The fiscal impact of the financial crisis on the UK state was severe: total UK public sector debt is 85.2 per cent of GDP, while the UK has the second highest level of debt among the industrialised nations. The growth of UK public debt is outlined in Figure 6.2.

The scale of public debt created a rationale for the Coalition government to roll back the frontiers of the state, with the initial objective of eliminating the public sector deficit by 2015–16 (since modified to 2016–17), entailing sharp reductions in year-on-year departmental expenditure. All Whitehall departments must reduce administrative budgets by 34 per cent over the lifetime of this parliament,[10] leading to dramatic headcount reductions, as Figure 6.3 indicates.

The Institute for Government (Paun and Halifax 2012) has claimed the scale of the retrenchment will have far-reaching consequences for

**UK gross public debt
(sterling, billions)**

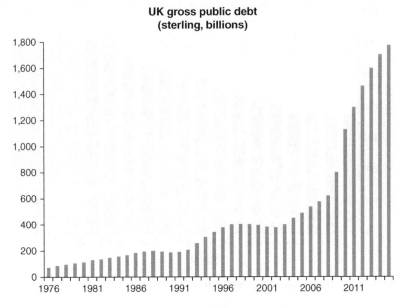

Figure 6.2   UK gross public debt 1976–2015[11]

Whitehall. The Cabinet Secretary Sir Jeremy Heywood acknowledges
that the process of fiscal consolidation requires fundamental reforms
of the state.[12] The fiscal crisis and the imperative of a post-bureaucratic
society entail major changes in the machinery of government and the
institutional apparatus of the core executive.

The Coalition government: Reshaping the Whitehall model?

This chapter avers that the Whitehall model has been impervious to
'root and branch' structural reform. The rhetoric of ministers demon-
strates a commitment to radically overhauling the Whitehall model.
This entails a narration of 'crisis' in which the fiscal pressures on the
state are addressed by fundamentally reshaping the institutions and
processes of central government. However, despite significant changes,
including the imposition of NPM, *Next Steps* and the pluralisation of
policy-making, traditional nostrums such as neutrality, integrity and
public service enunciated in Northcote-Trevelyan and Haldane have
endured (Wrisque-Cline 2008). Since 2010, it is evident that a disjuncture has emerged between the reforming rhetoric of political actors and

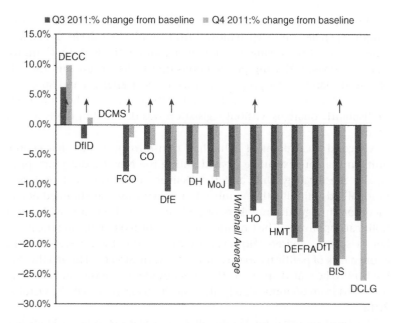

Figure 6.3 Percentage reductions in FTE staff in Whitehall since 2010[13]

the resilience of the Whitehall model, as can be observed in five key areas.

First, the Coalition was committed to abandoning targets, the audit culture and top-down delivery. This entailed a shift from 'bureaucratic' to 'democratic' accountability, involving greater transparency in performance data. The extension of competition and quasi-markets would ensure consumer preferences created pressure for change. Targets in the NHS were held to be unnecessary and bureaucratic. A key theme of the post-bureaucratic society is adopting non-governmental instruments to drive up standards in public services, including data transparency and price incentives.[14] However, in November 2011, Secretary of State for Health Andrew Lansley was forced to reintroduce central guidelines increasing the number of patients being treated within 18 weeks. The Department of Health subsequently imposed 60 NHS outcome measures.[15] Targets, albeit in moderated form, were back.

As well as scrapping targets, an intention was announced to cull the 'quango state'. The government initially proposed to cut 192 out of 901 public bodies, merging a further 118.[16] Nonetheless, ministers realised that shutting quangos was costly, delivering few up-front efficiency savings. They appreciated the strategic advantage of having 'arms-length' agencies one step removed from ministerial decision-making. 'The bonfire of the quangos' barely materialised: the Forestry Commission was saved following public opposition to its closure and the sale of forestry land.[17] The proposal to merge Sport England and Sport UK was abandoned.[18] Moreover, the Public Bodies Bill enabling ministers to dismantle quangos without legislation was defeated in the House of Lords.

A second focal point of Whitehall transformation was that central units in the core executive created during the New Labour years, principally the Strategy Unit and the Delivery Unit, were cut back and rationalised. Initially, the Number Ten Policy Unit was slimmed down, incorporating greater numbers of permanent civil servants with fewer political appointees. The Coalition was committed to reducing the number of special advisers. However, by early 2011, there were concerns about a lack of political capacity in 10 Downing Street.[19] This led the Policy Unit to be scaled up, while the total number of advisers in Whitehall increased from 66 immediately after the 2010 election to 85 by October 2012.[20]

The third proposal for Whitehall reform was creating an Efficiency and Reform Group (ERG) in the Cabinet Office under its Director-General, Iain Watmore. The aim of the ERG is to reduce administrative costs by £6 billion through improvements in efficiency and reductions in back-office capacity. Spending on ICT, recruitment, property and consultancy is being reduced through the centralisation of procurement. The challenge for the ERG, however, is to make an impact beyond Whitehall since local public sector bodies are not directly controlled by the centre (The Economist 2012). Moreover, there are concerns that reductions in back-office capacity may undermine operational effectiveness, as became apparent in the Care Quality Commission (CQC)'s failure to identify abuse in the care home sector.[21]

The fourth area of reform is transforming the career structure of the civil service through 'early exit' for poorly performing officials, accompanied by recruitment of outsiders into senior management positions. The cuts in headcount have been dramatic: since 2010, more than 17,800 civil servants have left their posts (27 per cent of the senior civil service).[22] This includes 43 per cent of staff in the Department for Communities and Local Government (DCLG), and 30 per cent of civil servants in the Treasury. Departmental management boards have been created: Lord Browne, former Chief Executive of British Petroleum

(BP), and Ian Davis, once head of the McKinsey management consultancy, joined the Cabinet Office board as non-executive directors (The Economist 2012). The infusion of outside talent into Whitehall is not wholly new, however, and has grown in importance since the mid-1980s. Moreover, doubt has been cast on how far senior appointments in the civil service are really being exposed to external competition.[23]

Finally, in order to make a reality of the post-bureaucratic state, philanthropists and charitable bodies are being encouraged to contribute to the delivery of public services and welfare reform. However, this continues the strategy of the previous Labour government, radically pluralising service delivery (Smith 2010). The *Civil Service Action Plan* proposes to extend pluralisation from delivery to policy analysis: a central fund has been created to pilot contestable policy-making, encouraging the development of innovative models such as mutual pathfinders. Nonetheless, by late 2012 Jeremy Heywood and the Head of the Civil Service Sir Bob Kerslake were diluting proposals to contract-out the policy process.[24]

The Cabinet Office minister Francis Maude signalled renewed interest in the New Zealand model, where there is a 'contractual' relationship between ministers and permanent secretaries. Officials have to meet delivery goals monitored by the State Services Commission based on five-year contracts. The civil service recently signalled its disenchantment with Maude's proposals. On appointments, both Kerslake and the Civil Service Commissioner Sir David Normington insist that although ministers have a role in the selection process, final decisions must rest with the Civil Service Commission.[25]

Moreover, there is evidence that Whitehall reforms are being weakened despite the severity of the fiscal crisis. Three years into the life of the Coalition government, the administration had confronted major obstacles in its attempt to overhaul the Whitehall model. There is an implementation gap between the rhetoric of parties in opposition and the actual practice of governing in the UK state. Indeed, key measures in the Coalition's *Civil Service Reform Plan* have unintended consequences which do not dismantle the Whitehall model – but arguably further entrench it.

The proposals do not challenge the constitutional status quo concerning the relationship between ministers and civil servants. The Haldane model stipulating an indivisible bond between ministers and civil servants remains undisturbed. The Coalition's proposals avoid addressing the doctrine of ministerial responsibility and the operational accountability of civil servants. While Maude expresses enthusiasm for the New Zealand system, the Cabinet Office minister Oliver Letwin emphasises retaining the traditional cadre of generalist policy-making officials at the centre of Whitehall.[26]

Nor is there a focus on major structural reorganisation in Whitehall. Despite concerns about the negative impact of 'silos' and the absence of 'joined-up' government, ministers are reluctant to dismantle Whitehall's federated structure based around departments. Similarly, there are no plans to further slim down and consolidate departments.

The structures designed to ensure efficient government under a coalition merely re-impose traditional collegiate decision-making arrangements on Whitehall. Rather than driving initiatives through departments and overseeing implementation, Number Ten has reverted to its traditional role of minimising intra-departmental conflict and coordinating the policy process. The Institute for Government has observed that Cabinet meets more frequently than before 2010, while key decisions are subject to more lengthy deliberation (Paun and Halifax 2012). The reality of a coalition makes governing through the Cabinet ever more necessary.

Number Ten and the Cabinet Office are led by a civil servant, Jeremy Heywood, rather than a political chief of staff. Whitehall mandarins have regained control over the political and administrative machinery of government. Dividing the post of Cabinet Secretary and Head of the domestic civil service following Sir Gus O'Donnell's retirement in 2011 has given Heywood greater latitude to drive through the Prime Minister's priorities.

The Whitehall status quo is reinforced by contingency, but also by fundamental weaknesses in the alternative conception of a post-bureaucratic society. The notion of the post-bureaucratic state is potentially contradictory. As Smith (2010) acknowledges, a conflict emerges between the rational choice ontology of the new right and the stress on social duty and responsibility. There is concern that shifting provision from state to non-state actors will result in 'abandonment', as occurred during the 'care in the community' reforms in adult mental health.[27] The libertarian paternalism of Thaler and Sunstein (2008) reflects American political culture, which is not easily transposed to the UK. Redrawing the parameters of the British state has been hard-going, as the Liberal Democrats have been determined to safeguard the Coalition's commitment to universal state provision. Neither has the administration developed a consistent approach to localism: UK politics remains 'hyper-centralised'. Fundamentally, ministers and officials do not trust local institutions' decisions: the Treasury is still responsible for 95 per cent of UK taxation.[28]

It may be that Cameron's instincts are anchored in the tradition of 'Whig-imperialism', rather than avowedly reformist (Marquand 2008). This alludes to ambivalence about the Whitehall machine among Conservative party ministers. The public choice framework of the New Right and NPM reform undermine traditional Tory principles focused on the preservation of the UK's constitutional inheritance and respect for the centuries-old stability of the UK's political institutions (Bale 2010). Many Conservatives have been inclined to regard Whitehall as a 'Rolls-Royce' machine which has bequeathed a remarkable legacy of strong and stable government marking the UK out from its continental European neighbours.

At the same time, Richards and Blunkett (2011) aver that confronted by a series of 'wicked' administrative challenges from dramatic reductions in public expenditure to the threat of Scottish independence, ministers have immersed themselves in the traditional 'comfort-blanket' of the Whitehall and Westminster model. Ministers and civil servants have a shared goal of defending their resources and power within the political system (Richards and Smith 2004, Marsh and Hall 2007). This strengthens the tendency towards institutional stability, continuity and inertia.

Whitehall: Pathology without crisis?

Despite the Coalition's objective of reshaping public administration in the wake of the post-2008 crisis, there was no consistent strategy for overhauling Whitehall and the civil service. Ministers narrate the 'crisis' in terms of the UK's perilous economic position, reducing the cost of government to sustain the confidence of the financial markets. Whitehall will undoubtedly be smaller as a result of the Coalition's reforms: the Thatcher government took 11 years to shrink the civil service headcount by 10 per cent – a figure achieved in two years by Coalition ministers (Paun and Halifax 2012).

As a result, there is dissatisfaction within the civil service about the prevailing climate of reform. The potential for loss of institutional capacity and collective memory has raised concerns (Riddell 2010). Alistair Darling indicated that the Treasury struggled to cope with the fall-out of the financial crisis following its 'slimming-down' during the post-2004 Gershon reforms. Not a single official was present who worked for the Treasury during the last major economic crisis following the UK's exit from the European Exchange Rate Mechanism (ERM) in 1992 (Darling 2010). The concern about a long-term erosion of civil service capability was confirmed in a recent Treasury report.[29] Nonetheless, reducing the size of the state need not denote a wholesale change in the Whitehall paradigm.

There are unresolved questions about fundamental constitutional conventions. The Coalition's proposals seek to redefine civil servants as delivery agents. However, officials are rarely accountable to MPs. Margaret Hodge, Chair of the House of Commons Public Accounts Committee (PAC), insists that civil servants should 'unambiguously answer to Parliament' (The Economist 2012). This is opposed by the Whitehall mandarinate fearing the Haldane principle of confidentiality between ministers and civil servants is being eroded (Foster 2005).[30] There is no immediately obvious resolution of this conundrum over ministerial and parliamentary accountability.

This chapter contends that the Coalition's reforms perpetuate a historical pattern of 'pathology without crises'. During the New Labour years, ministers raised concerns about Whitehall's performance, averring that the civil service had too little capacity for delivery. Officials insisted that traditional nostrums of 'good government' were being attacked and undermined. Yet, there seemed little prospect of a decisive resolution to the crisis. A crisis is usually defined as a moment of decision when medically the patient is either cured for good, or declines with no hope of recovery (Dunleavy 1993). The fundamental point of decision in Whitehall has never been reached, even in the aftermath of the 2008 crisis. The vision of a post-bureaucratic society has yet to be realised.

All crises have structural determinants, where a deadlock or impasse persists for a long period before resolution (Gamble 2009). While there are phases of stability and order, crises have the potential to erupt unpredictably leading to new regimes: 'New institutions, new alignments, new policies, and new ideologies' (Gamble 2009: 7). However, analysing change in Whitehall and the core executive through the concept of 'crisis' is rarely illuminating. More significant is how strategically calculating actors legitimate their position within the political system, operating within the dominant tradition of centralised statecraft, majoritarianism and executive dominance.

Conclusion

This chapter considered Whitehall reform in relation to contested conceptions of 'crisis' in UK politics, addressing how far the reform programme outlined by the Coalition represents a substantive challenge to the Whitehall paradigm. Ministers seized the opportunity to impose reforms on the permanent bureaucracy, initiating a post-bureaucratic society. Nonetheless, the impact of the reforms has been blunted. Moreover, key pillars of the Whitehall model have endured, especially the symbiotic relationship between civil servants and ministers.

The 'stem-cell' of UK government is provided by the Westminster model, underlining the salience of the BPT (Judge 2006). Despite espousing the rhetoric of reform, the Coalition is reasserting core tenets of the Westminster model and Whitehall paradigm: ministerial and collective responsibility, strong leadership, the capacity for 'command and control' through the core executive. The post-2008 crisis has major implications for the future of the state. However, there are limits to the reach of the Coalition's plans given the underlying attachment of the major parties to the dominant tradition in UK politics. The Whitehall model has been strengthened and reinforced by the Coalition's programme.

Other ambiguities in Whitehall remain. The paradox of modern governance is the aversion to risk coinciding with increased demands for operational efficiency and higher performance (Explorations in Governance 2012). The demand on the state to ensure security and resilience conflicts with the imperative in the public sector to deliver 'more for less'. These contradictory pressures aggravate underlying pathologies with the potential for spill-over effects and unintended consequences, destabilising the political and administrative machinery of government. This is not a moment of fundamental crisis, but such instability alludes to the potential for further upheaval in the UK's administrative state.

Notes

1. Greer has categorised the following features of NPM: a shift to disaggregation in public services organisation; limited term contract employment of senior staff over traditional career tenure; monetised incentives rather than the traditional structure of control in the public sector through non-monetary factors and uniform fixed salaries; top managerial 'freedom to manage'; the separation of provision from delivery in public services; an emphasis on cost cutting; a shift away from policy-making towards efficiency and cost of service delivery, emphasising quantifiable methods of performance measurement; a shift from 'process' to 'outputs' in accountability mechanisms (Greer 1994: 8).
2. See *The Better Government Initiative (BGI) Report* on good government: http://www.bettergovernmentinitiative.co.uk/sitedata/Misc/Good-government-17-October.pdf

3. Quasi-markets are institutional structures in public services such as health and education that combine the efficiency gains of free markets with the concern of the public sector for equity and fairness (Dixon and Le Grand 2006).
4. Quoted from Evidence to the Public Administration Committee, 15th January 2000.
5. More recently, the current Home Secretary Theresa May became embroiled in a serious dispute with the Chief Executive of the UK Border Agency Brodie Clark about speeding up immigration checks at ports and airports, a decision apparently unauthorised by ministers.
6. 'Reducing the deficit and reforming public services', speech to the Reform think tank, Francis Maude MP, 7 July 2010.
7. 'Big Society Not Big Government: Building a Big Society', Conservative Party election document launched by David Cameron MP, 31 March 2010, Conservative Party Central Office, Millbank, London.
8. http://media.conservatives.s3.amazonaws.com/manifesto/cpmanifesto2010_lowres.pdf
9. HM Treasury, Annual Budget Statement, March 2012.
10. This is set out in the June 2010 Public Expenditure Review: cdn.hmtreasury.gov.uk/sr2010_completereport.pdf
11. HM Treasury, Annual Budget Statement, March 2012.
12. Sir Jeremy Heywood, Speech to the Institute of Government, 12 June 2012: http://www.bbc.co.uk/news/uk-politics-18528945.
13. This is based on Paun and Halifax (2012).
14. http://www.publications.parliament.uk/pa/cm201011/cmselect/cmpubadm/writev/goodgov/gg04.htm
15. http://www.guardian.co.uk/society/2011/dec/07/andrew-lansley-patient-outcome-measures
16. http://www.guardian.co.uk/politics/2010/oct/14/government-to-reveal-which-quangos-will-be-scrapped
17. http://www.guardian.co.uk/environment/2011/feb/16/forests-sell-off-cameron-uturn
18. http://www.telegraph.co.uk/sport/olympics/9821609/Government-scraps-plans-to-merge-UK-Sport-and-Sport-England-funding-following-success-at-London-Olympics.html
19. http://www.independent.co.uk/news/uk/politics/no-10-under-cameron-the-three-acts-of-the-pms-leadership-2260819.html
20. https://www.gov.uk/government/publications/special-adviser-data-releases-numbers-and-costs-october-2012
21. http://www.kingsfund.org.uk/blog/2012/04/are-we-expecting-too-much-care-quality-commission
22. http://www.guardian.co.uk/politics/2012/apr/13/senior-civil-servants-exodus
23. https://www.gov.uk/government/publications/fair-access-to-professional-careers-a-progress-report
24. The Institute for Public Policy Research (IPPR) was recently awarded the contract to produce a comparative analysis of civil service accountability across jurisdictions. This is the first contract to be awarded under the government's Contestable Policy Fund: http://www.ippr.org/research-project/44/9627/civil-service-reform-lessons-from-overseas

25. http://www.civilserviceworld.com/appointment-reforms-blocked/
26. 'Why Mandarins Matter', keynote speech by Rt. Hon. Oliver Letwin MP, Institute of Government, 17 September 2012.
27. http://www.publications.parliament.uk/pa/cm201011/cmselect/cmpubadm/writev/goodgov/gg04.htm
28. http://blogs.lse.ac.uk/politicsandpolicy/archives/10884
29. http://www.hm-treasury.gov.uk/d/review_fincrisis_response_290312.pdf
30. Similarly, the outgoing Cabinet Secretary Gus O'Donnell recently argued that freedom of information legislation was weakening the ability of ministers and civil servants to engage in 'free and frank' discussion of policy options within government: http://www.guardian.co.uk/politics/2011/nov/23/freedom-of-information-act-government

7
A Crisis of the Union

Paul Cairney

Introduction

The election of a majority Scottish National Party (SNP) Government in Scotland in 2011 all but guaranteed that Scotland would vote on an independence referendum in 2014. The prospect of Scottish independence has triggered widespread concern about the potential emergence of a crisis of the Union following the departure of its second largest member. Scottish independence would force the other devolved territories, and perhaps English regions, to reconsider the role and value of the Union and what it stands for. Further, even an extension of Scottish devolution (a potential longer term consequence of a 'no to independence' vote in 2014) would raise new questions about the powers of Wales and Northern Ireland and the future of England within a new Union (Hazell 2006).

This chapter outlines three key qualifications to such arguments. First, Scottish independence is still unlikely: the rise in support for the SNP has not been accompanied by a rise in support for independence. In fact, support for independence *fell* in 2007 even though the SNP gained enough electoral support to form a minority government. By 2011, support for independence had risen, but only back to one-third of the population. The SNP's popularity can be better explained in terms of valence politics factors such as its image of governing competence. Consequently, there may be a crisis of the Union, but more in terms of an impending point of decision in 2014 than a realistic possibility of a sudden, fundamental constitutional change.

Second, to a large extent, the 'crisis of the Union' is 15–20 years out of sync with important aspects of the current debate on crisis in the UK. For example, the 'conservative conception of crisis' outlined in the

Introduction to this volume, regarding the general notion that politics has failed, was a key part of Scotland's (and Wales') 'new politics' narrative in the run up to the devolution referendums in 1997. This now almost forgotten narrative was already about a 'crisis' of representative government. Indeed, perhaps ironically, the modern Scottish experience may provide a corrective to the idea that traditional representative democracy in the UK is under threat. The Scottish experience shows us that 'new politics' is often little more than rhetoric and the Scottish Parliament has operated along Westminster lines despite being designed as a 'consensus democracy' with participative and deliberative elements (Cairney 2011: 39). In other words, in the light of the argument presented in the Introduction about the need for 'more participatory or deliberative models practised elsewhere', the case of Scotland may reveal there is a rhetorical gap between elites paying lip service to the notion of greater engagement and the actual political reality. In so doing, Scotland many not offer a sharp corrective to the British political tradition (BPT) argued elsewhere by some.

Third, the same sorts of crises associated with UK politics and representative government can be found in Scottish politics, suggesting that major political reform or constitutional change does not represent a solution to such problems. For example, the Scottish Parliament had its own expenses scandal and 'lobbygate' experience several years before Westminster and it also has representatives with similar levels of 'politics facilitating' backgrounds (Keating and Cairney 2006).

Overall, these qualifications suggest that a focus on the independence referendum in 2014, as a symbol of the crisis of the Union, does not give us the full picture. The more likely outcome of Scottish nationalism, articulated and addressed over centuries, is a further extension of political devolution. The cumulative effect of these (generally less visible) crises, addressed by the UK state, is a fundamental shift in the nature of the Union in incremental steps rather than a punctuation or big bang in 2014. The following section identifies the extent to which this discussion ties in with broader conceptions of crisis explored in the book, before outlining the three main qualifications to a focus on the referendum in 2014 as a symbol of the crisis of the Union.

Scotland as a source of crisis, a source of comparison and a source of information

The Scottish case provides two different points of reference for a wider discussion of UK crisis. First, devolution in 1999 is a key example of the UK state adapting to perceived crisis through modifications to the constitutional settlement, along the lines, outlined in the Introduction, of the 'Whiggish-like ability to adapt and incorporate new political and economic situations'. In this case, there is an unusual mix of perceived and created crisis. There may have been a growing desire in the 1990s to address rising levels of Scottish nationalism, linked to measures such as Scottish Social Attitudes surveys, which showed high and/ or increasing levels of 'Scottishness' (Cairney 2011: 146–7) and electoral behaviour from the 1970s, demonstrating a 'democratic deficit' when Scotland generally voted Labour but often received a Conservative UK Government. However, there was also an attempt by devolution supporters to reflect, reinforce and *construct* a 'conservative' sense of crisis, in which the public no longer trusts politicians to devise a particular form of devolution. Devolution was accompanied by a new series of measures to go beyond representative democracy towards new forms of participative and deliberative democracy. As the Scottish Constitutional Convention (the key body set up to advance devolution) argues, Scotland has, 'consistently declared through the ballot box the wish for an approach to public policy which accords more closely with its collective and community traditions' (SCC 1995).

Consequently, second, devolution provides a new source of comparison for the UK. At face value, we may expect that a new political system set up, in part, to solve a growing sense of crisis may be less subject to concerns about levels of public disillusionment with the political process. The 'conservative' sense of crisis should be less apparent in Scotland if there is not only a more collective political tradition but also a political system designed to address the limitations of representative democracy. Yet, as discussed below, the evidence for this sense of Scottish distinctiveness, in tradition and politics, is often overstated and we can identify similar indicators of dissatisfaction.

These two aspects may be closely related if we link current dissatisfaction with Scottish politics to dissatisfaction with its current devolution settlement. Surveys conducted or collated by John Curtice since 1999 (reported in Cairney 2011: Chapter 7) broadly suggest that respondents are ambivalent or unimpressed with the Scottish Parliament's achievements since devolution but that they have far greater trust in the Scottish Parliament or Scottish Government to act in Scotland's interests and would prefer Scottish institutions to have the greatest say in how Scotland is run. Consequently, the perceived solution to a disenchantment with Scottish politics may be to devolve more powers to the Scottish Parliament (short of full independence).

Overall, although Scottish independence is still unlikely, the current constitutional debate may reinforce the long-term, cumulative effect of the UK state's tradition of Whiggish-like adaptation and accomodation to new challenges. The UK state has a long history of accommodating Scottish nationalist demands and each measure has taken us further from a relatively unified Union towards significant political devolution and, potentially, a further devolved settlement that has a passing resemblance to Scottish independence (for a detailed history see Mitchell 2003). The Union took place in 1707 accompanied by various commitments to maintain distinctive Scottish institutions (the legal system, religion, local government and education). The Scottish Office was created in 1885 to take responsibility for a small number of government bodies and the post of Secretary of State for Scotland began as a symbolic gesture to address nationalistic grievances about the threat of UK assimilation (largely through 19th-century attempts to harmonise the education systems in Scotland and England). From 1926, the Scottish Secretary became established as a full member of the UK Cabinet. In the post-war period, the Scottish Office expanded in line with the growth of the UK welfare state. Political devolution in 1999 was therefore an opportunity to provide new scrutiny to the significant range of administrative responsibilities – in areas such as health, education, crime, housing and local government – that developed in this period. This was followed in 2012 by a new Scotland Act devolving more powers to the Scottish Parliament.

In this context, even if the 2014 referendum produces a 'no' vote, it is not unrealistic to see the formation of 'devo max' – the devolution of all responsibilities with the exception of foreign affairs (which may include dealings with the European Union), defence and some economic policies (including monetary policy, if Scotland uses the pound as currency) – in the near future. The UK state has shown an ability, over 300 years, to adapt to crises to maintain the Union, but the cumulative effect may be a fundamental change in the way that Scotland is governed within it.

Support for the SNP does not mean support for independence

The referendum on Scottish independence will take place on the 18th September 2014 following the 'Edinburgh Agreement' struck by the UK and Scottish Governments (Scottish Government 2012). The agreement ensures that the UK passes a Section 30 order (which alters reserved UK and devolved Scottish powers) to give responsibility for the administration of the referendum to the Scottish Parliament. The governments agreed to have a single question on independence (rather than a multi-option referendum including 'devo max'). The next step, in mid-2013, was for the Scottish Government to pass a Referendum Bill outlining the details, including setting the voting age at 16, and producing the final agreed question, 'Should Scotland be an independent country?' Yet, a lead for the SNP in opinion polls, and the decision to have a referendum, should not be confused with high support for independence.

Support for the SNP

The SNP won the Scottish Parliament election by one seat in 2007, forming a single party minority government with 36 per cent of seats (see Table 7.1). In 2011, it won a majority of seats (53.5 per cent) and formed a single party majority government. The 2011 majority may appear small in the UK context of single party majorities exaggerated by the plurality electoral system (at least until the 2010 General Election), but it is generally thought to represent an 'avalanche' win because Scotland's mixed member proportional (MMP) electoral system is designed to stop one party gaining a majority of seats (at least without a majority of votes – the SNP received 45 per cent of constituency votes and 44 per cent of regional votes). Consequently, the SNP argued (immediately after the win) that it had a clear mandate to introduce a referendum on independence – a position that no other party felt able to counter. Yet, the rise in SNP support should not be seen simply in those terms.

The SNP's popularity can best be explained in terms of valence politics, which relates to a tendency 'to vote in accordance with one's opinion of the party, the party leader, the government's record in office or one's prediction about another party's likely performance' (Cairney 2011: 22; on valence politics in Scotland see Johns et al. 2009; 2010; on the UK see Stokes 1992, Clarke et al. 2004). Voters in 2007 appeared to support the SNP based on its image, its leader's image, its vision and its likely record in government; the SNP offered 'a more positive and Scottish oriented agenda than Labour' (Curtice 2009, Johns et al. 2009: 207, 229, 2010). The same can be said for the SNP's landslide victory in 2011 (the Scottish Election Study's equivalent texts have yet to be published, but preliminary analysis suggests the same effect – see http://www.scottishelectionstudy.org.uk/ and Johns et al. 2011). It was 'based largely on voter perceptions of the competence of the SNP in

Table 7.1 Scottish Parliament election results 1999–2011

	1st vote (%)	Seats	2nd vote (%)	Seats	Total seats	% Seats
Labour						
1999	38.8	53	33.6	3	56	43.4
2003	34.6	46	29.6	4	50	38.8
2007	32.2	37	29.2	9	46	35.7
2011	31.7	15	26.3	22	37	28.7
Scottish National Party						
1999	28.7	7	27.3	28	35	27.1
2003	23.8	9	21.6	18	27	20.9
2007	32.9	21	31.0	26	47	36.4
2011	45.4	53	44.0	16	69	53.5
Conservative						
1999	15.6	0	15.4	18	18	14
2003	16.6	3	15.5	15	18	14
2007	16.6	4	13.9	13	17	13.2
2011	13.9	3	12.4	12	15	11.6
Liberal Democrat						
1999	14.2	12	12.4	5	17	13.2
2003	15.4	13	11.6	4	17	13.2
2007	16.2	11	13.9	5	16	12.4
2011	7.9	2	5.2	3	5	3.9
Green						
1999	0	0	3.6	1	1	0.8
2003	0	0	6.5	7	7	5.4
2007	0.2	0	4.0	2	2	1.6
2011	0	0	4.4	2	2	1.6
Scottish Socialist Party						
1999	1.0	0	2.0	1	1	0.8
2003	6.2	0	6.5	6	6	4.7
2007	0	0	0.6	0	0	0
2011	0	0	0.4	0	0	0
Other						
1999	1.7	1	5.7	0	1	3.1
2003	3.4	2	8.7	2	4	0.8
2007	3.1	0	7.4	1	1	0.8
2011	1.1	0	7.3	1	1	0.8

government' – a factor compounded by the SNP's ability to exploit the reduction in support for the Scottish Liberal Democrats, following the UK party's decision to engage in the UK Coalition Government (Cairney 2011: 22).

Support for independence

Put simply, there is not enough support for independence. This argument is best demonstrated using the results from polls asking people to choose between three main options: independence, devolution (status quo or further devolution) and no parliament. As Figure 7.1 (provided by John Curtice, in Cairney and McGarvey 2013) shows, there have only been two points since 1997 when devolution and independence have been within ten percentage points of each other – in September 1997, during the 'yes' to devolution campaign, and in 2005. Notably, the gap *widened* in 2007 (the first SNP election victory) and stayed rather wide in 2011 (the electoral avalanche).[1] While support for independence has risen since 2007 (using this measure), it is only because support was unusually low in 2007.

The SNP's broad plan was to win in 2007 and boost support for independence in office by presenting a strong image of governing competence before campaigning in 2010. It did not have the desired effect in terms of support for independence (although it helped explain its electoral win in 2011). Indeed, ironically, its successful first term may have had the opposite effect – by providing a stronger 'Scottish voice' and therefore reducing Scottish discontent within the Union; showing people that they could enjoy some of the benefits of independence without the risk of 'separation' (Curtice in Cairney 2011: 151, Curtice and Ormston 2011: 31).

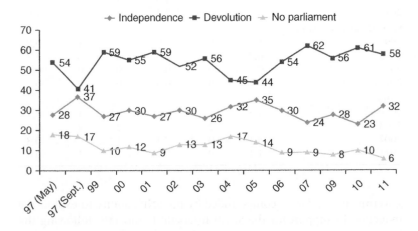

Figure 7.1   Constitutional preferences 1997–2011
Source: Cairney and McGarvey (2013) drawing on Curtice (2012a: 8) and Curtice (2012b: 2).[2]

Of course, this information is now less relevant following the decision not to have a multi-option referendum. Instead, our attention now moves to responses to a single yes/no question on independence. They still generally reveal insufficient support for independence, but the results are often close. Much depends on the question asked. Support for independence tends to be lowest (often below 30 per cent, compared to over 50 per cent against) when people are asked about a 'completely separate state outside the UK' (Cairney 2011: 153). They are generally higher when people are asked about an 'independent country' (the SNP's preferred wording). Yet, as Table 7.2 suggests, the response also varies over time to the same question. Further, this type of question has often produced a plurality in favour of independence (or a majority if we remove 'don't know'). Perhaps worryingly for the SNP, a plurality has not been achieved since 2006, while the highest levels of support were recorded as far back as 1998 (although this might provide some cause for optimism, since it followed the last constitutional change campaign).

Surveys from 2007–12, based on the SNP's previously favoured wording – in which respondents were asked about the Scottish Government negotiating independence with the UK Government (a less scary and more non-committal question) – tended to suggest that there is often little to separate the 'yes' and 'no' responses, with a small 'yes' victory in August 2011 followed by a larger 'no' victory in January 2012 (Table 7.3).

Table 7.2 Support for Scotland as an independent country

%	1998	1999	2000	2001	2006	2007	2009
For	48–56	38–49	47	45	51	33–46	38–42
Against	35–44	42–50	43	49	39	44–46	50–54

Source: Adapted from Curtice (2009: 16–17).[3]

Table 7.3 Support for a negotiated independence settlement, 2007–12

%	August 07	November 07	March 08	June 08	October 08	January 09	May 09	August 11	January 12
Agree	35	40	41	39	35	38	36	39	35
Disagree	50	44	40	41	43	40	39	38	44

Source: Adapted from Curtice in Cairney (2011: 154), Dinwoodie (2011), TNS-BRMB (2012).[4]

This issue has been made all the more important by the recent debate on the wording of the referendum. The Scottish Government's consultation document *Your Scotland, Your Referendum* (Scottish Government 2011) proposed to ask this question: 'Do you agree that Scotland should be an independent country?' The question was described in many party political, media and academic forums as a leading question and challenged in a (February 2012) survey financed by Lord Ashcroft (http://lordashcroft.com/pdf/02022012_referendum_poll_tables.pdf). Further, the SNP's preferred wording did not produce any recent plurality in favour of 'yes' (Ipsos Mori 2012a).

The final outcome, following recommendations from the Electoral Commission, was 'Should Scotland be an independent country? Yes/No' (Scottish Government 2013). Consequently, surveys from 2013 are likely to focus on the actual wording of the referendum, which presents an initial problem of comparability and the tendency of some media accounts to wrongly identify large swings in opinion based on responses to different questions. Still, the figures suggest that, based on the question to be asked, there is currently insufficient support for independence.

Scotland and the 'conservative' conception of crisis: 20 years on?

A significant aspect of elite support for devolution in the 1990s was built on the idea of a general crisis of legitimation, articulated by bodies such as the Scottish Constitutional Convention (SCC) – a (largely self-selected) set of political parties (Scottish Labour, Scottish Liberal Democrat, Green, plus occasional SNP involvement), interest groups (including, for example, the Scottish Council of Voluntary Organisations) and other prominent members of Scottish 'civil society' which formed in 1989 to 'promote the principle (and detailed workings of) of devolved government' (McGarvey and Cairney 2008: 12–13).

Much was made in Scotland of a 'democratic deficit', in which the Scottish population got a government for which it did not vote, particularly from 1979 when a period of Thatcherite government followed the first referendum on devolution; a small majority voted 'yes', but not enough to pass the required threshold of 40 per cent of the voting population (McCrone and Lewis 1999: 17). The relatively high levels of opposition to 'Thatcherism' in Scotland also became intertwined with support for devolution (Mitchell and Bennie 1996), and with narratives about replacing discredited forms of top-down politics based on the concentration and misuse of power associated with a Thatcherite interpretation of the Westminster model (McGarvey and Cairney 2008: 32–4). Devolution was accompanied by an electoral system designed to diffuse power (at least among parties likely to be forced to form coalition or minority governments) and a new series of measures to encourage new forms of participative and deliberative democracy.

In other words, a new Scottish politics would replace the old Westminster model. The SCC's final report in 1995 famously summed up the argument that 'The coming of a Scottish Parliament will usher in a way of politics that is radically different from the rituals of Westminster: more participative, more creative, less needlessly confrontational.'

Following the decision to introduce a Scottish Parliament (after the referendum in 1997), its agenda was followed by the Consultative Steering Group (CSG) – a cross-party group chaired by Henry McLeish (Labour minister and future Scottish First Minister) with members drawn from 'civil society' (associated with the SCC or devolution campaign). It was established by the UK Government (Scottish Office) to construct the standing orders of the Scottish Parliament and articulate the principles it would seek to uphold 'the sharing of power' (between government, parliament and 'the people'); accountability (of government to parliament and the people); accessibility; and, equal opportunity (CSG 1999: 6). Further, its statement of principles would not look out of place as a response to the current crises of representative government explored in Chapters 1 and 2:

> They aim to provide an open, accessible and, above all, participative Parliament, which will take a proactive approach to engaging with the Scottish people – in particular those groups traditionally excluded from the democratic process. To achieve this the Scottish Parliament must avoid adopting procedures which are obscure or archaic. It should adopt procedures and practices that people will understand, that will engage their interest, and that will encourage them to obtain information and exchange views. *We have detected a great deal of cynicism about and disillusionment with the democratic process*; it will require an effort both from the Parliament itself and from the people with whom it interacts to achieve the participative democracy many seek. We firmly believe that the Scottish Parliament should set itself the highest standards. Our key principles are intended to achieve a Parliament whose elected Members the Scottish people will trust and respect, and a Parliament with which they will want to engage.
>
> (CSG 1999: 6; emphasis added)

Notably, this 1990s rhetoric was largely developed by actors within Scotland. As Flinders (2010) suggests, devolution was not sold by the UK Government or Labour Party as the start of a new approach to, or rejection of, the core tenets of the Westminster model – that of representative and 'responsible' government. Indeed, Flinders (2010: 12) suggests the opposite: that a commitment to some constitutional changes (including devolution) may have provided some cover to the protection of majoritarian government in the UK – the Labour Party used a 'rhetorical commitment' to limit constitutional reform to 'win power' and then hoard it within central government. Indeed, one of the few direct and recent references in the UK to a 'new politics' is more closely related to a speech made by the new Deputy Prime Minister Nick Clegg (reported in Duffett 2010):

> So, three steps to new politics. First, sweeping legislation to restore the hard won liberties that have been taken, one by one, from the British people... Second, reform of our politics. Reform to reduce the power of political elites, and to drag Westminster into the 21st century... The third, and final step, is the redistribution of power away from the centre.

In both cases, the meaning of new politics is not precise, referring broadly to an alternative to the elitism practices associated with the BPT and the Westminster model and buzz words such as participatory and deliberative forms of democracy to address the alleged problems associated with representative democracy, which include (McGarvey and Cairney 2008: 12–13):

- a first-past-the-post system which exaggerates majorities and generally ensures that one party dominates proceedings
- a 'top-down' system, in which power is concentrated within government
- an adversarial style of politics with a charged partisan atmosphere in Westminster
- limited links between state and civic society; outside of the voting process, there are limited means for 'the people' to influence government
- an unrepresentative Parliament with a particular lack of women and a rise in candidates with no experience outside of the close world of politics.

Consequently, the Scottish new politics agenda includes the following aims:

- a proportional electoral system, with a strong likelihood of coalition and bargaining between parties
- a consensual style of politics, with an enhanced role for business-like committees and a reduced role for party conflict in plenary
- 'power-sharing' to address the problem of executive dominance in a system where power is concentrated within government
- fostering closer links between state and 'civic society' through parliament (e.g. with a focus on the right to petition parliament, a new civic forum and a new committee role to oblige the executive to consult widely) to reflect a Scottish system with a tradition of civic democracy and the diffusion of power (McGarvey and Cairney 2008: 12–13)
- There is also reference in the SCC to equality in the selection of candidates, perhaps as part of a wider move away from the idea of professional politicians (Keating and Cairney 2006).

The literature suggests two main reasons for this exposition of new politics. The first relates to the idea that Scotland has its own consensual 'political tradition' based on the pursuit of negotiated settlements rather than the imposition of policy (McGarvey and Cairney 2008: 13). In other words, it is presented as an alternative to the BPT of majoritarian representative democracy in which power is concentrated at the centre, leaders are strong and the government knows best (discussed in many other chapters throughout this volume).

This argument was made particularly strongly in the 1990s, following the era of Thatcherism and the tendency for Scottish interests to attempt to agree a common line to use to lobby in the UK and often oppose the UK Government policy (Midwinter et al. 1991). The description of a 'democratic deficit' combined with a Thatcherite policy style reinforced:

> a perception of governmental remoteness and antipathy towards the distinctiveness of Scottish policy traditions. The argument was that if the Scottish electorate was being denied democratic control (or at least government responsiveness), then there would be an alternative, more participatory, venue in which to articulate Scottish priorities.
>
> (Cairney et al. 2009: 105)

Second, the devolution agenda coincided with a political climate that was not conducive to the funding of simply another tier of democracy and politicians:

> A perception of popular disenchantment with politics and politicians suggested that a new Scottish Parliament should not replicate a political system discredited in the public eye...For politics to be participative and inclusive, its Parliament would have to play down party conflicts, assert its right to initiate as well as scrutinize legislation and prove to be a focal point for participation outwith the electoral cycle.
>
> (McGarvey and Cairney. 2008: 13)

The Scottish experience has the potential to provide valuable lessons for political reformers in the UK. In particular, it may provide a corrective to the idea that traditional representative democracy in the UK can be transformed quickly with the introduction of new institutions and processes. Instead, it shows that politicians can still revert to type, adopting a Westminster style of political culture (including power hoarding within government and adversarialism within Parliament) within a new institutional context.

The Scottish experience often seems to show us that new politics was little more than rhetoric; the Scottish political system has operated along 'old Westminster' lines despite being designed as a 'consensus democracy' with participative and deliberative elements. There are notable differences in the nature of Scottish political institutions (including the electoral system, the standing orders of the Scottish Parliament and the petitions process), but fewer notable attempts to ensure a change in behaviour.

In the Scottish Parliament, the relationship between the two main political parties (the SNP and Labour) has always been adversarial, contributing to a traditional (in Westminster terms) Scottish Government and Parliament relationship: 'The first eight years of devolution [1999–2007] were marked by a form of majoritarian (coalition) government that would not seem out of place in the UK' (Cairney 2011: 39). Indeed, Labour sought to form a coalition government to dominate Parliament and make sure that it could not be 'ambushed' by the SNP (Arter 2004: 83). The next four years, from 2007–11, were marked by minority government but a surprising degree of continuity in terms of governmental dominance: 'the Scottish Parliament plenary was used largely as an adversarial forum and committees were not particularly effective'

(Cairney 2011: 40; compare with Flinders 2010: 137–42). The next five years of majority government, from 2011–16, will reinforce that asymmetrical relationship in which Parliament is a peripheral part of the policy process.

In the wider sphere, there is little evidence of a shift towards more participation or deliberation in Scottish politics. Indeed, Cairney's (2011: 13) review of the first ten years of devolution (based on over 30 Scotland Devolution Monitoring Reports) finds almost no evidence of new forms of participation beyond the brief existence of the Scottish Civic Forum and a rather ineffective petitions process.

In other words, even in a Scottish system designed to contrast with old Westminster, the dominant notion associated with the BPT of representative and responsible government has become difficult to shake off. Partly, this is because new politics was accompanied by a fairly traditional political design in which the Scottish Government would produce most policy and the Scottish Parliament would provide scrutiny, with other forms of participation given few resources or institutional support. As Mitchell (2004: 39, 2005: 37) argues, such measures 'appear more symbolic than effective... an elaborate democratic veneer sitting atop long established processes'.

The 'crises' did not stop in Scotland after 1999

Consequently, the same sorts of crises currently associated with UK politics and representative government can be found in Scottish politics. First, the Scottish Parliament had its own 'lobbygate' scandal in 1999 when John Reid's son was caught suggesting to people that his lobbying firm (Beattie Media) could guarantee privileged access to Scottish ministers (Cairney 2011: 198). This attitude reflected a continuation of the sort of 'club government' we associate with UK politics and, perhaps in particular, a Labour party occupying government in the UK and Scotland.

Second, the Scottish Parliament had its own expenses scandal several years before Westminster (Cairney 2011: 7–8, on which this next section draws). There have been some vague calls for Westminster to learn from Holyrood's expenses and second-homes system when, in fact, the latter developed over time as much through partisan debates, self-interest and a response to media criticism as any higher sense of propriety that preceded public attention. For example, the Scottish Parliament has been dogged from 1999 by the issue of different allowances for constituency and regional Members of the Scottish Parliament (MSPs) – a debate made more contentious by the make-up of the Parliament in which most constituency MSPs were Scottish Labour and most regional MSPs were from the opposition parties (before the SNP reversed the trend in 2011). Media attention to MSP costs also became an annual event following the publication of expenses by the Scottish Parliament Corporate Body (SPCB). It reached a crisis point in 2005, following various freedom of information requests by journalists for more detailed breakdowns of expenses, which led to two resignations related to questionable claims – David McLetchie as Conservative leader and Keith Raffan as an MSP. Such cases produced a general feeling among politicians (and Presiding Officer George Reid in particular) that the constant attention undermined the Scottish Parliament's reputation as a transparent body. This prompted the SPCB to publish, in December 2005, a much more detailed account of expenses and initiate in June 2006 an online search facility on the Scottish Parliament's website.

Yet, the levels of unwanted attention did not end there. Instead, there was a shift in media attention to the possibility of MSPs making a profit from sales of their second homes in Edinburgh (the mortgage interest was funded via MSP expenses) which prompted First Minister Jack McConnell to write to George Reid to request that the SPCB consider how to reform the system. While the original intention of George Reid was for the SCPB to produce a legacy paper for consideration by the new Parliament in 2007, his successor Alex Fergusson commissioned an independent review to take a 'first principles' approach to the allowances of MSPs and party leaders, and the extent to which centrally provided services (particularly relating to office equipment) could replace allowances. The Langlands Review recommended abolishing the payment of an allowance to meet mortgage interest payments (by phasing it out by 2011) and setting a cap on claims for overnight stays for MSPs in eligible areas. While this was accepted by the Scottish Parliament in June 2008, the debate also took us back to the very first party conflicts over the office and staff allowances for list and constituency MSPs. Thus, again, the media was able to report that the parties were divided despite voting themselves a significant rise in allowances. The overall outcome is a transparent system that can be emulated by other legislatures, but it is one that resulted from external pressure and internal adversarial debate.

Third, the Scottish Parliament also has representatives with similar levels of 'politics facilitating' backgrounds, discussed in Chapters 4 and 5 (Keating and Cairney 2006). The issue of MP backgrounds is relevant to the popular idea that they have become a group of professional politicians recruited from an increasingly narrow pool, with limited experience of (and therefore a tendency to be detached from) the 'real world' (articulated most recently by Allen 2012 and Cowley 2012). This problem was addressed to some extent by Scottish parliamentary reformers (although the SCC focused primarily on greater gender parity) and, to a larger extent, by Scottish Labour which sought to recruit people from a wider pool (or, at least, fewer men and fewer former councillors). Yet, the Scottish Parliament does not highlight a markedly different experience from that of Westminster or wider European trends (Keating and Cairney 2006). While it elected proportionately more women (an important, if partial, achievement), it also 'accelerated the trend towards professional middle-class leadership' (2006: 56). Further, 'MSPs are more likely than MPs to be white, middle-aged, middle-class, and university-educated with a professional or "politics-facilitating" background' (McGarvey and Cairney 2008: 231). Indeed, one effect of a rise in Conservative MPs in the UK is that the number of narrowly political appointments has reduced somewhat (since they are more likely to have business backgrounds, albeit followed by a spell in politics).

Conclusion

The forthcoming referendum on Scottish independence in September 2014 has prompted consideration of a crisis of the Union in at least one way – in the sense that an important decision has to be made. The evidence does not suggest that the referendum will lead to a break-up of the Union. Rather, we are more likely to witness the longer term extension of devolution, into areas such as welfare and fiscal powers, after a 'no' vote. In this context, the more important effect of Scottish nationalism has been the much longer term effect of the ability of the UK state to adapt. The Union of 1707, which guaranteed some distinctively Scottish institutions, was followed by the introduction of a Scottish Office and Scottish Secretary in 1885, significant administrative devolution from 1945, political devolution in 1999 and (albeit limited) further devolution from 2012. A further extension of devolution may cement the long-term transformation of Scottish government after a series of incremental changes rather than a single post-crisis event.

This chapter argues that the Scottish experience may be as interesting for the comparisons it provides between Scottish and UK practices and the way that they relate to other conceptions of crisis (such as 'conservative'). In particular, the new Scottish political system was designed, in part, to break from the BPT – its type of representative government and its tradition of 'responsible' government. Scotland was designed as a consensus, not majoritarian, democracy and its 'architects' proposed a series of measures to move away from a 'government knows best' approach, in which power is concentrated in central government, to a more participative and deliberative democracy.

The consequences of this apparent contrast of institutional design are unclear. Scotland has a traditional government–parliament relationship. Its efforts to introduce a petitions system and a civic forum have produced few tangible outcomes. It had its own lobbygate expenses scandals. Its representatives are drawn largely from the same kind of pool of recruitment as its Westminster equivalent. In broader terms, the Scottish experience does not challenge the idea of the BPT, in particular, a central government 'club' which still processes the vast bulk of government business.

The Scottish experience shows us the limited extent to which the population (or key parts of it) and its parliament can pay attention to modern governments with huge resources and responsibilities. Instead, the public pays a lot of attention to a very small proportion of government business. This is the context for the political reform agenda in the UK, aimed at rebuilding trust in politicians by (somehow) bringing them closer to the people and encouraging greater participation in politics – the Scottish experience tells us that unrealistic expectations for change may simply produce greater disenchantment with politics.

Modern debates on independence have not been built, in the same way, on the criticisms of representative democracy and clubby politics that we witnessed in the 1990s. Instead, the independence agenda rests on a range of other arguments, from the simple desire for self-determination to, for example, the more complicated arguments about the alleged desire in Scotland for more 'social democratic' policies. There is little evidence to suggest that the independence debate is live because of crises of legitimation in the UK. There is also little evidence to suggest that a general sense of crisis in the UK can be exploited disproportionately to raise support for independence.

On the other hand, the formation of a Conservative-led UK government in 2010 raises the spectre of another 'democratic deficit' in Scotland which still tends to vote Labour in UK general elections. We may be able to identify important arguments linking economic crises to the need for constitutional change – such as the idea that the UK Government will fulfil its commitment to introduce austerity measures in non-devolved areas, raising the spectre of a return to 'Thatcherism', which (however defined) was relatively unpopular in

Scotland. However, we can also identify arguments linking crisis to the need to preserve the Union – such as the idea that small states struggle to deal with economic crises (e.g. the UK Labour government argued that an independent Scotland could not have 'bailed out' the Royal Bank of Scotland). Overall, the debate on constitutional change rests on a more mixed description of crisis in the UK.

Notes

1. See also Cairney 2011: 149–51 which provides a breakdown of categories – including independence in or out of the European Union, and devolution with or without tax powers – but showing very similar results.
2. Curtice produced the figures from Scottish Election Study (the May 1997); Scottish Referendum Study (September 1997) and Scottish Social Attitudes (1999–2011). Note: most years do not add up to 100 per cent because 'don't know' is excluded; May 1997 should read 51/26/17 (Curtice, in correspondence). Methodological note: respondents are asked to choose in a way that might put some people off independence – for Scotland to be 'independent, separate from the UK' (either within or outwith the European Union); for Scotland to 'remain part of the UK, with its own elected parliament' (either with or without taxation powers), or for Scotland to 'remain part of the UK without an elected parliament' (Curtice and Ormston 2011: 28). Support for independence seems to increase to 31 per cent (2007–10) if respondents are instead asked who should be responsible for defence and foreign affairs (2011: 29).
3. Note: the hyphens denote a range of scores from multiple polls taken in that year. In most cases the question is: 'In a referendum on independence for Scotland, how would you vote? I agree that Scotland should become an independent country; I do not agree that Scotland should become an independent country'. 'Don't know' varied from 9 to 18 per cent.
4. The question is: 'The SNP are outlining their plans for a possible referendum on Scottish independence in future. If such a referendum were to be held tomorrow, how would you vote? I agree [I do not agree] that the Scottish Government should negotiate a settlement with the government of the United Kingdom so that Scotland becomes an independent state'. Note: the figures do not add up to 100 per cent because many people 'don't know'.

8
A Crisis of Europe

Charles Dannreuther and Simon Lightfoot

Introduction

On making her way to the 1999 Conservative Party conference, Margaret Thatcher observed that 'In my lifetime all our problems have come from mainland Europe and all the solutions have come from the English-speaking nations across the world.' (The Guardian, 1999). This musing, in many ways, reveals some of the enduring issues defining the UK's relationship with the (European Union) EU. The current Eurozone crisis is just the last in a long line in 'problems from mainland Europe' that have had an impact on UK politics. This chapter examines whether the UK's way of dealing with the EU has changed at all since the economic crisis and whether the crisis in any sense at all challenged the orthodoxy of UK governmental practice. We conceptualise the 'crisis' within our analysis using the lens of two approaches to understanding the UK's relationship with the EU: statist and sociological. The chapter links this UK debate to the legitimacy crisis within the EU that has become exacerbated by the economic crisis, which has created problems for the UK government. The timeframe is linked to the financial and Eurozone crisis that was triggered in 2008 as this is identified as a potentially critical moment both in relation to European integration and the UK's membership of the EU. However, it is crucial to situate the current debates in previous crises in the relationship between the UK and the EU and the extent to which successive governments have failed to make the case for Europe.

The nature of the EU crisis

It is over 40 years since the UK joined the EU and during this period the UK has confirmed both its role in Europe and the durability of its political system under consistent influence from EU policies (Richards and Smith 2002, Bache and Jordan 2006). But by the same measure, the EU has also faced many challenges since its creation as the European Economic Community (EEC). The history of European integration has never been a linear process and the process has seen many setbacks (Geyer 2003). Webber argues that the European Defence Community debates in the 1950s, the empty chair issue in the 1960s, the period of Euro-sclerosis in the 1970s and the referenda defeats in the 1990s could all be seen as crises of European integration (Webber 2013). Optimists argue that out of these crises the EU emerged stronger. However, the level of economic integration between states as a result of the Euro means that writers as diverse as Habermas (2012) and Moravcsik (2012) both argue that the current crisis is perhaps the most serious crisis the EU has faced. The global economic crisis has exposed weaknesses in the Euro design, most notably the fact that it is a monetary union without a fiscal union (Gamble 2009a: 126). The way the EU has responded to the crisis has been documented (Buckley and Howarth 2010), but it is clear that the financial crisis, as the first major challenge for the Euro, has the potential to undermine all previous elements of integration and undermine the solidarity of the EU as a whole (Jones 2009).

The economic crisis is also connected to a legitimacy crisis with support for the European project declining. Gamble (1995) notes that the recession of the early 1990s saw a downturn in support for the EU across all member states. There was a view that

> political support for European integration is cyclical, and is linked directly to economic performance. In times of economic expansion, the gains from cooperation are more apparent and the political task of creation coalitions which will support new initiatives is easier. In times of recession, support is harder to obtain, the costs and burdens of European policies are more apparent, and protectionist, defensive reactions tend to predominate.
>
> (Gamble 1995: 163)

This view must be read alongside the nature of public opinion on the EU. There was said to be a detachment from the project based on a belief that elites knew best and that politics was seen to lie firmly at the national level. 'From the beginning the EU and the European project were primarily a project of national elites and the emerging European elite. Many commentators have observed how much the consensus on Europe, which legitimated the participation of member states in the

European project, was a permissive and passive consensus as far as national electorates were concerned' (Gamble 1995: 166). The permissive consensus perhaps reflected a more deferential time in European politics and much of the current research suggests the permissive consensus has been displaced by a 'constraining dissensus' (Hooghe and Marks 2008, Webber 2013).

The issue of European integration transcends ideology in UK politics and therefore impacts upon all three main political parties (Sherrington 2006). However, we tended to find that the permissive consensus held during time of prosperity, but that EU membership can also expose a lack of accountability in UK politics during time of recession, as the executive asserts its authority. The impact of the Eurozone crisis on UK politics has been likened to both the collapse of the Gold Standard and the Winter of Discontent in terms of its potential legacy for UK politics (Bogdanor 2012). The following sections explore this assertion through the lens of the differing approaches to the UK's relationship with the EU and the concept of dissensus to show to what extent the current crisis represents the potential for a critical juncture in both EU integration and the UK relationship with the EU.

Statecraft and society

The statecraft approach, and specifically that associated with Jim Bulpitt's *Territory and Power*, has endured in the study of UK politics (Bulpitt 1983). Statecraft is 'the art of winning elections and achieving a necessary semblance of governing competence in office' (Bulpitt 1986: 21) and offers 'an account of the nature of governing across the whole polity' (Bradbury and John 2010: 297). The concept of statecraft has been deployed to explain some of the key characteristics of the UK's political economy as one governed by a free economy and a strong state (Gamble 1979, Bonefeld 2010). Buller makes use of this framework to highlight how UK economic policy became Europeanised under successive Conservative administrations and to reveal how Tony Blair was able to deliver successive electoral victories through good statecraft (Buller 2000, Buller and James 2012). Statecraft, and specifically the free economy and strong state thesis (FESS), may have been rekindled by an interest in state centrist analyses (Krasner 1984, Evans. 1985) but these concepts have been increasingly dominant in explaining how the core executive managed EU relations in Whitehall (Bulmer and Burch 1998, 2009). From the statecraft perspective, we would therefore expect that in a crisis the core executive would exploit the opportunity to maximise the electoral chances of the prime minister in power. In other words, the core executive deploys a strategy of 'strategic adaptation' where 'the EU is conceived as an emerging political and administrative opportunity structure which can both empower and disempower domestic policy-makers in the pursuit of their strategic objectives' (Scott 2010: 821). As we shall see below, the UK's relationship with the EU is peppered with examples of this kind of practice, most notably as crises open up new opportunities in the EU that the UK can exploit. Crises create opportunities for the UK core executive to exploit agendas that maximise their popularity with the electorate, allowing them to exert greater control over local government especially through pro-market reforms or service to minimise current or future political costs in a visible way.

But the free economy and the strong state distinction asserts a separation between the state and economy that, typically in a liberal democracy, is false (Bonefeld 2010). It is this societal dimension that is particularly relevant in understanding the impact of the Euro crisis on the UK's political system, because UK society changed during the boom years that preceded the crisis. Europe provided the Thatcher administration (1979–90) with opportunities for achieving scale and scope in societal control by externalising the management of the national economy to the Commission's Directorate General for Competition. As Lord Young presented the Single European Market as the nation's industrial policy in the 1980s (DTI 1988), the EC's Social Policy presented an ally to an embattled trade union movement (Rosamond 1993). But as competitiveness agendas replaced free markets and as collective class identities were replaced by individualism, the New Labour project presented Europe as the best way to react to the forces of globalisation (Hay and Rosamond 2002). The period of finance-led growth that followed drew heavily on the European level to exercise change in society. This increased the power of the UK government against regional centres allowing the UK to focus on policy at the EU level over regional level. But it decreased the government's influence against financial markets so that electoral interest waned and government credibility subsided. As the Conservative Party collapsed over internal divisions, anti-establishment protest votes characterised the European parliamentary elections. By the time the crisis hit in 2007, Europe, which had been a source of strength for the core executive, had become too toxic for it to risk further exploiting. Brown's 'British jobs for British workers' was as ill-advised as Cameron and Hague's referendum pledges. Europe had become a political liability for the core executive as popular sovereignty has come to the economic and political sovereignty that the Court once enjoyed (Gifford 2010).

Stabilising statecraft through Europe policy

As analysts of statecraft, we would expect the core executive to prosecute these opportunities to enhance both the likelihood of re-election and the perception of government competence on each of these occasions. From the essentialist sociological account, we would expect exceptionalism to be driven more consistently by the historic, geographic and cultural distinctions that made UK national interests different from those of the majority of other member states.

The UK has never managed to fully reconcile its relationship with Europe or the EU (Wallace 1997, Schmidt 2006). Even before the UK joined the EU in 1973, the question of the relationship loomed large in UK politics. Churchill's speech to the House of Commons in 1953 summed up an attitude: 'We are with Europe but not of it; we are linked but not compromised. We are associated but not absorbed. If Britain must choose between Europe and the open sea, she must always choose the open sea.' The reconciliation of parliamentary sovereignty in both practice and in political rhetoric with the EU (Broad and Daddow 2010) has frequently attracted essentialist explanations highlighting geography, historic and cultural ties with the USA and the Commonwealth, and notions of identity and domestic politics that have combined to make the UK a 'reluctant European' (Geddes 2004). These essential narratives have persisted in the UK constraining the arguments that might have enabled new interpretations of the UK's relationship with the EU (Schmidt 2006). Without new ideas, the redefinition of the UK's interests as European could not emerge and so old national identities reinforced national territorial boundaries (Eder 2009).

Whilst the awkward partner thesis has become a standard way to examine the UK's relationship with the EU, the UK is no longer 'a minority of one', if it ever was. Sovereignty debates in the UK take on more forms than in those political systems with written constitutional courts to adjudicate on national European boundaries, such as Germany. The political organisation of the debate over sovereignty has been more complex organisationally. Gifford (2010) identifies three forms of sovereignty in the UK's relationship with the EU: *de jure*, or parliamentary sovereignty; economic, or *de facto*, sovereignty; and popular sovereignty. In each of these areas of debate over sovereignty, the core executive has derived greater potential for re-election or competence through its engagement with the EU. So for *de jure* sovereignty we would expect debates over Europe to increase the control of the core executive over parliament; for *de facto* sovereignty, we would anticipate the core executive using Europe to increase its reputation of competence; and finally for popular sovereignty we would expect the core executive to use Europe to maximise its opportunity to win in the ballot box. EU membership in the UK has tended to be elite driven, as in other member states. This also reflects the UK's majoritarian political system. The political elite has tended to adopt a lukewarm attitude towards EU membership since the early days of the project (Young 1998).

The 2008 crisis and elite politics in the UK

The EU is the largest market for UK exports (54 per cent) and the rules and standards for this market are set in the EU. Non-members such as Norway or Switzerland have to apply these rules and standards in relation to the single market without being able to influence them (Kux and Sverdrup 2000). Therefore, the 'British concern has always been to shape the single market in a liberal, Anglo-Saxon direction, building alliances to do so' (Gamble 2012: 475). Under Gordon Brown, the challenges were acute due to the 2008 financial crisis. The financial crisis in Andrew Gamble's terms 'struck like an earthquake at the heart of the institutions, practices and beliefs of those years' (Gamble 2009: 1). At a time when many states lacked the confidence to offer solutions, the UK's commitment to limited but coordinated state intervention under the broader philosophy of pro-market liberalism placed it well in-between the more coordinated economies of the EU and the G20 leadership. Thus, when Brown referred to equipping Europe for global competition it was on the basis of 'British ideas' of 'flexibility, openness and free trade' 'whose time has come' (Gifford 2010: 335). The solutions offered for the Eurozone crisis also had a UK hue, such as supporting liquidity, alongside a morality in its criticisms of debtor states (Hodson and Quaglia 2009). Quaglia (2009) highlights how the UK banking rescue plan announced in late 2008 set the pace for the adoption of similar banking rescue plans across the EU, despite not being particularly innovative. However, the impact of the recession, unfavourable public perception and a series of unfortunate events, meant that the Labour government was unable to translate winning the battle of ideas into winning the 2010 election.

The financial crisis and the subsequent recession therefore presented a clear problem for the incoming Coalition. They had to distance themselves from New Labour's previous policies but there were precious few alternative ideas other than austerity (see Chapter 3). When the recession initially took root in the UK, there was a degree of *schadenfreude* at the failures of the Anglo-American model. But as the US subprime crisis triggered secondary recession across European economies, and even relatively successful ones like Spain also began to suffer, the Eurozone presented the UK's measures as tough, necessary and far better than what was going on 'over there'. It also formed the background for any discussion of the Cameron administration's dealings with Europe. The promotion of austerity sits within the 'free economy' narrative, whilst veto of the fiscal treaty revealed the 'strong state'. We can see that 'the one consistent theme in Conservative approaches to Europe has been its commitment to the principle of a free trade Europe which is often cited as the original basis of Treaty of the Rome that has been distorted by European bureaucracy and regulation' (Gifford 2010: 335).

This bureaucracy feeds into a key theme of this chapter: the nature of the European project as an elite project. In recent parliamentary debates on EU membership, statements such as the UK public being 'fobbed off' by the political elite on the subject of Europe are not uncommon. Calls to give the 'British public a democratic vote on our future relationship with the EU' (Miller 2012) are also common. Indeed, the internal pressures exerted within the Conservatives on the party leadership over this issue led to David Cameron committing his party to an in/out referendum on the issue of EU membership in 2017, which he announced on 23 January 2013. Much of this debate is played out over the idea that the public has been misled over the nature of membership, although Wall argues these claims are 'wide of the mark' (Wall 2012: 330). A recent Eurobarometer showed that the UK public was split in its attitudes towards the EU: 42 per cent had a 'quite positive' or 'very positive' image of the EU, while almost as many respondents had a 'quite' – or 'very negative' view (39 per cent). Thirteen per cent took a neutral stance (neither positive nor negative) and 6 per cent had no opinion on this matter (EC 2011). In relation to the 2017 referendum on membership, recent polls appear to suggest that public opinion tends to be against (Miller and Barclay 2012 for an overview). However, pollsters also 'gently point out that when asked to rank the EU as an issue only 1 per cent of the electorate regard it as the most important issue facing the country and only 4 per cent put it in the top ten issues' (Gamble 2012).

The European Union Act of 2011 signals a significant departure for UK relations with the EU. Past legislation has not sought to make ratification conditional on a referendum in the UK, but proposed amendments have. The European Union Act is a significant departure from the norm, because it was a government-sponsored attempt to impose a referendum requirement in certain instances, such as new competences, certain moves away from unanimity, certain moves to the ordinary legislative procedure, other decisions (e.g. to join Euro). On 24 October 2011, a backbench business debate was held on a motion proposed by the Conservative David Nuttall, calling for a national referendum on whether the UK should:

(a) remain a member of the EU on the current terms
(b) leave the EU or
(c) renegotiate the terms of its membership in order to create a new relationship based on trade and cooperation.

The motion was defeated by 483 votes to 111, with 81 Conservatives defying the whips to vote for a referendum (Miller 2012). Perhaps the most interesting aspect of this rebellion was the number of new MPs who defied the whip to vote against the government, meaning the rebellion wasn't just restricted to usual suspects (Cowley and Stuart 2012). The European Union Act now means that a referendum would be automatic in cases prescribed under the Act and not left to Cabinet decision – the so-called 'referendum lock'. Basically any treaty change of substance that affects the UK will probably trigger a referendum, which at the present time could be lost, which might set in train a series of events that would ultimately lead to the UK leaving the EU – the so-called 'Brixit' (Ennis 2011, Bagehot 2012, Bale 2012).

There was some discussion in 2011 around the changes proposed to the Treaty on European Union in relation to the Euro crisis and the role of the UK government in these discussions. The Eurozone members wished to add change with the addition of a new paragraph 3 to Article 136 of the Treaty on the Functioning of the European Union stating, 'The Member States whose currency is the euro may establish a stability mechanism to be activated if indispensable to safeguard the stability of the euro area as a whole. The granting of any required financial assistance under the mechanism will be made subject to strict conditionality.' This was clearly outside the remit of the European Union Act but Cameron made it clear that he would only accept this change if certain safeguards relating to financial services were agreed by the others. The other states 'simply' decided to proceed with an extra-EU treaty. Cameron's problem here was therefore political: backbenchers were baying for blood/referendum and he was unwilling to make the case against there being a need for a referendum.

It is also clear that the coalition government, like the ones before, is trying to walk the tight rope of party management on the issue of Europe. The government wants to stay in but has to try to retain support and stop the Conservatives splitting on the issue. EU membership is often portrayed in solely negative terms. However, it is clear that the reality is more complex, more dynamic and more to do with the maintenance of credibility by the government than intrinsic characteristics of the UK political system. The debate, to a large extent, revolves around political sovereignty and economic free markets. The UK has been pushing an economic liberalisation agenda since the Single European Act of 1987, regardless of the political hue of the government of the day. The EU has worked for the UK in many ways. The UK government has been able to manage the relationship between the UK and the EU. For instance, during the Thatcher government the concern was to ensure the liberalisation of markets through the single market programme but also ensure limits on the EU's social programme and a significant rebate on payments to the EU. John Major managed to further limit the social impact of the EU with the opt-outs negotiated from the Treaty on European Union, a policy of non-cooperation with the EU institutions employed towards the end of his premiership,[1] and the continued implementation of the single market programme. It was with some optimism that the incoming Blair government started its dealings with the EU. The New Labour government was concerned with the challenges of globalisation and saw the EU as a mechanism for dealing with a complex and interdependent world. As a result, there was initially a positive approach to the EU with the end of the Social Chapter opt-out and a joint Anglo-French European security and defence policy initiative at St Malo. However, one of the first acts of the new government was to negotiate 'a case-by-case opt-in on the chapter on "freedom, security and justice" (Title IV TEC)' whilst retaining national border controls (Adler-Nissen 2008: 665). On a case-by-case basis, the UK government could demonstrate its autonomy and control of the relationship with the EU to the electorate rather than appearing to take the whole Treaty as a package. The other political issue for the Blair administration was membership of the Euro. The decision as to whether or not the UK would join the Euro was left in the hands of Gordon Brown, who designed his five economic tests to attempt to diffuse this difficult political issue (Oppermann 2008).

Under Labour there was a 're-articulation of the British belief in the desirability of an open global economy and acceptance that any European project should be subordinated to this wider goal. A key dimension of this is the emphasis on the inevitable logic of globalisation and the necessity of domestic accommodation' (Gifford 2007: 472). Matthew Watson and Colin Hay (2003 claim that the adoption by New Labour of a political project that ascribed the logic of necessity to globalisation was primarily motivated by electoral interests. It also affirmed the UK core executive's approval of further economic integration with precious little social integration. Kassim (2004) summarises UK dealings with the EU in this period as 'Winning the Battle, Losing the War'. The importance of institutional constraints at both the EU and national level produced a situation where, despite the perceived success of the Constitutional Treaty negotiations for the UK, failure to engage the public created problems for the future. Indeed, Allen goes as far as to blame 'the abject failure of the Blair government to project domestically the "case for Europe"' (Allen 2005: 126–7). In this though Blair is no different from previous prime ministers, none of whom have taken the political risks associated with making a case for Europe.

The future: the EU and the UK

Despite being a non-member of the Euro, the relationship between the UK and the EU is such that the UK still sees itself having a stake in the future of the Euro (FCO 2012). The view is that UK membership can produce solutions to policy problems that are of benefit to both the UK and her EU partners. This view is obvious in the current prime minister. He regards 'membership as something to be nudged by a cool cost-benefit analysis. And weighing those costs and benefits today, Mr Cameron thinks that the right of his party are simply miscalculating where the balance lies. For him, the benefits still trump the costs' (in Miller, 2012). There are clear positive 'national interest' elements of UK European policy from trade through security to political influence (both within the EU and beyond). Has the nation-state become less important? In many ways, the recession has highlighted the limitations of the nation-state. In the EU, we see the Euro economies are closer tied, but as a non-Euro member this does not apply to the UK. A good example of this was a recent 'Future of the Euro' speech by David Cameron. This speech has resonances of the famous speech by Churchill in Zurich where the message was a clear call for a United States of Europe – but a United States without the UK. In his speech, Cameron called for deeper fiscal integration amongst the Eurozone members but clearly with the UK watching from outside (Brittan 2011). In contrast, the UK has been actively utilising the EU context to put pressure on, amongst others, the Irish government to tighten its domestic tax laws, which are being used by large multinationals to minimise their tax liabilities in the UK.

The UK government has been proactive in trying to ensure these policy solutions sit comfortably with its view of how the EU should exit the crisis and then develop. To some extent, the enlargement process, of which the UK has long been a champion, has undermined the UK position. An EU of 28 countries is clearly a more complex beast than the six original members. Whilst the UK has been a long-standing supporter of enlargement to dilute the federal nature of the integration project, enlargement throws up huge challenges for both parties. The Labour Party is struggling to respond to policy challenges such as free movement and the subsequent migration. The current Labour leadership has to deal with the legacy of the decision to allow unlimited free movement in 2004 to the citizens of the new EU member states. The UK was one of only three EU countries to do so but the political cost has been high for the Labour Party as voters react to what many see as unfairness in the system. The issue is also problematic for the Conservatives, given David Cameroon's pledge to limit migration into the UK. EU migration is unrestricted so ensuring the pledge is met means that there has been a tightening up of migration rules from non-EU states.

In the UK, the debate has begun to focus on a possible renegotiating of UK terms of membership. The options range from repatriating EU powers and competences, more flexible integration, a new EU institutional structure, a trade-based relationship, an economic relationship, leaving the EU but staying in the European Economic Area and a single market plus a 'pick and mix' strategy towards EU policies (Miller 2012). Many of these options might be popular amongst certain sectors of the public and certain MPs, but there is a strong belief that many of these options would not be feasible as they would require support from the other 27 member states. As Phinnemore argues, 'there is one form of membership: membership' (in Miller 2012: 28). A good sense of the current debate is obtained by examining the government's audit of the balance of the EU's existing competences. The document does clearly state though that 'Membership of the European Union is in the UK's national interest'. However, it goes on to state that 'as others give thought to the future of the Eurozone and the EU, now is the right time to deliver the undertaking in the Coalition Programme for Government to "examine the balance of the EU's existing competences"' (FCO 2012: 5). The audit will report in 2014. What shape the EU will be in then will be fascinating given the huge political changes seen as a result of the Euro crisis.

Conclusion

Both the models used to understand the UK's relationship with the EU have been challenged by the recent crisis. Europe is no longer a place for politically expedient grandstanding as the momentous decisions being undertaken in the Eurozone are placing considerable political constraints on the UK, even challenging its credibility as a European actor. This has had the effect of forcing far greater transparency on the UK–EU relationship than before. The Review of the Balance of Competences is assessing each Treaty article against the national interest, while the European Act 2011 has legislated a step-by-step process to a referendum when new powers are transferred to the EU. The statecraft tradition that institutionalised core executive control over European policy has been challenged in an unprecedented way.

With 56 per cent of Britons voting to leave the EU (30 per cent to remain) (Boffey and Helm 2012), the UK Independence Party (UKIP) appears to have captured the voice of the disgruntled in UK politics. Furthermore the general malaise in UK political leadership, of which the Coalition is one consequence, has provided an opportunity for this political organisation to capture a politically central section of the electorate. The UKIP challenge also offers Conservative MPs a rationale for rebellion against the party (Lynch and Whitaker 2013). UKIP's single-issue agenda has been simple enough to distract the nation from the complex and confusing negotiations of Brussels with a stark and simplistic offer: a referendum to leave. But UKIP is not just appealing to Eurosceptics but also to political sceptics (Hayton 2010, Ford et al. 2012). The 2013 English County Elections results saw a very strong showing for UKIP, prompting John Curtice to label UKIP's rise the 'most serious fourth party incursion' into English politics since 1945. This has implications for all three major parties (Curtice 2013a), but the analysis highlights the rise of UKIP having a proportionally larger potential impact on the Conservatives (Curtis 2013a). Therefore, we can contextualise Cameron's referendum pledge in electoral terms. However, it also has a clear party unity focus. As Lynch and Whitaker (2013: 337) argue,

An enhanced referendum pledge linked to a route map to policy repatriation, building on the Fresh Start Project's work, may provide a basis for future policy. But if changes in the relationship with the EU are not forthcoming, differences between Conservative Eurosceptics may transform into a starker 'in' versus 'out' divide.

What UKIP and similar parties are offering is a vote of no confidence on the UK political system as well as the EU. It is for this reason that the sociological approach is also limited in interpreting the impact of the crisis because the anti-European vote appears to have little to do with the recession. Despite repeated accusations that the recession is all Europe's fault, few people are convinced of this when so much damaging activity clearly took place in London's 'square mile'. The slow exit from the recession may have something to do with the deflated Eurozone economies, but few, even the Labour Party, have found it easy to differentiate between the austerity measures of Number Eleven and the ordo-liberalism of the EU's Troika.

The Euro crisis in particular highlights the tension for UK government – economic need for access to the single market and risk of contagion from the Euro crisis versus the domestic political challenge of Eurosceptic MPs. A wider issue is the lack of trust in the UK polity clearly reflected through EU membership debate. An example of this was the decision in October 2012 to opt out of a wide range of European police and judicial matters, including the European Arrest Warrant. This signals further disengagement from the EU, although there are some suggestions that this decision might be a 'placatory gesture' to his backbenchers by David Cameron (*Economist* 6 October 2012). Further evidence of the power of Conservative Party backbenchers was seen in July 2013 when the leadership put no barriers in the way of James Wharton's private member bill on making the 2017 referendum pledge a binding law.[2]

The European issue is clearly one that has the potential to divide the two main parties, especially the Conservative Party (Lynch and Whitaker 2013). Yet the limited range of policy solutions is also evident. As other chapters have shown, the crisis also presents opportunities for the institutions of government to develop new powers. Having said this, it appears that the relationship with the EU has more to do with statecraft than awkwardness on the part of the UK. 'Europe has always been a two-level game, and British politicians have played it as gustily as anyone else. They show one face to their domestic parties and voters, and another to the Council of Ministers and the Commission . . . . Europe has become a scapegoat for innumerable ills at home, including many things that are nothing to do with the EU, such as the European Court of Human Rights, and even the Eurovision song contest' (Gamble 2012: 475). We have seen that previous governments have adopted a muddle through strategy and to some extent this has worked. The Europe issue does tend to be more prominent during times of recession than times of prosperity, with the Major government facing the last major recession.

In summary we can see that the Eurocrisis is linked to the crisis of legitimacy within UK institutions. A lack of trust is reflected in the end of the permissive consensus. This produces the situation where current crisis has two possible outcomes for the UK's relationship with the EU. Given the positive tone of the Foreign and Commonwealth Office paper, we might see the issue sink down again if the economy picks up. John Curtice (2013b) argues that David Cameron should encourage his party to focus more on the economy than Europe, but it is unlikely the Conservatives will allow him that luxury given the electoral success of UKIP and repeated opinion polls suggesting the UK public would vote to leave the EU. Cameron might be able to connect the possible renegotiation of the UK's relations with the EU, which he has explicitly linked to the 2017 referendum pledge, with the outcome of the Balance of Competences Review. The idea of a renegotiation has the tacit support of other EU states, notably the Dutch government, so the UK may not be isolated in its calls for change and therefore more likely to be able to show results.

It is clear that one scenario is to see the UK 'on the sidelines' in the EU, forced to apply rules it has no influence over. Yet this solution might ensure party or even Coalition government unity. The other possibility, one that is increasingly being discussed, is the Brixit. The length of the crisis within the Eurozone and the seeming inability of member states and the European institutions to restore faith in the project leads some to see a critical juncture in the process of integration (Bale 2012). The EU has, over its 60-year history, faced a number of crises which it has come through relatively unscathed. Possible solutions to the current crisis see the EU becoming stronger via fiscal union as a result. The total collapse of the integration project is unlikely (Moravcsik 2012), but we might see a smaller EU with states forced to leave or, in the case of the UK, deciding to leave. At the time of writing the future is far from certain, although it is clear that the current mood in the Conservative Party is hostile to EU membership on its current terms. What is clear is that Mr Cameron's political gamble to pledge to hold a referendum in 2017 is designed to maintain Conservative Party unity and ensure the Coalition government sees out its term of office. Whether the 2017 referendum ends the historical discussions around the UK's EU membership is something that only time will tell.

Notes

1. The policy of non-cooperation involved the UK government blocking EU legislation. Miller (1996) identified about 75 instances of UK blocking tactics, many in areas where there would otherwise have been strong UK support and in some cases where the UK had been the leading advocate.
2. The pledge to hold a referendum by the end of 2017, following a renegotiation of the UK's relationship with Brussels, cannot be made law in the form of a government bill because of Lib Dem opposition. The private members bill was backed unanimously by (mainly Conservative MPs) on its second reading on 5 July 2013.

9
A Crisis of the Financial Sector

Helen Thompson

Introduction

Perhaps no group in the UK has been more vilified over the past few years than bankers. The crisis of confidence in their working practices has manifested itself in widespread disgust at the individuals in the sector who enriched themselves and dismay at the immense consequences of their actions during the boom. If there is an epicentre to a more general crisis of confidence in UK institutions addressed throughout this volume, it is perhaps the banks. Yet there is a paradox here. Any examination of the underlying phenomenon that produced this political response must recognise that the banking sector is structurally prone to crisis and that such crises are inherently reputational because banks depend on maintaining confidence. As James Stewart in the film *It's a Wonderful Life* explains to panicking customers, 'the money's not here'. One person's money is in another's house and the citizens of Bedford Falls are lending each other the money to build homes and pay it back 'as best they can'. Only if they all 'have faith in each other' can the bank work. Nonetheless, even allowing for the fact that banking crises happen with some frequency, the banking crisis that began in the UK in the summer of 2007 has been exceptional in its fallout. The crisis followed a period in which banking had been a central foundation of the UK economy's growth for a decade and was also a significant component of a fiscal regime that had facilitated a sharp increase in the size of the public sector. As a succession of dramatic stories have come to the fore about exactly what the banks were doing during the pre-crisis years, the crisis has increasingly damaged the legitimacy of banking as a profit-making activity and precipitated a political backlash against both banks and the financial aspects of capitalism, and quite possibly some aspects of market economy and wealth-creation more generally.

Trying to understand the dynamics of the crisis raises several questions of analysis, both comparatively and temporally. Clearly, the UK banking crisis is part of a wider international financial crisis. Consequently, locating temporality and context in ways specific to the UK is difficult. Moreover, the temporal origins of the international financial crisis are contested. Some have argued that it has long historical roots either as part of a long-standing crisis generated by the structural contradictions between capitalism and democracy (Streek 2011), or in a crisis of the neo-liberalism that emerged out of the 1980s (Gamble 2009a). Yet there are aspects to the financial crisis that do not fit that comfortably into such general narratives of the present relationship between the economic and the political. There was a specific international economic context that made this particular financial crisis possible, not least a period of extraordinarily low interest rates, and that was generated by the recent, and historically unparalleled, economic relationship between East Asia and the United States. Meanwhile, much of the drive towards the rise of mortgage securitisation and subprime lending was actively encouraged and financially supported by the USA and is thus in itself hard to characterise as the product of neo-liberalism (Thompson 2012). There are also some particular difficulties of temporality in analysing the particular UK banking crisis as part of the shifts that took place in the UK economy in the 1980s. Whilst the 1986 Big Bang reforms to the City radically changed London as a financial centre, the institutional, international and regulatory changes that allowed the UK banking sector to develop as it did in the decade prior to the crisis occurred in the late 1990s and early 2000s, and did not necessarily follow from those reforms. The UK banking sector in 2007 was radically different from what it had been in the 1980s in practice, regulation and political perception and it was this sector that emerged in the pre-crisis decade that thereafter unravelled.

For this reason, this chapter concentrates on the crisis in the UK banking sector that emerged in the decade preceding the crisis of 2008, whilst recognising that this version of the banking sector developed within a broad context of a longer period of change in the UK economy and the politics around it. The first section traces the development of the UK banking crisis and the institutional response to it. The second considers the banking crisis as a systematic crisis of confidence in virtually every aspect of what banks do and the political fallout of that breakdown in trust. The final section seeks to situate the banking crisis in the context of a possibly much wider political crisis in the UK, as discussed in greater detail in Chapters 1 and 3.

The banking sector: From radical expansion to crisis

The financial services sector has long been important to the UK economy and banking has constituted a crucial part of the sector. In the early 1990s, the UK had in comparative terms a strong but not exceptional banking sector. In 1990, the balance sheets of UK banks were the equivalent of 75 per cent of GDP. By 2000, they amounted to 143 per cent and, in 2010, an astonishing 450 per cent (Bank of England 2010: 321). Of the G20 states, only Switzerland has banks that have balance sheets as large in relation to the economy. The UK's banks are now around four times larger in this respect than the US banks (Bank of England 2010: 324).

Structurally, from the late 1990s to 2007, the UK retail-banking sector changed in several fundamental ways. Most simply, a succession of building societies – including Northern Rock, Bradford and Bingley, and Halifax, which merged with Bank of Scotland to become HBOS – demutualised and turned themselves into banks. Meanwhile, the UK retail-banking sector was penetrated by investment banking. In the decade after the Big Bang reforms of 1986, UK investment banking had struggled to compete internationally. By the middle of the 1990s, a number of investment banks had been sold overseas and those commercial banks that had entered the sector were withdrawing. However, within a few years of what appeared to be the demise of serious investment banking in the UK, three commercial banks – Barclays, HSBC and RBS – began to operate as serious universal banks, engaging in large-scale investment activity as well as deposit-taking, with retail deposits providing capital for securities and derivatives trading. Barclays had sold its investment bank, BZW, in October 1997, but then recreated one in Barclays Capital and turned it into one of the largest investment banks in the world, a position strengthened by its purchase of the American assets of Lehman Brothers in 2008 after that bank's bankruptcy. Until the late 1990s, Barclays had been a bank driven by retail profitability, but more latterly it became a bank driven by its investment arm. For its part, RBS used its acquisition of NatWest in 2000 to turn itself into an investment banking operation, and took itself to another level in the sector by purchasing, as the lead bank in a consortium, the investment part of the Dutch bank ABN Amro. Meanwhile, after various earlier failed efforts at investment banking, HSBC moved systematically and ambitiously back into the sector in 2003. Even the UK commercial banks that eschewed the universal bank model also began, from the late 1990s, to use various investment banking methods, including the securitisation of their loans (Augar 2010: 130–7).

By the beginning of the 21st century, banks from across the restructured sector began to borrow far more heavily. Declared UK bank liabilities rose from £3.15 trillion in 2000 to £7.92 trillion in 2008, a rise of 151 per cent (OECD Banking Statistics). Whilst in 2000 UK banks covered virtually all their lending with customer deposits, in 2008 there was a £900 billion gap between deposits and the loans they had made (Institute for Fiscal Studies 2009: 153). Five of the UK banks that grew rapidly after 2000 – RBS, HBOS, Northern Rock, Alliance and Leicester, and Bradford and Bingley – were dependent in their business models on wholesale short-term debt (FSA 2009: 35). Among these banks, Northern Rock went even further, relying not on short-term wholesale markets but on securitisation for funding, leaving only a quarter of its loan book covered by retail deposits (Augar 2010: 154). Put simply, without regulatory encumbrance, the UK banks greatly increased their balance sheets and created a fundamental new risk in retail banking on top of the basic vulnerability created by holding long-term assets and short-term liabilities (Engelen et al. 2011: 119).

The expansion and structural transformation of the UK banking sector from the late 1990s was actively encouraged by the New Labour government. On coming to office in 1997, it stripped the Bank of England of responsibility for supervision of banks and gave regulatory authority to a newly created Financial Services Authority (FSA). The regulatory regime practised by the FSA was designed to be 'light-touch' on the fundamentals of banking activity whilst stacking up thousands of pages of rules on micro-matters on which banks had to be compliant. The FSA gave the banks a large amount of autonomy on the prudential issues of liquidity and capital and did not engage at all with the leverage-driven business models of those banks that were dependent on wholesale short-term debt (FSA 2011: 27). Even inside the weak regulatory framework, the FSA was willing to act as an effective facilitator of what banks wished to do. For example, from June 2006, Northern Rock was supervised in a unit within the FSA whose primary responsibility was insurance (FSA 2008: 2). When, at the end of March 2007, Northern Rock reported a capital position that was in breach of its regulatory requirement, the team supervising the bank acted as if the breach had not occurred (FSA 2008: 54).

New Labour Treasury ministers were explicit that the whole purpose of the regulatory regime was to create competitive advantages for London as a financial centre, particularly after the United States tightened accounting regulations after 2001 (Balls 2006, Brown 2006). When banks complained that the demands the FSA did make on them were too burdensome, New Labour ministers acted to help them. In 2005, Prime Minister Tony Blair wrote to the FSA complaining that it was 'hugely inhibiting of efficient and impeccable companies that have never defrauded anybody' (FSA 2007). The Pre-Budget Report of 2005 delivered by Chancellor of the Exchequer Gordon Brown contained a ten-point plan for reducing the burden of regulation on the financial sector, including lessening reporting requirements 'which reflect[ed] the greatest concerns that businesses have raised with the Government about the burden of financial services regulation' (HM Treasury 2005: 45). The New Labour government also facilitated the capture of the FSA by the bankers themselves. Between February 2003 and January 2004, the FSA fined HBOS three times over maladministration of PEPs and ISAs, serious inadequacies in monitoring and internal auditing failures, and money laundering rule breaches (FSA 2003a, 2003b).[1] In January 2004, the Chancellor nominated the Chief Executive Officer of HBOS, Sir James Crosby, to the FSA board. Thereafter, the FSA took no further action against HBOS until after the government had engineered a sale of a virtually insolvent HBOS to Lloyds TSB.

The New Labour government also worked to defuse criticism of the banks' practices and its own regulatory framework. In 1998, it commissioned a review into commercial banking in the UK. The review published a report that was highly critical of the banks, declaring that they were anti-competitive, overcharged personal and small business customers and procured higher profits than would otherwise be the case by doing so, and failed to provide customers with information that could allow accountability (HM Treasury 2000). The Cruickshank Report was also highly critical of the new FSA regulatory regime, arguing that

> Changes are required to ensure that the FSA is sufficiently independent from government and industry pressures' and that 'the Treasury should re-examine its relationship with the FSA ... ensuring its objectives, operations reflect the fact that the FSA is a regulator independent of Government'.
>
> (HM Treasury 2000: xi–xii)

Yet by the time the Treasury received the report, the Chancellor was committed to a growth model in which the banks were crucial. Consequently, Treasury ministers proceeded to ignore most of the review's general recommendations and all the recommendations on regulation both in the immediate aftermath of the review and as part of the review of the 2000 Financial Services and Markets Act, which had formally created the FSA (HM Treasury 2004).

By 2009 the UK banking sector was in deep crisis and unrecognisable in structure and ownership from what had emerged in the preceding decade. The crisis began in August 2007 and was triggered by the collapse of the mortgage-backed securities market in the United States and the subsequent tightening of wholesale funding markets. Northern Rock found itself closed out of all three of the wholesale markets in which it borrowed and asked the Bank of England for emergency support (House of Commons Treasury Committee 2008: 16–17). Within two years of the beginnings of the crisis at Northern Rock, few of the top UK banks were recognisable. Northern Rock and Bradford and Bingley were nationalised. Alliance and Leicester was sold to the Spanish bank Santander, and HBOS was sold, under government encouragement and after the suspension of competition rules, to Lloyds TSB. RBS and the Lloyds Banking Group, created out of the Lloyds TSB takeover of HBOS, had been recapitalised by the UK state, in the case of RBS leaving UK Financial Investments Limited with an 83 per cent share. Barclays was recapitalised by the China Development Bank and the Qatar Investment Authority. Only HSBC and Standard Chartered remained unscathed in this respect.

The financial crisis in 2008 and the need for the state to find large-scale resources to save various banks from insolvency have led to pressure for reform. Whilst some (Froud et al. 2010, 2011) have argued that these reforms have been cosmetic if the aim were a fundamental transformation of the place of finance in the UK economy, the UK banking sector in practical terms does not look as it did in the pre-crisis years.

Strikingly, part of the pressure for reform has come from those institutions, especially the Bank of England, most closely connected to the banking sector (Baker 2010: 656–7). Senior officials at the Bank of England have used strong language to condemn the banks. Andy Haldane (2010: 2), the Executive Director for Financial Stability, for example, published an official Bank paper in 2010 describing the banking industry as a 'pollutant' that 'endanger[ed] innocent bystanders'. Since coming to office, the Coalition government has pushed a substantive reform agenda. In June 2010, it announced that it would abolish the FSA and transfer responsibility for banking regulation by the end of 2012 to a new Prudential Regulation Authority located within the Bank of England. In October 2010, it legislated to turn its predecessor's one-off tax on bankers' bonuses into a permanent levy on the global balance sheets of UK banks and the UK operations of foreign banks. Meanwhile the UK government and regulatory institutions have taken a comparatively hard line on international regulatory change. When in 2010 the Basle Committee on Bank Supervision agreed a new international regulatory regime, Basle III, the then Governor of the Bank of England, Mervyn King, publically criticised the proposed capital standards as insufficient 'to prevent another crisis' and called for banks having to hold 'very much higher levels of capital' (King 2010). In terms of the implementation of Basle III, most EU member-states have looked to dilute some requirements, whilst, by contrast, the Coalition government in 2012 secured the right within the EU framework to implement Basle III in full.

The Coalition government has also acted on the separation of retail and investment banking. In June 2010, it set up an Independent Commission on Banking under the chairmanship of John Vickers. The September 2011 Vickers Report recommended, among other things, that banks ring-fence their retail operations from their investment activities. The Coalition government accepted the recommendations and committed to legislate by 2015 to force change upon the banks with a transition period up to 2019. In December 2011, it ordered RBS to shrink radically its investment activities, and four months later, RBS sold the Dutch investment operation of ABN Amro. Whilst there is no evidence that the Coalition government wishes to downsize the financial services sector, it has appeared determined to prevent the banks returning to important aspects of the pre-crisis years. In accepting the Vickers Report, the Coalition argued that whilst it wished to see the UK: 'at the heart of the international banking and finance sector' that this required 'establishing a stable financial system in the UK' and this could not come from providing implicit taxpayer subsidies to a small proportion of the financial institutions that constitute the City'. (HM Treasury 2011).

Whether this scale of commitment to reform of the banking sector can be maintained without an alternative short- to medium-term growth strategy must be open to question. It is one thing for a UK government to envisage a different kind of banking sector that is less fundamentally dangerous to the rest of the economy and the fiscal position of the state, and it is quite another to eschew the benefits the banks provided in the pre-crisis decade without an alternative source of provision for the same economic and political goods. The longer the recovery takes, the more any UK government will be caught between the competing imperatives of curtailing banks and acquiescing to them. Nonetheless, there can be no return to the banking sector as it was in the UK in 2007. Significant parts of it have simply disappeared or will remain under state control for the foreseeable future. Moreover, the banks are still too heavily exposed abroad to begin significantly expanding their balance sheets again any time soon, and the international financial and political context that supported the previous expansion has changed too profoundly to be re-established.

We have no faith

The practical crisis in the banking sector is inextricably linked to a breakdown of confidence in what banks do at all levels. This failure has multiple dimensions that have interacted with each other to produce an intense crisis of trust that goes to the heart of banks' legitimacy as profit-making corporations. At the centre of that crisis lies the relationship between banks and their stakeholders from customers to shareholders to creditors. For retail banks to operate at all, customers must have confidence in the safety of their deposits in them. The public face of the banking crisis began in September 2007 when this confidence among customers of Northern Rock evaporated, precipitating the first bank run in the UK for 146 years. Just over a year later, there was a corporate run on RBS with one oil corporation withdrawing several billion pounds in one transaction. Rumours of the run prompted a 20 per cent fall in the bank's share price, leaving RBS to tell the Treasury on the morning of 7 October 2008 that it would run out of cash in the afternoon (*Daily Telegraph* 2011a). That communication prompted the New Labour government to establish a bank recapitalisation fund that led to the UK state taking a stake in RBS and the Lloyds Banking Group. Almost five years after the crisis of the autumn of 2008, a YouGov *Sunday Times* poll found that 60 per cent of voters did not trust high-street banks to look after their money (YouGov 2012).

Beyond the financial crisis and all that it revealed about the breakdown of prudence in retail banking, bank customers were also given reasons for profound dissatisfaction with the services they received. In 2010, the FSA published a review into banks' practices for dealing with customer complaints, which severely criticised the banks for incentivising staff to ignore complaints to ensure bonuses and said that its enforcement division was looking at how the Bank of Scotland

and RBS dealt with customers' complaints (FSA 2010, *Financial Times* 2010a, 2010b). In the same year, the FSA reprimanded banks over the mis-selling of payment protection insurance after receiving 1.5 million complaints (*Financial Times* 2011). After the High Court ruled in March 2011 that the banks had to reopen previously dismissed claims for compensation for thousands of people sold such products, the big banks were forced to announce that they were putting billions of pounds aside for compensation on payment protection cases. In April 2012, after a campaign through a business action group called Bully-Banks, the FSA began investigating the mis-sale by banks of interest rate swap agreements to small- and medium-sized businesses that had left many firms with large liabilities and some bankrupt. Two months later, the FSA announced that it had found 'serious failings' in the sale of interest rate hedging products by Barclays, HSBC, Lloyds and RBS to some small- and medium-sized enterprises and had required the four banks to provide compensation (FSA 2012a).

The dissatisfaction of customers with banks was matched by shareholders in a number of banks where the value of shares had fallen dramatically since the autumn of 2008. This anger was particularly acute in the case of Lloyds Banking Group. In the summer of 2008, Lloyds TSB had no direct and a limited indirect vulnerability to the subprime mortgage-backed securities market, a modest exposure from securitisation, and a relatively small funding gap (Augar 2010: 187). After its takeover of HBOS and subsequent recapitalisation by UK Financial Investments Limited, the share price for Lloyds Banking Group collapsed and remained in mid-2012 at around 20 per cent of its value before the acquisition. In June 2010, a group of UK shareholders in Lloyds Banking Group signalled their intention to take legal action against the Lloyds TSB Board for the failure to disclose the effective bankruptcy of HBOS when, in 2008, Lloyds TSB put taking over the Scottish bank to its shareholders. In January 2012, US share holders in the bank filed a class action suit on the same grounds. Meanwhile, in March 2012, a shareholders' action group notified RSB and the bank's former directors that it wanted compensation for what it said was the bank's failure to disclose pertinent information in a rights issue that the bank made in April 2008.

Beyond this crisis of confidence of stakeholders, there has been much collective fury about virtually everything that banks do and the bankers who do it. Various investigations by the FSA and the House of Commons Treasury Committee after the autumn of 2008 exposed that senior people at failed banks were unqualified for the jobs they held. In February

2009, evidence at the Treasury Committee revealed that the former Chief Executive Officer (CEO) of RBS, Fred Goodwin, had no banking qualifications. In the same month, a former Head of Group Regulatory Risk at HBOS, Paul Moore, told the Treasury Committee that he had been sacked by the bank after telling the HBOS board that its practices posed a serious financial risk and that he had been replaced by a sales manager with no experience in risk management (*Financial Times* 2009). In its report on Northern Rock, the Treasury Committee stated that 'the Financial Services Authority should not have allowed nor ever again allow the two appointments of a Chairman and a Chief Executive to a "high-impact" financial institution where both candidates lack relevant financial qualifications' (House of Commons, Treasury Committee 2008: 33).

Public wrath was manifested most immediately and acutely in a huge backlash against bankers' pay, pensions and, in particular, bonuses. This anger was focused particularly sharply on Fred Goodwin, especially after the Treasury revealed in February 2009 that he had walked away from RBS's failure with a £700,000-a-year pension. Politicians from all three main parties thought they had to respond to the strong perception that bankers are motivated by greed and make at least some stance against the prevailing banking culture. The Brown government put significant pressure on Goodwin and eventually reduced his pension by around 50 per cent. In 2012 the Coalition government acted to strip Goodwin of his knighthood. This was followed a year later by James Crosby, the former boss of HBOS, asking for his knighthood to be revoked following the publication of a highly critical report into the collapse of HBOS by the Parliamentary Commission on Banking Standards, a request that was acceded to in June 2013. More generally, in December 2009, the then Chancellor of the Exchequer Alastair Darling introduced a 50 per cent tax on bankers' bonuses of more than £25,000 over and above the rate of income tax, and in early 2012, David Cameron intervened to persuade the CEO of RBS, Stephen Hestler, not to take an annual bonus.

As anger about remuneration mounted, public scrutiny also turned to banks' behaviour as taxpayers. In March 2009, *The Guardian* published leaked documents from a whistleblower about Barclay's tax affairs which suggested that the bank was engaged in tax avoidance in the UK and was at the centre of an international scheme of aggressive tax avoidance through tax havens (*The Guardian* 2009a). In the same month, RBS admitted that it had engaged in international tax avoidance schemes and announced that it was disbanding the department responsible (*The Guardian* 2009b). After ongoing pressure on the banks, and Barclays in particular, the then CEO of Barclays, Bob Diamond, admitted in 2011, in response to a question from the Treasury Committee, that in 2009 the bank had paid only £113 million in tax in a year when it made £11.6 billion in profit, a rate of 1 per cent (*Financial Times* 2012a). As with bonuses and pensions, politicians wanted to be seen to act. By the end of November 2010, the Coalition government had signed up the 15 largest banks to a code on taxation in which they agreed not to engage in tax avoidance, something that was not asked of any companies outside the banking sector despite a series of stories during the same period about tax avoidance by other large corporations. Most strikingly, the Coalition government used retrospective legislation in February 2012 to counter what it deemed to be aggressive tax avoidance by Barclays (*Financial Times* 2012b).

In the summer of 2012, the crisis of the banks' relationship with the public deepened further. Over the course of around a month, RBS left thousands of its customers without access to their accounts after a computer failure; a High Court judge ended a trial of former directors of a Christmas hamper business on the grounds of HBOS' behaviour in the run up to the company's bankruptcy; the FSA made its announcement on the mis-selling of interest rate hedging products to small- and medium-sized businesses; Barclays was fined a total of £290 million by the FSA, the US Justice Department and the US Commodity Futures Trading Commission for misconduct relating to the London Interbank Official Rate (LIBOR) and the Euro Interbank Official Rate (EURIBOR); the FSA revealed that other banks were under investigation for the same practices; a US Senate committee exposed HSBC's facilitation of the money-laundering activities of drug cartels and terrorist groups; and Standard Chartered Bank paid a $340 million fine to the New York Department of Financial Services for sanction-busting in regard to Iran. Political pressure, including from the Labour Party leadership, grew for a full judicial inquiry into the whole banking sector. Whilst parliament rejected the option, the pressure for criminal prosecution of bankers intensified, and in the media frenzy about the succession of scandals the Scottish prosecutor revealed that several Scottish banks were under criminal investigation (Reuters 2012).

The pressure for criminal investigation of the banks in part reflected a sense that bankers were getting away with fraudulent and corrupt behaviour that would be prosecuted in other walks of life. It also reflected a lack of confidence in the ability of those responsible for regulating the banks to hold the banks accountable or then themselves for failing to do so. In December 2010, the FSA said that after an internal investigation into RBS enforcement action would not be taken against the banks and that the internal report could not be published for reasons of confidentiality. It soon became clear that despite the FSA's investigation no report had been written. Under political pressure, the FSA promised a report by March 2011 which did not appear until some nine months later and when it did upheld the original decision against enforcement proceedings (FSA 2011). In July 2011, the FSA said that it would not report on Bradford and Bingley's collapse, claiming there were no lessons to learn and, five months later, it said it would only publish a report into HBOS if it found wrongdoing that required formal action (*The Guardian* 2011, *Daily Telegraph* 2011b). Even when the FSA did act on a number of bank practices, the punishment appeared limited. The fine imposed by the FSA on Barclays over LIBOR and EURIBOR was tiny in relation to the bank's profits. When the FSA censured the Bank of Scotland for 'very serious misconduct, which contributed to the circumstances that led to the UK government having to inject taxpayer funding into HBOS', it said that it would not fine the bank because that would punish taxpayers twice since HBOS had become part of Lloyds Banking Group which had been recapitalised through UK Financial Investments Limited (FSA 2012b).

Time and again since the crisis of the autumn of 2008 the message from majority public opinion in the UK has been that the banks are greedy and incompetent and that politicians have not done enough to punish them and force them to change. A YouGov poll in September 2011 (Figure 9.1) showed that more than 70 per cent of voters thought that governments had been too soft on the banks and this figure rose to more than 80 per cent among those over 40.

A further YouGov *Sunday Times* poll in late June 2012 (Figure 9.2), after the LIBOR revelations, showed that 82 per cent of all voters did not think that the banks had improved their behaviour since the banking crisis began in 2008. Again, older voters were more likely to have a negative view of the banks' ongoing behaviour.

What is perhaps striking about these survey results is how strong the belief among the vast of majority of citizens is that nothing has changed in the banking sector. Although politicians from all parties have been responsive to popular opinion on the banks both in the angry language they have used to describe banks and bankers and in the action they have taken from taxes on bonuses to regulatory reform, the perception persists that the status quo has prevailed. What began as a crisis of banking has, as the crisis developed, touched the broader question of whether

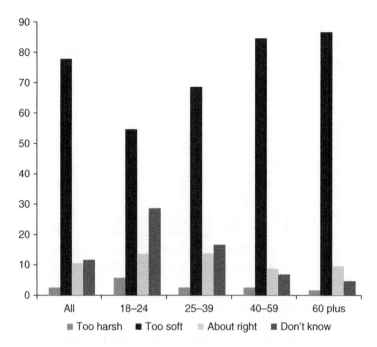

Figure 9.1 Attitudes to government handling of banks since the financial crisis
Source: YouGov for the *Sunday Times* September 2011.

the UK's political institutions and political class are disconnected from its citizens.

Conclusion: From a banking crisis to a crisis of politics?

As we saw in Chapters 1 and 3, in part the banking crisis extends into questions about UK's representative democracy because of the specific relationship between politics and the banks that developed in the decade before the crisis. Politicians in both main parties encouraged bank expansion because they believed it was central to growth and in so doing maintained close relations with bankers. Several bankers were given knighthoods and appointed to policy commissions. Gordon Brown, for example, not only put James Crosby, the disgraced CEO of HBOS, on the FSA, he appointed him to head a government forum and produce a report on identity cards and was a close personal friend of the banker. Even the upper echelons of the civil service appeared strongly connected to the financial services sector in new ways. Most

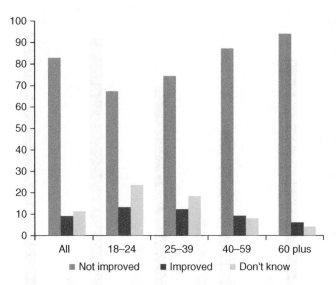

Figure 9.2   Attitudes to bank behaviour since 2008
Source: YouGov *Sunday Times* June 2012.

conspicuously, Sir Jeremy Heywood moved from being Principal Private Secretary to the Prime Minister from 1999 to 2003 to become Managing Director of Morgan Stanley before going back to the Cabinet Office in 2007.

But the political reach of the banking crisis is also broader. The revelations about the behaviour of banks and bankers have fitted into a larger narrative in recent years about self-enriching powerful elites. Like MPs and parts of the media, top bankers have appeared to act as if they believed that the rules and the law do not apply to them. Even more than with other parts of what Ferdinand Mount (2012) has called the 'new few', their excesses have made some of them extremely rich. If power and wealth have become increasingly concentrated in a new elite, then executive bankers, and indeed others in the financial services sector, are at the heart of the phenomenon. Over the past three decades, and the last one in particular, there has been a much higher differential between executive pay and that of others. One study suggested that the ratio of the remuneration of chief executive officers at FTSE companies to the average UK employee rose between 1998 and 2010 from 45;1 to 120:1 (*Forbes* 20 September 2011). Among executives and senior managers who saw their remuneration shoot up over the last decade, none did as well as those who worked in financial services.

The High Pay Commission (2011: 9), set up in 2010 by the pressure group Compass and the Joseph Rowntree Charitable Trust, calculated that between 1998 and 2007 60 per cent of the rise in the overall income share of the best paid 10 per cent came from those who worked in the financial services sector.

Perceptions of there being a wealthy and powerful elite apparently immune from the law are always likely to fuel distributive debates in times of economic difficulty whether that be in regard to income, fiscal policy or tax compliance. In this case, the reaction against bankers as part of an elite, whether or not that elite is in power terms new or not, was fuelled by the enormous size of the remuneration packages on offer to those at the top, when taxpayers became financially responsible for the spectacular failures of some of their beneficiaries. But the specific political fallout of the politicisation of high remuneration and its contribution to income inequality is unclear. Certainly, over the past few years, shareholders of some corporations have voted down remuneration reports and the Coalition government moved in early 2012 that it intended to legislate to reform company law to make the results of such votes binding. However, despite the amount of public anger focused on bonuses, the reform agenda of politicians has been more muted on pay than over the regulation of banks, and remuneration at the senior levels of banking remains extremely high. If little in practice changes, then the perception of many that a wealthy and politically well-connected elite has captured politics and that politics itself cannot produce significant economic and social change in the face of that is likely to persist.

Meanwhile the banking crisis and the political response to it are crucial components of both the crisis of growth discussed in Chapter 3 and the issues for UK politics generated by the depth of the ongoing problems of the UK economy. The banking crisis has exposed the reality of the weakness of much of the economy over much of the past two decades. Politicians in many advanced-economy states, not just in the UK, looked towards an expanding financial services sector as international competition in lower value-added production mounted in the wake of the rise of various non-Western economies, not least China and India. Although from 1993 to 2007 the UK economy as a whole saw 15 years of uninterrupted growth with only modest inflation in sharp contrast to the performance of the economy since the early 1970s, a significant amount of that growth was the product of leveraging by the financial services sector (Weale 2009). Put differently, growth in the UK economy in the decade before the crisis depended on the business models of the failed banks, which depended on the absence of prudence, which depended on regulatory failure. The UK economy has no substitute sector that can quickly replace the financial services sector generally and the banks in particular as an engine of growth. The weaker the banking sector is the slower the return to a growing economy will be.

The fallout of the growth crisis also has fiscal consequences. The financial services sector and banks in particular were crucial to the fiscal calculations of the New Labour government after the first term when it began to increase public expenditure significantly. The sector provided a volume of tax receipts through both corporation and income tax significantly higher than its proportion of national output (HM Treasury 2009). The longer the banking sector remains mired in crisis, the less tax revenue it will produce at a time when the UK is running a large budget deficit and when demographic change and the rising cost of health care are putting further long-term strain on the state's finances.

Even if the banks were to be replaced by a new growth model, then the need for them to act as a source of capital to the rest of the economy and to lend to the state remains. As it is, the nature of the banking crisis makes giving the banks the leeway to lead a recovery by pursuing profit-making through extending more credit impossible. Banks cannot simultaneously be significantly expanding lending, tightening capital and liquidity requirements, purchasing government bonds, and paying a high dividend to the state (in the case of RBS and Lloyds Banking Group). Banks might have existentially bankrupted themselves in the realm of public opinion, but the political expectations that are now heaped on them are also frequently incoherent. In this sense those, like Flinders (2012) and Riddell (2011), who have argued that contemporary politics suffers from a crisis of excessive expectations and that these expectations have been encouraged by the political class have a point if their argument is applied to this particular case, rather than the wider context of politics discussed in Chapter 1. During the decade prior to the crisis, banks were helping to provide many citizens at a macro level with things they wanted whether that be growth, cheap mortgages or increased public expenditure as the basic rate of income tax fell, and now the banks that did those things are being treated as problematic without the material goods in question being repudiated. But these expectations, incoherent as they are, have also arisen in part because of the sheer multi-dimensional nature of the practical and trust crisis that banks and the politicians who encouraged them brought into being. The banking sector developed in an unsustainable way, regardless of any expectations citizens have of it or of the politics around it. Banks cannot go back to acting as they were doing because the state could not withstand having to bail out what remains of the retail-banking sector in the UK. Yet at the same time the UK economy cannot mount a sustainable recovery if banks, as profit-seeking corporations, do not act as a trustworthy conduit of channelling money from savers to investors, and that, by the nature of banking itself, is a risk-based activity. Legitimacy issues require that politics is seen as a site of collective action that makes banks change and they also require that politics creates some buffers between banks and political anger about them.

Note

1. In 2012 the matter of the second fine in April 2003 became the subject of criminal proceedings and the content of the press release is no longer available (FSA 2003c).

10
A Crisis of Regulation
Daniel Fitzpatrick and Adam White

Introduction

State regulation – the use of standard setting, behaviour modification and information-gathering tools by state institutions to influence the everyday actions of public and private actors – has been a long-established feature of UK governance (Moran 2003). While its form and content have evolved over time, in line with the prevailing political-economic logic of the era, regulatory change is often particularly acute during periods of crisis. In many ways, regulation and crises are natural bedfellows. In moments of crisis, when the fabric of society is threatened, states (especially liberal democratic states with high public expectations placed upon them) need to act. Regulation has become a matter of recourse in these circumstances. Braithwaite (2008) accordingly observes that regulatory innovation and expansion often follows crises, and the recent global financial crisis – marked in the UK by the first run on a bank since the late 19th century – is no exception.

This chapter explores how the financial crisis and its aftermath have impacted upon the form and content of state regulation in the UK. It argues that there have been (at least) two notable shifts, each of which has important implications for the trajectory of state regulation. First, there has been a shift in the relative influence of the two narratives which have come to dominate regulatory discourse and practice over the past three decades or so: what Lodge and Wegrich (2011: 728–9) term the 'hierarchy' and 'individualist' narratives. The hierarchy narrative is more interventionist in orientation, viewing state regulation as a legitimate mechanism for realising social, economic and environmental objectives. The individualist narrative is more libertarian, regarding state regulation as an infringement on private autonomy that should only be employed to address specific market failures (such as inducing competition in monopolistic or oligopolistic markets). While these narratives are founded upon polarised assumptions and arguments, in reality political actors draw upon elements of both at the same time, usually guided by a mixture of ideological belief and a need to respond to political contingencies of the day. Half a decade after the onset of the financial crisis, it is becoming apparent that on balance political actors in the UK are drawing upon the individualist narrative with much more regularity than the hierarchy narrative. One notable consequence of this shift is that the more the individualist narrative takes hold, the more the financial crisis and its aftermath can be seen as giving rise to a subsequent crisis – or at the very least delegitimation – of state regulation.

In exploring this putative 'crisis of regulation', it is necessary to disaggregate between sectors, for at this level the relative influence of the two narratives can vary significantly. Indeed, it is at the sectoral level where the second shift in the post-2007 regulatory landscape can be found. In the wake of the financial crisis discussed in detail in Chapters 3 and 9, there has been a tendency for politicians of all colours to make a distinction, at least implicitly, between financial regulation and non-financial regulation, and to strike a very different balance between the individualist and hierarchical narratives with regard to each. In the strategically significant financial sector, the hierarchy narrative has been more prevalent, for it allows politicians to assume the popular (and many would argue necessary) position of chastising the Treasury, the Financial Service Authority (FSA) and the Bank of England for not imposing proper order on 'casino banking', and to propose the introduction of more robust regulation so as to avoid future crises. Put differently, it allows politicians to (be seen to) actively respond to what are commonly considered to be the main causes of the financial crisis. The individualist narrative has certainly not disappeared from this sector; the ongoing importance of financial services to the 'Anglo-liberal growth model' (see Chapter 3) means that any moves to tighten financial regulation are inevitably balanced with the more libertarian logic of innovation and entrepreneurship embedded within the individualist narrative. Elsewhere there is a different story to be told. In the less politically sensitive territory outside the financial sector, where the vast majority of state regulation takes place, the individualist narrative has been espoused in much bolder terms, with politicians across the spectrum pledging to strip back burdensome 'red tape' in order to promote growth and to ease the strain on the Exchequer.

These two shifts are by no means clear cut. They are rooted in broader historical contexts, subject to the fast-moving ebbs and flows of crisis politics, and distorted by the often sizeable distance between political rhetoric and reality. This chapter seeks to trace these shifts through the complex political-economic landscape of the financial crisis and its aftermath. It does so over four sections. The first examines the antecedent conditions which facilitated these particular shifts, emphasising that the individualist narrative was already on the rise and that the financial sector had already been accorded a special status before the crisis hit. The second traces key regulatory patterns from the onset of crisis to the 2010 General Election, focusing on the divergent rhetorical practice used in relation to financial regulation (which was guided by a complex mix of narratives) and non-financial regulation (which was guided by a strong version of the individualist narrative). The third analyses the distance between rhetoric and reality under the Coalition government, illustrating that while the government has so far largely realised its technocratic vision of regulatory reform in the financial sector, its attack on non-financial regulation has not been nearly as successful. The fourth concludes by considering the core question: To what extent has the financial crisis given rise to a broader crisis of state regulation?

Antecedents: regulation before the crisis

In most aspects of political decision-making, the Thatcher and Major governments were guided by a neo-liberal policy which emphasised the centrality of markets in the delivery of public services. They accordingly viewed state regulation as a necessary evil. In the Littlechild Report (1983: 7), which established the institutional basis for regulating the privatised telecommunications sectors – and set the pattern for subsequent privatisations – regulation was viewed as a means of 'holding the fort' until competition arrived. When it became clear that regulation was not going to wither away after a smooth transition to free market provision, the Conservatives took the view that regulation, as a constraint on the entrepreneurial freedom of market actors, should be stripped back. This position was made clear in a succession of Department of Trade and Industry (DTI) reports with such unambiguous titles as *Lifting the Burden* (1985), *Building Businesses not Barriers* (1986), *Releasing Enterprise* (1988) and *Deregulation: Cutting Red Tape* (1994). In Weatherill's (2007: 1) words, 'the rhetoric of deregulation dominated the day' – even though in reality the Conservatives often found it difficult to realise their deregulatory ambitions because many ministers had become dependent on the various regulatory bodies orbiting their departments (Flinders 2008: 75–81). Nevertheless, in this period the Conservatives were constructing and perpetuating a distinctly individualist narrative in line with their neo-liberal policy agenda which demonstrated a lack of faith in regulation and prioritised market freedom.

The emergence of New Labour and its 'Third Way' approach to public service delivery – a pragmatic blend of statist social democracy and market neo-liberalism – led to the individualist narrative becoming increasingly balanced against the assumptions and arguments of the hierarchy narrative. After 1997, the Labour government reformulated the 'deregulation' agenda into a 'better regulation' agenda, which reconceptualised regulatory governance in more positive terms. In addition to their ongoing role as facilitators of market competition, regulators also became 'governments in miniature' (Arthurs 1985), empowered to use discretionary rules to construct more effective partnerships between state, economy and society and to realise a wide range of social, economic and environmental outcomes. In Radaelli's (2007: 192–3) words,

> When Labour returned to office in the UK after the Conservative era, one of the first changes in the cabinet office was the reorganization of better regulation bodies and their mission, with an explicit emphasis on consultation, transparency, and regulatory quality (as opposed to the old deregulation agenda, based on 'quantity'). The old compliance cost assessment turned gradually into a more comprehensive appraisal of proposed legislation, based on the analysis of a wide range of benefits and costs affecting different stakeholders – not just the business community, but also citizens, civil society organizations, and public administration.

From 1997 onwards, it became the responsibility of the newly christened Better Regulation Unit (formerly the Deregulation Unit) to ensure that interconnections between economy and society were ordered more formally, effectively and democratically through state regulation, rather than operating on the institutional presumption that 'free' markets were the most efficient means of delivering public goods and services.

A key example of this reformulation was Labour's 1997–98 review of public utilities' governance, which proposed a number of regulatory reforms: a new statutory power for the secretary of state to issue guidance on social and environmental matters (HC 50, 1996/97); an organisational change from the Director-General model in which executive decisions are essentially made by one individual to a board model in which executive decisions are made by a number of expert individuals drawn from different backgrounds; and the establishment of separate consumer councils designed to feed into the regulatory decision-making process (HC 89, 1996/97). Although limited to the energy sector in the eventual Utilities Act 2000, it was claimed at the time that such reforms represented a shift towards 'a new regulation' (Gray and Jenkins 1998). These reforms not only illustrate how the hierarchical ordering capabilities of the public utilities regulators were being extended far beyond the narrow economic remit bequeathed by the Conservatives, but also that these capabilities were in theory being fashioned according to a democratic vision of regulation that was more deliberative, transparent and accountable (Black 2000, Prosser 2010). In reality, though, this democratic vision was to operate in the 'shadow of hierarchy' (Héritier and Rhodes 2011), so remaining within the elitist conception of democracy set out by the British political tradition (BPT). For in 'regulating the regulators' the better regulation agenda served to significantly enhance the powers of central actors, such as the Cabinet Office and the Treasury, in the regulatory sphere (Black 2007), thereby sustaining the power-hoarding model of UK government discussed in Chapter 1.

This more interventionist and 'deliberative' agenda came about largely as a result of three key factors. First, the reformulation of 'deregulation' into 'better regulation' was in terms of electoral statecraft (Bulpitt 1985) a rhetorically powerful way of defining Labour against the previous era of Conservative rule. It clearly signified a change in political direction, which was a central concern for a political party which had been out of office for almost two decades. Second, a commitment to more collaborative, democratic governance in the field of regulation was a core component of Labour's 'Third Way' ideology, which was predicated on the involvement of a wide range of stakeholders from the public, private and third sectors in the development of policy and the delivery of goods. Third, this new agenda was informed by and further reinforced a corresponding transformation taking place outside the UK. At the global level, the Organisation for Economic Cooperation and Development (1997) was beginning to emphasise the importance of improving the quality of regulation in a way that dovetailed with the Better Regulation agenda. At the European level, the Mandelkern Group on Better Regulation (2001) and the European Commission's White Paper on Governance (2001) were advocating high-quality – as opposed to low-quantity – regulatory governance arrangements (Radaelli 2007).

These initiatives in effect created a far-reaching epistemic community whose core beliefs were centred on open and democratic regulatory governance, thereby facilitating policy convergence on this issue (Knill 2005, Radaelli 2005).

It is important to note, however, that the ascendance of the hierarchy narrative did not eclipse the assumptions and arguments of the individualist narrative. While Labour were drawing from the hierarchy narrative in many aspects of their regulatory discourse and practice, they were simultaneously maintaining a commitment to neo-liberal ideology, free markets and a reduction in the size of the 'quango state',[1] emphasising that while regulation was being expanded to more effectively order relations between state, economy and society, this was not being done at the expense of market entrepreneurialism. Significantly, as we saw in the last chapter, these individualist undertones were especially evident in the financial sector, where the tripartite regulatory regime created by Labour in 1997 was immediately notable for its 'light-touch' character – an orientation in large part explained by the fact that the government's Anglo-liberal growth model was heavily dependent on freely available (or loosely regulated) bank credit (see Chapter 3 and Hay 2011). Nevertheless, the important example of the financial sector aside, the overall balance during the late 1990s and early 2000s appeared to be shifting in favour of the hierarchy narrative.

However, in the mid-2000s regulatory rhetoric and practice experienced another period of realignment as the assumptions and arguments individualist narrative once again entered into the political foreground – a trend which has been amplified in the post-financial crisis landscape. In 2004, Labour commissioned two reviews of the UK regulatory environment with the intention of exploring different methods of reducing the administrative burden of regulation on business. The first review, conducted by Sir Philip Hampton – a prominent figure in UK commerce – recommended that the regulatory state be streamlined through a narrowing of the criteria used by regulators to conduct inspections of and take enforcement actions against businesses; applying a risk-based approach to regulatory inspection and enforcement; and by simplifying the structure of the regulatory system more generally (Hampton 2005). The second review, conducted by the Better Regulation Task Force (BRTF), recommended that regulators employ a more sophisticated system for measuring the cost of regulatory action on business and that regulators adopt a 'one in, one out' policy whereby every new condition is offset with the removal of a pre-existing condition (BRTF 2005). Both sets of recommendations were readily accepted by the government, signalling what Baldwin (2006: 203) has called a 'fundamental shift of the UK Government's rhetoric on regulation'. Armed with these recommendations, the government set about reframing state regulation as a burden on private autonomy and market innovation – a position which, as Weatherill (2007: 2) notes, was reminiscent of the Thatcherite agenda of the 1980s. The umbrella term 'better regulation' was kept, but now 'better' meant 'less'. Turning this rhetoric into practice, the BRTF was reconstituted into the Better Regulation Commission and, alongside the newly created Better Regulative Executive, given the task of implementing this new regulatory philosophy.

As one might expect, the primary contextual driver behind this individualist shift was economic in nature. Quarter on quarter GDP growth in the UK economy fell throughout 2004, reaching lows not previously seen since the early 1990s. It was with this in mind that Labour sought to stimulate economic growth through the medium of regulatory reform. This was certainly the case in the increasingly important financial sector. The UK's economic growth over the previous decade was in large part dependent on the widespread availability of bank credit. So when growth began to slow, the government sought to stimulate recovery by further curbing the already light-touch regulations on bank lending (see Chapter 9). This explains the introduction of the Regulatory Reform (Financial Services and Markets Act 2000) Order 2007, which sought to 'streamline' requirements on the FSA to consult on changes to securities listings (Thain 2009: 436), and the Investment Entities Listing Review, which permitted 'a flexible, more principles-based approach to investment strategies' (FSA 2007). These decisions were to come under very close scrutiny in the coming months.

Reinforcing this economic rationale was a changing interpretation of risk among the UK's political elite. Dodds (2006) argues that during the late 1990s and early 2000s, it was becoming common practice for stakeholders to see state regulation as a way of eliminating risk to their organisations, in turn precipitating an unwelcome growth – or 'creep' – of state intervention. As Hampton and the BRTF were publishing their reviews, Blair and the Labour leadership were denouncing the unrealistic expectation that risk could be eliminated through state regulation and instead began promoting the notion of risk toleration (Dodds 2006). This concept was premised on the idea that where risks could be objectively quantified it was permissible for regulators to take action, but where risks took on a more subjective quality – which was frequently happening in the more deliberative regulatory forums created in Labour's first term – their management should be devolved to the organisational and individual level. It was against this backdrop that Tony Blair pledged to 'roll back the tide of regulation' (2005: 193–4) in a speech entitled 'Common Sense Culture, not Compensation Culture'. This shift in the understanding of risk further contributed to the reassertion of the individualist narrative in the mid-2000s. State regulation was now being criticised not only on the grounds that regulators curtailed the entrepreneurial ambitions of market actors, but also that a rules-based culture was eroding individual and organisational resilience, ingenuity and agility, turning private actors into risk-averse dependents of the state. It is clear, then, that by the time the financial crisis emerged in 2007, faith in state regulation was already on a downward trajectory. It is also evident that financial services were coming to occupy a privileged position in regulatory discourse and practice, giving this sector a different trajectory to other sectors of state regulation. Both trends were to be accentuated in the post-financial crisis landscape, though in often unpredictable ways.

From the crisis to the election

One of the defining characteristics of any crisis is that it catches those in power off-guard. This was certainly the case with the Labour government and the onset of financial crisis in 2007. Just weeks before the run on Northern Rock in September 2007, Gordon Brown could be found waxing lyrical about the 'golden age for the City of London' (Brown 2007), apparently unaware that equity prices in the banking sector were about to fall by 80 per cent over the next 18 months (Haldane 2010: 1). The government's initial regulatory response to the crisis therefore took the shape of day-to-day 'fire-fighting' rather than coherent and strategic planning, and this fire-fighting drew from both the hierarchy and individualist narratives in often contradictory ways, as politicians sought to navigate the twists and turns of the fast-changing circumstances of the financial crisis. Lodge and Wegrich (2011) note the emergence of two further regulatory narratives in post-2007 politics: what they term the 'egalitarian' and 'fatalist' narratives.[2] But, apart from a few appearances in speeches by state actors, these narratives have remained peripheral to the mainstream debate on state regulation, which has continued to coalesce around the dominant assumptions and arguments of the individualist and hierarchy narratives. In this sense, the shifts that have occurred in the post-financial crisis regulatory landscape have taken place within the existing parameters of state regulation.

The government's first response to the unravelling financial crisis was to establish arrangements for depositor protection in an effort to enhance financial stability while also maintaining the 'UK's reputation as the pre-eminent location for financial services' (Treasury, FSA and Bank of England 2007: 8). As the crisis escalated, the government was forced to change tack and, as we saw in Chapter 9, it nationalised Northern Rock and Bradford and Bingley, publicly funding capital investments in Lloyds TSB and the Royal Bank of Scotland and establishing the arms-length regulatory body United Kingdom Financial Investments (UKFI) to oversee these investments. The Treasury had previously avoided such policy options fearing that direct intervention in the banking system would irreparably damage the City's international reputation and credibility (Gamble 2009b). But the gradual realisation that the collapse of the entire financial system was not only possible but probable if action was not immediately taken resulted in a change in attitude, eventually leading to 'the largest UK government intervention in financial markets since the outbreak of the First World War' (Bank of England 2008).

These interventions were justified – in a largely post-hoc manner – by drawing upon the assumptions and arguments of the hierarchy narrative. Addressing the 2009 Labour Party Conference, Brown asserted that the government had been – and was still being – forced to decide 'whether markets left to themselves could sort out the crisis; or whether governments had to act' (Brown 2009b). Faced with this stark choice, the government was of course opting for the interventionist strategy. These broad-brush hierarchical sentiments were then reinforced by an appeal to the egalitarian narrative: 'Bankers', Brown (2009b) continued, 'had lost sight of basic British values, acting responsibly and acting fairly... And so this is our choice – to toughen the rules on those who break the rules... markets need morals'. This proved to be a popular line with a public whose confidence in the banking system had fallen from 90 per cent in 1983 (higher than any other institution) to just 19 per cent in 2009 (Curtice and Park 2011: 141, Johal, Moran and Williams 2012; see also Chapter 9).

On the surface, these positions represented a decisive break with the 'light-touch' individualist narrative which Labour had perpetuated in the financial sector over the previous decade. Yet at the level of 'deep politics' (Dale Scott 1996), the individualist narrative was still informing regulatory practice, if not official discourse (where it failed to resonate with the national mood). This is neatly illustrated by two key moments in the trajectory of post-crisis financial reform. First, the role of chairing the new regulatory body UKFI was given to Sir Philip Hampton, principal architect of the individualist regulatory strategy which had permeated governmental circles since the post-2004 reformulation of the Better Regulation agenda. Rather than searching for new figureheads with new ideas, the government was turning to familiar faces for more of the same. Second, instead of significantly redrawing the regulatory arrangements between the Treasury, FSA and Bank of England as many were calling for, the Treasury White Paper *Reforming Financial Markets* (2009) sought only to effect relatively minor changes to this tripartite structure, mostly by adding a few additional statutory powers to the already light-touch regime (Froud et al. 2010). The White Paper therefore signalled a largely 'business as usual' approach to financial regulation, or a 'timid rebranding' as one observer put it (McDonnell 2009). Though it should be noted that the actors populating these regulatory institutions were not necessarily left quite so unchanged. Mervyn King (2009), the then Governor of the Bank of England, argued that strong hierarchical banking reform was 'essential', in line with 'other industries [where] we separate those functions that are utility in nature – and are regulated – from those that can safely be left to the discipline of the market'. For Andrew Haldane (2010: 2), the executive director for financial stability, the systematic risk to the wider economy and general public created by the banking industry is a negative externality that should be subject to robust regulation and even prohibition, in the same way as other types of 'pollutant[s]'.

These important caveats aside, one explanation for the government's 'business as usual' approach to financial regulation in the face of much popular and expert opinion is that they lacked an alternative growth strategy in the wake of the financial crisis (see Chapter 3). Growth was still largely dependent on the widespread availability of bank credit, and so placing too many regulatory restrictions upon the financial sector would only serve to undermine this strategy. In addition to its central role in growing other sectors of the economy, the financial sector also remained significant in terms of its contribution to employment levels and tax revenues. Macartney (2011: 197) observes that in the year before the crisis hit, the financial sector employed 1.3 million people and contributed 11 per cent of income tax and 15 per cent of corporation tax. Against a backdrop of rising unemployment and escalating public debt, the government thus had further incentive not to regulate this sector too stringently. Complementing these instrumental rationales was the firmly embedded individualist culture running through the political and financial sector elites. Since the Big Bang reforms in 1986, political and financial elites have perpetuated a light-touch regulatory culture in this sector, as evidenced by Labour's permissive tripartite regime established in 1997. This culture has survived in the post-2007 era, as Froud et al. (2010: 32) remark, 'What makes the White Paper especially significant is that its approach to the regulatory system is not idiosyncratic; it reflects a consensus about the design of the regulatory system, and the meaning of the banking rescue, that has come to unite both regulatory and banking elites.'

As such, there was no single, unified narrative informing Labour's discourse and practice towards financial regulation in the wake of the crisis. Labour policy-makers were instead generating a hybrid narrative which drew heavily on state intervention (especially in rhetorical terms), reinforced where appropriate with egalitarian language, but also informed by a 'deep politics' of individualism. Taken together, Labour's narrative thus portrayed state regulation as part of the initial problem (lack of pre-crisis regulatory oversight in the financial sector), part of the post-crisis solution (more regulatory oversight) and part of a new post-crisis problem (balancing regulatory oversight with the Anglo-liberal growth model, the need for a competitive financial sector and a deep individualist culture). It was also a problematic amalgamation in political terms as, in the lead up to the 2010 General Election, it caused Gordon Brown to portray himself as the 'man-of-the-hour' who saved the country from the worst of the crisis, as the former Chancellor responsible for putting in place the light-touch regulatory arrangements which contributed towards the crisis in the first place and as the present Prime Minister allowing many of these arrangements to stand – a dissonance which almost inevitably resulted in electoral failure.

Yet though contradictory, it is important to emphasise this amalgamation does not amount to a crisis of state regulation in the financial sector. While state regulation was implicated in the causes of the financial crisis, it was always seen to be part of the solution. It was outside of the financial sector where a crisis of state regulation was taking shape. Interestingly, Labour was not an agent of this latent crisis. One of the most striking features of Labour's agenda in the pre-election debates is that their regulatory rhetoric did not extend much beyond the financial sector. Financial reform was a central pillar of their electoral statecraft, but state regulation as a whole was conspicuous in its absence, barely featuring at all in their manifesto (Labour 2010). In this regard, the Conservatives deviated sharply from Labour.

In terms of financial sector regulation, the Conservatives were in broad agreement with Labour. They saw lack of regulatory oversight in this sector as an important factor contributing towards the onset of crisis, and regarded the hierarchical strengthening of financial regulation as part of the solution – actually going further than Labour in this respect by proposing to abolish the FSA and to re-empower the Bank of England (Conservatives 2010: 29). But like Labour, they also lacked any alternative to the Anglo-liberal growth model – indeed, as Hay (2011: 3) remarks, the Conservatives are 'if anything more pure and pristine exponents of the old paradigm'. This, together with recognition of the sector's importance in terms of employment levels and tax contributions, and even closer ideological attachment than Labour to the individualist culture running through the City of London, meant that the Conservatives too interweaved their hierarchical assumptions and arguments with key components of the individualist narrative.

However, the Conservative's regulatory discourse went far beyond the financial sector, where it took on a very different character. Building on the generic lack of faith in regulation which had been accruing in recent years, they extended an untempered version of the individualist narrative into virtually every other sphere of state, economy and society, largely through their nebulous Big Society agenda. A key part of this agenda was substantially reducing the burden of the 'increasing amounts of red tape and complex regulation [which] have eroded Britain's reputation as a good place to invest, create jobs or start a business' (Conservatives 2010: 20). Another was 'curtailing the quango state', where a sizeable proportion of the UK's regulatory bodies could be found (Conservatives 2010: 70). In their sanguine vision of a Conservative-led country, these attacks on state regulation would serve to stimulate economic enterprise and decrease public spending, and any problems which seeped into the regulatory vacuum left behind would be solved by a 'bigger society' motivated by duty and volunteerism (Smith 2010).

Significantly, this powerful individualist rhetoric found resonance not only with the political and economic elite but also with the public. The Big Society agenda lacked popular support. Public attitudes surveys consistently revealed that Big Society rhetoric did not enjoy a great deal of traction amongst the electorate, with the majority of the public often confused about what it actually meant (Ipsos Mori 2010, YouGov 2011). Yet the more specific agenda of rolling back state regulation did attract popular support. As Curtice and Park (2011: 141) reflect, 'despite the furore about bankers' bonuses and the need for the government to nationalise some banks, there is no sign of a renewed enthusiasm for greater government intervention in the economy'. It can therefore be reasoned that the success of the Conservative's critique of state regulation lay not in its electoral packaging but in its ability to connect with the individualist sentiments which had become deeply ingrained in popular and elite consciousness prior to the onset of crisis. Outside of the financial sector, a new set of individualist assumptions and arguments were thus marginalising the hierarchy narrative and delegitimating state regulation.

As the 2010 General Election approached, one key issue at stake was the future trajectory of the regulatory state. A Labour victory was likely to bring about further hierarchical reordering of financial regulation informed by a 'deep politics' of individualism, with largely unknown consequences for state regulation outside of the financial sector – though as Flinders and Skelcher (2012: 328) point out, when the Conservatives first announced their plans to abolish sizeable sections of the quango state (and by extension a significant number of public regulators), Labour soon followed with similar commitments. A Conservative victory would result in a similar balancing act in the sphere of financial regulation, but promised a profound retrenchment of the remainder of the regulatory state. The subsequent emergence of a Conservative-led coalition government would therefore appear to throw the wider regulatory state into crisis. However, in the event this was not necessarily to be the case.

Rhetoric and reality: the Coalition and regulation

In forming a coalition government with the Liberal Democrats, the Conservatives had to make concessions on some issues. Their regulatory objectives were not among them, for their new coalition partners were also committed (in a slightly more muted manner) to balancing 'better global financial regulation' with 'reduc[ing] the burden of unnecessary red tape by properly assessing the cost and effectiveness of regulation' and 'cut[ting] quangos across government' to make cost savings (Liberal Democrats 2010: 57, 25 and 103). Yet despite this favourable context for bringing about real change, there has been an uneven relationship between pre-election rhetoric on state regulation and the post-election reality.

In the sphere of financial reform, there has so far been a relatively close correlation between rhetoric and reality, in large part because a sizeable amount of political attention and resources has been targeted at this strategically significant and electorally sensitive sector. As we saw in Chapter 9, one month after coming to power the new Chancellor George Osborne asked Sir John Vickers (Chief Economist at the

Bank of England during Labour's first term) to chair an Independent Commission on Banking (ICB) to consider the reform of financial regulation. Acting on the ICB's recommendations, the Coalition government made a commitment to separate (or ring-fence) the retail and investment activities of the banks and to establish a new regulator – the Financial Conduct Authority, to be housed in the Bank of England – to promote competition (ICB 2011, Treasury 2012). As such, far from a crisis of state regulation, this reform represented a rejection of the light-touch approach of the tripartite regime and a re-regulation of the City. Yet, importantly, any such regulatory reforms had to be consistent with the logic of the Anglo-liberal growth model in which banks were not so much 'too big' as 'too important to fail' (King 2009: 3). This in turn caused Vickers to accuse the government of 'watering down' (Treanor 2012) the agenda for regulatory reform, which the chair of the now abolished FSA, Lord Turner, also criticised for being too focused on market competitiveness (Moore 2012). In the financial sector, then, the Coalition government sought to balance the need to increase regulatory oversight with the importance of an ongoing supply of bank credit in order to stimulate growth.

In the vast regulatory hinterland outside the financial sector, the distance between rhetoric and reality has been much greater. Progress on 'cutting red tape and complex regulation' and 'curtailing the quango state' has to date been rather piecemeal. The flagship policy for reducing the 21,000 non-EU regulations in place when the Coalition assumed office has been the 'Red Tape Challenge'. This interactive online policy process hosted by the Cabinet Office was launched in April 2011 and provides individual citizens with the opportunity to comment in detail on the value or otherwise of a specific set of regulations. Ministers then have three months to act on these comments, with the default position being abolition: 'If Ministers want to keep them, they have to make a very good case for them to stay'.[3]

As Table 10.1 shows, two years into power – and one year into the scheme – the government had succeeded in putting 1,497 of the approximately 21,000 non-EU regulations through the scheme (roughly 7 per cent of total non-EU regulations) and of these 22 per cent had been scrapped (roughly 1.6 per cent of total non-EU regulations). When considered against the backdrop of the strong pre-election posturing on this issue, and the fact that EU regulations (which are said to account for between 15 per cent and 50 per cent of all UK regulation depending on the method of calculation[4]) are outside the remit of the Red Tape Challenge, it can be reasoned that the scheme has made only marginal gains

Table 10.1   Red Tape Challenge April 2011–May 2012

Theme	No. of Regs.	Scrap	Improve	Keep	% Scrap
Retail	257	114	56	87	44
Hospitality, food and drink	114	12	69	33	11
Road transport	376	58	83	235	15
Health & safety	207	31	144	32	15
Manufacturing	128	47	18	63	37
Employment-related law	160	12	57	91	8
Environment	255	53	132	70	21
Total	1,497	327	559	611	22

Source: Adapted from Cabinet Office (2012) *The Red Tape Challenge in Summary (as of 15 May 2012)* (London: Cabinet Office).

in its attempt to curtail the size and scope of the regulatory state. Indeed, in terms of the non-scrapped regulations about half stayed the same and the rest were 'improved'. As such, it could actually be argued that if anything the Red Tape challenge has breathed new life into state regulation by reformulating a large number of measures in line with current economic and social needs. This of course is no bad thing and could be claimed as a policy achievement (especially from a hierarchical perspective), but it is some distance from the Big Society individualist rhetoric espoused by the Conservatives in the wake of the financial crisis.

A similar picture emerges with regard to the proposed culling of the hundreds of arm's length bodies which collectively make up the quango state. The ostensible motivation behind what became popularly known as the 'bonfire of quangos' was to make cost savings and to downsize those parts of the state operating beyond the ministerial accountability structures which lie at the heart of the Westminster Model. Yet for all intents and purposes this rhetoric also represented a concerted attack on the regulatory state, for while only some quangos are classified as 'regulators' in formal terms (Flinders 2008: 333–6), most perform some kind of regulatory function, whether that be standard-setting, behaviour-modification or information-gathering (Lodge and Wegrich 2012: 25). If the Coalition government was able to translate its anti-quango rhetoric into reality, state regulation would experience a huge reduction in size.

To begin with it seemed as though this might be the case. Just one month after assuming power, the Cabinet Office launched its wide-ranging Structural Reform Plan, which proposed to abolish or merge into government departments no less than 904 non-departmental public bodies (commonly referred to as quangos) which failed to meet a series of functionality tests. After a short review period by the relevant departments, the Public Bodies Bill was presented to Parliament to legislate for this reform. The resulting Public Bodies Act 2011 identified 262 quangos for abolition, and by August 2012 106 had been formally closed (Cabinet Office 2012, National Audit Office 2012: 12–14). On the surface, this appears to represent a significant reduction in the 'quango headcount' (Sklecher et al. 2013: 5), with 11 per cent of quangos under review already abolished and another 98[5] marked for closure in the next phase of the reform process.

Once these headline figures are unpacked, however, the claim that they amount to a 'radical reform…of the landscape of public bodies' (Maude 2010) appears to be a highly contestable one. To begin with, the review was only designed to focus on one part of the quango state: non-department public bodies (NDPBs).[6] Most non-ministerial departments (e.g. the Food Standards Agency, Office of Gas and Electricity, OFWAT [Office of Water Services]) and executive agencies (e.g. the Teaching Agency and Medicines and Healthcare Products Regulatory Agency) were not included among the 904 public bodies which were subject to the functionality tests and so were excluded from remit of the review, despite their obvious regulatory functions. As a result, a large proportion of the quango state was actually exempt from the start. Also, while 106 public bodies have been closed to date, most of the functions they performed have been either (re)assimilated into central departments or transferred to other arm's length bodies, and in a few cases delegated to local government (e.g. the London Thames Gateway Development Corporation), the private sector (e.g. the sale of the Horserace Totalisator Board – the Tote – to Betfred) and voluntary organisations and charities (e.g. the replacement of the British Waterways Board with the Canals and Rivers Trust). Indeed, only 80 quangos (9 per cent of the overall total) have seen their functions abolished in addition to the closure of the body itself (Skelcher et al. 2013: 10).

Furthermore, the pace of the review and the lack of clarity about how it was to be implemented across different departments meant the functionality tests at the heart of the review were not applied consistently. As a result, some public bodies were designated for abolition while others escaped without a clear rationale or explanation (Flinders and Skelcher 2012: 329–33). Consistent with previous deregulatory reforms (such as those during the Thatcher era), it could easily be that ministers and public servants simply wanted to keep their quangos for political reasons – for instance, to depoliticise contentious political activities

(Flinders and Buller, 2006) – and as a consequence manipulated the tests. Moreover, quangos are not equal in terms of budget, staffing or function, so a hypothetical 23 per cent reduction in the number of quangos does not necessarily equate to a 23 per cent reduction in the size of the quango state itself, neatly illustrated by the fact that the bulk of the predicted savings in the review are accounted for by the abolition of eight regional development agencies and the British Education Communications and Technology Agency (Becta), which was actually set for abolition before the public bodies review began (NAO 2012; see also Flinders and Skelcher 2012). Taken together these qualifications suggest that the public bodies reform programme is unlikely to achieve the radical overhaul of the quango state – and by extension state regulation – envisaged in the post-financial crisis 'bonfire' rhetoric of the Coalition government.

Thus, while the public bodies reform programme is ostensibly about a rationalisation of the quango landscape to make costs savings, the centralisation of many functions back to the departmental level, under the auspices of enhancing accountability, means it dovetails with the hierarchical narrative as much as the individualist. The (re)assimilation of functions back into departments, allied to the increased oversight role of the Cabinet Office over public bodies, has led some to suggest that ' "the arm" in the arm's-length relationship has been shortened' (Skelcher et al. 2013: 6). Therefore, if we take the perspective that 'politics is performance' (Hajer 2005), the public bodies reform process can be seen as the discursive construction of both 'front stage' and 'back stage' narratives: the individualist narrative has occupied the public facing 'front stage' as the justification for the streamlining of the quango landscape; however at the 'back stage' a more hierarchical narrative has dominated, where the drivers of the process have been focused on centralising control and tightening the levers of arm's-length governance.

Conclusion

To what extent has the financial crisis given rise to a crisis of state regulation? This question needs to be addressed with regard to financial and non-financial regulation. Outside the financial sector, where the vast majority of state regulation takes place, it is possible to reason that the financial crisis has to some degree contributed towards a sense of regulatory crisis, but with a few notable qualifications. It is important to first emphasise that for a decade or so before the financial crisis, elite and popular faith in state regulation was already on a downward trajectory, with politicians across the political spectrum drawing on the assumptions and arguments of the individualist narrative in their regulatory discourse and practice. This trend was intensified in the wake of the financial crisis. Driven by a desperate need to cut public spending and stimulate growth, together with the decentralising Big Society ideology, the Conservatives led the way in renewing the individualist attack on the regulatory state. Yet while this may have resulted in something approaching a crisis of state regulation in rhetorical terms, the reality has for the most part been a different matter. The Red Tape Challenge has, if anything, served to highlight the ongoing relevance of many regulations on the statute books, and the bonfire of quangos has illustrated how difficult it is to reshape the nebulous institutional structures of the regulatory sphere. So although criticisms of state regulation may represent a popular rhetorical target, in practice the institutions and norms of regulation continue to be deeply embedded. From this perspective, the pattern of regulatory reform post-crisis and under the current Coalition cannot be regarded as offering a serious challenge to the BPT.

Indeed, a consolidation of the regulatory state has been occurring during the recent spate of 'crises' in other domains of UK politics. The wanton neglect of patients in the Mid-Staffordshire Hospital Trust, the discovery of horsemeat in supermarket beef products, and the role of journalists and the police in the 'phone-hacking' scandal have all brought with them calls for stronger state regulation. While the government has in each case been reticent about introducing further regulation, holding firm to its individualist leanings, it has ultimately conceded ground. This is because, as with all liberal democratic states facing any sort of crisis, the government needs to (be seen to) actively address any ruptures in the fabric of society – an enduring need which will always sustain state regulation, even in the context of a predominant individualist narrative. Therefore, while the Coalition government has launched a consistent attack on non-financial state regulation, this mode of intervention has continued to be an active and important tool of governance.

The logic at play in each of these further crises is important for our understanding of the regulatory dynamics inside the financial sector. While the financial crisis was in many respects a consequence of regulatory failure, it was seen to be a failure of too little regulation rather than too much. As such, more state regulation was regarded as at least part of the solution. With both political-economic and electoral necessity in mind, politicians once again felt compelled to (be seen to) actively manage the crisis, and regulating the behaviour of those actors who were widely perceived to be responsible for causing the crisis – most notably the bankers – became a core political objective. This explains the resurgence of the assumptions and arguments of the hierarchy narrative in this sector during the financial crisis and its immediate aftermath – even if these were balanced by the countervailing influence of the individualist narrative to protect the integrity of the Anglo-liberal growth model.

Lastly, it is valuable to take a step back from these dynamics to explore some of the broader regulatory trajectories taking place. One consequence of the two specific shifts examined in this chapter is that there are now perhaps more commonalities between the form and content of regulation in the financial and non-financial sectors than there were pre-crisis. As financial regulation moves from the individualist towards the hierarchy end of the regulatory spectrum, and non-financial regulation moves from the hierarchy towards the individualist end of the spectrum, these different sectors are, for a period at least, seemingly converging in their regulatory orientation. This convergence is in turn a reflection of the fact that political debates about post-financial crisis state regulation have for the most part been taking place within this very familiar spectrum, with the individualist narrative at one end and the hierarchy narrative at the other (Lodge and Wegrich 2011). Despite the fact that crises often precipitate regulatory innovation and expansion, in the wake of the financial crisis, we have only witnessed innovation and expansion within long-established parameters. We have not seen the emergence of a radically new vision of state regulation that offers a decisive paradigm shift away from the dominant individualist and hierarchy narratives. As such, the regulatory discourse in the UK remains embedded within the structured context of the BPT.

Notes

1. 'Quango' being the acronym for quasi-autonomous non-governmental organisation.
2. The egalitarian narrative depicts the crisis as the outcome of excessive individualism, or 'ostentation and material indulgence on a grand scale' (Gamble 2009a: 4), and seeks to bring about an alternative social order more firmly centred upon the values of social solidarity, participation and transparency. The fatalist narrative regards the dynamic complexity of markets as being beyond the reach of regulation, at least in the long term, and in the final analysis is resigned to the 'inherent folly, futility and unpredictability under which all human affairs are conducted' (Hood 1998: 15). The former New York Federal Reserve President Gerald Corrigan neatly encapsulated the fatalist position

when he told an audience in 2007 that 'anyone who thinks they understand this stuff is living in la-la land' (cited in Hindmoor 2010: 451).
3. www.redtapechallenge.cabinetoffice.gov.uk
4. See House of Commons Library (2010), *How much legislation comes from Europe?* RESEARCH PAPER 10/62.
5. The current target stands at 204 abolitions (Cabinet Office 2012), which would account for approximately 23 per cent of the overall total (904).
6. However, a small number of public corporations and non-ministerial depart-ments were also included (Cabinet Office 2011).

11
A Crisis of the Media

Ralph Negrine

Introduction

Of the institutions explored in this volume, the media potentially divides opinion more than most. It tends to generate conflicting views, as two contrasting observations taken from the year the Leveson Inquiry was conducted reveal. On the one hand, Robert Jay, lead QC at the Leveson Inquiry (Leveson 2012), commented:

> My impression is that the press in the UK could well qualify as the most unruly and irreverent in the world...; it is fearless, and it speaks its mind... To be described as 'unruly and irreverent' would be regarded by most editors and journalists as a badge of honour, not of aspersion. Many would argue that these qualities make the press in the UK the best in the world, because the dividing line between fearlessness in holding power to account and unruliness in disparaging the rights of private individuals is almost impossible to draw.
>
> (Jay 2013)

Here, the self-image of the press is highlighted: fearless, fighting for justice and the little person in the street, relentlessly pursuing stories, etc. Conversely, this view given by an ex-Prime Minister tarnishes that image:

> the press to me [when I was in office] was a source of wonder. I woke up each morning and I opened the morning papers and I learned what I thought that I didn't think, what I said that I hadn't said, what I was about to do that I wasn't about to do.
>
> (Major 2012: 8)

For Major, the press may be 'fearless, and it speaks its mind' but it's a mirage, a fiction. As the Leveson Inquiry amply showed, the press did indeed have many strong points and it had done a public service in revealing, for example, the sometimes questionable expenses of MPs, but its 'culture, practices and ethics' deserved very close scrutiny. The press was under attack precisely because it transgressed in a systemic way: computer accounts were illegally hacked, mobile phones messages intercepted, the privacy of individuals was intruded upon, members of the police were paid for stories and leads, stories were made up, and so on.

However, the press was not alone in the spotlight as evidence of close links between the press, the police and politicians tumbled out during the Leveson Inquiry. Towards the end of 2012, the focus suddenly shifted to the BBC when it was revealed that an investigation into sexual abuse by the late DJ Jimmy Savile had been shelved. The investigation into this affair illustrated both the BBC's strengths and weaknesses: its editorial staff and Director General were grilled on air as the story was forensically examined by its own reporters at the same time as it became clear that the story had become a scandal precisely because of an opaque management structure and a leadership that was wanting (Pollard, 2012). When the Director General was forced to resign because of this affair with a substantial pay-off, the ensuing publicity was all negative.

These sometimes isolated incidents are important not necessarily because they add up to a deep crisis in institutions but because they can be used to illustrate a general point about the media losing their way or becoming embroiled in unpleasant events and dubious practices: the hacking into the mobile phone of the then missing teenager Milly Dowler, subsequent revelations of widespread hacking of phones and computer accounts, payments to police for information, invasions of privacy, misreporting events, issues of companies (Sky) lobbying for preferential treatment in pending legislation . . . all create a sense of crisis or, at the very least, of things having gone terribly wrong. When political, commercial and public reaction to one of these incidents – that of the hacking of the mobile phone of Milly Dowler – led to Rupert Murdoch shutting down the *News of the World* in an attempt to draw a line under the affair, it set off a series of inquiries which brought about even closer scrutiny of journalistic activity. For instance, the Murdochs were forced to appear in front of inquiries and, in due course, the net was extended to others close to them (including politicians). Under pressure to do something to deal with these matters, the Prime Minister set up the Leveson Inquiry which, in the event, did little to douse the flames of concern: the longer the inquiry sat, the more the evidence was problematic for much of the tabloid press, for the police, for politicians and for journalists.

It would be easy to take all these incidents, serious as they are, as a sign that not only were things not well with the media but that they were in crisis. Such a conclusion would be simplifying a set of complex and sometimes contradictory events. Several reasons can be put forward in support of this position. First, we need a much better understanding of what we mean by a 'crisis' in/of the media. Second, we need to take note of the existence of different media (some untouched by the events mentioned above). Third, we need to be careful to separate short-term events, e.g. the Savile affair, from longer term forces that introduce their own momentum, e.g. new technologies. Fourth, and this is a critical point, it is not possible to understand the nature of issues, problems, even crisis in the media or in the world of politics without acknowledging that the one is somehow implicated in the misfortunes of the other. The world of politics was rocked not only by the substance of the expenses scandal revelations in 2009 but also by the way these were made public; the troubles in the Murdoch empire and the issues aired at Leveson were inflamed by many with strong political convictions. Sometimes the media are also happy to go for one of their own as when the right-wing press revels in the problems at the BBC. This means, first, that problems can be easily exaggerated and inflamed beyond what could be regarded as appropriate and, second, there is always a media/politics dimension to public, political and media scandals as different actors seek advantage.

These preliminary comments frame much of what this chapter seeks to argue, namely, that we should not confuse the appearance of things with the underlying structures and processes that do play a part in determining the future of the media. This is not to say that the superficial cannot also be important but, in the nature of the media-news business, it can soon be forgotten and superseded by tomorrow's big story.

The next section of this chapter outlines some of the key issues that underpin any analysis of the contemporary media: What do we mean by 'crisis' and are all the media in 'crisis'? Are there different forms of 'crisis' and are some more significant than others? Do the events mentioned above – hacking, the expenses scandal of 2009, the Savile sex abuse scandal, and so on – amount to a 'crisis'? The chapter then explores the media–politics relationship and to the possibility that the media are not sufficiently and institutionally separate from those they seek to hold to

account. The final section looks at responses to the Leveson Inquiry recommendations as representing a denial on the part of the press of the
existence of a problem, let alone a crisis.

The media in 'crisis'

Perhaps the first point to dispel is the idea that the media, as a whole
sector, is in crisis; the second point to dispel is that all incidents are
worthy of the label 'crisis'. In reality, many different sectors make up
'the media' and a blanket statement to the effect that 'the media are
in crisis' seems both inappropriate and an exaggeration. It is necessary,
therefore, not only to develop a more nuanced understanding of the
meaning of 'crisis' but also to pinpoint more accurately what sections of
the media might be thought to be in 'crisis'. In carelessly over-using the
word 'crisis' – ironically, in the way the media themselves do – we may
be devaluing its true meaning and change-shifting properties.

If, as has been argued elsewhere in this volume, we understand a crisis
as a set of circumstances that can bring about some sort of transformative change in the structure, organisation, behaviour and governance of
institutions, then we need to offer a more precise analysis of the sets of
factors that will bring about such change. In fact, it is possible to identify
several possible ways in which (sections of) the media might be said to
be 'in crisis'. One could, for example, argue that newspapers are in crisis
because they are no longer able to function as they used to: the old business model that sustained them for nigh on two centuries is no longer
robust enough to guarantee their future economic survival. For newspapers, this truly is a 'crisis' as it questions their ability to survive in the
long term as newer media ('disruptive technologies' (Dickinson et al.
2013)), different consumption habits and newer practices play havoc
with age-old practices and systems.

Such a crisis is less likely in the broadcasting sector. For a start, the
major providers of entertainment and news are structured in such a way
that they rely on different sources of revenue: the BBC on the license
fee, Sky on advertising and subscriptions, and the commercial television companies (ITV, Channel Four, etc.) mainly on advertising. As a
result, they do not usually compete directly for the same sources of
revenue, unlike the newspaper industry where newspapers are often in
direct competition. This means, in effect, that the broadcast media do
not face challenges to their very existence; even governments have now
shied away from directly challenging the BBC. While there are always
issues about funding, there is not a structural or financial crisis of the

scale that is impacting on newspapers. Furthermore, while broadcasters have always faced some level of scrutiny of their output and practices – reaching a crescendo with the BBC 'dodgy dossier' over the Iraq controversy in 2003 – recent attacks on the media have almost entirely focused on the national press.

Both print and commercial broadcasters do, nonetheless, face one common challenge – even possibly leading to a 'crisis' – in that they are both seeing readers and viewers accessing free news content on the web and, in doing so, diverting revenues away from them. Those who read or view freely available news on the web do not contribute to the payment of journalists. The provision of news on traditional media can be said to be at risk because the news organisations that sustained journalism are themselves struggling for survival. This state of affairs, though, is no different from the condition of the multitude of web services that compete on a daily basis for hits and revenue. The difference is that political and elite concerns are mainly voiced about the travails of traditional print and broadcasting media and the 'new' media are overlooked; as many remarked, the Leveson Inquiry report devoted only one page out of 2000 to the web. It was, it could be argued, a report seeking to deal with yesterday's problems.

Irrespective of whether the media in question are print or broadcast, new or old, the availability of free news online damages the ability of traditional news providers to pay for the collection and dissemination of news. This suggests that a different interpretation of the media 'in crisis' would focus on the increasingly precarious place of journalism and of news provision in traditional media and in the public domain. Lower revenues can lead to less funding being available for journalists and thus journalism. Whilst general entertainment or niche services (e.g. consumer magazines, film channels, etc.) can survive with a minimum of news content, media that pride themselves on being news providers (e.g. newspapers) need news content to sustain themselves as such. Cutbacks and closures make it difficult for journalism to survive and thrive in a democratic society. Put differently, it becomes difficult for traditional news providers to pay to employ journalists to collect news, when news is freely available and accessed through services such as Google which does not spend anything on journalism. (See Currah 2009).

Alongside this longer term 'crisis' brought about by 'disruptive technologies', the intense scrutiny of the culture and practices of national newspapers during the Leveson Inquiry following revelations of transgressions (mentioned above) has contributed to a general debate about their ability to accurately and honestly reflect a complex and troubled social and political landscape. It has also highlighted the question of whether existing governance structures are sufficiently robust: What needs to replace the 'failed' Press Complaints Commission (PCC) and how can the BBC Trust ensure that there is no repetition of editorial lapses as there was around the Jimmy Savile affair? Such questions point to institutional crises in that they highlight practices, relations and governance issues rather than economic and structural ones.

A different sort of media 'crisis' would arise if new forms of governance proposed on the back of intense public scrutiny of media transgressions have a 'chilling effect' on the ability of journalists to carry out their traditional roles. So, for example, greater transparency vis-à-vis meetings with sources (e.g. politicians, police, councillors) could curtail the supply of information and ultimately have a detrimental impact on what can/cannot be published. If that were to happen, journalists would not be able to fulfil their traditional roles – as 'watchdogs' – and the place of the media in democratic systems would be severely undermined. A more extreme version of this crisis would be the imposition of state controls on media either through, say, direct appointments to editorial bodies or forms of licensing. The obvious danger here is that a legitimate inquiry into 'Who guards the guardians' (Leveson 2012) could lead, or be seen to lead, to unwelcome and restrictive recommendations. Herein lies the fight back against the Leveson Inquiry proposals for some form of statutory oversight of newspapers (see below).

These versions of crises – and they are connected – not only highlight the fragile existence of news media *per se* but, paradoxically, also the ways in which privately-run, profit-maximising organisations have taken on the mantle of protectors of democratic societies. Whilst it is obviously true that, without a vibrant, inquisitive, awkward media, citizens are less well informed and the public interest is less well protected, it is not abundantly obvious why those organisations should not, in some way, be governed by some sort of regulatory framework. That a battle for the freedom of the press – in reality the 'freedom of privately-owned media' – has become synonymous with the battle for freedom of speech is by no means an insignificant interpolation of words.

In contrast to the above accounts of crises, it is possible to put forward a different and a more relaxed version of the media 'in crisis' thesis. This version does not deny the severity of the problems highlighted above; instead, it emphasises ever-present processes of adaptation of media to different circumstances and conditions. Newspapers changed in the wake of the introduction of radio in the 1920s and of television in the 1950s; terrestrial television changed when cable and satellite – then seen as a threat to the BBC – came along in the 1980s (Negrine 1985); and all media are now, in a sense, adapting to the world of the web. Change, including technological change, disrupts practices and organisations but is this suggestive of a 'crisis' or a more benign, albeit painful, 'adaptation' to different circumstances?

It follows that using different timescales and historical analyses can provide us with competing narratives that do not easily fit into a 'crisis' thesis. On the contrary, they present us with the possibilities of the new: new structures, new arrangements, new challenges. At the extreme, a 'crisis' affecting 'old' media is not a 'crisis' affecting *the* media. Nevertheless, even a process of 'adaptation' is not without its losers (and winners) and it should not conceal some of the potential risks that arise from change. The risks that arise principally from technological change and from the changes in patterns of consumption of news media are explored in the next section, the structural crisis. Following that, we focus on changes that may arise from the scrutiny of the media's 'culture and practices' particularly in the context of the coverage of politics, the institutional crisis.

A 'structural crisis': The challenge to the 'old' media

Arguably the greatest threat to news media today, particularly print media, comes from the fact that fewer people are prepared to pay for their news content. Without a guaranteed and plentiful supply of revenue from paying customers and/or advertisers, the whole model on which news media has traditionally based itself becomes unsustainable. This structural transformation of the news media is producing a crisis precisely because some news media can no longer be sustained as before, until and unless, that is, some way is found to meet the challenge of disappearing readers and of the 'disruptive technologies' that are bringing about changes in patterns of news production and its consumption. The former arises out of the possibilities of individuals producing content in a plethora of ways – blogs, Tweets, user-generated content (UGC), for example – and so forcing traditional news producers to recognise that others can help shape the news agenda; the latter out of a sharp decline in sales of newspapers in particular.

However, the decline in sales of newspapers is not of recent origin, as Table 11.1 and Figure 11.1 show, and despite this longer term trend, it is important to acknowledge that national newspapers are still bought by about ten million people in the UK each and every day. Given the way in which the media agenda is often driven by the newspaper agenda, their

Table 11.1   Circulation of national newspapers in the UK (in thousands)

Title	1961	1976	1980	2000	2012	2013 (Average daily browsers)
The Sun	N/A	3,708	3,741	3,557	2,582	1,698
Daily Mail	2,610	1,755	1,948	2,354	1,945	7,833 (Mail Online)
Daily Mirror	4,561	3,851	3,625	2,271	1,103	1,176
Daily Star	N/A	N/A	1,034	503	617	N/A
Daily Telegraph	1,248	1,308	1,439	1,040	578	3,041
Daily Express	4,328	2,594	2,194	1,051	577	n/a
The Times	253	310	297	726	397	113 subscribers[1]
The Financial Times	132	174	197	435	316	328 subscribers[2]
i	N/A	N/A	N/A	N/A	264	N/A
The Guardian	245	306	377	402	216	4,771
The Independent			N/A	222	105	1,131

Sources: http://en.wikipedia.org/wiki/List_of_newspapers_in_the_United_Kingdom_by_ circulation, and for online data relating to groups e.g. Telegraph.co.uk from Press Gazette http://www.pressgazette.co.uk/adoption-metered-paywall-has-little-effect-telegraphs-overall-website-traffic;
[1] http://nicommercial.co.uk/news/times-digital-subscribers-continue-to-grow;
[2] http://aboutus.ft.com/corporate-information/ft-company/#axzz2Ui8Ga3rT.

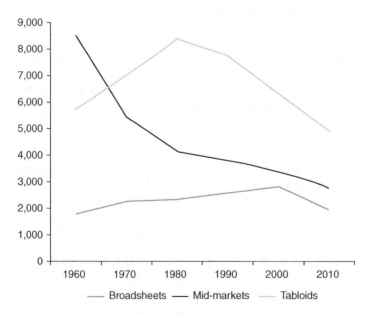

Figure 11.1   Circulation by sector 1960–2010

place in social and political life is thus by no means insignificant. Importantly, Table 11.1 also charts the growth of online visitors to newspaper websites and this provides an insight into the growing importance of the web for newspaper organisations even though the resultant growth has not yet generated significant revenue streams. New and different ways to fund profitably the collection and delivery of news have yet to be devised and until such a time newspapers in particular are at risk.

But is this 'crisis' any more significant than past 'crises'? If this present 'crisis' heralds the beginning of the end of newspapers, then it will surely be a crisis of an unprecedented kind. On the other hand, if this 'crisis' leads to a new set of circumstances and contexts for those newspapers that will probably continue to exist, then it is no different from previous moments of panic. It is worth recalling here that in the 1960s and 1970s, the national newspaper industry went through turmoil. Concerns about costs, practices, new technology – then computerisation – gave rise to fearful predictions of title closures and a narrowing of choice (Negrine 1998: 138–146). In the event, newspapers adapted. The fundamentals of the national press have remained broadly unchanged since: newspapers are still in private ownership, the range of titles is broadly similar across this period (Table 11.1) and they still mainly lose money despite not insignificant sales. However, given that newspapers have never been run primarily for profit, the reality of continuing losses – then or now – does not unduly impact on their futures: published losses produce a frisson of concern and some panic (or delight) but generally things carry on, more or less.

Where such losses are not sustainable and have had more immediate consequences is in respect of the local and regional press. In this sector of the newspaper industry, declining sales and declining profitability – again the result of a loss of advertising revenue in particular as advertising has migrated to the web – have brought about significant changes. In 2012, the industry's magazine *Press Gazette* reported that 'at least 242 local newspapers closed between 2005 and the end of 2011. This compares with just 70 launches.' (*Press Gazette* 2012) One specific example of the scale of the transition in the fortunes of local newspapers was provided by the General Secretary of the National Union of Journalists. 'Forty years ago', she pointed out, 'the *Yorkshire Evening Post* had a staff of 1,350, eight editions and a daily circulation of 230,000. Today there are fewer than 400 and it has two editions a day.' [Its circulation in 2012 hovered around the 40,000 mark] (Stanistreet 2012). It is obvious that, as she put it, 'further cuts and attacks on editorial is not the panacea for increased circulation' but this seems to be an inevitable strategy in an effort to stay alive. The consequences of this pattern of decline were noted in one parliamentary committee report which pointed out that the 'importance of reporting on local institutions and local authority cannot be overstated; *without it there is little accountability*. This reporting must be independent and good quality in order to inform the public and maintain their confidence' (Select Committee Culture, Media and Sport 2010; emphasis added). This comment is equally applicable to the national print and broadcast media.

In these ways, a structural crisis in the industry quickly translates into a crisis of journalism, and if journalism cannot be funded to do what it is meant to do and make institutions accountable, then one key feature of democratic life is damaged. Hence the urgency of finding new ways to fund news-gathering and news distribution organisations that can serve the public better.

By contrast to newspapers, as has been pointed out above, the different funding and regulatory regimes that surround the broadcast media (e.g. through OFCOM or the BBC Trust) give them a greater measure of security. Whilst the patterns of television consumption have certainly changed dramatically over the last 40 years with, say, the advent of satellite, the 'traditional' broadcasters – the BBC and ITV – are still dominant, albeit with a smaller share of the audience. Competition has fragmented the once 'national' 'mass' audience (http://www.barb.co.uk/facts/annual-share-of-viewing?_s=4) and access to television via the web has also opened up new ways to watch television and also new ways for traditional broadcasters to reach viewers. (http://www.thinkbox.tv/server/show/nav.1435#.Tzlk8jwfJEE.email)

More significantly, broadcast news provision has been seen, by and large, to be less problematic than news provision in print and now on the web. The regulatory framework governing broadcast news provision ('impartiality', fairness, etc.) ensures that public concerns are lessened and that political concerns, for example over the 2003 Iraq 'dodgy dossier', are treated as mainly politically motivated concerns. This helps to explain why the Leveson Inquiry was essentially focused on public and political concerns about the press, though some would argue that the press is under greater scrutiny precisely because it is more 'unruly and irreverent' than broadcasting. Moreover, support for public broadcasting continues to remain high as does confidence and trust in its journalism. A recent comparative study of broadcasting in Finland, Denmark, the UK and the USA has persuasively argued that European public service television channels – of which the BBC is the prime example – still continue to play a vital role in the provision of news and education for its many publics. In their news output, they devote time to overseas news events and they are also more hard news oriented, at least when compared with US television (Curran et al. 2009: 12–13). As Barnett et al. (2012: 3) have also pointed out in their longitudinal study of changes in the nature and content of news output over a 35 year period (1975–2009): 'within a predominantly serious framework, there remains a diversity of news output' across the broadcasting sector.

The general public seems, on the whole, to echo the findings in academic studies that highlight the continuing value of public broad-casting. Although public opinion fluctuates from year to year, the broad pattern suggests that a higher percentage of the public expressed trust in television than in print media, in broadcast journalism than in print journalism, and in print journalists on 'serious' newspapers as compared with those working for tabloid newspapers (Audit Commission 2003, MORI 2008, 2009).

Some have argued that this sort of evidence is really not very substan-tial (Coleman et al. 2009: 7) and that it masks a sense of bewilderment amongst the public when they consume news. Coleman et al. (2009: 20) observe:

> When we encountered distrust in the news, it was because people felt that their expectations were not shared by news producers; that they were being told stories that were not properly explained; that their lives were reported in ways that were not adequately researched; or that they could find more useful, reliable or amusing information elsewhere. Public trust in the media was lost when they were imag-ined and approached in ways that ignored or devalued their everyday experiences.

Coleman et al. (2009: 41) rightly label this a 'crisis of political efficacy' (in that it may reflect a sense of disconnection between the public and the media and people and events that they report on). This is not a crisis in the media *per se* although it does raise fundamental issues about how the public should be included in wider political conversations and decisions rather than as onlookers. In the coverage of the 2009 expenses scandal, for example, only 5 per cent of total BBC broadcast news time over a period of three weeks was taken up by members of the public and then only as members of a chorus mouthing words of disgust (Negrine and Bull, forthcoming).

Ensuring that public concerns, issues and experiences are properly reflected by the media is probably part of a longer list of desirables for a functioning democracy, yet shortcomings across the media do not necessarily damage these expectations. Herein lies a paradox: despite public disquiet about journalists and media in general, sales and viewing patterns do not appear to fluctuate in such a way as to be taken to represent comments on media activities. Similarly, and despite shortcomings etc., the more the media expose weaknesses in other institutions of governance (e.g. banks, parliament, local councils, football clubs), the better their reputation, at the same time as they contribute to a general sense of crisis and malaise. Even when their own practices come under scrutiny, as they did in the course of the Leveson Inquiry, the opaque nature of their own links to these other institutions and their shortcomings that govern our lives, never seem to damage their fortunes significantly: How did they fail to spot the problems of the banks, of sexual abuse among high-profile media folk, of tax-avoidance...and how did they not notice the 'abuse' of the expenses system by MPs? In other words, despite being very close to the world of politics – the theme of the next section – journalism displayed some serious shortcomings when it came to fulfilling its role.

Journalism and politics: A relationship in crisis?

The relationship between media and politics is punctuated by extremes. There are moments of adversarialism, but there are many instances of proximity and closeness. The press, by and large, likes to portray itself as separate from politicians and holding them to account but the reality, as seen during the Leveson Inquiry, can often be very different. Importantly, that relationship has continued to evolve in a climate in which pressures on the media have accelerated certain tendencies. As Alastair Campbell, formerly Blair's Director of Communications, and a well-known and controversial critic of the media, has argued:

> The centre of gravity in our press has moved to a bad place; the combined forces of technological change, intense competition, an obsession with celebrity, a culture of negativity, and amorality among some of the industry's leaders and practitioners have accelerated a downmarket trend, and accelerated too the sense of desperation in the pursuit of stories...[T]he impact upon our culture and our public life of what the press in Britain has become has a large debit side alongside the credit that freedom brings.
>
> (Campbell 2012)

Whilst Campbell's critique is of the press as a whole, evidence produced at the Leveson Inquiry highlighted other questionable practices: there were allegations of entrapment of politicians, invasions of privacy, alleged requests (and granting) of special (political) favours, and stories written for political impact (e.g. Major 2012, and top of this chapter). This pointed to a crisis in journalism in general and in political journalism; more specifically, it pointed to a crisis in the ways in which journalists and politicians interacted, and posed questions about who benefitted from the interaction.

As the Introduction to this volume notes, at its heart the issue is about power: Who had it and who did not? The voluminous evidence produced by, and for, the Leveson Inquiry seemed to suggest that the media had it and that politicians did not. These were not two institutions of roughly equal size eyeballing one another. There were certainly tensions between journalists and politicians as well as suspicions about the motives of the other. This was not new and, in a sense, only to be expected and welcomed since both institutions had different parts to play in the polity. Yet enmity and suspicion was counter-balanced by injudicious and unwise proximity. Here was evidence, once again, of the extremes: the coverage of the expenses scandal in 2009, at one end, and the LOL[1] text messages between the Prime Minister and a newspaper executive (see below) at the other.

The extremes: Adversarialism

During the months of May and June 2009, the daily outpourings of information about what MPs had claimed for in expenses did little to endear them to the public. That parliament had sought to hide the information from public scrutiny had made matters only worse. The revelations under such headlines as 'It's Payback Time' (*Daily Telegraph* 2009) confirmed what the public had already seemingly known, namely, that politicians were untrustworthy and taking liberties within a system that they themselves had created.

The coverage of the scandal reinforced the image of the press as being on the side of the public and 'holding truth to power'. MPs, who were now publicly humiliated, were angered by the tone and style of coverage. Acts of criminality aside, for example in submitting false claims, many felt that allegations were often made without substance, that they were not given time to properly respond to criticisms and that they were all, as a group, tarnished with the same brush. For a while, it is possible to argue, the long-established relationship between these two institutions was strained and, no doubt, that some relationships were irretrievably broken.

Yet, it is worth noting, first, that the *Daily Telegraph* was only able to publish the original information because it had paid for the disc containing the information which had been stolen from parliament, and, second, that political journalists who had close on-going relations with politicians seemed to be unaware of the scale of the problem (and/ or had not revealed that information beforehand). Both points are suggestive of a news media either not working as they perhaps ought to have done and/or of a political class not fully aware of the way their actions might look to others. Irrespective of such speculation, it is possible to see that journalists would argue that they were only doing their job on behalf of the public in revealing the information on the expenses of MPs and that MPs were duty bound to respond to public concern and outrage. In essence then this could be interpreted as a very serious falling out in a generally uneasy relationship in which the overall benefits of the trade in information and favours ultimately keep the partners together.

The extremes: Proximity

Proximity is a key feature of the troubled relationship because it remains the best way to obtain information, but it has a darker side. The evidence at Leveson confirmed this: the press was closely linked to and not separate from those in politics and not as independent or as impartial as appearances might suggest. Furthermore, the falling out over the expenses scandal coverage made little difference to the long-standing nature of the relationship. Rather than keeping away from the press in the wake of the expenses scandal coverage in 2009 – a reasonable assumption if one's reputation was shredded in public – ministerial diary entries post-2009 revealed lists of meetings between politicians and media (journalists and proprietors) (Gaber 2012). Prime Minister Cameron's own relationship with Rebekah Wade/Brooks (sometime editor of the *News of the World*, deputy editor of the *Sun*, very close confidante of Rupert Murdoch) had its own soap opera quality in revelations of numerous friendly text messages ending with LOLs.

Whilst everyone seemed to acknowledge that the relationship between the press and politicians was not quite right, few seemed bothered enough to do anything about it either because it was too difficult to create an appropriate framework to deal with it and/or because it suited both partners best to maintain things as they are. In his evidence to Leveson, David Cameron accepted that the relationship had been an issue 'for years' and had 'not been right' and that there was a need to try and get it on a better footing (Cameron 2012: 14). This view was echoed somewhat by Tony Blair, also in evidence to Leveson, who described the relationship as 'unhealthy' (Blair 2012). In such circumstances, one could be forgiven for thinking that the two sides in this relationship might wish to take a break and let the dust settle before re-engaging, yet within two months of the publication of the Leveson Inquiry report, there were newspaper reports of the Chancellor of the Exchequer having meetings with newspaper executives (*Private Eye* 2013: 12) and having a 'private dinner...with Rupert Murdoch', London Mayor Boris Johnson and newspaper editors. (*The Guardian* 2013).

If the press could be excused for wishing to pursue its object in the relationship because it was part of the process of getting close to sources and of 'trading in information', those in politics seemed to argue that they had to do it because they were, in effect, powerless to do otherwise. As Tony Blair pointed out,

> what, in a sense, happens is not necessarily that you become particu-
> larly close, but the relationship is one in which you feel this... pretty
> intense power and the need to try and deal with that... I decided, as
> a political leader – and this was a strategic decision – that I was going
> to manage that and not confront it.
>
> (Blair 2012: 4)

It had, to all intents and purposes, the qualities of a forced marriage with the public (the children?) occupying the role of bystander. All this echoed the findings of the 2004 Phillis Review of government communi-cation and its comment that there was a worrying 'three-way breakdown in trust between government and politicians, the media and the general public' with politicians and media inhabiting a world of their own, dis-trustful of one another, and seemingly not interested in the welfare of the public at large.

The fundamental problem, in the eyes of a veteran observer of the press, was that newspapers had become detached ('unhinged') from their traditional points of anchorage in political parties and were 'open to capture by interest groups and factions' (Seymour-Ure 1998: 49). According to Seymour-Ure, the experiences of Blair and Major – to which we can now add Brown and Cameron – reflect:

> the extent to which, arguably, (media) barons commit themselves
> nowadays more to leaders or to causes than to parties. This could be
> because parties are less ideological and leaders more 'presidential', or
> because the barons themselves are less locked on to the system which
> kept them, in Baldwin's word, 'responsible'.
>
> (Seymour-Ure 2003: 113)

Little wonder then that readers of newspapers need to 'understand the factors influencing their role as evaluators' (Seymour-Ure 1998: 53) which, following the Leveson Inquiry, included their political allegiances and deal-making.

Though the crisis in political journalism may be born out of a troubled and uneasy relationship, its real impact is felt in the 'collateral damage': in its detachment from the public that the Phillis Review (2004) highlighted and the systemic suspicions it engenders; in the 'damage' it has done to our politics (Lloyd 2004) and in the fact that it had brought us to the 'bad place' that Campbell referred to in his evidence to Leveson. That is not to say that the 'too close' 'unhealthy' relationship does not merit some sort of attention but only that, in the absence of a specific template setting out what it should be like, it is best to let it re-calibrate itself over time whilst taking into account different political and journalistic styles, for example.

It is perhaps the bigger concerns about the consequences of super-adversarial journalism, at one extreme, and proximity, at the other, that we need to pay attention to and to consider as part of a crisis in politics and journalism. This may raise issues about style and tone, perspectives on politics and the debasing of political dialogue which are more important than the occasional dinner with a newspaper proprietor. Such concerns, though, go beyond newspapers and must take in broadcasters and now the web, where the world of politics is exposed to the full force of critique from many who are not party to a 'cosy', 'too close' and 'unhealthy' relationship. In this bigger universe, newspapers remain important but given their structural problems and the challenges to their pre-eminence from the 'new kids on the block', the old may indeed be giving way to new forms of political journalism that is less closely tied up with traditional media and traditional allegiances.

Conclusion: read all about it – 'Media Crisis in Fleet Street' (Few hurt)

Recognising the existence of problems – even crises – is far easier than finding remedies; no more so than in a sector where one of the key participants – the national press – has its own strong views about what should and should not be done. As I have argued above, the structural problems of newspapers are specific to it and do not extend to the broadcasting sector or to new media. It is perhaps no more than a matter of the old adapting to new circumstances rather than a terminal crisis. The institutional crisis, on the other hand, is more troubling because its impact can be felt so far and so wide: it impacts on the quality of the political conversations that we have and on who is included in, or excluded from, those conversations.

In the process of exploring these issues, the Leveson Inquiry sought to provide a framework for recalibrating relationships and existing arrangements. Lord Justice Leveson's key proposal was for the setting up of a new governance structure with some form of statutory underpinning to an independent regulator as a mechanism for rebuilding public trust in the press and its practices. The recommendations stressed the need for independence and separation from those in political power and the need to include all media players (Leveson 2012a). It was not, however, warmly received: major press players and Prime Minister David Cameron openly rejected any suggestions of minimal system repair. This was indicative of at least two things: first, of a fear that any attempts to introduce new governance structures would have detrimental consequences for press freedom; second, that the industry and sections of the government failed to acknowledge or recognise that there was a problem, even perhaps a crisis.

Journalists are justifiably concerned that requiring greater transparency regarding their frequency of meetings with politicians, say, would have a 'chilling effect' on their ability to do their work. Indeed, any proposals that limit what the press should legitimately do in the public interest is a matter of grave concern. But Leveson's key proposal was designed not to do any of these things but to create a framework whereby newspaper groups would create a system of independent regulation that had some force behind it, unlike the former PCC. That it might be difficult to design such a framework was acknowledged by all but dismissal of the proposals *tout court* suggested unwillingness on the part of many newspaper interests to give up their powers. The proposal was criticised – by the press! – for being no more than a tool for politicians to control the press. Those who felt brave enough to support some form of underpinning of independent regulation were branded censors and against age-old, hard-won media freedoms. If any evidence was needed that Lord Leveson had lost the 'war of words', one could simply turn to the title of a debate at *The Spectator* in January 2013. The motion was: 'Leveson is a fundamental threat to the free press.'

In the six months since the publication of the report and the recommendations, battle lines were clearly drawn between those who supported the proposals and those who did not. Alternative proposals were produced to avoid the element of statute that Leveson had called for but these went nowhere. In a last-minute deal to resurrect and act on the Leveson proposals, in March 2013 the leaders of the political parties drew up proposals for a Royal Charter that, they felt, guaranteed the separation of powers that Leveson had asked for and that also provided elements of statute.

This fared no better with the press and, once again, many newspaper groups objected and threatened not to take part in the framework, so making the system unworkable. At the time of writing, it remains unclear where the key recommendations of the Leveson Inquiry stand. Parliament has accepted the idea of a Royal Charter for the press but major newspaper groups – not all – are still threatening to make the whole thing unworkable. And not for the first time, commentators have suggested that '(David) Cameron has let down a generation by allowing Leveson to fail. Media barons have bent parliament to their will.' (Kettle 2013).

The debate around, and antipathy to, Leveson's recommendations show that newspapers will seek to continue to behave as before, more or less, and that they do not, in effect, recognise that there is even a problem. Hacking, they would argue, was outside the law and should have been punished; similarly, paying for information. The law, in other words, should have dealt with law-breaking by journalists; the culture and ethics of the press did not contribute to any of that. Even before Leveson was set up, the public sensed that this would be the outcome of all these deliberations. In July 2011, after hacking and press misdemeanours became public, Reuters/Mori (2011) asked members of the public whether or not they thought these events would bring about change. Just over half (51 per cent) responded 'Yes', 41 per cent said 'No', with the difference made up of 'Don't Knows'. The public was certainly not convinced that the media would change their 'cultures, practices and ethics'.

Perhaps, then, the crisis in the media has a clear discursive element to it, residing in the manner in which the press (and other 'traditional' media) are telling us that there is no crisis in the media. The real consequences of structural and institutional problems for a democratic system are rarely given the treatment they deserve. The self-obsession of the media, especially the traditional mainstream media, make it difficult to ask bigger questions and to discuss bigger issues.

Should we be overly exercised by this? The obvious answer is 'Yes' precisely because the 'old' media are still dominant and they still play an important part in our democratic systems. But they are no longer the only players. The web has brought about a dramatic change in communication structures and practices. The news environment, for example, is significantly different from what it was even five years ago. Traditional sources of news and information are being challenged by those who blog or Tweet and by those who offer different perspectives, different news, and even more detailed and better informed news. The availability of information through a myriad of sources will begin to reshape the news environment: MPs and journalists will be able to communicate directly with members of the public; campaign groups will be able to set up their own networks, and so on. At the same time, individuals have been offered the power to communicate directly with others, including to journalists and those in power. The top-down model of communication has been supplemented by horizontal, open networks of communication.

The process of adaptation of the old to the new is at an early stage but it provides us with different perspectives on the theme of the 'media in crisis'. We might wish to mourn the loss of this or that newspaper– as we have done throughout the last two centuries – but the prospect of newer and possibly better forms of communication should dissuade us from mourning for too long. The loss of journalism as an activity taking place within established and hierarchical organisations may similarly be mourned (Flinders 2012: 142–58), but there are other means to deliver the content, including through well-connected individuals using mobile devices, for example.

The institutional crisis, if we accept that there is one, presents other issues and highlights the need to open up the channels of communication to different voices and to move contra Flinders (2012) from a long, settled, albeit troubled, relationship between the world of media and politics to an open-marriage: to be more inclusive of new media and new voices, to be almost promiscuous in the choice of partners, topics and voices. In the process, one hopes that journalism as an activity can continue to survive and thrive and can establish an appropriate space for grown-up conversations about political matters and individual lives; to move, in other words, away from the 'bad place' that Campbell described to somewhere better.

If the media are in crisis, that crisis is not about individual lapses of judgment or law-breaking. It is, on the one hand, a structural crisis of a long-term nature and, on the other, a crisis of identity. The former is about economics and business models, the latter, as I have argued, is about where the media are located within the many institutions that govern our lives. In the new media environment where all can participate in the production of news and we can consume an unlimited and varied diet of news, the old media – the national newspapers, television – should begin to ask important questions not only about their long-term economic viability but about how best they can serve the public and democratic systems.

Note

1. Brooks revealed that Cameron thought LOL stood for Lots of Love. She corrected him.

12
A Crisis of Policing

Layla Skinns

Introduction

In recent times, hardly a week or even a day has passed without a story in the media exploring controversy, criticism or concern in relation to the police. This has ranged from phone-hacking and police corruption to racism in the police; from misuse of police powers and officers operating outside the law to overly favourable pay and conditions; or from incompetence in the policing of public order or in the investigation of high-profile crimes to the contracting-out to the private sector of key police functions. Even in the brief period taken to write the present chapter, the police have been the focus of much public ire. For instance, the ethicality of the infiltration of protest groups by undercover police officers – who formed intimate relationships with some of the protestors, even having children with them, as well as acting as 'agent provocateurs' – is a news story about the police which has raised its head time and again. In its latest incarnation, in June 2013, the media reported that an undercover officer allegedly co-wrote the leaflet criticising the McDonalds food chain, which later became the focus of the three-year 'McLibel' case, which cost taxpayers and McDonalds millions of pounds (Lewis and Evans 2013a). In the same month, a former Metropolitan police officer has come forward to say that he worked undercover in the aftermath of Stephen Lawrence's death to collect hearsay information on the Lawrence family and others campaigning for a fuller investigation into his racially aggravated murder, with the aim being for the police to use this information to impugn campaigners' reputations.[1] In September 2012, South Yorkshire Police were criticised in the report of the Hillsborough Independent

Panel both for their policing of the event (e.g. their persistent focus on crowd control of 'drunken' fans rather than crowd safety) and their handling of its aftermath (e.g. their attempts to blame allegedly disorderly ticketless fans for the disaster and the alteration of police officers' statements to cover up their errors). The 'plebgate' affair, also in September 2012, in which the Chief Whip for the Conservative Party resigned after allegedly calling police officers 'plebs' has been revealing as to the level of antipathy between the police and the Conservative Party. When taken together, it might seem, therefore, as if the police are an institution in crisis.

In relation to the penal system, Cavadino and Dignan (1997: 9) define a crisis, first, as a state of affairs that constitutes a danger and a moral challenge, which makes it the most pressing social issue of the day and, second, as a critical juncture or turning point. These definitions are useful, but they fail to explore to whom these social issues pose a danger and a moral challenge. In the context of the police, the 'crisis' needs to be thought of not only in terms of its impact on the police, but also in terms of its impact on the public, and public perceptions of the police and the state.

The purpose of this chapter is to explore whether the seemingly endless stream of criticism and controversy amounts to a crisis in the police in England.[2] In particular, it addresses three questions. First, what evidence is there of a shift from the police being seen as revered defenders of social order to an institution currently in 'crisis'? Second, what factors have contributed to this shift? Third, what are the wider ramifications of this? My argument is that it is hard to ignore the intensification of criticism and controversy about the police in the last decade, which is indicative of a 'crisis' of sorts. However, as the previous chapter on the media points out, the issue of temporality has an important bearing on the way in which the notion of crisis can be understood. For example, by expanding the focus to the period from the late 1960s to the present, that is, by situating recent criticism and concerns about the police in England in debates about the police over the last 40 years, rather than just the last decade, it is possible to see that there is more continuity with the past than the current 'crisis' suggests and that the current 'crisis' is part of a more longstanding trend or series of crises, which have implications for the police, other criminal justice agencies and perhaps the state too.

Before I address these matters, it is necessary to put the police in context by exploring the police mandate and the intimate connection between the police and society.

The police in context

The police are fundamental to the governance of democratic societies. Just how fundamental they are remains a controversial issue, not least because of a tendency to slip into fetishising the police; that is, to assume that the police are a necessary prerequisite for social order and that chaos would ensue without them (Reiner 2010: 3–4). In fact, the police's contribution to the reduction of crime is limited, as various academic studies – for example of low detection rates and the limited impact of police patrols on crime – have shown (e.g. Kelling et al. 1972, 1981, Bayley 1996, Radcliffe et al. 2011). Furthermore, policing and, more broadly, social control are in fact carried out by a variety of actors and organisations, from social workers to families to neighbourhood wardens to schools, meaning that the police are only one part, albeit an important one, of the broader processes of policing and social control.

Nonetheless, with the creation of the 'new police' – a change set in motion by Sir Robert Peel who was instrumental to the creation of the Metropolitan Police Act 1829 – policing came to be seen as primarily a state-sponsored activity performed by a hierarchically organised, uniformed workforce and new recruits were instructed that the prevention of crime was their principal responsibility, together with the protection of life and property and the preservation of public tranquillity (Mawby 2008, Reiner 2012). Since their inception, the meaning of this mandate has varied. Most recently, in public discourse the tendency has been primarily to see the police as 'crime-fighters'; for example, Theresa May announced at the Police Federation conference in July 2010 that the police's mission is to 'cut crime; no more, no less'. Yet this pronouncement fails to appreciate the wide-ranging nature of the police mandate, which also encompasses acting as an emergency service and at times a social service, as well as engaging in peace-keeping and public order maintenance, state security and public reassurance (e.g. Banton 1964: 127, Cain 1973: 33–45, 53–79, Shapland and Vagg 1988: 36–9, Bayley 1996, Waddington 1999: 4–20, Johnston 2000: 36–43, Newburn and Reiner 2007, Reiner 2012).

Intrinsic to Sir Robert Peel's notion of the 'new police' was the idea or, some might argue, ideology of policing by consent. Indeed, this was one of the primary reasons why the Metropolitan Police, from their inception, gave the impression of being disarmed:[3] it led to the belief that police officers were merely citizens in uniform, relying on the consent of the public rather than the possibility of the use of force. This image of the police was used to reduce widespread public opposition to their introduction. Tales of the surveillance capabilities of the police in pre-revolutionary France, who relied on a network of informants (*sous-mouche*), were enough to make the public nervous about the potential for police forces in England also to become an arm of a totalitarian state (Brodeur 2010: 52, 67–8). Disarming the police was thus of symbolic significance, setting the police in England apart from the police institutions springing up in France, as well as in other jurisdictions in the same period, such as in Ireland, America and Australia (e.g. Walsh 1998: 6–12, Finnane 2005, Brodeur 2010: 68–72).

The intimate connection between the police and broader social, economic and political conditions is also evident in more recent times. As Reiner (1992: 762) says, the police are like a 'social litmus paper, reflecting sensitively the unfolding dynamics of a society'. Over the last 40 years, the police have had to adapt to a series of changes which have affected how the public perceive the police and how the police perform their role as protectors of dominant conceptions of social order. In the mid-1970s, free market economics and deregulation of increasingly globalised and fragile markets have contributed to an increase in inequality, socioeconomic polarisation, long-term exclusion from employment and the creation of a so-called under-class (Reiner 2010: 241). These social and economic dislocations have increasingly led to the police being called on to police conflict and disorder (e.g. the miners' strikes), meaning that they have become viewed as acting in political and partisan ways, as well as contributing to the over-policing and under-protecting of certain social groups, notably, young, ethnic minority, inner-city populations (Reiner 1995). In addition, growing desubordination (or perhaps a democratisation of sentiments) has contributed to a decrease in traditional patterns of deference and a more questioning attitude towards those in positions of authority, including the police, thereby creating an almost impossible challenge for the police in terms of meeting the demands of what has also become an increasingly diverse population (Reiner 1995).

Next, I examine the extent to which there is merely a crisis or, in fact, a series of crises in the police in England. The primary focus is on policing from the late 1960s to the present.

Crisis or crises?

To an extent the recent intensification of controversy, criticism and concern about the police can be seen as a 'crisis' in the police institution. The last decade has been punctuated by periods of intense difficulty affecting the police, the public and the state. Public debate has alighted on certain key issues, which are the focus of this chapter, namely, racism in the police; police incompetence, particularly in the policing of the riots in August 2011; police corruption, especially in relation to the phone-hacking scandal; and the need for organisational reform connected to governmental austerity measures.[4]

A crisis about racism in the police is evident in the way that the police have dealt with minority ethnic victims, suspects and police officers. It is exemplified by the flawed investigation into the racially aggravated murder of the young black teenager Stephen Lawrence in 1993, in which no one was initially convicted, and the subsequent public inquiry, the Macpherson Inquiry, which concluded that the Metropolitan Police Service (MPS) were 'institutionally racist'.[5] This conclusion about the MPS has continued to resonate to the present day, not only for those connected to the Stephen Lawrence case, as illustrated by the revelations in June 2013 about attempts at the time of the investigation to impugn the reputations of anti-racist campaigners, but also for the public, more generally, during their everyday interactions with the police. Of particular concern are inequalities in police stop and search practices. Though there is some debate about how proportionality can best be measured (e.g. Waddington, Stenson and Don 2004), the general picture is that black and Asian citizens tend to be over-represented in the figures relative to white citizens. For example, government statistics show that, in 2009/10, per 1000 of the population, black people were seven times more likely than white people to be stopped and searched under the Police and Criminal Evidence Act 1984 which requires there to be 'reasonable suspicion' (MOJ 2011: 38). Moreover, the low visibility of this type of police work, often involving only a low-ranking police officer and the citizen themselves, and the vagaries of the law, even when 'reasonable' suspicion is required, mean that discretionary stop and search decisions can be readily influenced by stereotyping of particular ethnic groups. For example, Cashmore (2001: 652) notes a police officer in his research who was advised to stop 'black kids with baseball caps, wearing all the jewellery' (see also Quinton 2011).

A crisis about the competence of the police in performing a key aspect of their mandate (i.e. maintaining social order) was also highlighted by the policing of five days of rioting in London and other major cities in England in August 2011. The riots were sparked by the death of Mark Duggan who was shot by armed police who believed him to be carrying a firearm, though it remains unclear whether he was.[6] Shortly after his death, the police and the Independent Police Complaints Commission (IPCC) failed to communicate properly with the wider community about the circumstances in which Mark Duggan died, for example, giving the public the incorrect impression that he had been held down and shot by the police (MPS 2012: 24). In the context of a history of poor police–citizen relations in Tottenham, particularly between the police and the black community, this is likely to have escalated the situation.[7] Their competence was also called into question by mistakes being made in the allocation and deployment of resources in the days that followed Mark Duggan's death, leaving the public to feel under-protected and possibly even facilitating the escalation of rioting. For example, in the first day of rioting in Tottenham, it took several hours to mobilise and deploy an appropriate number of officers in view of the size of the disorder. On subsequent days, the MPS based their predictions about appropriate staffing levels on the scale and location of rioting on the previous day, not anticipating that it might spread to other areas and grow in scale (MPS 2012: 64–5). As such, they were ill-prepared.

The phone-hacking scandal – in particular allegations that a child murder victim's mobile phone messages had been listened to and deleted by members of the press, which prompted further allegations that unnamed police officers had received illegal payments in exchange for confidential information – suggests, as we saw in the previous chapter, a crisis about integrity and corruption in the police as a result of their relationships with the press.[8] Concerns stretched up to the highest level of the largest police force in the country, culminating in the resignation of the Commissioner of the MPS, Sir Paul Stephenson, in July 2011, along with other senior members of the force, including John Yates, Andy Hayman and Peter Clarke, shortly before the August riots. They also prompted a flurry of activity in terms of inquiries, investigations and reports, nearly all of which are ongoing at the time of writing, such as various investigations by the MPS;[9] independent inquiries and reports by Her Majesty's Inspectorate of Constabularies (HMIC),[10] the IPCC,[11] and Dame Elizabeth Filkin on behalf of the MPS.[12] One exception is the Leveson Inquiry which concluded, in relation to the police,[13] that poor decisions were taken and mistakes made in police relations with News International which contributed to the 'perception' that this relationship was too close. For example, the decision not to further investigate the extent of phone-hacking at News International, following Glen Mulcaire's arrest and conviction, was mistaken but understandable, according to Leveson, in the light of the pressures on the police as a result of their counter-terrorist activities (Leveson 2012: 18).

That said, the nature and extent of police corruption in England may be more widespread and more serious than the phone-hacking scandal and Leveson's conclusions suggest, even based on official data. Whilst both the police and the IPCC record complaints about police corruption, with the IPCC recording and investigating the more serious matters, these figures will only ever include a fraction of incidences. These official data are likely to reflect recording practices, rather than the 'true' extent of the problem (IPCC 2012: 45), with an unknown amount of police corruption occurring below the radar, going unreported and unrecorded by anyone. Nonetheless, some of the matters that come to the attention of the IPCC are of serious concern. Between 2008/9 and 2010/11, the IPCC received 837 referrals. The majority of these (33 per cent) were for perverting the course of justice, for example, through the falsification of records, perjury at trials and tampering with evidence. The remainder were for theft and fraud (30 per cent), abuse of authority (15 per cent), unauthorised disclosure of information (13 per cent) and misuse of systems (9 per cent). Of all the types of corruption that the IPCC records, perverting the course of justice is the gravest because it is likely to have the most frequent impact on citizens and their perceptions of the police as a troubled institution in crisis.

The police also appear to be in crisis at present because of the speed and scale of organisational reform which is expected of them. The fragility of global markets and the ensuing recession, together with the dominance of the neo-liberal ideological paradigm identified in Chapter 3, has prompted governmental cuts to budgets and 'efficiency savings' in a bid to create a smaller, leaner and less costly public sector. The Comprehensive Spending Review (CSR) in 2010 announced a cut of central government funding for policing of £1.9 billion between 2010/11 and 2014/15, amounting to a 20 per cent cut in police budgets. The scale and pace of these cuts has created challenging conditions for the police. Moreover, neither the National Audit Office (NAO) nor HMIC are confident that all police forces will be able to make the necessary cuts in the specified time scale. In particular, HMIC note that Devon and Cornwall, Gwent, Nottinghamshire, Sussex, West Mercia, Greater Manchester and West Midlands Police will struggle to make the necessary cuts whilst protecting the jobs of frontline staff (2011b: 23). In addition, only 17 forces have firm plans in place to make the necessary savings by 2014/15. Furthermore, 26 forces have shortfalls in their budgets totalling £0.5 billion (HMIC 2011b: 15).

Police pay and conditions have also come under sustained critique which, again, is suggestive of an organisation in crisis. The Winsor reports (2011 and 2012) have recommended, for example, a lower starting salary for new recruits of between £19,000 and £21,000 depending on qualifications and relevant service experience (Winsor 2012: 22–4); a pension age of 60 years; and the introduction of a pay scale which reflects the physical and mental capacity of the police to do the job, including direct entry for inspectors and superintendents and reduced pay for those who fail fitness tests or who are on restricted duties (e.g. due to injury) for more than a year.[14] The Winsor Reports also signal that from the perspective of government, the police are 'fair game' and have to pay their dues just like the rest of the public sector in shouldering the burden of cuts and changes to their working conditions. For example, the reports directly compare the police to other public sector workers, saying that they are 10–15 per cent better paid than them. This higher level of pay, along with the fact that there is less crime and the police work fewer unsocial hours than they did in the past, is then used to make a case for introducing a two-year progression freeze in which police officers would no longer receive their annual increment (Winsor 2011: 15). This progression freeze would be on top of the public sector pay freeze announced in June 2010.

As the 30,000 strong protest of off-duty officers demonstrated on 10 May 2012, the Winsor Report has not been well received by the police. However, the police do not have the same bargaining power that they once had with Conservative governments during the 1980s and 1990s, perhaps because of the support that the police showed Thatcher during the miners' strikes in this period. As such, there is less incentive for the present government to keep the police on board and more reason for them to go ahead with Winsor's recommendations, which also fit with the realisation of their neo-liberal aspirations across the public sector.

These crises over the last decade about racism in the police, police competence in the policing of disorder, police integrity and organisational reforms seem to paint a picture of an organisation in crisis. However, these current crises are not a new phenomenon. Whilst the police institution may seem as if it is in crisis, there is more continuity with the past than this 'crisis' suggests. It is not the first time in the past 40 years that there has been a crisis about racism, incompetence or corruption in the police or the need for organisational reform, and the current 'crisis' in English policing that has been critically assessed over the preceding pages must be seen against this historical backdrop.

In the context of an increasingly multi-ethnic post-war society – in which successive waves of migrants from former British colonies in the West Indies, India, Pakistan and Africa answered the UK's call for workers for difficult-to-fill jobs – racism in the police is an issue which has continuously been of concern. For example, stop and search practices have long been noted as a source of discrimination, dating back at least to the 1970s. In the 1970s, the 'Sus' laws of the Vagrancy Act 1824 were used to arrest and prosecute people for frequenting or loitering in a public place with the intent to commit an arrestable offence. These laws were used particularly against minority ethnic communities particularly black people, including during Operation Swamp which precipitated the Brixton riots (Scarman 1981: 3.27). Following sustained critique of their use in the Royal Commission on Criminal Procedure in 1981, this led to current provisions, which require 'reasonable suspicion' in the Police and Criminal Evidence Act 1984. Nonetheless, this has far from eradicated the problems associated with their use, as the discussion above highlights. Police stop and search practices past and present and their sustained critique over the last 40 years suggest that the police have struggled to adapt to the changing social conditions of policing. As Whitfield notes,

> [a] conservative, inward-looking, largely inexperienced post-war police service, whose priorities lay elsewhere than in the field of community relations, was tasked with policing the nation's transition to an ethnically and culturally diverse society without the legislative support to ensure its success. In such circumstances, it was perhaps inevitable that the transition would be painful for those most directly involved.
>
> (2007: 15)

Similarly, riotous behaviour and the policing of it have also been a source of concern in the past. Some of the first riots, in the period that is the focus of this chapter, were connected to the concerns of more recent migrants and/or the racist attitudes and behaviour of white residents such as in Chapeltown, Notting Hill and Liverpool in 1976, and in Southall in 1979. Later, in the context of Thatcherism, growing deprivation, unemployment, particularly for young black people, social inequality and widespread social unrest arose in the 1980s. These riots were also a manifestation of the increasingly strained relationship between the police and black communities. Rioting broke out first in Bristol in 1980 and then in Brixton in 1981, followed by Manchester, Liverpool and Birmingham. Rioting in Handsworth, Birmingham in 1985 led to the deaths of two Asian men and injury of 100 people and was soon followed in 1985 by the Broadwater Farm riots discussed above (Bowling, Parmar and Phillips 2008).

However, rioting in the 1980s was not just race-related. In the Miners' strikes 1984–5, Northern working-class communities bore the brunt of unjust police practices; MPS officers and officers from other forces were drafted in precisely because they were less likely to be sympathetic towards the miners, unlike local officers. Indeed, the ensuing antipathy towards the police may have continued to have a bearing on police–community relations in these areas, especially in the light of the 'Northern' riots in working-class areas affected by de-industrialisation in Bradford, Burnley and Oldham in 2001.

Furthermore, whilst the recent phone-hacking scandal has been revealing as to the improper relations between the press and the police, police corruption is not new or unique to the police in England. As with racism in the police and to a lesser extent incompetence in the policing of disorder, it is important to note that police corruption has also been a longstanding phenomenon in England and one that has been hard to quantify. Over the last four decades, policing has been affected by high-profile police corruption scandals relating to receiving payments from organised crime (e.g. the Obscene Publications Squad and the Drugs Squad during the 1970s), the suppression of evidence, the assaulting of suspects, the tampering with evidence and perjury (e.g. the Birmingham Six and the Guildford Four during the 1970s). Indeed, Newburn (1999: 45) concludes:

> Police corruption is not new, it has been part of policing for as long as we have had policing. It is also pervasive. It is unlikely that there are many police organisations that are completely corruption-free. That said, although most police organisations are likely to be able to find examples of corruption within their ranks, examples of organised corruption do not reach the public domain all that frequently. In part, because 'individual cases' of corruption are more visible, the idea of 'bad apples' in otherwise clean barrels continues to have considerable currency. This is reinforced by a reluctance on the part of police agencies to admit to organisational corruption, even where there is evidence to suggest that corrupt activities are entrenched.

Finally, organisational reform whether through cutting costs and altering police pay and conditions has also long been a preoccupation of successive governments over the last 40 years, though not always one that directly impacted on the police. For example, the Sheehy Inquiry in 1993 into police pay and rewards and the more recent Winsor Report in 2010/11 bear a number of similarities. Like Winsor, the Sheehy Inquiry had managerialist overtones and was headed by someone supportive of the private sector: Patrick Sheehy was the head of British American Tobacco. It also recommended short-term contracts, reduced starting salaries for new recruits, performance-related pay and the abolition of three ranks. Furthermore, at the time, the police were outraged by the manner in which the Sheehy Report was foisted on them with little consultation as well as by the sustained assault on UK policing that it signalled. However, perhaps one key point of variation between the Winsor and Sheehy Reports is that most of Sheehy's recommendations were shelved or watered down, in the end, due to Police Federation resistance, a protest rally supported by chief officers and a government which at the time was receptive to their concerns. Nonetheless, like Winsor, the report signalled that policing was no longer seen as sacrosanct by government (Loader and Mulcahy 2006: 291–2).

Taken together, this continuity between the past and present in relation racism in the police, the policing of disorder, police corruption and organisational reform suggests that there is not so much 'a crisis' in English policing, but rather there have been a series of crises over the last 40 years. The current so-called crisis is part of a longstanding trend, rather than being a stand-alone event and is suggestive of a more generalised sense of crisis in the police in England.

Contributing factors and wider ramifications

This series of crises in policing over the last 40 years, as explored above, can be explained in two main ways. First, the police have been edging and are now seemingly hurtling towards their current predicament since the 1970s, if not before, as evidenced by declining trust in the police since the heyday of the English bobby in the 1950s (Reiner 1995, Bradford et al. 2009). This demystification of the police as revered defenders of the social order is known as the desacralisation thesis. The desacralisation of policing means that it is easier and more likely for the police to be knocked off their proverbial 'perch', as they are no longer regarded by the public as the sacred and revered totem that they once were in the 1950s. Second, these crises and the decline in trust in the police that underlie them have been set in motion by wider social, economic and political changes particularly over the last 40 years; society has become increasingly unequal, less deferential, multi-ethnic, individualist and neo-liberal. The less deferential attitude of the public towards the police is particularly significant; it suggests that no matter what the police do, their actions will be questioned by citizens. Politicians have similarly demonstrated an increasingly questioning and less deferential attitude towards the police, as shown by successive governments' withdrawal of unconditional support for the police over the last 40 years and their support for more robust forms of police governance.

However, the increasingly diverse nature of English society means that the decline in trust and deference towards the police over the last 40 years has not been a uniform process, as critics of the desacralisation thesis note. In fact, the decline in trust in the police is not necessarily a one-way street from the sacred to the profane and, in addition, support for the police remains high amongst certain sections of the population but not others (Loader and Mulcahy 2006: 32–6). Through their exploration of the culture of English policing,[15] Loader and Mulcahy (2006) offer an alternative explanation for this decline in trust in the police. In particular, they identify three sets of dispositions towards English policing expressed by the public, the police and government officials[16] – dominant, residual and emergent – which reveal a complex mixture of sacred and profane world views of policing.[17] The co-existence of these different dispositions towards English policing also helps to explain why it is that, in spite of the general decline in trust in the police in the post-war period, some parts of the public – in particular, those who express the residual world view, in Loader and Mulcahy's terminology – continue to express a commitment to English policing, for example, by routinely demanding more bobbies on the beat.

The implication is that whilst the research evidence suggests that objectively there have been a series of crises in the police over the last 40 years, not all of the public necessarily view the police institution as in crisis. For the majority of the public who subscribe to the dominant world view of English policing that Loader and Mulcahy (2006: 305–11) identify, they are more likely to find fault with the police and thus view the series of concerns and controversies about the police over the last 40 years as indicative of an institution in crisis. At the same time, there is a small albeit significant minority of dissenting voices amongst those whose world view of policing harks back to the bobbies of the past (residual) or looks forward to the possibility of democratic policing of the future (emergent). For this minority, in spite of the series of crises in policing that have arisen over the last 40 years, the police institution continues to have purchase and they may be less likely to view them as in crisis. Indeed perhaps these world views, which encompass support for the police, are something that should be encouraged amongst the wider populace, if the most recent crisis in the police institution is to become a much needed turning point and used to galvanise change and increase the public's trust in the police once again. As discussed below, more trusting relationships between police and citizens might be encouraged, for example, by requiring the police to treat citizens in a more equitable manner during their day-to-day interactions with them.

What the preceding discussion highlights is that what is important is perhaps not so much whether there is a crisis or series of crises, which can be objectively documented and evidenced through research, but rather whether the public perceives and understands them as such; that is, public opinions of the police are vitally important. Indeed, this is something that police services, particularly under the last government, had begun increasingly to recognise with moves to measure police performance in terms of public confidence in the police, rather than crime rates. Though the concept of confidence in the police is somewhat vague, this attempt by the police to impact on public opinions of and trust in them was perhaps too little too late and might be read as those within the police institution taking the public's trust in them for granted and losing touch with the principles on which the police institution was founded. After all, the public's opinions of the police are so vitally important because they offer a window into the extent to which the public consent to being policed which, as noted earlier, was one of the defining principles of the 'new police'. More fundamentally, public opinions of the police perhaps also offer a window into the health or otherwise of the relationship between citizens and the state, the police being one of the main manifestations of the state, with the police and the state mirroring each other respectively at the micro- and macro-level (Brodeur 2010: 109–10).

Therefore, in response to the third question about wider ramifications, the generalised sense of crisis in the police institution which has arisen over the last 40 years is important because of the fundamental role that the police play in the governance of democratic societies. As noted at the beginning of the chapter, the police are part of a network of organisations which contribute to the broader processes of social control. A breakdown in the relationship between police and citizens is likely to undermine the capacity of the police (and others) to perform this important role. In particular, the current predicament suggests that some sections of society – including 'police property', those on the receiving end of unfair police practices and, more worryingly, a substantial number of people who subscribe to the dominant world view of policing – may be in the process of withdrawing their consent to being policed. As one of the founding principles of the 'new police', the crises in policing over the last 40 years therefore have the potential to rock the foundation of the modern police institution. Moreover, unless this perceived crisis can be successfully averted, the symbiotic nature of the relationship between the police, other criminal justice agencies and the state means that the 'crisis' also has the potential to erode the legitimacy of other parts of the criminal justice process, including prosecutorial processes and the penal system, and perhaps even the state as a whole. This possibility seems all the more likely given the cumulative effect of the crises in policing, in combination with crises arising in the other institutions that are the focus of this book.

Conclusion

The aim of this chapter is to address three key questions. First, what evidence is there of a shift from the police being seen as revered defenders of the social order to an institution currently in 'crisis'? Second, what factors have contributed to this shift? Third, what are the wider ramifications of this? In relation to racism in the police, the policing of disorder, police corruption and organisational reform, the current so-called crisis in English policing does suggest that the police are no longer the revered defenders of the social order that they used to be in their heyday, but then so do the string of other crises in policing over the last 40 years. The current so-called crisis must be seen in the context of a series of crises in English policing and not in isolation from the past. This is because the origins of this current crisis do no merely emanate from present-day social conditions, but rather from shifts and changes that have emerged over the last 40 years. As one of the most visible manifestations of the state, this growing lack of trust and regard for the police suggests that it is not just the police institution that is coming under a sustained critique from citizens in whose trust and on whose consent it depends, but prosecutorial processes, the penal system and perhaps even the state too.

This raises a key question about the extent to which the police can claw their way back from this string of crises over the past 40 years and the extent to which the present-day crisis might act as a turning point for the police institution and be used to galvanise reform. It is beyond the scope of this chapter to discuss how recent socio-political changes that have contributed to the current crisis in policing might be altered. Instead, the focus is on more practical steps that could be taken to improve the way that the police interact with citizens and improve the public's opinion of them, which are more broadly situated within attempts to improve the governance of the police.[18] One way would be to encourage the police to alter the way that they interact with citizens on a day-to-day basis; a growing body of empirical research shows that the police are more likely to be viewed as being legitimate if they act in procedurally just ways towards citizens, for example, talking politely to them and treating them with dignity and respect (e.g. Tyler 2003, Bottoms and Tankebe 2012). Moreover, it has also been found that this is more likely to encourage citizen consent to policing and compliance with the law, than the effectiveness of the police, for example (Tyler 2003).

Such procedurally just treatment of citizens might be encouraged by developing a publicly known framework which encourages a more ethical approach to policing and also acknowledges the ethical dilemmas that police officers face. This emphasis on ethics in policing is particularly applicable to police corruption, though it is also of relevance to the other aspects of policing considered in this chapter, whether that is when conducting stop and searches or participating in public order policing or when dealing with the press or protesting about police reforms. For example, it is clearly relevant to decisions about the deployment of tactics like water cannons and attenuated energy projectiles (rubber bullets) in public order situations, which are being mooted as a possibility in the future (HMIC 2011a: 4–5). Newburn (1999: 48) notes that police organisations might learn from the Nolan Committee which was set up in 1995 to explore standards in public life and identified principles such as selflessness, objectivity, accountability, openness, honesty and leadership. As such, the review of the original Committee's recommendations announced on 29 May 2012 holds out much promise (Committee on Standards in Public Life 2012); if applied to the police, as well as other institutions that are perceived to be in crisis, it could create parity across these institutions in terms of the ethical principles guiding actions and behaviour and help to alter the perception of the police and other institutions as being in crisis.

However, encouraging the police to act in procedurally just ways – for example, through a framework of ethics which cuts across public institutions – may be insufficient on its own. This is because compliance with such frameworks would depend to a large degree on individual officers' discretion. There are two ways to bolster such discretion one depending on boosting internal restraint and the other on external regulation. There are many ways to bolster internal restraint but a significant approach would be to establish a graduate profession which has and enforces its own ethical requirements much like nurses and medical doctors. Turning to external regulation of individual officers and forces, the recent introduction of police and crime commissioners and the plans to further increase the independence and powers of the Independent

Police Complaints Commission (IPCC) might help the police to act and be perceived as acting in a fair manner towards citizens and in the conduct of their duties more generally.[19] It is also necessary to have additional mechanisms which more formally regulate the way police interact with citizens, particularly during social crises in which the police play a repressive role. Human rights conventions and legislation are important in this regard, as the Gillan and Quinton vs. the United Kingdom case shows.[20] In the future, human rights values should be given a central place in police policies in the way that Patten (1998) suggested in relation to policing in Northern Ireland.[21] The Human Rights Act and the European Convention/Court on/of Human Rights should be defended for enhancing the legitimacy of public institutions like the police, rather than being discredited for undermining national sovereignty.

Taken together these measures can be thought of as being more broadly concerned with improving the governance of the police. After a string of crises in the police in England over the last 40 years, improved police governance is vital if the present crisis is to be a turning point for the police institution. The improvements to police governance discussed above might reshape the police institution into something in which the public can once again trust and believe in; for example, an emphasis on ethics and the creation of a publicly known ethical code, which is backed up by individual officers' sense of responsibility towards it, as well as external oversight of compliance with it, might help the public to recognise that contrary to what the crises in the police have revealed, the police operate with a similar set of values to the rest of society. Such improvements to police governance may also contribute to them being an organisation with which the public will cooperate, as well as to a sense of policing by consent. These improvements might also go some way towards redressing the readiness to criticise and question the police which has arisen over the last 40 years. Ultimately, what is at stake here is the legitimacy of the police, as well as the other institutions with which they are associated including the other criminal justice agencies and the state too. The series of crises in the police over the last 40 years means that there is much hard work to be done by those within the police institution and beyond to win over the public and to reignite widespread public support for the police in England.

Notes

1. For example, this police officer was responsible for finding out information that led to Stephen Lawrence's friend, Duwayne Brooks, being charged with criminal damage, although the case was later thrown at court (Evans and Lewis 2013, Lewis and Evans 2013b).

2. This chapter refers to policing in England as opposed to the UK as the history and legal position of the police in the rest of the UK is specific to each nation.
3. Initially, they were lightly armed with a truncheon and a rattle. Following a spate of murders, they were later covertly armed with a pistol and, eventually, disarmed again once the danger passed (Waddington 1999). This contrasts with some of the present-day armoury available to the police including Tasers and incapacitant spray, as well as to specialist armed units such as SO19, both of which suggest a shift towards the militarisation of the police.
4. Whilst the Coalition government may argue that this need for austerity stems from the triple dip recession, this rolling back of the state began in the 1980s under Margaret Thatcher and arguably stems from an ideological commitment to these kind of neo-liberal policies, rather than on an assessment of the current situation.
5. By this, Macpherson meant 'the collective failure of an organisation to provide an appropriate and professional service to people because of their colour, culture or ethnic origin. It can be seen or detected in processes, attitudes and behaviour, which amount to discrimination through unwitting prejudice, ignorance, thoughtlessness, and racist stereotyping which disadvantage minority ethnic people' (1999: 6.34, 28).
6. The obligatory independent investigation into his death will clarify the circumstances and lawfulness of his death, though at the time of writing it has yet to be published.
7. The location of his death was not far from the Broadwater Farm Estate which was the location of race-related rioting in 1985, sparked by the death of Cynthia Jarrett following police contact. She was the mother of Floyd Jarrett, who was arrested for having a counterfeit tax disc on his car, which led the police to search his house. During the search and in a disturbance between his family and the police, his mother died. During the riot, a community policeman, PC Keith Blakelock, was stabbed to death.
8. Corruption is notoriously difficult to define. Nonetheless, Newburn (1999: 7–8) offers some useful identifiers. First, attention must be paid to the means, ends and motivations behind corruption. In particular, he suggests that the motivation behind an act is corrupt when the primary intention is to further private or organisational advantage. Second, corruption need not only involve illegal acts, but can also include 'approved' goals, such as 'catching bad guys', no matter what. This can lead to a kind of 'noble cause' corruption. Third, corruption may involve the use/abuse of organisational authority and, fourth, can be both internal and external in its effects.
9. They are undertaking investigations into phone-hacking (Operation Weeting), inappropriate payments of police officers by the media (Operation Eleveden), and computer hacking by the media (Operation Tuleta).
10. See HMIC (2011b).
11. See, for example, IPCC (2011a) and IPCC (2012).
12. See Filkin (2011).
13. Between August 2011 and July 2012, Lord Justice Leveson explored the culture, practices and ethics of the press, in relation to the public, the police, and politicians.

14. After a further year, those who are on restricted duties could be dismissed, retired or asked to resign and immediately take up a police staff role (on lower pay) if one is available.
15. They define it as 'the amalgam of institutions, practices and policies, myths, memories, meanings, and values that, at any given time, constitute the idea of policing within English society' (Loader and Mulcahy 2006: 303).
16. One set of views that is missing from their analysis are the views of academics. It would have been of interest to examine their comparability with the world views of those who were included in their study and the direction of influence. For instance, to what extent do academic perspectives on the police influence public sentiments towards them?
17. Dominant world views reflect the culture of scrutiny and complaint exhibited towards the police, though these complaints are made in an individualised way which is unconnected to the democratic process. By contrast, residual world views express a reverence for the local beat bobby of the past and thus for locally delivered and accountable policing, whilst emergent dispositions are connected to a more democratic understanding of policing, which emphasises things like equality and political accountability.
18. Police governance refers to more than the 'constitutional and institutional arrangements for framing and directing the policies of the police' (Jones 2003: 605), which include legal regulation and organisational accountability mechanisms. It also includes the wider patterns of social ordering in which the police play a part and which also apply to them too in the way they conduct their duties. After all, the police play a role in upholding the norms and values of society, as set out in the criminal law, in order to maintain a particular social order. These norms and values apply as much to police officers as to other citizens. In this sense, police governance and the processes of governance in which the police engage are simultaneously separate but overlapping.
19. Police and crime commissioners (PCCs) were elected for the first time in November 2012 as a new form of supposedly more democratic police governance. At the time of writing, their impact remains unclear, though some appear to have begun flexing their muscles, for example, the Chief Constable of Avon and Somerset Police stepped down having been asked to re-apply for his job by the PCC.
20. Gillan & Quinton vs. UK 50 EHRR 45.
21. Patten said that policing 'should be based on principles of protection of human rights and professional integrity and should be unambiguously accepted and actively supported by the entire community' (1998: para 1.9, p. 5).

Conclusion: Après le Deluge? Crisis, Continuity and Change in UK Institutions

David Richards, Martin Smith and Colin Hay

Introduction

Throughout this volume on institutions and crisis, there have been a number of comparisons drawn between the 1970s and the present day. Yet, one of the paradoxes to emerge during the course of the 1970s was the extent to which, while a sense of both political and economic crisis particularly in the latter stages of that decade loomed large, many of the institutions explored in this volume were at the same time still robustly defended. Indeed, for those with long memories, a popular refrain, not exclusive to the political class, was that 'Britain had the best armed forces, police force, judiciary, civil service [or any of the above] in the world'. Supporting evidence substantiating such claims was mainly conspicuous by its absence and was more often than not the product of a still lingering imperial superiority.

The contrast with the present is striking. For what we have seen throughout the contributing chapters in this book is that a wide range of UK institutions have faced a period of crisis in the sense that a critical event or set of events has led to a questioning of the functioning and effectiveness of the institution. These events have often led to resignations, inquests and reforms, many of which remain ongoing. In some cases the crises are acute, as in the case of the banks; in others they are more chronic, as in the case of political parties or police. Sometime crises are overtly political – as in the case of Whitehall where the crisis is partly a reflection of a power battle between politicians and ministers and at other times they may be media creations. What is striking is that today apologists have replaced the 1970s' antediluvian voices which once so stridently proclaimed that the major institutions of the UK were paragons of best practice that others would do well to replicate.

Rightly or wrongly the word 'crisis' has been applied to a wide range of events and institutions and the liberal use of the word raises the question of whether the notion of crisis has any analytical weight. Nevertheless, there is little doubt that a number of key institutions in the UK have suffered notable failures in recent years – and that these failures have been or have become intensely politicised. In some cases, these manifest as multiple failures – for example the police, the media, the banks and the parliament – where there seems to be a continual flow of stories of misjudgement, mismanagement and at times illegality. There are also other institutional pathologies that the constraint of a single volume has not afforded the opportunity to explore: child protection; failures of hospitals within the NHS; reoccurring crises in education; child abuse in both the Church and media organisations; rising child poverty; and continuing challenges to the role and functions of local government being some of the more prominent. Today, it is rare to find a UK institution in which some type of failure or pathology has not contributed to a wider sense of crisis.

Approaches to explaining crisis

One central question of the book is whether there is a connection between these crises. Has there been a series of unconnected events that are exacerbated and exaggerated by the scrutiny of the media or is there something more fundamental here about the character of the major UK institutions? In a sense, this is the claim of the risk society approach which sees crisis as endemic within the late modern world. However, there is a range of responses. One is that the present proliferation of crises is an outcome of the financial crisis, that the sudden rupture of the economic crash of 2008 has had a knock-on effect in the confidence and functioning of a far greater range of UK institutions. Certainly public expenditure cuts have impacted on the ability of institutions to fulfil their functions (e.g. the delivery of accident and emergency in hospitals or the growing crisis over housing). However the problem with putting the focus on the 2007–08 financial crisis and its aftermath is one of causality. In many cases, the crises explored throughout this volume predate 2008 and in others, the way crisis has unfurled has had little directly to do with the economy. However, as we discuss below, there is a way in which the recent financial crisis has contributed to a wider loss of faith in government, the political class and, at times, in other sets of actors associated with the institutions we have explored throughout this volume. In so doing, it has reaffirmed a general dissatisfaction with the working practices associated with these formal institutions and more specifically the way in which politics is conducted.

The second possibility is that this is, as Richards highlights in Chapter 1, an issue of expectations. This is not a debate simply confined to concerns over the way in which democratic politics currently functions, as the chapters in this volume on the financial sector, the media and police reveal, although it does tend to draw the lion's share of attention. In terms then of the political, as we outlined in the Introduction, the conservative approach to crisis places the blame for popular dislocation from formal democratic practices on the demands of a simplistic electorate who expect too much and are disappointed when institutions fail. Such an approach alights upon a failure to appreciate the contingencies involved. Elsewhere, as we have seen, policing is a challenging and complex occupation and there are bound to be failures. Governing the country involves compromises and complexities and, as such, what is ultimately delivered is perceived as sub-optimal. As (2012a: 7) muses, 'Is it possible that we "hate" politics because we have forgotten its specific and limited nature, its overwhelming value, and also its innate fragility? Could it be that our expectations are so high that politics appears almost destined to disappoint?' He then points out that politicians have often fed rather than dampened these expectations. However, two big questions arise from this view. First, are the crises outlined in this book really a product of unrealistic expectations? Is it unrealistic to expect banks not to purse high-risk investment strategies well beyond their current assets, police not to give misleading or in some cases fallacious accounts of the death of citizens, journalists not to hack into mobile phones or politicians not to make false expense claims? How limited should expectations be in a democratic system? What evidence is there to suggest that lowering expectations encourages public leaders to behave in a more appropriate fashion?

A related theme is whether disappointment and disillusionment in formal politics is the fault of the voters or the political system and the politicians. Both Flinders and Riddell claim that politicians are 'normal' people, but in what sense are they normal? The former New Labour strategist and pollster, Deborah Mattinson (2010: 5) highlights that her focus group work in the mid-1980s on how the public perceived politicians revealed a 'very clear pen portrait' invoking such characteristics as upper-class, male, pinstriped suit, rich, went to Eton, lives in a mansion, works in the City, etc. Clearly, there is a gap here between perception and the demographic reality. But to what extent can the lives of politicians – be it Macmillan, Thatcher, Blair, Cameron, Clegg, Miliband, etc. – ever really be expected to resonate with the lives of ordinary voters? What is their connection with the normal voters? Even when they meet 'ordinary' people, they tend to be people interested in politics or community activities. They react to events through a filter of the media and Westminster.

For Mattinson (2010: 289–91), this is an issue that is more acute now than it was three decades ago. Her extensive survey work throughout this period leads her to conclude that

> the relationship between the voter and politician is more dysfunctional now than ever before. The ... Westminster village has changed. It has become more rarefied; increasingly made up of politicians and journalists who have a singly minded focus on political process ... The Westminster-based political class lead lives that are vastly different from those whom they purport to represent, with different aims, different views, different attitudes.

In a similar vein, Docx (2013) suggests that to be convincing, party leaders today have had to adopt particular personas. But in so doing, rather than convince, they illustrate the leader's lack of authenticity: 'Now because both Cameron and Miliband – for their different reasons – suffer from this distracting dissonance between public and private personality, neither is able naturally to connect with the public.' Mattinson (2010: 287) offers a rather different perspective, but draws a similar conclusion:

> Voters demand to see politicians in the round: to know about their backgrounds, their families, their hobbies, their homes – to get to know them as people. Unsurprisingly, many politicians fail to live up to this kind of scrutiny. Fearing failure, some cannot resist sacrificing authenticity in favour of a more saleable back-up story.

Elsewhere, the three main political parties' responses to the success of UKIP in the 2013 local election are revealing. What has transpired is almost a knee-jerk reaction to UKIP's policies rather than any attempt to understand the concerns of citizens. The Conservatives seek a more sceptical line on Europe and Labour a harder line on immigration, but this is done as if people voted ideologically for UKIP and not as a protest vote against current mainstream politics in relatively small numbers. Similarly Andrew Adonis' account of the formation of the Coalition, *5 Days in May*, perhaps unwittingly reveals how insular and inward looking the political class is 'concerned about their own political fortunes with little reference to the voters. The voters have produced a result that they have to sort out' (Adonis 2013: 4).

Institutional crisis and the pathology of the BPT

Rather than focus on the recent financial tsunami or public expectations as the main drivers behind the current set of crisis operating across the various institutions explored in this volume (although both may have played a contributing role), instead the main argument presented here focuses on what is seen as a set of deeply embedded, pathological failings within the UK political settlement. Their emergence has long been visible. Indeed, what each of the individual chapters more often than not reveals is that the roots of the current multiple crises confronting UK's institutions first became visible in the 1960s.

The question of the crisis of the UK state was initiated by Perry Anderson who wrote in 1964:

> The present crisis is a general malady of the whole society, infrastructure and superstructure – not a sudden breakdown, but a slow, sickening entropy. All the conditions which constituted the unique good fortune of the ruling bloc in the 19th century have turned against it. The 'law' of uneven development has produced its customary dialectical reversal – with a vengeance. Today, Britain stands revealed as a sclerosed, archaic society, trapped and burdened by its past successes, now for the first time aware of its lassitude, but as yet unable to overcome it.

The 1960s was the beginning of the realisation that the UK was no longer a world political or economic power. The Second World War had left the UK exhausted and led to the final dissolution of the Empire (which was a slow post-war process) and growing dependence on the USA. The 1950s and 60s saw the UK overtaken by France and Germany economically. The UK's uncomfortable journey to full-blown membership of what was then the European Common Market in 1973 reveals the difficulties of the political leaders reconciling themselves to the loss of its world power status (George 1988, Young 1999). At the same time, during this period, changes in society and culture lead to the first sustained popular challenge to the UK's governing class.

However, it was the 1970s which saw a more fundamental questioning of the post-1945 polity. The combination of low UK growth, the end of the post-war boom and a global oil crisis exposed the fundamental weaknesses of the UK economy. The Keynesianism of the post-war political economy was undermined by the development of sustained bouts of stagflation (Gamble 1994a). In addition, the delicate consensus between business and the unions was pulled apart by trade union attempts to maintain living standards when faced with high inflation. The welfare bargain of both the Wilson and later the Callaghan Labour governments was also questioned by seeming rising costs and continued failure to tackle deep-seated social problems.

The besetting sins of club regulation and secrecy

The dominant theme to emerge from the various contributions to this volume and underlying the re-occurring of crises is a failure to adapt both the political system and its associated institutions to the changing world. Perceptions of risk may have changed. It may be that citizens expect to be better informed but the governance of UK institutions has remained relatively stable. Put another way, the fault lies in the sustaining of the British political tradition (BPT) and with it the stoking-up of a series of pathologies that have led to the present crisis. We would argue that many of the characteristics associated with the BPT and its related system of government manifested in the Westminster model are ones that have been replicated elsewhere in the institutions explored through this volume.

In bringing these arguments together, our focus is drawn to what we consider to be the pathologies that emerged from the BPT. Crucial to the normative ideas underpinning the BPT is the notion that the political class should operate within a self-regulating arena to protect against outside, potentially undemocratic, influence (Judge 1993, Moran 2003). This *modus operandi* can be traced back to the 19th century, where, alongside the emergence of a new democratic settlement, was the embedding first of what Moran (2003) refers to as a system of 'club regulation' among the UK's political elite but also what Vincent (1998) identifies as the principle of 'honourable secrecy'. In terms of the former, Moran (2003: 32) notes that one of the original accounts of the BPT by David Marquand portrayed the Westminster model as

> a synonym for the 'club model'...The atmosphere of British government was that of a club, whose members trusted each other to observe the spirit of the club rules: the notion that the principles underlying the rules should be clearly defined and publicly proclaimed was profoundly alien.
>
> (Moran 2003: 32)

The emergence of a culture of club regulation is coupled with the development by the UK's political elite of an ethical code of honourable secrecy which Vincent (1998) traces back to the 1860s. This code was formulated on the creation of a culture of 'instinctive self-censorship which... would render unnecessary the overt use of formal regulations' (Vincent, 1998: 28–9). Such a code was based on the notion of 'gentlemanly honour' and all the social, hierarchical and class characteristics of mid-19th century UK such a concept evokes. It was originally used to defend against the need for an Official Secrets Act, but after 1911 its legacy, as an ethos espousing 'discreet reserve' and the 'negation of personal interest', particularly in matters concerning public policy negotiations, continued to shape the outlook of the UK's political class (Vincent 1998: 315).

In practice, what followed over the next 150 years was the political class resolutely defending the principle that it alone should act as its own judge and jury. This was captured in key characteristics of the Westminster model: the doctrine of ministerial responsibility meant that only democratically elected politicians faced public accountability for their actions, though in practice the secrecy surrounding the policy-making process offered a welcome comfort blanket of protection; civil servants remained anonymous, shielded from public view. Crucially, responsibility for this self-regulating system was vested in Whitehall's senior elite who were imbued with the values associated with gentlemanly honour. Chapman (1993: 104), quoting from an *Establishment's Officers Guide*, highlights the self-reverence of this approach: 'It has never been thought necessary to lay down a precise code of conduct because civil servants jealously maintain their professional standards', opting instead for 'the maintenance of a general code of conduct which, although to some extent intangible and unwritten, is of very real influence'. The 'arbiter of last resort' in this system is the Cabinet Secretary (Hennessy 1995). It is perhaps indicative of the insularity of this approach that former Cabinet Secretary William Armstrong could say without any sense of irony that he was accountable to himself, the great taskmaster: 'I am accountable to my own ideal of a civil servant' (Richards and Smith 2000: 61).

Some notable characteristics then of the BPT, appearing in various guises throughout the chapters in this volume, include that of elitism, a lack of transparency and accountability, and an aloof detachment between the governors and the governed. Such characteristics could only operate in a less deferential era. Today, in an era of increasing demystification, their contradictions, indeed pathologies, are increasingly hard to sustain. As Marquand (2004: 5) observes,

> Upright and conscientious though they were, the elites that ran its institutions were often aloof and condescending. Accountability was often lacking. Above all, the operational codes and tacit understandings of the central state were saturated with pre-democratic, essentially monarchical assumptions and values, which became increasingly out of joint with the attitudes of a better-educated and less deferential citizenry; and as the state sank in esteem, the public domain all too often sank with it.

Yet, despite numerous question raised about the institutional structure of the UK political system, there has been little attempt to reform the system. The broad structure of the current system of UK government is one based on a 19th-century model of democracy which sees a clear distinction between rulers and rules. It is based on a considerable distance between voter and governor. The connection was mainly through voting but a more intense connection was created by political parties. However, whilst the Westminster system has largely remained intact, the process of governing bears almost no relation to 19th-century governance. The levels of intervention of the state in everyday life are manifestly different now compared to the 19th-century. Moreover, state intervention does not come from a centralised government (which oversees the process) but from an almost infinite range of fragmented institutions that deliver policy – and these days this can range from private bodies to local government, to regional organisations, to semi-independent NHS trusts, free schools and universities. Indeed, Marquand (2004: 2) goes so far as to suggest that over recent decades what has emerged is:

> a relentless *kulturkampf* designed to root out the culture of service and citizenship which had become part of the social fabric. De-regulation, privatisation, so-called public-private partnerships, proxy markets, performance indicators mimicking those of the private corporate sector, and a systematic assault on professional autonomy narrowed the public domain and blurred the distinction between it and the market domain. Public functions of all kinds were farmed out to unaccountable appointed bodies, dominated by business interests and managed according to market principles. Intermediate institutions

like the BBC, the universities, the schools, the museums and the health service were forced, so far as possible into a market mould.

What has emerged in this complex, more diverse arena is an ever-expanding dissonance between the elector, voting for a particular potential government and the final delivery of public services. Voters have marginal, if no control or participation in how policies are made or how they are delivered. Indeed, many may be confused or unaware over who is delivering a particular service. Lines of accountability are not transparent. In this sense, we reject the determinism of the risk society approach – increased perceptions of risk are not inevitable in later modernity. However, if people do not trust their institutions, they are less likely to believe the reassurances they are offered over, for example, genetically modified food, fracking or a death in custody. From this perspective, there is a relationship between secrecy and institutional failure and trust. The former leads people to perceive that there is something to hide and that institutions are not being truthful about risk (which is what happened in the case of Bovine spongiform encephalitis in the 1990s).

Yet, at the same time the scrutiny of institutions is greater than before. As noted above, the 19th-century model was based on the ideal of club government (see Chapter 6). In other words, the rulers were allowed to get on with ruling without interference because they were 'good chaps' who could be trusted. This 'good chaps' (sic!) model of governing or leadership was one whereby elements of which could be discerned to varying degrees in the majority of UK political institutions (Moran 2003) and essentially meant that appointments and decisions were made with little public justification or accountability. Why would accountability be necessary when the rulers could be trusted to do what was best? To give one striking example of the impact and secrecy of club government: between 1947 and 1967 10,000 children were taken from mainly single mothers and forcibly deported to Australia. Neither the mothers nor the children were told the truth about what happened and the whole process was covered up. Such decisions were taken on the basis that the authorities knew what was best for the children. But this is just one emotive example of many cases where decisions have been made in closed secretive ways ranging from decisions on nuclear weapons, the selling of arms to Iraq, mad cow disease and, more recently, issues in relation to weapons of mass destruction in Iraq.

The traditional elite model of government with a closed, relatively small and connected group of individuals is in charge of key decisions with only limited scrutiny – as the chapters of this book illustrate. Parallels could be drawn with what C. Wright Mills, in the 1950s, described as the power elite in the USA:

> Composed of men whose positions enable them to transcend the ordinary environments of ordinary men and women; they are in positions to make decisions having major consequences. Whether they do or do not make such decisions is less important than the fact that they do occupy such pivotal positions: their failure to act, their failure to make decisions, is itself an act that is often of greater consequence than the decisions they do make. For they are in command of the major hierarchies and organisations of modern society. They rule the big corporations. They run the machinery of the state and claim its prerogatives. They direct the military establishment. They occupy the strategic command posts of the social structure, in which are now centred the effective means of the power and the wealth and the celebrity which they enjoy.

Yet, while such a model has been increasingly hard to sustain, core features still remain today. We continue to see decisions made by small groups of inter-related individuals from similar backgrounds and with close connections that have a sizeable influence over key institutions in UK society (Marsh 2002, Marsh, Richards and Smith 2003, Cohen 2004, Walden 2006, Oborne 2008, Richards, Blunkett and Mathers 2008, McGuiness 2010, Mount 2013). At the same time, the levels of inequality in the UK have increased and in particular the gap between the rich and the rest has grown. As Dorling (2013) points out, in 1945 the richest 0.01 received 123 times the national average, by 1978 it had fallen to 28 times, but by 1997 it had increased 99 times and by 2007 the rich had regained all their losses and more with their income being 144 times the national average. Since 1979, we have seen the well-off becoming richer and at the same time the political class has become a more closed and uniformed group (see Chapter 5). An enlightening revelation of the Leveson Inquiry was the extent to which the police, media and politicians maintained not only close political relations but also close personal relations. At the same time working-class and socially deprived communities have been come increasingly alienated from political processes and their associated political and social elites. As Jones (2011) illustrates, the working class has become increasingly demonised. This demonisation has led to a growing moral politics where the working class are blamed for their unemployment and ill health (through smoking, drinking and obesity), alongside the emergence of increasing social and political differences between those at the top and bottom of the social structure (Dorling 2013).

The economic crisis reveals the nature of the inequality even more starkly. As we saw in Chapter 9, bankers continue to claim astronomical severance packages and those who still work up the upper echelons of banks continue to receive large bonuses, while the population endures the brunt of the cuts. The austerity programme in effect leaves the general public paying for the mistakes of the political and economic classes. In this context, it is perverse to be surprised at the dissatisfaction of the ordinary voter expressed in disengagement from the formal political arenas. To try to sideline such a response as 'cynical' and 'anti-political', reflecting a civic decadence on the part of the electorate is demeaning. In past times, the BPT has always sort to ensure power was in the hands of the elite, but it was legitimised by the participation of citizens in voting and in effect subscribing or endorsing a set of informal rules of the game. The danger for that tradition revealed by this current crisis is that it has been demystified over time and so lost or at least is increasingly losing its legitimacy, as the electorate are more willing to question and challenge existing (previously unrevealed) practices. The end game in this process is an electorate less inclined to vote or, if it does vote, to no longer support the traditional mainstream parties.

The erosion of secrecy and the fading of the old rules of club government

One of the responses to the changes wrought by the contemporary crises discussed throughout this volume is that the modern elites have become more insular. It is a response to the changes in the media, interest groups, digital technology, the constitution (with freedom of information) and continued institutional failure each of which has contributed to a process of undermining the old social mores underpinning the club government. In recent times, the most symbolic example of club government failure is provided by the parliamentary expenses scandal. Here was a classic 'club government' system. The system of expenses was determined, regulated and distributed by MPs. Much of the claiming was done through a set of unspoken rules about the nature of the claims and how they could be used to supplement for the fact that MPs salaries would not be increased. In this sense, it was not a failure of individual MPs but a systemic failure of openness. It would have continued unquestioned had not the Freedom of Information Act enabled the freelance journalist Heather Brook and others to pursue information on MPs expenses (and illustratively, the initial response from parliament was to try to get MPs exempted from the freedom of information to prevent the revealing of claims). The shining of a light exposed a practise that had little legitimacy with the public and indeed the issue was that politicians were not honest about what was happening. As Engelen et al. (2012) highlight, a similar sort of hubris and technocratic policy-making can be identified in the banking crisis with the banks and regulators overseeing internalised governance on a subject seen as too complicated for public engagement. In the cases of the Hillsborough disaster, the shooting of Jean de Menzies and the killing of Ian Tomlinson, it appears that the initial response of the police was even cruder with the manipulation of information being released in the period following deaths and, in the case of Hillsborough, a systematic attempt to prevent the truth being revealed. Elsewhere, in June 2013, another lobbying scandal involving both MPs and peers being seen to accept cash from special interests again reveals the weakness of self-imposed, 'voluntary' regulation. What these examples and many elsewhere in this book highlight is that closed decision-making often leads to questionable decisions and the exposure of those decisions undermines the legitimacy of the institutions.

The problem with all these cases is that the truth has been revealed after the event. There is a pattern of bad decisions being taken in closed political systems which when investigated and exposed have created a crisis that has produced a loss of faith in the political system (Marquand 2004: 8–36). What these crises share is a distance between the public and the policy-makers and attempts by policy-makers to make decisions effectively in secret and then to cover up where failures have occurred. Yet it is increasingly difficult for institutions to control information. The nature of Ian Tomlinson's death was revealed by mobile phone footage. The mistakes of Hillsborough were revealed by a long campaign involving the relatives of the victims.

Hence the crisis of UK institutions can be understood in terms of an increasing perception of a gap between citizens and decision-makers and with it, the failure of political institutions to adapt to the demands and pressures of 21st-century democracy. Elite government sits uncomfortably with what Castell (2000) identifies as the rise of the networked society based on a sharing of information driven by the rise of new digital technologies. Moreover, whilst inequality has increased since 1979, citizens now have more control over their own lives. Standards of living have increased since 1945, people own their houses, they have their own cars and they travel abroad. Elite government may have been able to function in a world of limited horizons and the ability to control information, but it is increasingly difficult to sustain in a climate in which people have greater expectations for themselves and their children.

The problem is that the 'club government' model on which many of the UK's institutions operated has been revealed, but it has not been replaced by an alternative form of legitimation. Unsustainable elite practices have been exposed. A process of demystification has led to a loss of faith by the public. What we have seen in recent years is not, as is so often claimed, a depoliticisation but in reality a politicisation as through different mechanisms, institutions are opened up to greater scrutiny over how they operate. Decisions which in the past were made behind closed doors are increasingly coming under the spotlight and whatever the many faults, limitations and self-referencing of digital politics, new media, as we saw in Chapter 11, is making a difference to political responses. Information is transmitted more rapidly and disparate groups or people are able to respond at low cost. Smart phones and tablets have become an instrument of accountability of the police and freedom of information and large data sets are allowing challenges to the arguments of elites at the apex of large institutions. An illustrative example of this dynamic, revealed by a freedom of information request, is the revelation that in 2013 Michael Gove, the Education Secretary's policy on reform of the school History curriculum was driven by data and information on teenage historical knowledge based on a poll commissioned by UKTV Gold and not properly conducted research. As Bartlett (2013) illustrates,

> The size, diversity and dynamism of social media platforms allow people to connect and form social movements outside the existing political channels far more quickly and easily than ever before. New social movements are emerging using social media, and challenging existing parties in a way unthinkable a decade ago. Beppe Grillo's Movimento 5 Stelle in Italy used social media to coordinate and organise so smartly it helped him gain over 25 per cent of the national vote – without a single interview with Italian broadcast or print media, confounding PR advisers across the continent. Closer to home Goerge Galloway attributes his success in the Bradford by-election to Twitter. The Grillo tsunami (his words, not mine) might yet recede, but others will be sure to follow.

As Chapters 1, 2 and 5 highlight, the 'crisis' for politics is that the 19th-century model no longer fits. As political and policy leaders are exposed without a mechanism of legitimacy, faith in politics declines further and populist organisation such as UKIP are able to capture the disillusioned voters. As Marsh et al. set out in Chapter 2, what is required is not a suppression of the demands of citizens but an idealism that demands a new form of politics and participation which engages votes in decisions that affect citizens' daily lives. Contrary to the defenders of the current model such as Riddell (2011) and Flinders (2012a), the accepting of our democracy as the 'least worst form' is not enough because it is alienating the voters (particularly the young) and producing a dangerous exit from politics. The UK has never had a participatory and democratic culture; it has a politics of holding a circulating elite to account. But a more sophisticated electorate in a world of information overload is no longer convinced by this system. There is a need to build a new system of politics for the 21st century rather than sustaining a model organised round the mores of the 19th century. Of course, the track record on change is not good. Even in the case of outstanding anomalies of 19th-century governance, the House of Lords, politicians have found it intractable to move from a pre-democratic institution to one vaguely reflecting a democratic body.

Re-legitimising the political system means giving people a sense of efficacy in relation to decisions that affect their lives and in so doing connecting the ordinary voter to the policy-making process. For too long in the UK, decisions have been made by a small elite based in London or, if not in London, based on authority that derives from London. The two traditional and dominant mainstream parties have seen participatory politics in negative terms. For Anthony Crosland, it was bound to be dominated by the middle classes. The informal socialisation effect by the Westminster model on today's political class can still be identified as operating in a similar way to 50 years ago (Richards and Smith 2002, 2004, Richards, Blunkett and Mathers 2008). It is the perception that politicians are taking a burden off the people by making decisions on their behalf. In the early post-war years, this was symbolised by the much misquoted aphorism associated with Douglas Jay that 'the man in Whitehall knows best', but evidenced today, for example, in the covert paternalism of 'nudging' promoted across Whitehall by the Cabinet Office's Behavioural Insight Team (Wilkinson 2013). The low turnout for the 2013 police commissioner elections suggests that democracy cannot be forced on people. Yet, if people are to regain faith in UK institutions, there is a need for new forms of engagement.

Three problems arise here. One is that the electorate has been infantalised; as Almond and Verba (1963) observed 50 years ago, the UK's civic culture was best characterised as one of deference, not vibrant activity. This of course chimes with the BPT in which 'subjects' have never been afforded meaningful channels to engage in decisions and therefore accommodation of their desires and experiences have not been properly nurtured. The second is that there has been little attempt to develop the mechanisms of participation and when they have, such as online petitions or police commissioners, they are done in such a way as to undermine further the credibility of participatory mechanisms. The debate over the degree to which citizens want a direct role in decision-making remains contested. But what Hay and Stoker's (2013) focus group research reveals on this theme is a pressing demand on the part of the general public to be able to have greater trust in politics than is currently the case. Third, politics in the UK has almost always been adversarial; it is not about reaching a consensus that takes account of different interests. It is about winners and losers and, unsurprisingly, the losers feel that they are not represented.

Participation requires people to become involved in decisions that are salient to what is important to them, that are not party political in a way that one party monopolises the process and the outcomes and that are about allowing 'normal' citizens to become involved in politics and decision-making. It may be that it has to take account of new media, that it may be populist and result in decisions that the elite do not like. It may be that it has to be much more flexible and responsive than existing institutions allow. It may be that participation varies from issue to issue. What blogs and Twitter and comments on websites show is that there are many people who have views; that people are not anti-politics when it is about issues that interest or affect them and perhaps that they think they can have some control over.

Conclusion: Crisis, continuity and change

In many ways, the crises described in this book are not connected and in some cases, there is more the accumulation of various pathologies within institutions, rather than a crisis acting as a juncture leading to transition. In this sense, we do not regard crisis as stemming from a riskier and more uncertain world. Instead, what we have seen is a continual repetition of institutional failure or underperformance to the extent that it has undermined the faith of citizens in those institutions. What we have also seen is that decisions are often not very sound, being made in secret and subsequently revealed and highlighted, at the least, as poor practice by leaders. The dilemma for our rulers is that whilst closed decision-making is often easier, and some may argue more effective, it is losing its legitimacy. The collapse in deference, the quantum change in available information and with it the demystification of how institutions have operated have presented a serious challenge for those wishing to sustain the status quo.

In terms of the political settlement, the problem, as an editorial in *The Observer* (2 June 2013) pointed out, is that we have a system which combines a centralised bureaucracy which is governed by a party system, where the winning parties only achieve a small proportion of the vote of the electorate. UK governments command sizeable power for very little support. Yet, greater transparency, via freedom of information and scrutiny in its many different forms, has opened up apertures revealing the informal 'club' practices shaping the operating practices of the institutions explored throughout this book. Once demystified, it is unlikely that this aperture can be reduced again given it has revealed some of the inner working practices previously shut off from public view.

Yet, this creates a dilemma. The old order and the old way of doing things are increasingly hard to sustain in the current climate, yet it is unclear what might emerge instead from this current crisis epoch. The history of institutional reform within the UK is one predicated very much on an evolutionary and piecemeal approach rather than any Big Bang transformational occurrence. The legacy of the 1970s crisis was slow in revealing itself and when it did materialise the emphasis was as much on continuity as change. The key question underpinning this crisis is the extent to which within a decade or more the tenets of the BPT continue to persist. For if the contours of the BPT can still be clearly discerned, continuity will have won the day. The problem of course remains of how to change a political culture. How do you get the political elite to be more open and the citizens to be more engaged? This is clearly a long and slow process that requires real debate about the nature of politics and other institutions. How do they engage those that they serve? How do we establish new mechanism of legitimacy? As *The Observer* (2 June 2013) points out,

> According to the Hansard Society's most recent Audit of Political Engagement, civic engagement – 'direct democracy' – is healthy. The public are far from apathetic...Trade union membership had increased for the first time in years, up by 59,000 to 6.5m. Far from its 13m peak, but lessons are being learned. 'We have to let go,' says TUC national organiser Carl Roper. 'We have to work with members, not tell them what to do.'

In order to re-legitimise the political system, we need to find ways of ensuring that engagement has an impact. This involves a proper localising of political decisions, a proper discussion of the electoral system, an opening up of the policy process in Whitehall, a much more easily navigable system of information disclosure, a review of accountability systems, and a transformation in the organisation of political parties. After nearly 200 years, it is time to properly revise the Westminster model and escape the trap of the BPT.

References

Abrams, M. and Rose, R. (1960) *Must Labour Lose?* London: Penguin Books.

Achterberg, P. (2008) 'Class Voting in the New Political Culture: Economic, Cultural and Environmental Voting in 20 Western Countries', *International Sociology*, Vol.21/2, pp.237–261.

Achterberg, P. and Houtman, D. (2006). 'Why Do So Many People Vote "Unnaturally"? A Cultural Explanation for Voting Behaviour', *European Journal of Political Research*, Vol.45/1, pp.75–92.

Adler-Nissen, R. (2008) 'The Diplomacy of Opting Out: A Bourdieudian Approach to National Integration Strategies', *Journal of Common Market Studies*, Vol.46, pp.663–684.

Adonis, A. (2012) *Education, Education, Education: Reforming England's Schools*, London: Biteback.

Adonis, A. (2013) *Five Days in May: The Coalition and Beyond,* London: Biteback.

Aitchenson, G. (2012) 'Why State-Funded Political Parties Would Be a Disaster for our Democracy', Available at: http://www.opendemocracy.net/ourkingdom/third-estate/why-state-funded-political-parties-would-be-disaster-for-our-democracy.

Akram, S. (2009) ' "Riots" or "Urban Disorders"? The Case for Re-Politicising Urban Disorders' in A. Furlong (ed.), *Handbook of Youth and Young Adulthood: New Perspectives and Agendas*, London: Routledge, pp.313–320.

Allen, D. (2005) 'The United Kingdom: A Europeanized Government in a Non-Europeanized Polity', in S. Bulmer and C. Lequesne (eds.), *The Member States of the European Union*, Oxford: Oxford University Press, pp.119–141.

Allen, P. (2012) 'Linking Pre-Parliamentary Political Experience and the Career Trajectories of the 1997 General Election Cohort', *Parliamentary Affairs,* Vol.66/1, pp.1–23.

Almond, G. A. and Verba, S. (1963) *The Civic Culture: Political Attitudes and Democracy in Five Nations*, Princeton, NJ: Princeton University Press.

Alonso, S., Keane, J. and Merkel, W. 'Rethinking the Future of Representative Democracy', in S. Alonso, J. Keane and W. Merkel (eds.), *The Future of Representative Democracy*, Cambridge: Cambridge University Press, pp.1–22.

Anderson, P. (1964) 'The Origins of the Present Crisis', *New Left Review,* Vol.23, pp.26–53.

Ansolabehere, S., Rodden, J. and Snyder, J. (2008) 'The Strength of Issues: Using Multiple Measures to Gauge Preference Stability', *American Political Science Review,* Vol.102/2, pp.215–232.

Armstrong, K. (2006) 'The "Europeanisation" of Social Exclusion: British Adaptation to EU Co-ordination', *British Journal of Politics and International Relations*, Vol.8, pp.79–100.

Arter, D. (2004) 'The Scottish Committees and the Goal of a "New Politics": A Verdict on the First Four Years of the Devolved Scottish Parliament', *Journal of Contemporary European Studies*, Vol.12/1, April, 71–91.

Arthurs, H. (1985) *Without the Law: Administrative Justice and Legal Pluralism in Nineteenth Century England*, Toronto: University of Toronto Press.

Audit Commission (2003) 'Trust in Public Institutions', Available at: http://www.ipsos-mori.com/DownloadPublication/1180_sri_trust_in_public_institutions_2003.PDF.

Augar, P. (2010) *Reckless: The Rise and Fall of the City*, London: Vintage.

Bache, I. and Jordan, Andrew (2006) *The Europeanization of British Politics*, Basingstoke: Palgrave.

Bache, I. and Flinders, M. (2004) 'Multi-Level Governance and British Politics', in I. Bache and M. Flinders (eds.), *Multi-level Governance*, Oxford: Oxford University Press.

Bagehot. (2012) 'A Brixit looms', *The Economist,* 23 June 2012.

Baker, A. (2010) 'Restraining Regulatory Capture? Anglo-America, Crisis Politics and Trajectories of Change in Global Financial Governance', *International Affairs*, Vol.86/3, pp.647–663.

Baldwin, R. (2006) 'Better Regulation in Troubled Times', *Health Economics Policy & Law*, Vol.1, pp.203–207.

Baldwin, R. (2007) 'Better Regulation: Tensions Aboard the Enterprise', in S. Weatherill (ed.), *Better Regulation*, Oxford: Hart, pp.27–47.

Bale, T. (2010) *The Conservative Party: From Thatcher to Cameron*, Cambridge: Polity.

Bale, T. (2012) 'Britain Leaving the EU Is now a Serious Possibility', Available at: http://blogs.lse.ac.uk/europpblog/2012/06/11/britain-leaving-the-eu-is-now-a-serious-possibility/ (Accessed 29 September 2012).

Bale, T., Taggart, P. and Webb, P. (2006) 'You Can't Always Get What You Want: Populism and the Power Inquiry', *The Political Quarterly*, Vol.77/2, pp.195–203.

Balls, E. (2006) 'The City as a Global Financial Centre: Risks and Opportunities', Speech at Bloomberg, 14 August 2006.

Bang, P. H. (2009) ' "Yes We Can": Identity Politics and Project Politics for a Late-Modern World', *Urban Research and Practice*, Vol.2/2, pp.117–137.

Bang, P. H. (2011) 'The Politics of Threat: Late-Modern Politics in the Shadow of Neo-Liberalism', *Critical Policy Studies*, Vol.5/4, pp.434–448.

Bank of England (2008) *Financial Stability Report*, October 2008, Issue no. 24, London: Bank of England.

Bank of England (2010) *Quarterly Bulletin 2010* Q 4, London: Bank of England.

Banton, M. (1964) *The Policeman in the Community*, London: Tavistock Publications.

Barber, M. (2007) *Instruction to Deliver: Tony Blair, Public Services and the Challenge of Achieving Targets*, London: Politicos.

Barnes, S. and Kaase, M. (eds.) (1979) *Political Action: Mass Participation in Five Western Democracies,* Beverly Hills, CA: Sage.

Barnett, S., Ramsay, G. N. and Gaber, I. (2012) 'From Callaghan to Credit Crunch.: Changing Trends in British Television News 1975–2009', Available at: http://www.westminster.ac.uk/__data/assets/pdf_file/0009/124785/From-Callaghan-To-Credit-Crunch-Final-Report.pdf.

Barry, B. (1965) *Political Argument,* London: Routledge and Keegan Paul.

Bartlett, J. (2013) 'The Internet Is Radically Changing the Nature of Collective Action and Political Organisation', Available at: http://blogs.lse.ac.uk/politicsandpolicy/archives/32914.

Baston, L. (2013) *The Bradford Earthquake*, Liverpool: Democratic Audit.

Bayley, D. (1996) 'What Do the Police Do?' in W. Saulsbury, J. Mott and T. Newburn (eds.), *Themes in Contemporary Policing*, London: Policy Studies Institute.

Beck, U. (1992) *The Risk Society: Towards A New Modernity*, London: Sage.

Beck, U. (2005). *Power in the Global Age: A New Global Political Economy*, Oxford: Polity.

Beer, S. (1965) *Modern British Politics*, London: Faber and Faber.

Beer, S. (1982) *Modern British Politics* (3rd edn), London: Faber and Faber.

Beetham, D. (2011) 'Do Parliaments Have a Future?', in S. Alonso, J. Keane and W. Merkel (eds.), *The Future of Representative Democracy*, Cambridge: Cambridge University Press, pp.124–143.

Bennett, L.W. and Segerberg, A. (2012) 'The Logic of Connective Action: Digital Media and the Personalization of Contentious Politics', *Information, Communication & Society*, Vol.15/5, pp.739–768.

Bentley, T. (2005) *Everyday Democracy: Why We Get the Politicians We Deserve*, London: Demos.

Berrington, H. (2004) 'Role of Political Parties', *BBC News*, Available at: http://news.bbc.co.uk/1/hi/programmes/bbc_parliament/2443563.stm.

Better Regulation Task Force (2005) *Regulation – Less Is More: Reducing Burdens, Improving Outcomes*, London: Cabinet Office.

Bevir, M. (2010) *Democratic Governance*, Princeton: Princeton University Press.

Bevir, M. and Rhodes, R. A. W. (2003) *Interpreting British Governance*, London: Routledge.

Biezen, van I., Mair, P. and Poguntke, T. (2012) 'Going, Going,...Gone? The Decline of Party Membership in Contemporary Europe', *European Journal of Political Research*, Vol.51/1, pp.24–56.

Birch, A. (1964) *Representative and Responsible Government*, London: Allen and Unwin.

Birch, A. (1984) 'Overload, Ungovernability and Delegitimation: The Theories and the British Case', *British Journal of Political Science*, Vol.14/2, pp.135–160.

Black, J. (2000) 'Proceduralizing Regulation', *Oxford Journal of Legal Studies*, Vol.20, pp.597–614.

Black, J. (2007) 'Tensions in the Regulatory State', *Public Law*, 2007 (Spring), pp.58–73.

Blair, T. (2005) 'Common Sense Culture, Not Compensation Culture'. Speech, IPPR, Available at: www.guardian.co.uk/politics/2005/may/26/speeches.media.

Blair, T. (2010) *A Journey*, London: Hutchinson.

Blair, T. (2012) Transcript of Hearing at Leveson Inquiry, 28 May 2012.

Blakeley, G. and Evans, B. (2009) 'Who Participates, How and Why in Urban Regeneration Projects? The Case of the New "City" of East Manchester', *Social Policy and Administration*, Vol.43/1, pp.15–32.

Blond, P. (2010) *Red Tory: How Left and Right Have Broken Britain and How We Can Fix It*, London: Faber and Faber.

Blunkett, D. (2006) *The Blunkett Tapes: My Life in the Bear Pit*, London: Bloomsbury.

Blyth, Mark (2002) *Great Transformations: Economic Ideas and Institutional Change in the Twentieth Century*, New York: Cambridge University Press.

Bogdanor, V. (2012) 'For UK Politics the Eurozone Crisis Will Bring the Deluge', *The Guardian*, 27 June.

Boin, A. (2004) 'Lessons From Crisis Research', *International Studies Review*, Vol.6/1, 165–174.

Boin, A. and 't Hart, P. (2000) 'Institutional Crises and Reforms', in H. Wagenaar (ed.), *Policy Sectors in Government Institutions: Effects, Changes and Normative Foundations*, Dordrecht, the Netherlands: Kluwer Academic Publishers.

Bolleyer, N. (2009) 'Inside the Cartel Party: Party Organisation in Government and Opposition', *Political Studies*, Vol.57/3, pp.559–579.

Bonefeld, W. (2010) 'Free Economy and The Strong State: Some Notes on the State' *Capital and Class*, Vol.34/1, pp.15–24.

Bottoms, A. E. B. and Tankebe, J. (2012) 'Beyond Procedural Justice: Dialogic Approach to Legitimacy in Criminal Justice', *Journal of Criminal Law and Criminology*, Vol.102/1, pp.119–170.

Bourdieu, P. (1986) 'The Forms of Capital' in J. Richardson (ed.), *Handbook of Theory and Research for the Sociology of Education*, New York: Greenwood, pp.241–258.

Bowling, B., Parmar, A. and Phillips, J. (2008) 'Policing Ethnic Minority Communities', in T. Newburn (ed.), *The Handbook of Policing*, Cullompton: Willan.

Bracher, K. D. (1967) 'Problems of Parliamentary Democracy in Europe', in S. R. Graubard (ed.), *A New Europe?* Boston: Beacon Press.

Bradbury, J. and John, P. (2010) 'Territory and Power: Critiques and Reassessments of a Classic Work', *Government and Opposition*, Vol.45, pp.295–317.

Bradford, B., Jackson, J., Hough, M. and Farrall, S. (2009) 'Trust and Confidence in Criminal Justice: A. Review of the British literature', in A. Jokinen and E. Ruuskanen (eds.), *JUSTIS Project Working Papers: Indicators of Public Confidence in Criminal Justice for Police Assessment*, Helsinki: European Institute of Crime Prevention and Control.

Braithwaite, J. (2008) *Regulatory Capitalism: How It Works, Ideas for Making It Work Better*, Cheltenham: Edward Elgar.

Brittan, L. (2011) 'Cameron Is Not Playing Games: Fiscal Union Is Vital', *Financial Times*, 18 November 2011.

Brittan, S. (1975) 'The Economic Contradictions of Democracy', *British Journal of Political Science*, Vol.5, pp.129–159.

Brittan, S. (1983) *The Role and Limits of Government*, London: Temple Smith.

Broad, M. and Daddow, O. (2010) 'Half-Remembered Quotations From Mostly Forgotten Speeches: The Limits of Labour's European Policy Discourse', *British Journal of Politics and International Relations*, Vol.12, pp.205–222.

Brodeur, J.-P. (2010) *The Policing Web*, Oxford: Oxford University Press.

Brown, G. (2006) Speech By the Chancellor of the Exchequer at the Mansion House, 21 June 2006.

Brown, G. (2007) Mansion House Speech, 20 June 2007, London, Available at: http://ukingermany.fco.gov.uk/en/news/?view=Speech&id=4616377 (Accessed 1 June 2012)

Brown, G. (2009a) PM Speech to European Parliament, 24 March 2009, London: Prime.

Brown, G. (2009b) 'Gordon Brown's Speech to Labour Conference', Available at: http://www.labour.org.uk/gordon-brown-speech-conference (Accessed 4 June 2012)

Brummer, A. (2009) *The Crunch*, New York: Random House.

Buckley, A. (2011) *Financial Crisis*, London: Prentice Hall/FT Publishing.

Buckley, J. and Howarth, D. (2010) 'Internal Market: Gesture Politics? Explaining the EU's Response to the Financial Crisis', *Journal of Common Market Studies*, Vol.48, pp.119–141.

Buller, J. (2000) *National Statecraft and European Integration; The Conservative Government and European integration 1979–1997*, London: Continuum.

Buller, J. and James, Toby S. (2012) 'Statecraft and the Assessment of National Political Leaders: The Case of New Labour and Tony Blair', *British Journal of Politics and International Relations*, Vol.14, pp.534–555.

Bulmer, S. (2008) 'New Labour, New European Policy? Blair, Brown and Utilitarian Supranationalism', *Parliamentary Affairs*, Vol.61/4, pp.597–620.

Bulmer, S. and Burch, M. (1998) 'Organizing for Europe: Whitehall, the British State and European Union', *Public Administration*, Vol.76, pp.601–628.

Bulmer, S. and Burch, M. (2009) *The Europeanisation of Whitehall: UK Central Government and the European Union*, Manchester: Manchester University Press.

Bulpitt, J. (1983) *Territory and Power in the United Kingdom*, Manchester: Manchester University Press.

Bulpitt, J. (1985) 'The Discipline of the New Democracy: Mrs Thatcher's Domestic Statecraft', *Political Studies*, Vol.34/1, pp.19–39.

Burnham, P. and Pyper, J. (2008) *Britain's Modernised Civil Service*, Basingstoke: Palgrave Macmillan.

Butler, R. (2004) *Review of Intelligence on Weapons of Mass Destruction*, London: The Stationary Office, 14 July 2004.

Cabinet Conclusions (1949) 'Conclusions of a Meeting of the Cabinet Held at 10 Downing Street, S.W.1, on Wednesday, 12 January, 1949, at 3 p.m', National Archive CAB 128/15 Original Reference CM 1 (49)–43 (49), 1949 1 January–30 June [accessed 14 March 2013–13 at http://filestore.nationalarchives.gov.uk/pdfs/large/cab-128–15.pdf]

Cabinet Office (2011) *The Cabinet Manual: A Guide to the Laws, Conventions and Rules on the Operation of Government*, London: Cabinet Office.

Cabinet Office (2012) 'Quango Clampdown Saving Billions or the Taxpayer', Available at: http://www.cabinetoffice.gov.uk/news/quango-clampdown-saving-billions-taxpayer.

Cabinet Office (2012) *The Red Tape Challenge in Summary*, London: Cabinet Office.

Cable, Vince (2009) *The Storm: The World Economic Crisis and What It Means*, London: Atlantic Books.

Cain, M. (1973) *Society and the Policeman's Role*, London: Routledge.

Cairney, P. (2011) *The Scottish Political System Since Devolution: From New Politics to the New Scottish Government*, Exeter: Imprint Academic.

Cairney, P. and McGarvey, N. (2013) *Scottish Politics* (2nd edn), Basingstoke: Palgrave.

Cairney, P., Halpin, D. and Jordan, G. (2009) 'New Scottish Parliament, Same Old Interest Group Politics?', in C. Jeffery and J. Mitchell (eds.), *The Scottish Parliament, 1999–2009: The First Decade*, Edinburgh: Luath Press.

Cameron, D. (2012) Transcript of Hearing at Leveson Inquiry, 14 June 2012.

Cameron, S. (2009) 'Wither Whitehall', *The Hidden Wiring*, Mile End Group Newsletter, pp.7–8.

Campbell, A. (2012) 'Debating Flinders', *Contemporary Politics*, Vol.18/1, pp.22–24.

Campbell, A. (2012) Submission to the Leveson Inquiry.

Campbell, C. and Wilson, G. (1995) *The End of Whitehall: Death of a Paradigm?* Oxford: Blackwell.

Cashmore, E. (2001) 'The Experiences of Ethnic Minority Police Officers in Britain: Under-Recruitment and Racial Profiling in a Performance Culture', *Ethnic and Racial Studies*, Vol.24/4, pp.642–659.

Castells, M. (2000) *The Rise of the Network Society, The Information Age: Economy, Society and Culture, Vol.1* (2nd edn), Oxford: Blackwell.

Castells, M. and Cordoso, G. (2006) *The Network Society*, Baltimore: John Hopkins University Press.

Cavadino, M. and Dignan J. (1997) *The Penal System: An Introduction*, London: Sage.

Centre for Women and Democracy (2013) *Sex and Power 2013: Who Runs Britain?* London: Centre for Women and Democracy.

Chapman, R. (ed.) (1993) *Ethics in Public Service*, Edinburgh: Edinburgh University Press.

Churchill, W. (1947) *House of Commons Hansard Debates*, 11 November 1947, Vol.444, pp.203–321.

Clarke, H., Saunders, D., Stewart, M. and Whiteley, P. (2004) *Political Choice in Britain*, Oxford: Oxford University Press.

Clarke, H., Sanders, D., Stewart, M. and Whiteley, P. (2009) 'The American Voter's British Cousin', *Electoral Studies*, Vol.28, pp.632–641.

Cm8208 (2011) *Political Party Finance: Ending the Big Donor Culture*, London: The Stationary Office.

Coates, D. (1994) *The Question of UK Decline*, Brighton: Harvester Wheatsheaf.

Coates, D. (2009) 'Chickens Coming Home to Roost? New Labour at the Eleventh Hour', *British Politics*, Vol.4/4, pp.421–433.

Coates, D. and Hillard, J. (1986) *The Economic Decline of Modern Britain: The Debate Between Left and Right*, Brighton: Wheatsheaf Books.

Coates, D., Johnston, G. and Bush, R. (eds.) (1985) *A Socialist Anatomy of Britain*, London: Polity Press.

Cohen, N. (2004) *Pretty Straight Guys*, London: Faber and Faber.

Coleman, S., Anthony, S. and Morrison, D. E. (2009) *Public Trust in the News. A Constructivist Study of The Social Life of the News*, Reuters Institute for the Study of Journalism: Oxford.

Committee of Public Accounts (1997) *The Work of the Directors General of Telecommunications, Gas Supply, Water Services and Electricity Supply: Sixteenth Report, Session 1996–1997*, HC.89 London: HMSO.

Committee on Standards in Public Life (2011) *Survey of Public Attitudes Towards Conduct in Public Life in 2010*, London: Committee on Standards in Public Life.

Committee on Standard in Public Life (2012) *Press Notice – Ethics and Best Practice in Public Life – What Works?* Available at: http://www.public-standards.gov.uk/ [last accessed 18 June 2012]

Conservatives (2010) *A New Economic Model: Eight Benchmarks for Britain*, Available at: http://www.conservatives.com/news/news_stories/2010/02/~/media/Files/Downloadable%20Files/new-economic-model.ashx.

Conservatives (2010) *The Conservative Manifesto 2010: An Invitation to Join the Government of Britain,* Conservative Party.

Consultative Steering Group (1999) *Shaping Scotland's Parliament: Report of the Consultative Steering Group,* Edinburgh: The Stationery Office, Available at: http://www.scottish.parliament.uk/PublicInformationdocuments/Report_of_the_Consultative_Steering_Group.pdf.

Cook, R. (2004) *The Point of Departure: Diaries From the Front Bench,* London: Pocket Books.

Cousins, A. (2011) 'The Crisis of the British Regime: Democracy, Protest and the Unions', Available at: http://www.counterfire.org/index.php/theory/37-theory/14906-the-crisis-of-the-british-regime-democracy-protest-and-the-unions.

Cowley, P. (2012) 'Arise, Novice Leader! The Continuing Rise of the Career Politician in Britain', *Politics,* Vol. 30, pp.31–38.

Cowley, P. & Stuart, M. (2012) 'The Cambusters: The Conservative European Union Referendum Rebellion of October 2011', *The Political Quarterly,* Vol.83/2, April–June 2012.

Crewe, I., Sarlvik, B. and Alt, J. (1977) 'Partisan Realignment in Britain', *British Journal of Political Science,* Vol.7, pp.129–190.

Crouch, C. (2008) 'What Will Follow the Demise of Privatised Keynesianism?', *Political Quarterly,* Vol.79/4, pp.476–487.

Crouch, C. (2009) 'Privatised Keynesianism: An Unacknowledged Policy Regime', *British Journal of Politics and International Relations,* Vol11/3, pp.82–399.

Crozier, M. (1975) *The Crisis of Democracy,* New York: New York University Press.

Currah, A. (2009) *Navigating the Crisis in Local and Regional News: A Critical Review of Solutions,* Reuters Institute for the Study of Journalism Working Essay, Oxford.

Curran, J., Iyengar, S., Brink Lund, A. and Salovaara-Moring, I. (2009) 'Media System, Public Knowldege and Democracy. A Comparative Study', *European Journal of Communication,* Vol.24/1, pp.5–26.

Curtice, J. (2009) 'Devolution, the SNP and the Electorate' in G. Hassan (ed.), *The Modern SNP: From Protest to Power,* Edinburgh: Edinburgh University Press.

Curtice, J. (2012a) 'Is There Still a Basis for a Stable Union?', WISERD Third Annual Conference, 28 March, Available at: http://wiserd.comp.glam.ac.uk/TCB/Data/Sites/1/coursedocumentation/conference2012/istherestillabasisforastableunion.pdf.

Curtice, J. (2012b) 'Is Scotland Heading for Independence? Evidence from the Scottish Social Attitudes Survey', *ScotCen,* 14 March.

Curtice, J. (2013a) Ukip's Popularity Will Hit Tories Hardest, *Theguardian.com,* Wednesday 24 April 2013, Available at: http://www.theguardian.com/politics/2013/apr/24/ukip-election-success-tories-farage (Accessed 12 September 2013).

Curtice, J. (2013b) 'If the Conservatives Are to Counter the Challenge of UKIP, They Need to Turn Around the Economy Rather Than Fret Obsessively About Europe', Available at: http://blogs.lse.ac.uk/politicsandpolicy/archives/33177 (Accessed 12 September 2013).

Curtice, J. and Ormston, R. (2011) 'So Who Is Winning the Debate? Constitutional Preferences in Scotland After Four Years of Nationalist Government', *Scottish Affairs,* 74, Winter, pp.24–44.

Curtice, J. and Park, A. (2011) 'A Tale Of Two Crises: Banks, MPs' Expenses and Public Opinion', in A. Park, J. Curtice, E. Clery and C. Bryson (eds), *British Social Attitudes – the 27th Report: Exploring Labour's Legacy,* London: Sage.

Curtice, J., Park, A., Clery, E. and Bryson, C. (2010) *British Social Attitudes: Exploring Labour's Legacy,* London: National Centre for Social Research.

Curtice, J., Park, A., Thomson, K., Phillips, M., Clery, E. and Butt, B. (2010), *British Social Attitudes: The 26th Report,* London: Sage.

Daalder, H. (1992) 'A Crisis of Party?' *Scandinavian Political Studies,* Vol.15/4, pp.269–288.

Daily Telegraph (2009) 'Payback Time', 13 May 2009, p.1.

Daily Telegraph (2010) 'Top Conservative: Recession? You've Never Had It So Good', 18 November 2010, Available at: http://www.telegraph.co.uk/news/politics/conservative/8144515/Top-Conservative-recession-Youve-never-had-it-so-good.html.

Daily Telegraph (2011a) 'Royal Bank of Scotland Investigation: The Full Story of How the "World's Biggest Bank" Went Bust', 5 March 2011.

Daily Telegraph (2011b) 'FSA Says No Lessons to Be Learned From Investigating Collapse Of Bradford And Bingley', 22 July 2011.

Dale Scott, P. (1996) *Deep Politics and the Death of JFK,* Berkeley, CA: University of California Press.

Dalton, R. (2008) 'Citizenship Norms And the Expansion of Political Participation', *Political Studies,* Vol.56, pp.76–98.

Daniel, B. and Helm, T. (2012) *The Observer,* Saturday 17 November 2012.

Darling, A. (2010) *Back From the Brink: One Thousand Days at Number 11,* London: Atlantic Books.

Darling, A. (2011) *Back from the Brink: 1000 Days at No.10,* London: Atlantic Books.

Daugbjerg, C. and Marsh, D. (1998) 'Explaining Policy Outcomes: Integrating the Policy Network Approach with Macro-level and Micro-Level Analysis', in D. Marsh (ed.), *Comparing Policy Networks*: Buckingham: Open University Press.

Davies, H. (2010) *The Financial Crisis: Who's to Blame?* Cambridge: Polity.

Davis, R. (2012) 'Arnie Graf: The Man Ed Milliband Asked to Rebuild the Labour Party', *The Guardian,* 21 November.

Department of Trade and Industry (1985) *Lifting the Burden,* Cmnd 9571, London: HMSO.

Department of Trade and Industry (1986) *Building Businesses not Barriers,* Cmnd 9794, London: HMSO.

Department of Trade and Industry (1988) *Releasing Enterprise,* CM 512, London: HMSO.

Department of Trade and Industry (1994) *Deregulation: Cutting Red Tape,* London: HMSO.

Diamond, P. (2011) 'Beyond the Westminster Model: The Labour Party and the Machinery of the British Parliamentary State', *Renewal,* Vol.19/1, pp.64–74.

Diamond, P. (2013) *Governing Britain: Power, Politics and the Prime Minister,* London: I.B. Taurus.

Diamond, P. and Richards, D. (2012) 'The Case for Theoretical and Methodological Pluralism in British Political Studies: New Labour's Political Memoirs and The British Tradition', *Political Studies Review,* Vol.10/2, pp.177–94.

Dickinson, R., Matthews, J. and K. Saltzis (2013) 'Studying Journalists in Changing Times. Understanding News Work as Socially Situated Practice', *International Communication Gazette*, Vol.75/1, pp.3–18.

Dinwoodie, R. (2011) 'Yes Voters Take Lead in New Independence Poll' *The Herald*, 5 September, Available at: http://www.heraldscotland.com/news/politics/yes-voters-takelead-in-new-independence-poll-1.1121712.

Dixon, A. and Le Grand, J. (2006) *Is Greater Patient Choice Consistent with Equity? The Case of the English NHS*. Journal of Health Services Research & Policy, 11(3), 162–166.

Docking, M. and Tuffin, R. (2005) *Racist Incidents: Progress Since the Lawrence Inquiry*, Home Office Online Report 42/05, London: HMSO.

Docx, E. (2013) 'The Relentless Charm of Nigel Farage', *Prospect*, 20 May 2013.

Dodds, A. (2006) 'The Core Executive's Approach to Regulation: From 'Better Regulation' to 'Risk Tolerant Deregulation', *Social Policy and Administration*, Vol.40/5, pp.526–542.

Dolphin, T. (2011) *Debts and Deficits: How Much Is Labour to Blame?* London: Institute for Public Policy Research.

Dorey, P. (1995) *British Politics Since 1945*, Oxford: Blackwell.

Dorling, D. (2013) 'How Social Mobility Got Stuck', *New Statesman*, 16 May 2013.

Douglas, J. (1976) 'The Overloaded Crown', *British Journal of Political Science*, Vol.6/4, pp.483–505.

Douglas, M. (1986). *How Institutions Think*, Syracuse: Syracuse University Press.

Drennan, L. T. and McConnell, A. (2007) *Risk and Crisis Management in the Public Sector*, London: Routledge.

Driver, S. (2011) *Understanding British Party Politics*, Cambridge: Polity.

Dubnik, M. J. (2011) 'Move Over Daniel: We Need Some "Accountability Space"', *Administration and Society*, Vol.43/6, pp.704–716.

Duffett, H. (2010) 'A Power Revolution: Nick Clegg's "New Politics" Speech in Full', *Liberal Democrat Voice*, 19 May 2010, Available at: http://www.libdem voice.org/power-revolution-nick-clegg-new-politics-speech-19604.html.

Dunleavy, P. (1983) 'Stability, Crisis or Decline?', in P. Dunleavy, A. Gamble, I. Holliday, and G. Peele (eds.), *Developments in British Politics 4*, Basingstoke: Palgrave Macmillan.

Durose, C., Gains, F., Richardson, L., Combs, R., Broome, K. and Eason, C. (2011) *Pathways to Politics*, Manchester: EHRC.

Easton, D. (1965) *A Systems Analysis of Political Life*, New York: Wiley.

Economist (2012) 'The Guns of War', 6 October.

Eder, K. (2009) 'A Theory of Collective Identity. Making Sense of the Debate on a "European Identity"', *European Journal of Social Theory*, Vol.12/4, pp.1–21.

Engelen, E., Ertürk, I., Julie Froud, J. and Sukhdev Johal, S. (2011) *After the Great Complacence: Financial Crisis and the Politics of Reform*, Oxford: Oxford University Press.

Engelen, E., Ertürk, I., Froud, J., Johal, S., Leaver, A., Moran, M. and Williams, K. (2012) 'Misrule of Experts? The Financial Crisis as Elite Debacle', *Economy and Society*, Vol.41/3, pp.360–382.

English, R. and Kenny, M. (2000) *Rethinking British Decline*, Basingstoke: Macmillan.

Ennis, D. (2011) 'Cameron Used the Veto to Keep Us in the EU 13 December 2011', Available at: http://www.mhpc.com/blog/cameron-used-veto-keep-us-eu/ (Accessed 11 September 2012).

Eurobarometer (2001) *Standard Eurobarometer* 56, Brussels: European Commission.

Eurobarometer (2007) *Standard Eurobarometer* 68, Brussels: European Commission.

Eurobarometer (2008) *Standard Eurobarometer* 70, Brussels: European Commission.

Eurobarometer (2009) *Standard Eurobarometer* 71, Brussels: European Commission.

Eurobarometer (2012a) *Standard Eurobarometer* 77, Brussels: European Commission.

Eurobarometer (2012b) *Standard Eurobarometer* 78, Brussels: European Commission.

European Commission (2001) *European Governance: A White Paper*, COM 2001 428, Brussels: European Commission.

European Commission (2011) Attitudes towards the EU in the United Kingdom, Analytical Report, European Commission, Available at: http://ec.europa.eu/public_opinion/flash/fl_318_en.pdf.

Evans, M. (2003) *Constitution-Making and the Labour Party*, Basingstoke: Palgrave Macmillan.

Evans, P. B., Rueschemeyer, D. and Skocpol, T. (eds.) (1985) *Bringing the State Back In*, Cambridge: Cambridge University Press.

Evans, R. and Lewis, P. (2012) 'Call for Police Links to Animal Rights Firebombing to be Investigated', *Guardian Online*, Available at: http://www.guardian.co.uk/uk/2012/jun/13/police (Accessed 14 June 2012).

Evans, R. and Lewis, P. (2013) 'Police "Smear" Campaign Targeted Stephen Lawrence's Friends and Family', *Guardian Online*, Available at http://www.guardian.co.uk/uk/2013/jun/23/stephen-lawrence-undercover-police-smears (Accessed 28 June 2013).

Explorations in Governance (2012) 'A collection of papers in honour of Christopher Hood', London: Institute of Government, March 2012.

Fawcett, P. and Marsh, D. (2013) 'Depoliticisation, Governance and Political Participation', *Policy and Politics*, forthcoming.

FCO (2012) *Review of the Balance of Competences Between the United Kingdom*, Available at: https://www.gov.uk/government/publications/review-of-the-balance-of-competences.

Fielding, S. (2010) 'The Permanent Crisis of Party'. *Twentieth Century British History*, Vol.21/1, pp.102–109.

Filkin, E. (2011) *The Ethical Issues Arising From the Relationship Between the Police and the Media*, London: MPS.

Financial Services Authority (2007) 'FSA Publishes Feedback and Further Consultation on Listing Review for Investment Entities', Available at: http://www.fsa.gov.uk/library/communication/pr/2007/078.shtml (Accessed 5 June 2012).

Financial Services and Markets Act (2000) *Great Britain*. Chapter 8, London: HMSO.

Financial Times (2009) 'Paul Moore's Memo in Full', 11 February 2009.

Financial Times (2010a) 'Banks Face Action Over Customer Complaints', 28 April 2010.

Financial Times (2010b) 'Lloyds and RBS Face Complaints Handling Probe', 29 April 2010.

Financial Times (2011) 'Banks Braced for Deluge of PPI Complaints', 20 April 2011.

Financial Times (2012a) 'Barclays Tax Plans Clash With Sentiment', 28 February 2012.

Financial Times (2012b) 'Barclays Faces Block on Tax Schemes', 27 February 2012.

Finnane, M. (2005) 'A "New Police" in Australia', in T. Newburn (ed.), *Policing: Key Readings*, Cullompton: Willan.

Fisher, J. (2010) 'Seven Myths about Political Parties', Lecture, Brunel University, 9 November.

Fisher, J. (2011) 'Review of Party Funding', Written Evidence E18, Available at: http://www.public-standards.org.uk/Library/All_written_evidence_political_party_finance_21_11_11.pdf.

Fisher, J. and Denver, D. (2009). 'Evaluating the Electoral Effects of Traditional and Modern Modes of Constituency Campaigning in Britain 1992–2005', *Parliamentary Affairs*, Vol.62/2, pp.196–210.

Flinders, M. (2008) *Delegating Governance and the British State: Walking Without Order*, Oxford: Oxford University Press.

Flinders, M. (2010) 'In Defence of Politics', *The Political Quarterly*, Volume 81/3, pp.309–326, July–September 2010.

Flinders, M. (2010) *Democratic Drift: Majoritarian Modification and Democratic Anomie in the United Kingdom*, Oxford: Oxford University Press.

Flinders, M. (2012a) *Defending Politics: Why Democracy Matters in the Twenty-First Century*, Oxford: Oxford University Press.

Flinders, M. (2012b) 'In Defence of Politics: Fifty Years On', *The Political Quarterly*, Vol.83/4, October–December 2012, pp.639–644.

Flinders, M. (2012c) 'The Demonisation of Politicians: Moral Panics, Folk Devils and MPs' Expenses', *Contemporary Politics*, Vol.18/1, pp.1–17.

Flinders, M. and Buller, J. (2006) 'Depoliticisation: Principles, Tactics and Tools', *British Politics*, Vol.1/3, pp.293–318.

Flinders, M. and Kelso, A. (2011) 'Mind the Gap: Political Analysis, Public Expectations and the Parliamentary Decline Thesis', *British Journal of Politics and International Relations*, Vol.13/2, pp.249–268.

Flinders, M. and Skelcher, C. (2012) 'Shrinking the Quango State: Five Challenges in Reforming Quangos', *Public Money & Management*, Vol.32/5, pp.327–334.

Flinders, M. and Wood, M. (2013) 'Depoliticisation', *Policy and Politics*, forthcoming.

Forbes (2011) 'UK Politicians Lash Out at "Lavish" Executive Pay Packages', 20 September. 2011, Available at: http://www.forbes.com/sites/nathanielparishflannery/2011/09/20/u-k-politicians-lash-out-at-lavish-executive-pay-packages/.

Ford, R., Goodwin, M. J. and Cutts, D. (2012) Strategic Eurosceptics and Polite Xenophobes: Support for the United Kingdom Independence Party (UKIP) in the 2009 European Parliament Elections, *European Journal of Political Research*, Vol.51, pp.204–234.

Foster, C. (2005) *British Government in Crisis: Or the Third English Revolution*, Oxford: Hart.

Foster, C. and Plowden, W. (1998) *The State Under Stress*, Buckingham: Open University.

Fox, R. (2010) *What's Trust Got to Do With it? Public Trust in and Expectations of Politicians and Parliament*, London: Hansard Society.

Franklin, M. (2004) *Voter Turnout and the Dynamics of Electoral Competition in Established Democracies since 1945*, Cambridge: Cambridge University Press.

Franklin, M. N. (1985) *The Decline of Class Voting in Britain: Changes in the Basis of Electoral Choice, 1964–1983*, Oxford: Clarendon Press.

Franklin, M. N. and Mughan, A. (1978). 'The Decline of Class Voting in Britain: Problems of Analysis and Interpretation', *The American Political Science Review*, Vol.72/2, pp.523–534.

Froud, J., Moran, M., Nilsson, A., Williams, K. (2010) 'Wasting a Crisis?: Democracy and Markets in Britain after 2007', *Political Quarterly*, Vol.81/1 pp.25–38.

Froud, J., Johal, S., Leaver, A., Moran, M. and Williams, K. (2011) *Groundhog Day: Elite Power, Democratic Disconnects and the Failure of Financial Reform in the UK*, CRESC Working Paper Series No. 118.

Froud, J., Moran, M., Nilsson, A. and Williams, K. (2010) 'Wasting a Crisis? Democracy and Markets in Britain After 2007', *Political Quarterly*, Vol.81/1, pp.25–38.

FSA (2009) *The Turner Review: A Regulatory Response to the Global Banking Crisis*, London: FSA.

FSA (2011) *The Failure of the Royal Bank of Scotland: FSA Board Report*, London: FSA.

FSA (2003a) Press Release 'FSA Fines Bank of Scotland 750,000 for Maladministration of PEPs and ISAs', 13 February 2003.

FSA (2003b) Press Release 'FSA Fines Bank of Scotland Plc 1,250, 000 for Money Laundering Rule Breaches', 15 January 2004.

FSA (2003c) Press Release, 9 April 2003.

FSA (2007) Freedom of Information Request, Sir Callum McCarthy's Letter to the Prime Minister, 31 May 2005.

FSA (2008) *The Supervision of Northern Rock: A Lessons Learned Review*, London: FSA.

FSA (2010) *Review of Complaint Handling In Banking Groups*, London: FSA.

FSA (2012a) Press Release, 'FSA Agrees Settlement with Four Banks Over Interest Rate Hedging Products', 29 June.

FSA (2012b) Press Release, 'FSA Publishes Censure against Bank of Scotland plc in Respect of Failings within its Corporate Division between January 2006 and December 2008', 9 March.

Furlong, A. and Cartmel, F. (2012) 'Social Change and Political Engagement among Young People: Generation and the 2009/2010 British Election Survey', *Parliamentary Affairs*, Vol.65/1, pp.13–28.

Gaber, I. (2012) 'Moment of Truth: What Hackgate Tells Us about the Changing Relations between the Media and Politics', Paper presented at Political studies Association Annual Conference, Belfast, April 2012, Available at: http://www.psa.ac.uk/journals/pdf/5/2012/622_265.pdf.

Gainsborough, M. (2012) 'Debating Flinders', *Contemporary Politics*, Vol.18/1, pp.24–26.

Gallup, George H. (1976) *The Gallup International Public Opinion Polls: Great Britain 1937–1975*, New York: Random House, Vol. 1.

Gamble, A. (1979) 'The Free Economy and the Strong State: The Rise of the Social Market Economy' in R. Miliband and J. Savile (eds.), *The Socialist Register*, London, The Merlin Press, 1–25.

Gamble, A. (1990) 'Theories of British Politics', *Political Studies*, Vol.37/3, pp.404–420.

Gamble, A. (1994a) *Britain in Decline* (4th edn), Basingstoke: Macmillan.

Gamble, A. (1994b) *The Free Economy and the Strong State* (2nd edn), London: Macmillan.

Gamble, A. (1995) 'Economic Recession and Disenchantment with Europe', *West European Politics*, Vol.18/3, pp.101–117.

Gamble, A. (2000) *Politics and Fate,* Cambridge: Polity.

Gamble, A. (2009a) *The Spectre at the Feast: Capitalist Crisis and the Politics of Recession,* Basingstoke: Palgrave Macmillan.

Gamble, A. (2009b) 'British Politics and the Financial Crisis', *British Politics,* Vol.4/4, pp.450–462.

Gamble, A. (2012) 'Better Off Out? Britain and Europe', *Political Quarterly*, Vol.83/3, pp.468–477.

Geddes, A. (2004) *The EU and British Politics*, Basingstoke: Palgrave.

Geddes, A. and Tonge, J. (1997) *General Election 1997: Labour's Landslide*, Manchester: Manchester University Press.

George, S. (1988) *An Awkward Partner*, Oxford: Oxford University Press.

Geyer, R. (2003) 'European Integration, Complexity and the Revision of Theory', *Journal of Common Market Studies*, Vol.41/1, p. 15–35.

Giddens, A., (1990) *The Consequences of Modernity,* Cambridge: Polity Press.

Giddens, A. (1994) 'Living in a Post-Traditional Society' in B. Ulrich, A. Giddens and S. Lash (eds.), *Reflexive Modernization: Politics, Tradition and Aesthetics in the Modern Social Order*, Cambridge: Polity.

Giddens, A. (1998) 'Risk Society: The Context of British Society', in J. Franklin (ed.), *The Politics of Risk Society*, Cambridge: Polity Press.

Gifford, C. (2007) 'Political Economy and the Study of Britain and European Integration: A Global-National Perspective', *British Journal of Politics and International Relations*, Vol.9/3, pp.461–476.

Gifford, C. (2010) 'The UK and the European Union: Dimensions of Sovereignty and the Problem of Eurosceptic Britishness', *Parliamentary Affairs*, Vol.63/2, 2010, pp.321–338.

Gough, I. (2010) 'Economic Crisis, Climate Change and the Future of Welfare States', *Twenty-First Century Society*, Vol.5/1, pp.51–64.

Gough, I. (2011) 'From Financial Crisis to Fiscal Crisis', in K. Farnsworth, and Z. Irving (eds.), *Social Policy in Challenging Times*, Bristol: The Policy Press.

Grant, W. (2000) *Pressure Groups and British Politics*, London, Macmillan.

Gray, A. and Jenkins, B. (1998) 'New Labour, New Government: Change and Continuity in Public Administration and Government 1997', *Parliamentary Affairs*, Vol.51/2, pp.111–130.

Greenleaf, W. (1983a) *The British Political Tradition: The Rise of Collectivism*, Vol. 1, London: Methuen.

Greenleaf, W. (1983b) *The British Political Tradition: The Ideological Heritage*, Vol. 2, London: Methuen.

Greenleaf, W. (1987) *The British Political Tradition: A Much Governed Nation*, Vol. 3 (Parts I and II), London: Methuen.

Greer, P. (1994) *Transforming Central Government: The Next Steps Initiative*, Buckingham, Philadelphia: Open University Press.

Grugel, J. (2011) *Democratisation: A Critical Introduction* (2nd edn), Basingstoke: Palgrave.

Guardian (2009a) 'Barclays Gags Guardian Over Tax', 17 March 2009.

Guardian (2009b) 'RBS Avoided £500M of tax in Global Deals', 13 March 2009.

Guardian (2011) 'Financial Services Authority may keep HBOS Report Secret', 6 December 2011.

Guardian (2011) Reading the Riots, *Guardian Online*, 5 November 2011, Available at: http://www.guardian.co.uk/uk/interactive/2011/dec/14/reading-the-riots-investigating-england-s-summer-of-disorder-full-report (Accessed 19 June 2012).

Guardian (2013) George Osborne and Rupert Murdoch Enjoyed Private Dinner in Mayfair, 28 January 2013.

Habermas, J. (1975) *Legitimation Crisis*, Boston: Beacon Press.

Habermas, J. (2012) *The Crisis of the European Union: A Response*, Oxford: Polity Press.

Hajer, M. A. (2005) 'Setting the Stage: A Dramaturgy of Policy Deliberation', *Administration and Society*, Vol.36, pp.624–647.

Haldane, A.G. (2010) 'The Debt Hangover', Speech by Mr Andrew G Haldane, Executive Director, Financial Stability, Bank of England, at a Professional Dinner, Liverpool, 27 January 2010.

Haldane, A. (2010) 'The $100 Billion Question, Speech at the Institution of Regulation and Risk', Hong Kong, 30 March.

Hall, M. (2011) *Political Traditions and UK Politics*, Basingstoke: Palgrave Macmillan.

Hall, Peter A. (1993) 'Policy Paradigms, Social Learning and the State: The Case of Economic Policy-Making in Britain', *Comparative Politics*, Vol.25, pp.275–296.

Halpern, D. (2010) *The Hidden Wealth of Nations*, Cambridge: Polity Press.

Hampton, P. (2005) *Reducing Administrative Burdens: Effective Inspection and Enforcement*, London: HM Treasury.

Hansard Society (2009) *Audit of Political Engagement 6: The 2009 Report*, London: Hansard Society.

Hansard Society (2010) *Audit of Political Engagement 7: The 2010 Report*, London: Hansard Society.

Hansard Society (2012) *Audit of Political Engagement 9: The 2012 Report*, London: Hansard Society.

Hansard Society (2013) *Audit of Political Engagement 10: The 2013 Report*, London: Hansard Society.

Hatier, C. (2012) ' "Them" and "Us": Demonising Politicians by Moral Double Standards', *Contemporary Politics*, Vol.18/4, December 2012, pp.467–480.

Hay, C. (1996) *Restating Social and Political Change*, Buckingham: Open University Press.

Hay, C. (2001) *Political Analysis*, Basingstoke: Palgrave.

Hay, C. (2006) 'Managing Economic Interdependence: The Political Economy of New Labour', in P. Dunleavy, R. Heffernan, P. Cowley, and C. Hay (eds.), *Developments in British Politics 8*, Basingstoke: Palgrave Macmillan.

Hay, C. (2007) *Why We Hate Politics*, Cambridge: Polity Press.

Hay, C. (2011) 'The 2010 Leonard Schapiro Lecture: Pathology Without Crisis? The Strange Demise of the Neo-Liberal Growth Model', *Government and Opposition*, Vol.46/1, pp.317–344.

Hay, C. (2012) 'Treating the Symptom not the Condition: Crisis Definition, Deficit Reduction and the Search for a New British Growth Model', *British Journal of Politics and International Relations*, Vol.15/1, pp.23–37.

Hay, C. (2013) *A Very British Crisis*, Basingstoke: PIVOT/Palgrave Macmillan.

Hay, C. and Rosamond, B. (2002) 'Globalization, European Integration and the Discursive Construction of Economic Imperatives,' *Journal of European Public Policy*, Vol.9/2, pp.147–167.

Hay, C. and Smith, N. (2013a) 'The Story of a North Sea Bubble: The Strange Demise of the Anglo-liberal Growth Model in the United Kingdom and Ireland', *European Political Science Review*, Vol.5/3, pp.401–430.

Hay, C. and Smith, N. (2013b) 'The Resilience of Anglo-Liberalism in the Absence of Growth: The UK and Irish Cases', in V. Schmidt and M. Thatcher (eds.), *Resilient Liberalism*, Cambridge: Cambridge University Press.

Hay, C. and Stoker, G. (2013) 'Can Politics Be Rescued from Anti-politics? Evidence from Recent Research', *Political Studies Association Annual International Conference*, Cardiff, 25–27 March 2013.

Hay, C. and Wincott, D. (2012) *The Political Economy of European Welfare Capitalism*, Basingstoke: Palgrave Macmillan.

Hayton, R. (2010) 'Towards the Mainstream? UKIP and the 2009 Elections to the European Parliament', *Politics*, Vol.30/1, 26–35.

Hazell, R. (2006) *The English Question*, London: The Constitution Unit www.ucl.ac.uk/spp/publications/unit-publications/130.pdf.

Hazell, R. (2007) 'The Continuing Dynamism of Constitutional Reform', *Parliamentary Affairs*, Vol.60/1, pp.3–25.

Healey, J., Gill, M. and McHugh, D. (2005) *MPs and Politics in Our Time*, London: Dod's Parliamentary Communications.

Helm, T. (2013) 'I was Elected to Speak My Mind So Why Does Cameron Keep on Ignoring Me', *The Observer*, 16 June.

Hendriks, F. and Tops, P. (2005) 'Everyday Fixers as Local Heroes: A Case Study of Vital Interaction in Urban Governance', *Local Government Studies*, Vol.31/4, 475–490.

Hennessy, P. (1995) *The Hidden Wiring: Unearthing the British Constitution*, London: Victor Gollancz.

Héritier, A. and Rhodes, M. (2011) *New Modes of Governance in Europe: Governing in the Shadow of Hierarchy*, Basingstoke: Palgrave Macmillan.

Hestletine, M. (2012) *No Stone Unturned: In Pursuit of Growth*, London: Department for Business, Innovation and Skills.

Heywood, J. and Kerslake, B. (2013) 'Margaret Thatcher: Our Kindly Boss by Britain's Top Civil Servants', *The Daily Telegraph*, 15 April 2013, www.telegraph.co.uk/news/politics/margaret-thatcher/9994375/Margaret-Thatcher-our-kindly-boss-by-Britains-top-civil-servants.html.

High Pay Commission (2011) *Cheques with Balances: Why Tackling High Pay Is in the National Interest, Final Report of the High Pay Commission*, London: High Pay Commission.

Hindmoor (2010) 'The Banking Crisis: Grid, Group and the State of the Debate', *The Australian Journal of Public Administration*, Vol.69/4, pp.442–456.

HM Treasury (2000) *Cruickshank Report: Competition in UK Banking: A Report to the Chancellor*, London: HM Treasury.

HM Treasury (2004) *Competition in UK Banking: the Cruickshank Report – The Government's Response*, London: HM Treasury.

HM Treasury (2005) *Pre-Budget Report*, London: HM Treasury.

HM Treasury (2009) *UK International Financial Services – the Future*, London: HM Treasury.

HM Treasury (2011) Press Release 'Government Sets out Plans to Reform the Structure of Banking in the UK', 19 December 2011.

HMIC (2011a) *The Rules of Engagement: A Review of the August 2011 Disorder*, London: HMIC.

HMIC (2011b) *Adapting to Austerity: A Review of Police Force and Authority Preparedness for the 2011/12–2014/15 CSR Period*, London: HMIC.

HMIC (2011c) *Without Fear of Favour: A Review of Police Relationships*, London: HMIC.

HMSO (2012) *Review of the Balance of Competences between the United Kingdom*, London: HMIC.

Hodson, D. and Quaglia, L. (2009) 'European Perspectives on the Global Financial Crisis', *Journal of Common Market Studies*, Vol.47/5, pp.939–953.

Hood, C. (1991) 'A Public Management for all Seasons?', *Public Administration*, Vol.69, pp.3–19.

Hood, C. (1998) *The Art of the State: Culture, Rhetoric and Public Management*, Oxford: Clarendon Press.

Hood, C. (2007) 'What Happens When Transparency Meets Blame-Avoidance?', *Public Management Review*, Vol.9/2, pp.191–210.

Hooghe, L. and Marks, G. (2009) 'A Postfunctionalist Theory of European Integration: From Permissive Consensus to Constraining Dissensus', *British Journal of Political Science*, Vol.39/1 pp.1–23.

Hooghe, M. (2011) 'Why There Is Basically Only One Form of Political Trust', *British Journal of Politics and International Relations*, Vol. 13/2, pp.269–275.

Hoskyns, J. (2000) *Just in Time: Inside the Thatcher Revolution*, London: Aurum.

House of Commons Committee of Public Accounts (2012) *Reorganising Central Government Bodies*, HC 1082, London: TSO.

House of Commons Library (2010) 'How Much Legislation Comes from Europe?', *Research Paper* 10/62.

House of Commons Treasury Committee (2008) *The Run on the Rock, HC 56–1 Fifth Report of Session 2007–2008*, London: House of Commons.

Hyman, P. (2004) *One in Ten: From Downing Street to Classroom Reality*, London: Random House.

Ignazi, P. (1996) 'The Crisis of Parties and the Rise of New Political Parties', *Party Politics*, Vol.2/4, pp.549–566.

IMF (2013) *World Economic Outlook: Coping with High Debt and Sluggish Growth*, October, Washington, DC: International Monetary Fund.

Independent Commission on Banking (2011) *Interim Report: Consultation on Reform Options*, London: Independent Commission on Banking.

Inglehart, R. (1999) 'Postmodernization Erodes Respect for Authority, But Increases Support for Democracy' in P. Norris (ed.), *Critical Citizens: Global Support for Democratic Government*, Oxford: Oxford University Press.

Inspector Gadget (2012) Winsor, Vested Interests and Privatization. Inspector Gadget Blog, Available at: http://inspectorgadget.wordpress.com/2012/05/13/winsor-vested-interests-and-privatisation/ (Accessed 15 June 2012)

Institute for Fiscal Studies (2009) *Green Budget 2009,* London: Institute for Fiscal Studies.

IPCC (2011a) *Corruption in the Police Service in England: First Report,* London: HMSO.

IPCC (2011b) *Report of the Investigation into a Complaint Made by the Family of Mark Duggan about Contact with Them Immediately after His Death,* London: IPCC.

IPCC (2012) *Corruption in the Police Service in England: Second Report – A Report based on the IPCC's Experience from 2008 to 2011,* London: HMSO.

Ipsos Mori (2008) *BBC Survey on Trust Issues.*

Ipsos Mori (2010) *IPSOS MORI poll for RSA,* 10–12 September 2010, Available at: http://www.ipsos-mori.com/Assets/Docs/Polls/big-society-poll-for-RSA-september-2010-topline.pdf (Accessed 5 May 2012).

Ipsos Mori (2012a) 'Four in Ten Scots Back Independence', Available at: http://www.ipsos-mori.com/researchpublications/researcharchive/2912/Four-in-ten-Scots-back-independence.aspx.

Jay, P. (1977) 'Englanditis', in R. E. Tyrell (ed.), *The Future that Doesn't Work,* London: Doublesday.

Jay, R. (2013) Leveson's Chief Inquisitor Calls UK Press 'Most Unruly and Irreverent in World', *The Guardian,* 21 January 2013.

Johal, S., Moran, M. and Williams, K. (2012) 'The Future Has Been Postponed: The Great Financial Crisis and British Politics', *British Politics,* Vol.7/1, pp.69–80.

John, Peter (2010) 'Central State Power and its Limits in Bulpitt's Territory and Power' *Government and Opposition,* Vol.45/3, pp.345–364.

Johns, R., Denver, D., Mitchell, J. and Pattie, C. (2010) *Voting for a Scottish Government: The Scottish Parliament Elections of 2007,* Manchester: Manchester University Press.

Johns, R., Mitchell, J. and Carman, C. (2011) 'The Scottish National Party's Success in Winning an Outright Majority at Holyrood in May 2011 Was an Extraordinary Result in an "ordinary" Election', Available at: http://blogs.lse.ac.uk/politicsandpolicy/archives/12865.

Johns, R., Mitchell, J., Denver, D. and Pattie, C. (2009) 'Valence Politics in Scotland: Towards an Explanation of the 2007 Election', *Political Studies,* Vol.57, pp.207–233.

Johnston, L. (2000) *Policing Britain: Risk, Security and Governance,* London: Longman.

Jones, E. (2009) 'The Euro and the Financial Crisis', *Survival,* Vol.51/2, April–May 2009, pp.41–54.

Jones, J. (2012) *The Report of the Hillsborough Independent Panel,* London: The Stationery Office.

Jones, O. (2011) *Chavs: The Demonisation of the Working Class,* London: Verso.

Jones, R. W. and Scully, R. (2006) 'Devolution and Electoral Politics in Scotland and Wales', *Publius: The Journal of Federalism,* Vol.36/1, 115–134.

Jones, T. (2003) 'The Governance and Accountability of Policing', in T. Newburn (ed.), *Handbook of Policing,* Cullompton: Willan.

Jones, T. and Newburn, T. (2002) 'The Transformation of Policing: Understanding Current Trends in Policing Systems', *British Journal of Criminology*, Vol.42, pp.129–146.

Jordan, A. G. (1990) 'Policy Community Realism versus "New" Institutionalist Ambiguity', *Political Studies*, Vol.38/3, pp.470–485.

Jordan, A. G. and Richardson, J. J. (1987) *Government and Pressure Groups in Britain*, Oxford: Clarendon Press.

Jowit, J. (2013) 'We're Not Axe Muderers: MP Tries to Find Why Everyone Hates Politicians', *The Guardian*, 1 January.

Judge, D. (1993) *The Parliamentary State*, London: Sage.

Judge, D. (1999) *Representation: Theory and Practice in Britain*, London: Routledge.

Judge, D. (2005) *Political Institutions in the United Kingdom*, Oxford: Oxford University Press.

Judge, D. (2006) 'This Is What Democracy Looks Like: New Labour's Blind Spot and Peripheral Vision', *British Politics*, Vol.1/3, pp.367–396.

Judge, D. (2013) ' "Word from the Street": When Nonelectoral Representative Claims Meet Electoral Representation in the UK', *British Politics*, advance online publication, doi: 10.1057/bp.2013.8.

Karpf, D. (2010) 'Online Political Mobilization from the Advocacy Group's Perspective. Looking Beyond Clicktivism', *Policy and Internet*, Vol.2/4, pp.7–41.

Kassim, Hussein (2004) 'The United Kingdom and the Future of Europe: Winning the Battle, Losing the War', *Comparative European Politics*, Vol.2/3, pp.261–281.

Katz, R. S. and Mair, P. (1995) 'Changing Models of Party Organization and Party Democracy The Emergence of the Cartel Party', *Party Politics*, Vol.11, pp.5–28.

Keane, J. (2009a) *The Life and Death of Democracy*, London, Pocket Books.

Keane, J. (2009b) 'Monitory Democracy and Media-Saturated Societies', *Griffith Review 24: Participation Society*, Brisbane: Griffith University.

Keane, J. (2011) 'Monitory Democracy?', in S. Alonso, J. Keane, and W. Merkel (eds.), *The Future of Representative Democracy*, Cambridge: Cambridge University Press.

Keating, M. (2008) 'Culture and Social Science', in D. Porta and M. Keating (eds.), *Approaches and Methodologies in the Social Sciences*, Cambridge: Cambridge University Press.

Keating, M. and Cairney, P. (2006) 'A New Elite? Politicians and Civil Servants in Scotland after Devolution', *Parliamentary Affairs*, Vol.59/1, pp.43–59.

Kelling, G. L., Pate, A., Dieckman, D. and Brown, C. E. (1972) *The Kansas City Preventative Patrol Experiment*, Washington, DC: Police Foundation.

Kelling, G. L., Pate, A., Ferrara, A., Utne, M. and Brown, C. E. (1981) *Newark Foot Patrol Experiment*, Washington, DC: Police Foundation.

Kellner, P. (2011) 'The Death of Class-based Politics', *The Political Quarterly*, Vol.81/1, pp.152–164.

Kellner, P. (2012) *Democracy on Trial: What Voters Really Think of Parliament and Our Politicians*, Oxford: Reuters Institute for the Study of Journalism.

Kenny, M. (2009) 'Taking the Temperature of the UK's Political Elite', *Parliamentary Affairs*, Vol.62/1, pp.149–161.

Kerr, P. (2001) *Postwar British Politics: From Conflict to Consensus,* London: Routledge.

Kettle, M. (2013) 'Like the Unions, the Press has shown us who Governs', *The Guardian,* 2 May 2013, p. 35.

Keynes, J. M. (1926) *The End of Laissez-Faire: The Economic Consequences of the Peace,* London: Macmillan.

King, A. (1975) 'Overload: Problems of Governing in the 1970s', *Political Studies,* Vol.23 2/3 pp.284–96.

King, A. (2007) *The British Constitution,* Oxford: Oxford University Press.

King, M. (2009) 'Speech to Scottish Business Organisations', Edinburgh, Tuesday 20 October 2009, Available at: http://www.bankofengland.co.uk/publications/Documents/speeches/2009/speech406.pdf.

King, M. (2010) 'Banking: From Bagehot to Basel, and Back Again', *The Second Bagehot Lecture,* Buttonwood Gathering, New York City, 25 October.

Knill, C. (2005) 'Cross-national Policy Convergence: Concepts, Approaches and Explanatory Factors', *Journal of European Public Policy,* Vol.12/5, pp.746–774.

Krasner, S. D. (1984) 'Approaches to the State', *Comparative Politics,* Vol.16/2, pp.223–246.

Krugman, P. (2008) *The Return of Depression Economics and the Crisis of 2008,* London: Penguin.

Kux, S. and Ulf S. (2000) 'Fuzzy Borders and Adaptive Outsiders: Norway, Switzerland and the EU', *Journal of European Integration,* Vol.22/3, pp.237–270.

Labour (2010) *The Labour Party Manifesto 2010: Future Fair For All,* London: The Labour Party.

Lawrence, D. (2012) 'Interview with Doreen Lawrence', *Woman's Hour,* BBC Radio Four, 15 March 2012.

Laws, D. and Marshall, P. *The Orange Book: Reclaiming Liberalism,* London: Profile Books, 2004.

Leftwich, A. (2004) *What Is Politics?: The Activity and Its Study,* Cambridge: Polity.

Leveson (2012a) *Executive Summary,* Available at: http://www.official-documents.gov.uk/document/hc1213/hc07/0779/0779.pdf.

Leveson, B. H. (2012) *An Inquiry into the Culture, Practices and Ethics of the Press,* London: Stationery Office, Available at: www.levesoninquiry.org.uk.

Lewis, P. and Evans, P. (2013a) McLibel leaflet was co-written by undercover officer Bob Lambert. *Guardian Online,* Available at: http://www.guardian.co.uk/uk/2013/jun/21/mclibel-leaflet-police-bob-lambert-mcdonalds (Accessed 1 July 2013)

Lewis, P. and Evans, P. (2013b) *Undercover: The true story of Britain's Secret Police,* London: Faber and Faber.

Lewis, P., Dodd, V. and Evans, R. (2012) 'Police Recorded 8,500 Corruption Allegations in Three Years', *Guardian Online,* Available at: http://www.guardian.co.uk/politics/2012/may/24/police-watchdog-corruption-complaints (Accessed 15 June 2012)

Leys, C. (2003) *Market Driven Politics: Neoliberal Democracy and the Public Interest,* London: Verso Books.

Li, Y. and Marsh, D. (2008) 'New Forms of Political Participation: Searching for Expert Citizens and Everyday Makers', *British Journal of Political Science,* Vol.38, pp.247–272.

Liberal Democrats (2010) *Liberal Democrat Manifesto 2010*, London: The Liberal Democrats.

Lijphart, A. (1999) *Patterns of Democracy: Government Forms and Performance in Thirty-Six Countries*, New Haven: Yale University Press.

Littlechild, S. (1983) *Regulation of British Telecommunications' Profitability, Report to the Secretary of State*, London: Department of Industry.

Lloyd, J. (2004) *What the Media Doing to our Politics*, London: Constable.

Loader, I. and Mulcahy, A. (2006) *Policing and the Condition of England: Memory, Politics And Culture*, Oxford: Oxford University Press.

Lodge, M. and Hood, C. (2010) *Regulation Inside Government: Retro-Theory Vindicated or Outdated?*, in Baldwin, Robert, Cave, Martin and Lodge, Martin, (eds.), *The Oxford Handbook of Regulation. Oxford Handbooks in Business and Management*, Oxford, UK: Oxford University Press.

Lodge, M. and Wegrich, K. (2011) 'Arguing about Financial Regulation: Comparing National Discourses on the Global Financial Crisis', *PS: Political Science & Politics*, Vol.44/4, pp.726–730.

Lodge, M. and Wegrich, K. (2012) *Managing Regulation: Regulatory Analysis, Politics and Policy*, Basingstoke: Palgrave Macmillan.

Loewenberg, G. (1971) 'The Role of Parliaments in Modern Political Systems', in G. Loewenberg (ed.), *Modern Parliaments: Change or Decline*, New York: Aldine.

Ludlow, P. (2006) *The European Community and the Crises of the 1960s: Negotiating the Gaullist Challenge*, London: Routledge.

Ludlow, Piers (1999) 'Challenging French Leadership in Europe: Germany, Italy, the Netherlands and the Outbreak of the Empty Chair Crisis of 1965–1966', *Contemporary European History*, Vol.8, pp.231–248.

Lynch, P. and Whitaker, R. (2012) 'Where There Is Discord, Can they Bring Harmony? Managing Intra-party Dissent on European Integration in the Conservative Party', *British Journal of Politics and International Relations*, Vol.15/3, pp.317–339.

Lynch, P. and Whitaker, R. (2013) 'Where There Is Discord, Can They Bring Harmony? Managing Intra-party Dissent on European Integration in the Conservative Party', *The British Journal of Politics & International Relations*, 15, 317–339, doi: 10.1111/j.1467-856X.2012.00526.x.

Macartney, H. (2011) 'Crisis for the State or Crisis of the State?', *Political Quarterly*, Vol.38/2, pp.193–203.

Macedo, S. et al. (2005) *Democracy at Risk: How Political Choices Undermine Citizen Participation, and What We Can Do About It*, Washington, DC: Brookings Institution Press.

Macpherson, Sir W. (1999) *The Stephen Lawrence Inquiry: Report of an Inquiry by Sir William Macpherson of Cluny*, CM 4262–1, London: Home Office.

Mainwaring, S., Bejarano, A. M. and Pizarro Leongómez, E. (2006) 'The Crisis of Democratic Representation in the Andes: An Overview', in S. Mainwaring, A. M. Bejarano, and E. Pizarro Leongómez (eds.), *The Crisis of Democratic Representation in the Andes*, Stanford, CA: Stanford University Press.

Major, J. (2012) *Leveson Inquiry, First Witness statement*, 14 May 2012.

Mandelkern Group on Better Regulation (2001) *Final Report*, Brussels: European Commission.

Mandelson, P. (2010) *The Third Man*, London: Harper Collins.

Margach, J. (1979) *The Anatomy of Power*, London: W.H. Allen.

Margetts, H., John, P., Escher, T. and Reissfelder, S. (2011) 'Social Information and Political Participation on the Internet: An Experiment', *European Political Science Review*, Vol.3, pp.321–344.

Marien, S. and Hooghe, M. (2011) 'The Effect of Declining Levels of Political Trust on the Governability of Liberal Democracies', *Paper Presented at the Annual Conference of the Political Studies Association*, London, 19–21 April.

Marquand, D. (1988) *The Unprincipled Society: New Demands and Old Politics*, London: Fontana Press.

Marquand, D. (2004) *Decline of the Public: The Hollowing Out of Citizenship*, Cambridge: Polity Press.

Marquand, D. (2008) *Britain Since 1918: The Strange Career of British Democracy*, London: Weidenfeld & Nicholson.

Marsh, D. (1995) 'Explaining Thatcherite Policies: Beyond Uni-Dimensional Explanation', *Political Studies*, Vol.43/4, pp.596–613.

Marsh, D. (2002) 'It's Always Happy Hour' in C. Hay (ed.), *British Politics Today*, London: Polity.

Marsh, D. (2010) 'The New Orthodoxy: The Differentiated Polity Model', *Public Administration*, Vol.89/1, pp.32–48.

Marsh, D. (2011) 'Late Modernity and the Changing Nature of Politics: Two Cheers for Henrik Bang', *Critical Policy Studies*, Vol.5/1, pp.74–89.

Marsh, D. (2012) 'British Politics: A View from Afar', *British Politics*, Vol.7/1, pp.43–54.

Marsh, D. and Hall, M. (2007) 'The British Political Tradition: Explaining the Fate of New Labour's Constitutional Reform Agenda', *British Politics*, Vol.2/3, pp.215–238.

Marsh, D. and Rhodes, R. A. W. (1992) *Policy Networks in British Government*, Oxford: Oxford University Press.

Marsh, D. and Tant, A. (1989) 'There Is No Alternative: Mrs Thatcher and the British Tradition', *Essex Paper No. 69*, Colchester: Department of Government, University of Essex.

Marsh, D. and Vromen, A. (2013) 'Everyday Makers with a Difference? Contemporary Cases of Political Participation', Available at: david.marsh@canberra.edu.au.

Marsh, D., O'Toole, T. and Jones, S. (2007) *Young People and Politics in the UK. Apathy or Alienation?* Basingstoke: Palgrave.

Marsh, D., Richards, D. and Smith, M. J. (2001) *Changing Patterns of Governance*, Basingstoke: Palgrave.

Marsh, D., Richards, D. and Smith, M. J. (2003) 'Unequal Power: Towards an Asymmetric Power Model of the British Polity', *Government and Opposition*, Vol.38/3, pp.306–322.

Marsh, D., Buller, J., Hay, C., Johnston, J., Kerr, P., McAnulla, S. and Watson, M. (1999) *Postwar British Politics in Perspective,* Polity: Cambridge.

Mason, Paul (2010) *Meltdown*, London: Verso.

Mattinson, D. (2010) *Talking to a Brick Wall: How New Labour Stopped Listening to the Voter and Why We Need a New Politics*, London: Biteback Publishing Ltd.

Maude, F. (2010) 'Ministerial Statement on Transforming Government Services to Make Them More Efficient and Effective for Users', 14 October

2010, Available at: https://www.gov.uk/government/news/public-body-review-published.

Mawby, R. C. (2008) 'The Police Organisation', in T. Newburn (ed.), *Handbook of Policing* (2n edn), Cullompton: Willan.

McAnulla, S. (2010) 'Heirs to Blair's Third Way; David Cameron's Triangulating Conservatism', *British Politics*, Vol.5/3, pp.286–314.

McCrone, D. and B. Lewis (1999) 'The 1997 Scottish Referendum Vote', in B. Taylor and K. Thompson (eds.), *Scotland and Wales: Nations Again?* Cardiff: University of Wales Press.

McDonnell, J. (2009) 'The Banking White Paper: What the Experts Say', *The Guardian*, 8 July 2009, Available at: http://www.guardian.co.uk/business/2009/jul/08/banking-regulation-alistair-darling (Accessed 11 June 2012)

McFarland, M. and Michelleti, A. (2011) *Creative Participation: Responsibility-Taking in the Political World*, Colorado: Paradigm Printers.

McGarvey, N. and Cairney, P. (2008) *Scottish Politics*, Basingstoke: Palgrave.

McGuinness, F. (2010) 'The Social Background of MPs', *House of Commons Research Paper*, SN/SG/1528.

McHugh, D. (2006) 'Wanting to Be Heard but Not Wanting to Act? Addressing Political Engagement', *Parliamentary Affairs*, Vol.59/3, pp.546–552.

McLaverty, P. (2009) 'Is Deliberative Democracy the Answer to Representative Democracy's Problems? A Consideration of the UK Government's Programme of Citizens' Juries', *Representation*, Vol.45/4, pp.379–389.

McLennan, G, Held, D. and Hall, S. (eds.) (1984) *State and Society in Contemporary Britain: A Critical Introduction*, London: Polity Press.

Middlemas, K. (1979) *Politics in Industrial Society: The Experience of the British system since 1911*, London: A. Deutsch.

Midwinter A., Keating, M. and Mitchell, J. (1991) *Politics and Public Policy in Scotland*, Basingstoke: Macmillan.

Miliband, R. (1961) *Parliamentary Socialism*, London: George Allen & Unwin.

Miliband, D. (2012) *Speaker's Lecture: Ministers and Politics in a Time of Crisis*, 20 June 2012, http://www.voicegig.com/speakers-lecture-ministers-and-politics-in-a-time-of-crisis/.

Miller, V. (1996) 'The Policy of Non-Cooperation with the EU' House of Commons Library, Research Paper 96/74.

Miller, V. (2012) *The UK and Europe: Time for a New Relationship?* Standard Note: SN/IA/6393.

Miller, V. and Barclay, L. (2012) UK Public Opinion on the European Union, House of Commons Library. Standard Note: SN/IA/5442.

Mills, J. (2010) 'Why Labour Would Do Well to Favour Working-class Candidates', *The Guardian*, 13 June 2010.

Milne, K. (2005) *Manufacturing Dissent*, London: Demos.

Ministry of Justice (2011) *Statistics on Race and the Criminal Justice System 2010, A Ministry of Justice Publication under Section 95 of the Criminal Justice Act 1991*, London: MOJ.

Mitchell, J. (2003) *Governing Scotland*, Basingstoke: Palgrave.

Mitchell, J. (2004) 'Scotland: Expectations, Policy Types and Devolution', in A. Trench (ed.), *Has Devolution Made a Difference? The State of the Nations 2004*, Exeter: Imprint Academic.

Mitchell, J. (2005) 'Scotland: Devolution Is Not Just for Christmas', in A. Trench (ed.), *The Dynamics of Devolution: The State of the Nations 2005*, Exeter: Imprint Academic.

Mitchell, J. and L. Bennie (1996) 'Thatcherism and the Scottish Question', in *British Elections and Parties Yearbook 1995*, London: Frank Cass.

Moore, J. (2012) 'Turner's Candour May Shut Bank Door', *Independent*, 25 July.

Moran, M. (2003*) The British Regulatory State: High Modernism and Hyper-Innovation*, Oxford: Oxford University Press.

Moravcsik, A. (2012) 'Europe After the Crisis.' *Foreign Affairs*, Vol.91/3, pp.54–68.

Mori (2009) Available at: http://www.ipsos-mori.com/newsevents/ca/32/Only-One-in-Five-Say-They-Trust-Journalists-to-Tell-The-Truth.aspx.

Moss, R. (1976) *The Collapse of Democracy*, London: Abacus.

Mount, F. (2012) *The New Few: Or a Very British Oligarchy*, London: Simon & Schuster.

MPS (2012) *Four days in August: Metropolitan Police Service Strategic Review into the Disorder of August 2011: Final Report*, March 2012, London: MPS.

National Audit Office (2012) *Financial Management in the Home Office*, 26 April 2012, London: HMSO.

National Audit Office (2012) *Reorganising Central Government Bodies*, HC 1703, London: TSO.

Negrine, R. (ed.) (1985) *Cable Television and the Future of Broadcasting*, London: Routledge.

Negrine, R. (1998) *Television and the press since 1945*, Manchester: Manchester University Press.

Nevitte, N. (1996) *The Decline of Deference*, Peterborough: Broadview Press.

Newburn, T. (1999) 'Understanding and Preventing Police Corruption: Lessons from the Literature', *Police Research Series*, Paper 110. London, HMSO.

Newburn, T. and Reiner, R. (2007) 'Policing and the Police', in M. Maguire et al. (eds.), *The Oxford Handbook of Criminology* (4th edn), Oxford: Oxford University Press.

Nohrstedt, D. and Weible, C. M. (2010) 'The Logic of Policy Change after Crisis: Proximity and Subsystem Interaction Risk', *Hazards & Crisis' Public Policy*, Vol.1/2, pp.1–32.

Norman, J. and Ganesh, J. (2006) *Compassionate Conservatism: What It Is, Why We Need it*, London: Policy Exchange.

Norris, P. (ed.) (1999) *Critical Citizens: Global Support for Democratic Governance*, Oxford: Oxford University Press.

Norris, P. (2002) *Democratic Phoenix: Reinventing Political Activism*, Cambridge: Cambridge University Press.

Norris, P. (2003) 'Young People and Political Activism: From the Politics of Loyalties to the Politics of Choice', *Report for the Council of Europe Symposium*, 27–28 November, Strasbourg.

Norris, P. (2011) *Democratic Deficit: Critical Citizens Revisited*, Cambridge: Cambridge University Press.

Norton, P. (2012) 'Speaking for the People: A Conservative Narrative of Democracy', *Policy Studies*, Vol.33/2, March 2012, pp.121–132.

Oakeshott, M. (1962) *Rationalism in Politics and Other Essays*, Indianapolis, IN: Liberty Press.

Oborne, P. (2008) *The Triumph of the Political Class*, London: Pocket Books.

Offe, C. (1975) 'The Theory of the Capitalist State and the Problem of Policy Formulation' in L. N. Lindberg et al. (eds.), *Stress and Contradiction in Modern Capitalism*, Washington DC: Heath.

Offe, C. (1984) *Contradictions of the Welfare State*, London: Hutchinson.

Oppermann, K. (2008) 'The Blair Government and Europe: The Policy of Containing the Salience of European Integration', *British Politics*, Vol.3, pp. 173–174.

Organisation for Economic Cooperation and Development (1997) *The OECD Report on Regulatory Reform: Synthesis*, Paris: OECD.

Oxford English Dictionary (2004) 'Crisis'. *Oxford English Dictionary* (11th edn), Oxford: Oxford University Press.

Page, E. (2010) 'Has the Whitehall Model Survived?', *International Review of Administrative Sciences*, Vol.76/3, pp.407–423.

Painter, C. (2008) 'A Government Department in Meltdown: Crisis at the Home Office', *Public Money and Management*, Vol.28/5, pp.275–282.

Park, A. (2005) *Young People's Social Attitudes 1998: ESRC, Full Report of Research Activities and Results* [R000237765], Available at: http://www.esrc. ac.uk/my-esrc/grants/R000237765/outputs/Read/5de98403-2b85-472e-89ea-a2240b4f6048.

Parmar, A. (2011) 'Stop and Search in London: Counter-terrorist or Counter-productive?' *Policing and Society*, Vol.21/4, pp.369–382.

Parr, H. (2005) *Britain's Policy Towards the European Community: Harold Wilson and Britain's World Role, 1964–1967*, Abingdon: Routledge.

Parsons, W. (1982) 'Politics without Promises: The Crisis of Overload and Ungovernability', *Parliamentary Affairs*, Vol.35/4, pp.421–435.

Patten, C. (1998) *A New Beginning: Policing in Northern Ireland. The Report of the Independent Commission on Policing for Northern Ireland*, Belfast: Patten Commission.

Pattie, C., Seyd, P. and Whiteley, P. (2004) *Citizenship in Britain: Values, Participation and Democracy*, Cambridge: Cambridge University Press,

Paun, A. and Halifax, S. (2012) *A Game of Two Halves: How Coalition Governments Renew in Mid-term and Last the Whole Term*, Institute of Government, June 2012.

Pemberton, Hugh (2009) 'Macroeconomic Crisis and Policy Revolution', *Renewal*, Vol.17/4, pp.46–56.

Phillis Review (Chaired by Sir Robert Phillis) (2004) *Independent Review of Government Communications*, January 2004, Available at: http://www.publications. parliament.uk/pa/ld200809/ldselect/ldcomuni/7/704.htm.

Pierson, C. (1991) *Beyond the Welfare State?: The New Political Economy of Welfare*, Cambridge: Polity Press.

Pollard, N. (2012) *The Pollard Review*, Available at: http://www.bbc.co.uk/news/ uk-20782889, Available at: http://downloads.bbc.co.uk/bbctrust/assets/files/ pdf/our_work/pollard_review/pollard_review.pdf.

Powell, J. (2010) *The New Machiavelli: How to Wield Power in the Modern World*, London: Bodley Head.

Power Commission (2006) *Power to the People*, London: Power Commission.

Power, M. (2007) *Organized Uncertainty: Designing a World of Risk Management*, Oxford: Oxford University Press.

Press Gazette (2012) Available at: http://www.pressgazette.co.uk/story.asp? storycode=49215.

Private Eye (2013) No. 1332, 25 January–7 February 2013, p.5.

Prosser, T. (2010) *The Regulatory Enterprise: Government, Regulation and Legitimacy,* Oxford: Oxford University Press.

Putnam, R. (2000) *Bowling Alone. The Collapse and Revival of American Community,* New York: Simon & Schuster.

Quaglia, L. (2009) 'The 'British Plan' as a Pace-Setter: The Europeanization of Banking Rescue Plans in the EU?' *Journal of Common Market Studies*, Vol.47, pp.1063–1083.

Quinton, P. (2011) 'The Formation of Suspicions: Police Stop And Search Practices In England', *Policing and Society*, Vol.21/4, pp.357–368.

Radaelli, C. M. (2005) 'Diffusion Without Convergence: How Political Context Shapes the Adoption of Regulatory Impact Assessment', *Journal of European Public Policy,* Vol.12/5, pp.924–943.

Radaelli, C. M. (2007) 'Whither Better Regulation for the Lisbon Agenda?' *Journal of European Public Policy*, Vol.14/2, pp.190–207.

Rainie, L., Purcell, K. and Smith, A. (2011) *The Social Side of the Internet*, Washington: Pew Research Centre.

Ratcliffe, J. H., Taniguchi, T. and Groff, E. R. (2011) 'The Philadelphia Foot Patrol Experiment: A Randomized Controlled Trial of Police Patrol Effectiveness in Violent Crime Hotspots', *Criminology*, Vol.49/3, pp.795–831.

Rawnsley, A. (2001) *Servants of the People: The Inside Story of New Labour,* London: Hamish Hamilton.

Rawnsley, A. (2006) *Servants of the People: The Inside Story of New Labour*, London: Penguin.

Rehfeld, A. (2006) 'Towards a General Theory of Political Representation', *The Journal of Politics*, Vol.68/1, pp.1–21.

Reiner, R. (1992) 'Policing a Postmodern Society', *Modern Law Review*, Vol.55, pp.761–781.

Reiner, R. (1995) 'From Sacred to Profane: The Thirty Years' War of the British Police', *Policing and Society*, Vol.5/2, pp.121–128.

Reiner, R. (2010) *The Politics of the Police*, Brighton: Harvester.

Reiner, R. (2012) *In Praise of Fire Brigade Policing: Challenging The Role of the Police. What if Pamphlets*, London: Howard League for Penal Reform, Available at: http://www.howardleague.org/what-if/ (Accessed 15 June 2012)

Reuters (2012) 'Scottish Prosecutor Confirms Banking Investigation', *Reuters,* 3 July 2012.

Reuters/Ipsos (2011) *Mori Political Monitor*, July 2011, Available at: http://www.ipsos-mori.com/researchpublications/researcharchive/2828/ReutersIpsos-MORI-Political-Monitor-July-2011.aspx.

Rhodes, R. A. W. (1994) 'The Hollowing-Out of the State: The Changing Nature of the Public Service in Britain', *Political Quarterly*, Vol.65/2, pp.138–151.

Rhodes, R. A. W. (1997) *Understanding Governance: Policy Networks, Governance, Reflexivity and Accountability*, London: Open University Press.

Rhodes, R. A. W. (2011) *Everyday Life in British Government*, Oxford: Oxford University Press.

Rhodes, R. A. W. and Marsh, D. (1992) 'Policy Networks in British Politics', in D. Marsh and R. A. W. Rhodes (eds.), *Policy Networks in British Government*, Oxford: Oxford University Press.

Rhodes, R. A. W., Wanna, J. and Weller, P. (2009) *Comparing Westminster*, Oxford: Oxford University Press.

Richards, D. (2004) 'The Civil Service in Britain: A Case-Study in Path Dependency', in J. Halligan (ed.), *Civil Service Systems in Anglo-American Countries*, London: Edward Elgar, pp.30–71.

Richards, D. (2008) *New Labour and the Civil Service: Reconstituting the Westminster Model*, Basingstoke: Palgrave Macmillan.

Richards, D and Blunkett, D. (2011) 'Labour in and Out of Government: Political Ideas, Political Practice and the British Political Tradition,' *Political Studies Review*, Vol.9/2, pp.180–192.

Richards, D. and Kavanagh, D. (2001) 'Departmentalism and Joined-Up Government: Back to the Future?', *Parliamentary Affairs*, Vol.54/1, pp.1–18.

Richards, D. and Mathers, H. (2010) 'Political Memoirs and New Labour: Interpretations of Power and "Club Rules" ', *British Journal of Politics and International Relations*, Vol.12/4, pp.498–522.

Richards, D. and Smith, M. J. (2000) 'Power, Knowledge and the Core Executive: The Living Chimera of the Public Service Ethos and the Role of the British Civil Service', *West European Politics*, Vol.23/3, pp.45–66.

Richards, D. and Smith, M. (2002) *Governance and Public Policy in the UK*, Oxford: Oxford University Press.

Richards, D. and Smith, M. J. (2004) 'Interpreting the World of Political Elites: Some Methodological Issues', *Public Administration*, Vol.82/4, p.777–800.

Richards, D. and Smith, M. (2010) 'Back to the Future: New Labour, Sovereignty and the Plurality of the Party's Ideological Tradition', *British Politics*, Vol.5/3, pp.239–264.

Richards, D., Blunkett, D. and Mathers, H. (2008) 'Old and New Labour Narratives of Whitehall: Radicals, Reactionaries and Defenders of the Westminster Model', *Political Quarterly*, Vol.79/4, pp.488–498.

Richardson, J. J. (1993) 'Introduction: Pressure Groups and Government', in J. J. Richardson (ed.), *Pressure Groups*, Oxford: Oxford University Press.

Richardson, J. J. (2000) 'Government, Interest Groups and Policy Change', *Political Studies*, Vol.48/5, pp.1006–1025.

Richardson, J. J. and Jordan, A. G. (1979) *Governing Under Pressure: The Policy Process in a Post-Parliamentary Democracy*, Oxford: Martin Robertson.

Riddell, P. (2007) *The Unfulfilled Prime Minister: Tony Blair's Quest for a Legacy*, London: Methuen.

Riddell (2010) 'In Defence of Politicians: In Spite of Themselves', *Parliamentary Affairs*, Vol.63/3, pp.545–557.

Riddell (2011) *In Defence of Politicians in Spite of Themselves*, London: Biteback Publishing.

Riddell, P. (2012) 'Debating Flinders', *Contemporary Politics*, Vol.18/1, pp. 26–28.

Riots Panel (2011) *Five days in August: Interim Report*, 26 November 2011, London: Riots, Communities and Victims Panel.

Riots Panel (2012) *After the Riots: The Final Report of the Riots, Communities and Victims Panel*, London: Riots, Communities and Victims Panel.

Rokkan, S. (1970) *Citizens, Elections, Parties: Approaches to the Comparative Study of Political Development*, Oslo: Universitetsforlaget.

Rosamond, B. (1993) 'National Labour Organizations and European Integration: British Trade Unions and "1992" ', *Political Studies*, Vol.41, pp.420–434.

Rosamond, B. (2002) 'Britain's European Future?' in C. Hay (ed.), *British Politics Today*, Cambridge: Cambridge University Press, pp.185–215.

Rose, R. (1975) 'Overloaded Governments: The Problem Outlined', *European Studies Newsletter*, Vol.5/3, pp.13–18.

Rowe, M. and Garland, J. (2003) 'Have You Been Diversified Yet? Developments in Police Community and Race Relations Training in England', *Policing and Society*, Vol.13/4, pp.399–411.

Saramago, J. (2004) *Seeing*, London: Vintage.

Saward, M. (2008) 'The Subject of Representation', *Representation*, Vol.44/2, pp.93–97.

Saward, M. (2009) 'Authorisation and Authenticity: Representation and the Unelected', *The Journal of Political Philosophy*, Vol.17/1, pp.1–22.

Saward, M. (2010) *The Representative Claim*, Oxford: Oxford University Press.

Saward, M. (2011) 'The Wider Canvas: Representation and Democracy in State and Society', in S. Alonso, J. Keane, and W. Merkel (eds.), *The Future of Representative Democracy*, Cambridge: Cambridge University Press.

Scarman OBE, Rt. Hon. Lord. (1981) *The Brixton Disorders*, 10–12 April 1981, London: HMSO.

Scharpf, F. (2002) 'The European Social Model: Coping with the Challenges of Diversity', *Journal of Common Market Studies*, Vol.40/4, pp.645–670.

Schmidt, V. A. (2006) 'Adapting to Europe: Is it Harder for Britain?' *The British Journal of Politics & International Relations*, Vol.8, pp.15–33.

Scott, J. (2010) 'Adapting to Brussels: Europeanization of the Core Executive and the "Strategic-Projection" Model', *Journal of European Public Policy*, Vol.17/6, pp.818–835.

Scottish Constitutional Convention (1995) *Scotland's Parliament: Scotland's Right*, Edinburgh: Convention of Scottish Local Authorities.

Scottish Government (2011) *Your Scotland, Your Referendum*, Edinburgh: Scottish Government.

Scottish Government (2012) 'Historic Edinburgh Agreement on Referendum Signed' 15 October 2012, Available at: http://www.scotland.gov.uk/News/Releases/2012/10/referendum15102012.

Scottish Government (2013) 'Scotland's Referendum', Available at: http://www.scotreferendum.com/.

Seldon, A. (2006) *Tony Blair*, London: Harper Collins.

Select Committee Culture, Media and Sport (2010) Select Committee, 2010 HC 43-I, para. 87.

Selle, P. (1991) 'Membership in Party Organizations and the Problem of the Decline of Parties', *Comparative Political Studies*, Vol.23/4, pp.459–477.

Seymour-Ure, C. K. (1998) 'Are the Broadsheets becoming Unhinged?' In J. Seaton (ed.), *Politics and the Media. Harlots and Prerogatives at the Turn of the Millennium*, Oxford: Blackwell.

Seymour-Ure, C. K. (2003) *Prime Ministers and the Media. Issues of Power and Control*, Oxford: Blackwell.

Shapland, J. and Vagg, J. (1988) *Policing by the Public*, London: Routledge.

Sherrington, P. (2006) 'Confronting Europe: UK Political Parties and the EU 2000–2005', *British Journal of Politics and International Relations*, Vol.8, pp.69–78.

Skelcher, C., Flinders, M., Tonkiss, K. and Dommett, K. (2013) 'Public Bodies Reform by the UK Government 2010–2013: Initial Findings', *Shrinking the State Research Paper* 1 (July 2013)

Smith, M. J. (1999) *The Core Executive in Britain*, Palgrave Macmillan.

Smith, M. J. (2005) 'It's Not the Economy, Stupid! The Disappearance of the Economy from the 2005 Campaign', in A. Geddes and J. Tonge (eds.), *Britain Decides: The UK General Election 2005*, London: Palgrave.

Smith, M. J. (2008) 'Re-centring British Government: Beliefs, Traditions and Dilemmas in Political Science', *Political Studies Review*, Vol.6/2, pp.143–154.

Smith, M. J. (2009) *Power and the State*, Basingstoke: Palgrave Macmillan.

Smith, M. J. (2010) 'From Big Government to Big Society: Changing the State-Society Balance', *Parliamentary Affairs*, Vol.63/4, pp.818–833.

Smith, M. J. (2013) 'Globalisation and the Resilience of Social Democracy', *British Journal of Politics and International Relations*, Article first published online: 16 APR 2013, doi: 10.1111/1467-856X.12020.

Snow, D, A. and Soule, A. S. (2010) *A Primer on Social Movements*, New York: W. W. Norton.

Stanistreet, M. (2012) NUJ calls on readers to rise up against culling of editors. NUJ, Available at: http://union-news.co.uk/2012/04/nuj-calls-on-readers-to-rise-up-against-culling-of-editors/.

Stark, A. (2010) 'Legislatures, Legitimacy and Crises: The Relationship between Representation and Crisis Management', *Journal of Contingencies and Crisis Management*, Vol.18/1, pp.2–13.

Stark, A. (2011) 'The Tradition of Ministerial Responsibility and Its Role in the Bureaucratic Management of Crises', *Public Administration*, Vol.89/3, pp.1148–1163.

Stoker, G. (2006) *Why Politics Matters: Making Democracy Work*, Basingstoke: Palgrave Macmillan.

Stoker, G. (2010) 'The Rise of Political Disenchantment', in C. Hay (ed.), *New Directions in Political Science: Responding to the Challenges of an Interdependent World*, Basingstoke: Palgrave.

Stoker, G. (2011) *Building A New Politics: A Report Prepared for the British Academy*, London: The British Academy.

Stoker, G. (2012) 'Debating Flinders', *Contemporary Politics*, Vol.18/1 pp.32–34.

Stokes, D. (1992) 'Valence Politics', in D. Kavanagh (ed.), *Electoral Politics*, Oxford: Clarendon, pp.141–164.

Streek, W. (2011) 'The crisis of Democratic Capitalism', *New Left Review* 71, September–October 2011, pp.5–29.

Studlar, D. T. and Waltman, J. L. (eds.) (1984) *Dilemmas of Change in British Politics*, London: Macmillan.

Tant, A. (1993) *British Government: The Triumph of Elitism: A Study of the British Political Tradition and Its Major Challenges*, Aldershot: Dartmouth.

Tarrow, G, S. (2011) *Power in Social Movements: Social Movements and Contentious Politics*, Cambridge: Cambridge University Press.

Thain, C. (2009) 'A Very Peculiar British Crisis?: Institutions, Ideas and Policy Responses to the Credit Crunch', *British Politics*, Vol.4/4, pp.434–449.

Thaler, R. H. and Sunstein, C. (2008) *Nudge: Improving Decisions about Health, Wealth and Happiness*, Yale: Yale University Press.

'tHart, P. and Boin, A. (2001) 'Between Crisis and Normalcy: The Long Shadow of Post-Crisis Politics', in U. Rosenthal, A. Boin, and L. K. Comfort (eds.), *Managing Crises: Threats, Dilemmas, Opportunities*, Springfield: Charles C Thomas.

The Economist (2012) 'Learning Mandarin', 21st April: https://www.economist.com/node/21553069

The Guardian (1999) 'Thatcher Returns to Fight Old Battles', Wednesday 6 October.

Thompson, H. (2012) 'The Limits of Blaming Neo-liberalism: Fannie Mae, Freddie Mac, and the Financial Crisis', *New Political Economy*, Vol.17/4, pp.399–419.

TNS-BRMB (2012) July 2012 Independence Poll http://www.tns-bmrb.co.uk/assets-uploaded/documents/july-2012-independence-poll-press-release_1341823401.pdf

Tomlinson, J. (2002) 'The British "Productivity Problem" in the 1960s', *Past and Present*, Vol.175, pp.189–210.

Tonge, J., Mycovk, J. (2012) 'Does Citizenship Education Make Young People Better-Engaged Citizens?' *Political Studies*, Vol.60/3, pp.578–602.

Trade and Industry Select Committee (1997) *Energy Regulation: First Report*, HC. 50, Session 1996–1997, London: HMSO.

Treanor, J. (2012) 'John Vicker's Says Osborne Reforms Don't Go Far Enough', *The Guardian*, 14 June 2012.

Treasury (2009) *Reforming Financial Markets*, CM 7667, London: TSO.

Treasury (2012) *Banking Reform: Delivery Stability and Supporting a Sustainable Economy*, CM 8356, London: TSO.

Treasury, Financial Services Authority and Bank of England (2007) *Banking Reform – Protecting Depositors: A Discussion Paper*, London: HMSO.

Trench (ed.) (2004) *Has Devolution Made a Difference? The State of the Nations Yearbook 2004*, London: Imprint Academic.

Turner, A. (2009) *A Regulatory Response to the Global Banking Crisis*, London: FSA.

Tyler, T. R. (2003) 'Procedural Justice, Legitimacy and the Effective Rule of Law', in M. Tonry (ed.), *Criminal Justice*, Chicago: University of Chicago Press.

Urbinati, N. (2006) *Representative Democracy*, Chicago, University of Chicago Press.

Urbinati, N. and Warren, M. E. (2008) 'The Concept of Representation in Contemporary Democratic Theory', *Annual Review of Political Science*, Vol.11, pp.387–412.

Van Biezen, I., Mair, P., and Poguntke, T. (2011) 'Going, going,...gone? The Decline of Party Membership in Contemporary Europe', *European Journal of Political Research*, Vol.22, pp.148.

Van Laer, J. and Van Aelst, P. (2010) 'Internet and Social Movement Action Repertoires: Opportunities and Limitations', *Information, Communication & Society*, Vol.14/8, pp.1146–1171.

Vegh, S. (2003) 'Classifying Forms of Online Activism: The Case of Cyberprotests Against the World Bank' in M. McCaughey, and D. M. Ayers (eds.), *Cyberactivism: Online Activism in Theory and Practice*, New York: Routledge, pp.71–95.

Verba, S. and Nie, N. (1972), *Participation in America: Political Democracy and Social Equality*, New York: Harper and Row.

Vincent, D. (1998) *The Culture of Secrecy in Britain 1832–1998*, Oxford: Oxford University Press.

Vromen, A. and Coleman, W. (2011) 'Online Movement Mobilisation and Electoral Politics. The Case of GetUp!', *Communication, Politics and Culture*, Vol.44/2, pp.76–94.

Vromen, A. and Coleman, W. (2013) 'Online Campaigning Organisations and Storytelling Strategies: GetUp! in Australia', *Policy and Internet*, Vol.5/1, pp.76–100.

Vromen, A. and Collins, P. (2010) 'Everyday Youth Participation?: Contrasting Views from Australian Policy Makers and Young People', *Young*, Vol.18/1, pp.97–112.

Waddington, P. A. J. (1999) 'Armed and Unarmed Policing', in R. I. Mawby (ed.), *Policing Across The World: Issues For The Twenty-First Century*, London: UCL Press limited.

Waddington, P. A. J. (1999) *Policing Citizens*, London: UCL Press.

Waddington, P. A. J., Stenson, K. and Don, D. (2004) 'In Proportion: Race, and Police Stop and Search', *British Journal of Criminology*, Vol.44/6, pp.889–914.

Wahl, A. (2011) *The Fall and Rise of the Welfare State*, London: Pluto.

Walden, G. (2006) *The New Elites: A Career in the Masses*, London: Gibson Square.

Wall, S. (2012) 'Britain and Europe' *The Political Quarterly*, Vol.83/2, pp. 247–255.

Wallace, H. (1997) 'At Odds with Europe', *Political Studies*, Vol.45, pp. 677–688.

Walsh, D. (1998) *The Irish Police*, Dublin: Sweet and Maxwell.

Watson, M. (2010) 'House Price Keynesianism and the Contradictions of the Modern Investor Subject', *Housing Studies*, Vol.25/3, pp.413–426.

Watson, M. and Hay, C. (2003) 'The Discourse of Globalisation and the Logic of No Alternative: Rendering the Contingent Necessary in the Political Economy of New Labour', *Policy and Politics*, Vol.31/3, pp.289–305.

Weale, M. (2009) 'Commentary: Growth prospects and Financial Services', *National Institute of Economic Review*, Vol.207, pp.4–9.

Weatherill, S. (2007) 'The Challenge of Better Regulation', in S. Weatherill (ed.), *Better Regulation*, Oxford: Hart, pp.1–17.

Webber, D. (2013) 'How Likely Is It That the European Union Will Disintegrate? A Critical Analysis of Competing Theoretical Perspectives', *European Journal of International Relations*, Janaury 2013, doi: 10.1177/1354066112461286.

Whiteley, P. (2011) 'Is the Party Over? The Decline of Party Activism and Membership across the Democratic World', *Party Politics*, Vol.17/1, pp.21–44.

Whiteley, P. (2012) *Political Participation in Britain*, London: Palgrave.

Whitfield, J. (2007) 'The Historical Context: Policing and Black People in Post-war Britain', in M. Rowe (ed.), *Policing beyond Macpherson*, Cullompton: Willan.

Wilkinson, T. M. (2013) 'Nudging and Manipulation', *Political Studies*, Vol. 61/2, pp.341–355.

Wilks-Heeg, S. and Crone, S. (2010) *Funding Political Parties in Great Britain: A Pathway to Reform*, London: Democratic Audit.

Wilks-Heeg, S., Blick, A. and Crone, S. (2012) *How Democratic Is the UK? The 2012 Audit*, Liverpool: Democratic Audit.

Winsor, T. (2011) *Independent Review of Police Officer's and Staff Remuneration and Conditions: Part 1*, Available at: http://review.police.uk/publications/index.html (Accessed 13 June 2012).

Winsor, T. (2012) *Independent Review of Police Officer's and Staff Remuneration and Conditions: Part 2*, Available at http://review.police.uk/publications/index.html (Accessed 13 June 2012).

Wood, M. and Flinders, M. (2012) 'From Folk Devils to Folk Heroes: Rethinking the Theory of Moral Panics', *Moral Panic Studies Working Paper Series*, London: Brunel University, December 2012, Vol. 2012/2, pp.1–26.

Wrisque-Cline, A. (2008) 'The Modernisation of British Government in Historical Perspective', *Parliamentary Affairs*, Vol. 61/2, pp.144–159.

YouGov (2011) *YouGov/The Sun Survey Results*, Available at: http://cdn.yougov.com/today_uk_import/YG-Archives-Pol-Sun-BigSociety-150211.pdf (Accessed 5 May 2012).

YouGov (2012) YouGov/*Sunday Times* Survey Results.

Young, H. (1998) *This Blessed Plot*, Basingstoke: MacMillan.

Index

Note: Locators in **bold type** indicate figures or illustrations, those in *italics* indicate tables and letter 'n' refers to notes.